SPACE SPIRITS
空間との対話

内藤 廣　SPACE SPIRITS　石元泰博

NAITO Hiroshi + ISHIMOTO Yasuhiro

空間との対話

ADP

目次　内藤廣＋石元泰博　空間との対話

004　言葉なき対話のかけらを探して
　　　内藤 廣

015　海の博物館──撮影1992
　　　021　展示棟　　039　重要有形民俗文化財 収蔵庫

053　安曇野ちひろ美術館──撮影1998

077　牧野富太郎記念館──撮影1999
　　　083　本館　　099　展示館

119　倫理研究所富士高原研修所──撮影2001

[プロセス]
159　海の博物館──1985-1992
170　失われた時を求めて
177　安曇野ちひろ美術館──1993-1996
184　倉庫のようなもの…
195　牧野富太郎記念館──1994-1999
202　伏せる様態
209　倫理研究所富士高原研修所──1998-2001
218　「形」から「仕組み」へ

　　　224　石元泰博略歴
　　　225　内藤 廣略歴
　　　226　あとがき

contents　NAITO Hiroshi + ISHIMOTO Yasuhiro　SPACE SPIRITS

004　Looking for Fragments of the Wordless Dialogue
　　　Hiroshi Naito

015　Sea-Folk Museum──photo1992
　　　021　Exhibition Hall　　039　Repository

053　Chihiro Art Museum Azumino──photo1998

077　Makino Museum of Plants and People──photo1999
　　　083　Museum Building　　099　Exhibition Hall

119　Fuji RINRI Seminar House──photo2001

[PROCESS]
159　Sea-Folk Museum──1985-1992
172　In Search of a Lost Moment
177　Chihiro Art Museum Azumino──1993-1996
188　A Building Like a Storehouse…
195　Makino Museum of Plants and People──1994-1999
204　Embracing the Ground
209　Fuji RINRI Seminar House──1998-2001
220　From "Form" to "Construction Method"

　　　224　BIOGRAPHY of Yasuhiro Ishimoto
　　　225　BIOGRAPHY of Hiroshi Naito
　　　226　Postscript

言葉なき対話のかけらを探して

内藤 廣

　自然は美しい。自明のことである。しかし，はたして人が介在したこの世界は美しいのだろうか。石元泰博のすべての写真に，この問いが含まれている。伝説の写真集『シカゴ，シカゴ』のビルの谷間に差し込んでくる光，新聞を舞い上がらせる風，自動車にうっすらと降り積もる雪。自然は人が造り出したものに，ささやくように語りかける。それは言葉のない詩のようなものである。人や建物や街を撮りながら，そこに光や風や雪といった自然が訪れる瞬間を切り取ろうとしている。その詩をフィルムに掬い取り，印画紙に刻み込もうとする。

　人そのものがそうであるように，人が造り出すものは美しいとは限らない。むしろそうでないものがほとんどだ。しかし，その美しいとは限らないものにも自然はささやきかける。その一瞬は，たとえどのようなものであれ，輝きを増し，この上なく美しい。雨に濡れた路上のつぶされた空き缶でさえ…。その瞬間さえ見逃さなければ対象は何でもよかったに違いない。

　こういう写真家の被写体になるには覚悟が要る。たいていのことは見透かされてしまう。その刹那を捉えようとする眼に応えるだけの資質を，建物は持ち得ているのか。たしかに，どのようなものにでも自然は語りかけるだろう。しかし，そのささやきに建物が的確に応えたとき，はじめて自然との言葉にならない対話が成り立つのである。より良きものは，より良き対話を生む。実は，その対話こそ写真家が写し取ろうとしているものなのではないか。

　法律上の制約，経済的な制約，技術的な制約，敷地の制約，建て主が与える制約。建築は無数の妥協の果ての産物である。しかし，だからこそもっとも生身の人間に近い創造物ともいえる。建築家は，この様々に混ざりあった要素を調え，あるべき方向へ調整し，そこに意志を込めようとする。それが充分でなければ，建物は自然のささやきに応えるだけの美しさを獲得することが出来ない。自分の生み出した建物が被写体にふさわしいのかどうか。撮影を依頼するにあたって，怯まぬはずがない。

　石元さんに初めてお目にかかったとき，わたしは無名で何の実績もない35歳の若造の建築家だった。その時，石元さんは64歳。桂離宮を撮り，丹下健三を撮り，建築界においてその

名を知らぬ者のない巨匠だった。この不釣り合いな関係を結んでくれたのが，西洋環境開発の伊勢志摩芸術村構想だった。三重県の鳥羽市郊外の半島の山林に芸術村を立ち上げるということで招集された文化人グループの中に，石元さんもわたしもいた。
　芸術村の構想は途中で頓挫するが，そのなかに誘致した「海の博物館」は，七年半の孤立無援の歳月を経てなんとか完成した。設計から完成までの歳月は，ちょうど狂乱のバブル経済の時期と重なる。浮かれる世の中に背を向けて，鳥羽に立て籠もるような気持ちでこの建物に打ち込んだ。完成して撮影をお願いした92年当時は，式年遷宮される伊勢神宮の撮影の準備に余念がなかった。
　漁労用具を収集し漁民の生活文化を展示するという内容，都会から遠く離れた僻地というロケーションと極限のローコスト。どれも当時の時流からは遥かに遠い。いかにも都会的でない風貌をもった簡素きわまりない建物は，当時の建築の常識からもかけ離れていた。
　開発が頓挫した造成地の中，世の中から見捨てられたような場所に，時代からも孤立して，この建物はポツンと建っている。完成した海の博物館は，まるで大海原で遭難した時代遅れの難破船のようであった。この難破船に，せめて少しでも光を当てたい。支えてくれた事務所のスタッフはもちろん，協力を惜しまなかった現場の職人たちにも報いたい気持ちがあった。

　たぶんまともに取り上げてくれるメディアもないだろうからと自費出版を決意して，大胆にも石元さんにその撮影をお願いした。過酷な条件の下で様々な妥協を重ねた末に出来上がった被写体は，建物としては充分ではないかも知れない。しかし，その取り組んだ精神には曇りがなかった。よく受けてくださったと思う。奥様の滋子さんの後押しの一言で撮影が決まった。カラーでどうか，と聞かれたときに，是非とも白黒でお願いします，と言った。カラーなら現像はラボに行ってしまう。石元さん自身に焼いてもらいたい。そのためには白黒でなければならない。わたしが言ったひとつだけのわがままである。
　一泊二日の撮影は三回に及んだ。石元さんはもう何回か行くつもりだったようだが，経済的に困窮を極めていた事務所では，三回の撮影に留めていただくしかなかった。

早朝から始まった撮影は，驚くことばかりだった。あらかじめ図面を頭に入れていたとしか思えない。天候を読み，雲の流れを読み，それに合わせて特定の時刻にあらかじめ決めていた場所に立ってカメラを構える。この光でこの場所を撮る，と決めている。われわれには見えない石元さんの頭の中にある緻密なプログラムで動くのだ。だから，次の撮影の立ち位置は予測がつかない。そして，それぞれの動きが分刻みだ。まごまごしていると怒られる。俊敏に動かねばならない。いったんカメラを手にすれば一切の妥協はない。昼飯も休憩もない。日のあるうちは動き続ける。

　変化し続ける光と影との一期一会の格闘。自然と建物が語り合う瞬間を切り取ろうとする。その対話の瞬間が多ければ多いほど，石元さんにとって撮るに足る建物であるに違いない。この建物がそれに適うものであったかどうかは分からない。しかし，ワンカットに対して十数枚の焼きがあった。紙焼きの総数はこの建物だけで数百枚に上るはずだ。

　この後，ある程度の規模があって力を入れた建物があれば撮影をお願いし，そのたびに写真集を作った。安曇野ちひろ美術館，牧野富太郎記念館，倫理研究所富士高原研修所。撮影のときはいつも緊張した。襟を正し，虚心坦懐に臨まねばならない。どれだけ自然はささやきかけてくれるだろうか。対話は成り立っているのか。その都度，厳しい目線で自らの仕事の密度を測る機会にしてきた。

　ここに収録したのは，撮影していただいた四つの建物の写真集を集め再編集したものである。本当は，この後，五年を費やし，全力を傾けた島根県芸術文化センターの撮影をお願いしたかったのだが，すでに体調を崩され，かなわなかった。この建物は，それまでの総決算のようなもので，時々刻々変わる自然を映し込むような建物である。この対話を石元さんの目がどのように捉えるのか見てみたかった。

　牧野富太郎記念館で村野藤吾賞をいただいたとき，記念にと村野藤吾の肖像写真を石元さんから頂戴した。村野さんが品川プリンスホテルの現場を廻るわずかな隙間で撮ったという。91

歳という巨匠晩年の数少ないポートレートだ。

　現場用と思われるスリッパのようなソフト靴。スーツにネクタイ，それにヨレヨレのコートを着ている。高齢にもかかわらず，いったん現場に出れば隅から隅まで一日かけて歩いたという。若い所員がついて行けないほどだったと聞いている。現場を歩いた途中での突然の撮影だからだろう。着衣はやや乱れている。疲労の色は隠せない。機嫌も悪そうだ。しかし，疲労した体と戦うように，その眼鏡の奥の厳しい眼差しには隙がない。

　すばらしいポートレートである。カメラは被写体の本質が現れるその瞬間を見逃さなかった。仕事に向き合うもっとも村野藤吾らしい姿が印画紙の上に留められている。この姿は，撮影現場での石元さんと重なる。この写真をいただいた意味をいまだに考え続けている。

　はたして世界は美しいのだろうか。2011年の3月11日から間を置かずして，被災地の陸前高田の渚に立った。空は晴れ，すべてを洗い流した海は湖のように凪いでいた。背後には学校のグラウンドのような大地が山裾まで広がっている。情けは人が抱く感情だが，ここには一切それがない。剥き出しの自然がもたらした情け容赦のない風景だ。それは美しい。しかし，温度がない。人の温もりの欠片もない。ここには言葉なき対話は成立していない。

　自然そのものには冷厳な美しさがあるが，人が生み出す建物や街や風景には，不完全ではあるが温度がある。人が介在してもなお，そこにより良き対話を見いだすことができるのかどうか。不完全ではあるが温度のある美しさは可能なのだろうか。自然がささやきかけたとき，それに応える人の温もりを留める温かな美しさはありうるのだろうか。情け容赦のない風景に身を晒すと，ことさらその存在を信じてみたくなる。また，それこそが建築や街や風景に向けられた石元さんの生涯の問いであったように思えてならない。

Looking for Fragments of the Wordless Dialogue

Hiroshi Naito

Nature is beautiful. It goes without saying; but is this intervening world of human endeavor beautiful? The question is present in every photograph by Yasuhiro Ishimoto. In his legendary photographic book, *Chicago, Chicago*, sunlight penetrates the canyons among buildings, a wind blows two newspaper pages aloft, and snow lightly dusts a car. Nature whispers to manmade things, and the effect is like a wordless poem. When photographing people, architecture, and cities, Ishimoto waits to capture the moment when nature in the form of light, wind, or snow comes into play. Holding this poem on film, he endeavors to commit it to the photographic paper.

Just as people are not always beautiful, neither are their productions. In nearly all cases, their productions are not beautiful. Yet, nature whispers to those not always beautiful manmade things. At that moment, regardless of what thing it may be, its glow is awakened and it becomes an object of infinite wonder and beauty. Even a flattened can on a road wet from rain. If the photographer but captures that moment, it will not matter what his subject is.

You have to prepare yourself, then, when such a photographer trains his camera on you. He will generally see through his subject's intentions. Does your building have the content necessary to reply to that photographer's eye when he is stalking such a moment? Nature will speak to any object at all, but for the wordless dialogue with nature to begin, a building must confidently respond to its whispering. The better the building, the richer the dialogue. It is, in fact, that dialogue itself the photographer seeks to capture.

Legal limitations, financial limitations, technical limitations, and limitations posed by the site and project owner—architecture is a product of countless compromises. For this very reason, however, as a creation it is much like a living, flesh and blood person. The architect undertakes to order this jumble of elements, lead it in the proper direction, and invest his will in it. When this is not sufficiently achieved, the building will lack the necessary beauty to reply to the whispering voice of nature. Is the building you have created qualified to be photographed? When asking him to shoot for you, you have to flinch.

When I first met Yasuhiro Ishimoto, I was an unknown young architect of thirty-five with no track record. Ishimoto was sixty-four, a master renowned throughout the architecture world who had photographed Katsura Imperial Villa and Kenzo Tange. What occasioned our disproportionate relationship was Seiyo Corporation's project to construct the Ise-Shima Art Village in forest surroundings on a peninsula near Toba City in Mie

Prefecture. Both Ishimoto and I were on the panel of cultural experts invited to the project.

The art village project was terminated midway, but working alone and unaided for seven and a half years, I somehow completed one element of it, the Sea-Folk Museum. The period of my engagement, from commencing the design to the building's completion, overlapped with the era of Japan's frenzied asset-inflated bubble economy. Turning my back on that crazed world, I had closed myself up in Toba and thrown myself into the building. On completing the Sea-Folk Museum in 1992, I asked Ishimoto to photograph it. At the time, he was absorbed in preparing to photograph the Shikinen-sengu (regular removal) of the grand shrine of Ise.

From its purpose—preserving and exhibiting the fishing equipment and culture of a fishing community—to its remote location far from a city and its extremely low budget construction, the Sea-Folk Museum was a project out of step with the times in every way. Even the building, with its simple appearance and complete lack of urban sophistication, deviated from what was considered common sense in architectural circles at the time.

The building stood alone in a remote, abandoned land development project, isolated from its times and forgotten by the busy world. It was like an out-of-date lifeboat stranded at sea. I wanted to throw some illumination on that lifeboat. I also wanted to acknowledge the support of my office staff and that of the craftsmen who had labored tirelessly at the construction site.

Feeling certain I could not find a publisher who would take the building seriously, I decided to pay the cost of publication myself and boldly asked Yasuhiro Ishimoto to undertake the photography. To complete the building, I had made compromise after compromise in surmounting the harsh conditions, so it doubtless left much to be desired as a photographic subject. Yet, my commitment to the building had been total. To think of it now, it was extraordinary that Ishimoto accepted my request. With only a little urging from his wife, Shigeruko, the shooting was set. When he asked if I wanted color, I requested that he shoot it in black and white. If he used color film, the negatives would be sent to a photo lab, and I wanted Ishimoto to develop the prints himself. Therefore, only black and white would do. This was my one selfish request of him.

Three shooting sessions were held during the course of two days. Ishimoto apparently intended to visit the building many times, but my office, in difficult financial straits, had to ask him to limit the sessions to three.

The sessions, which began early each morning, were a continual surprise. One could only think he had memorized the architectural drawings beforehand. Watching the weather and the clouds, he would position himself with his camera in a pre-decided place at a specific time, in line with his observations. Under this particular light, he would say, we have to shoot this particular facet of the building. He seemed to have a detailed program of action in his head that we were not party to. Subsequently, we could never foresee where the next shoot would take place. Each move to a new position was, moreover, worked out to the minute. If we became flurried, he would get angry. We had to move decisively. Once he had his camera in hand, there was no compromising, whatsoever. He took no lunch or rests. As long as there was light, he kept working.

Each shoot was a unique battle with light and shadow in his effort to capture the moment when nature and building fell into dialogue. The more of such moments there are, surely the more sufficient a building is, as a photographic subject. I do not know if my building made a suitable subject or not. Yet, for every shot, he made a dozen prints. He must have made several hundred prints for this one building.

Thereafter, I asked Ishimoto for photography whenever there was a building of scale I had invested time and energy in. Chihiro Art Museum Azumino, Makino Museum of Plants and People, and Fuji RINRI Seminar House. During the shoots I was always tense. They forced me to confront my building sincerely with an empty mind. To what degree would nature deign to whisper to it? Would a dialogue actually develop? I took each session as a chance to measure the quality of my work with a harshly objective eye.

Re-edited and compiled in this volume are the photographic books of the four buildings I asked Ishimoto to photograph. Actually, I had also hoped to ask him to photograph the Shimane Arts Center, a building I poured my energies into for five years, but he had grown ill by then and my wish went unrealized. Shimane Arts Center is like a final settlement of accounts for all I had done up to that time, a building that reflects the incremental changes in nature. I had wanted to know how Ishimoto would view that dialogue.

To commemorate my reception of the Murano Togo Award for Makino Museum of Plants and People, Ishimoto sent me a portrait photograph of Murano Togo. He had taken it during a pause when Murano was inspecting the Shinagawa Prince Hotel construction site. Murano was 91. It is one of the few portraits of the master architect in his late years.

The soft, slipper-like shoes, perhaps for site use. Over the suit and necktie, a rumpled coat. Despite his advanced age, Murano, once at the site, would spend the entire day walking about and inspecting every corner. The younger personnel, it is said, could hardly keep up with him. It is therefore probably a quick photograph taken during one his walks. His clothing is a little disheveled. He cannot hide his fatigue. He appears to be in a bad temper. Yet, behind the glasses, the glint in his eyes is unrelenting, as if he were locked in a battle with his tired body.

It is a superb photograph. The photographer has captured that moment when his subject's essential nature was revealed. On the photographic paper, he has fixed an apt portrait of Murano Togo at work. It is an image calling to mind Ishimoto, himself, when he was at work. I continue to ponder, even now, the significance of my receiving this photograph.

Is the world, in truth, beautiful? Soon after the earthquake and tsunami of March 11, 2011, I stood on a beach in the stricken Rikuzentakata area. The sky was cloudless and the ocean, after having swept everything away, was serene like a lake. Behind me, an empty flat area, like an elementary school athletic ground, extended to the foot of the mountains. Compassion is a human emotion. There was none of that here. It was a pitiless landscape, produced by unbridled nature. It was beautiful. But it was without warmth. Nowhere was there a fragment of that warm human presence. Here, the wordless dialogue did not take place.

Nature itself has a cold, stark beauty, but there is warmth, albeit incomplete, in buildings, towns, and landscapes created by people. Is it possible to find that richer dialogue even where human endeavor intervenes? Can there be beauty with warmth, albeit a beauty incomplete? Can there be beauty imbued with the warmth of human presence, responsive to nature when it commences to whisper? When exposed to such a pitiless, cold landscape, we want to believe there can. This, I cannot help feeling, was the great inquiry of Ishimoto's career, the question he continually asked of architecture, cities, and landscapes.

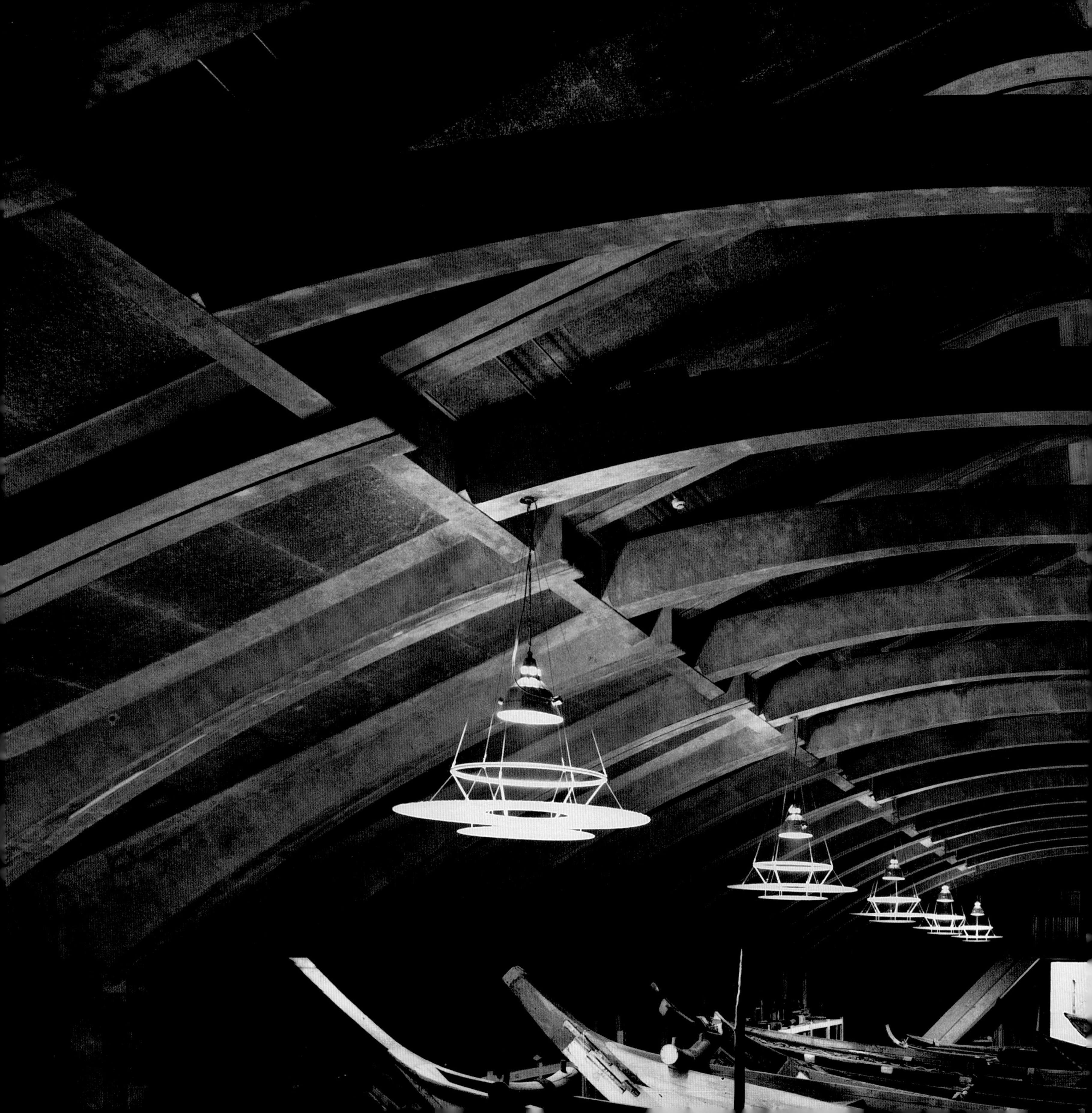

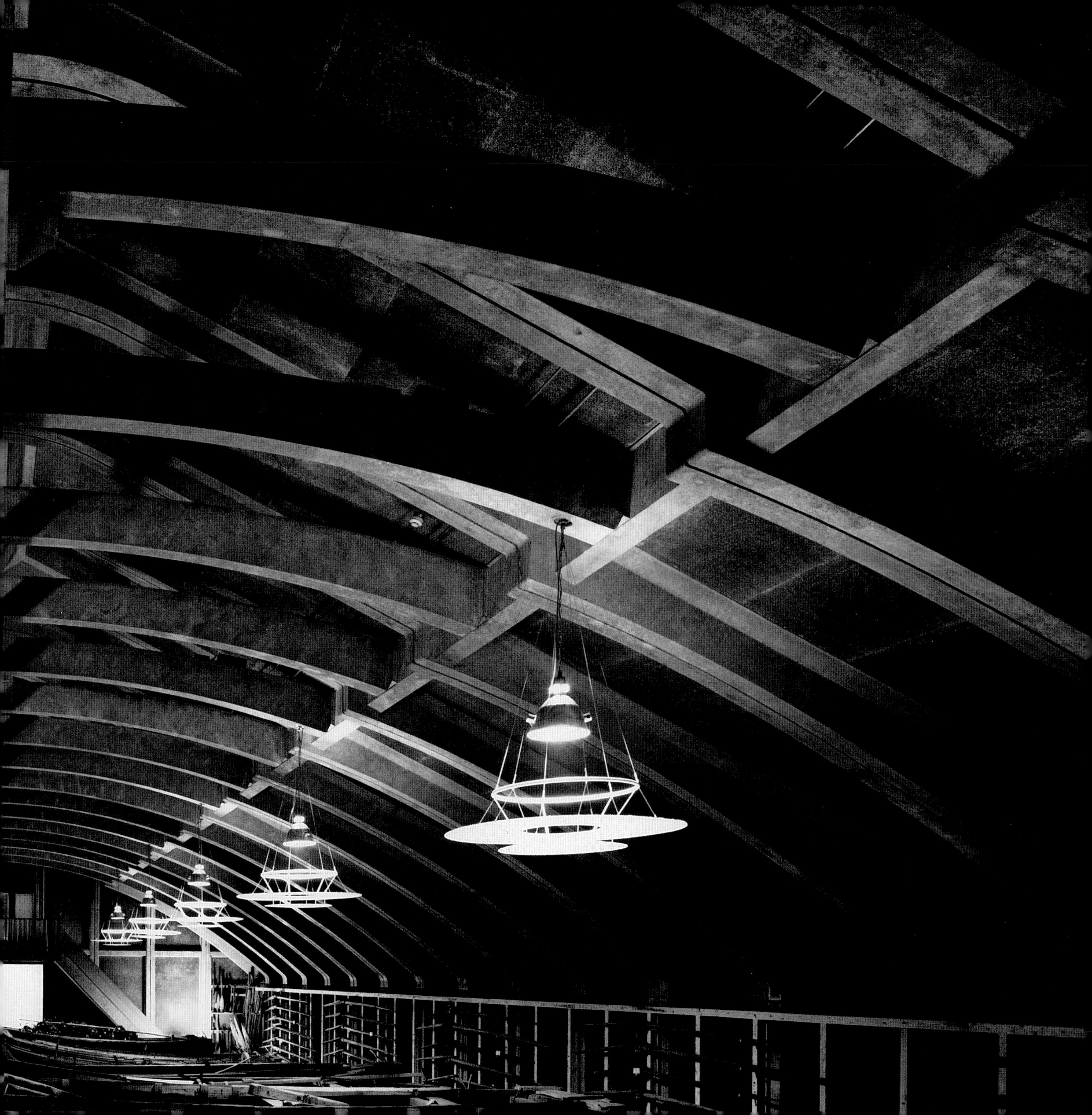

Sea-Folk Museum

海の博物館　撮影■1992

016

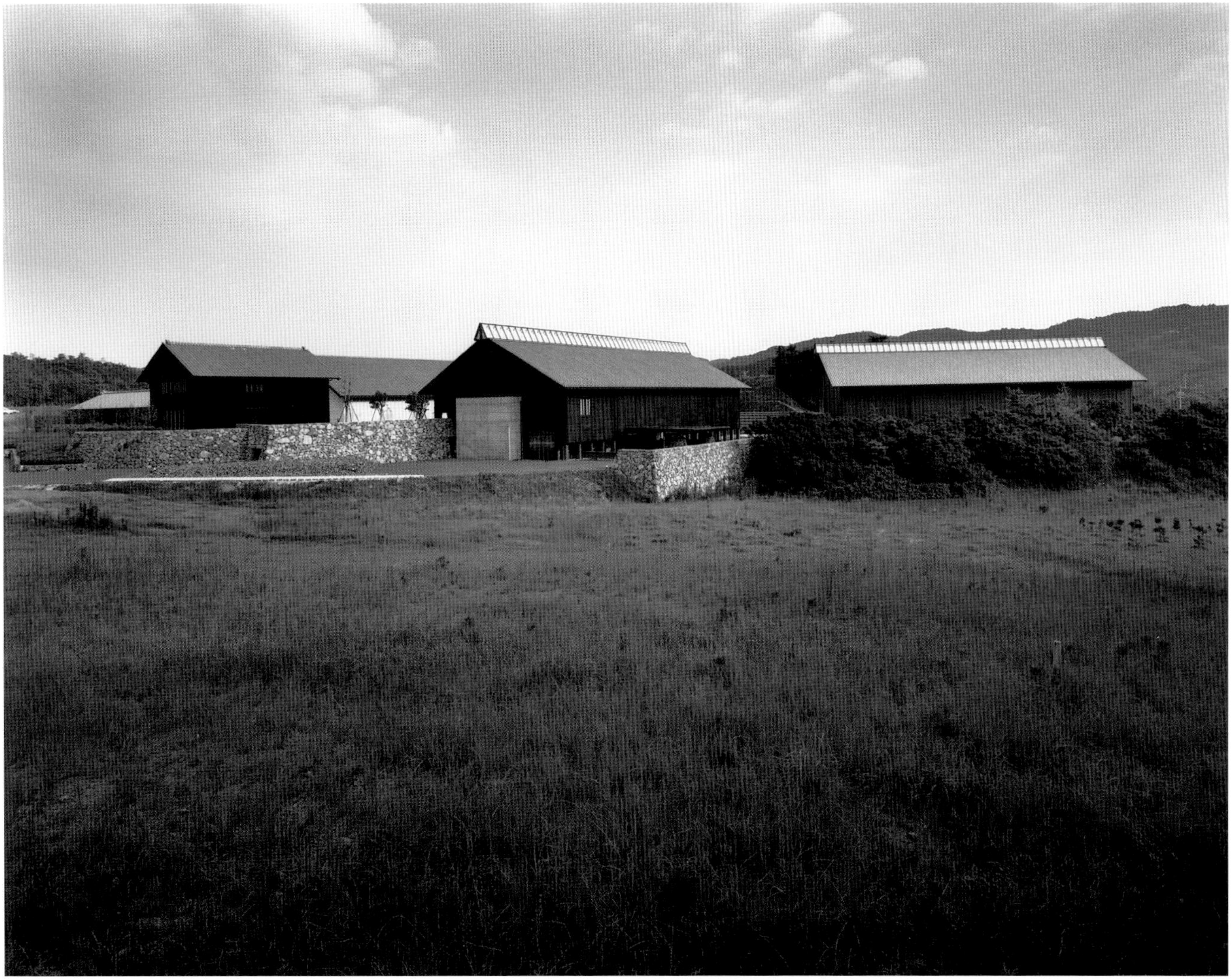

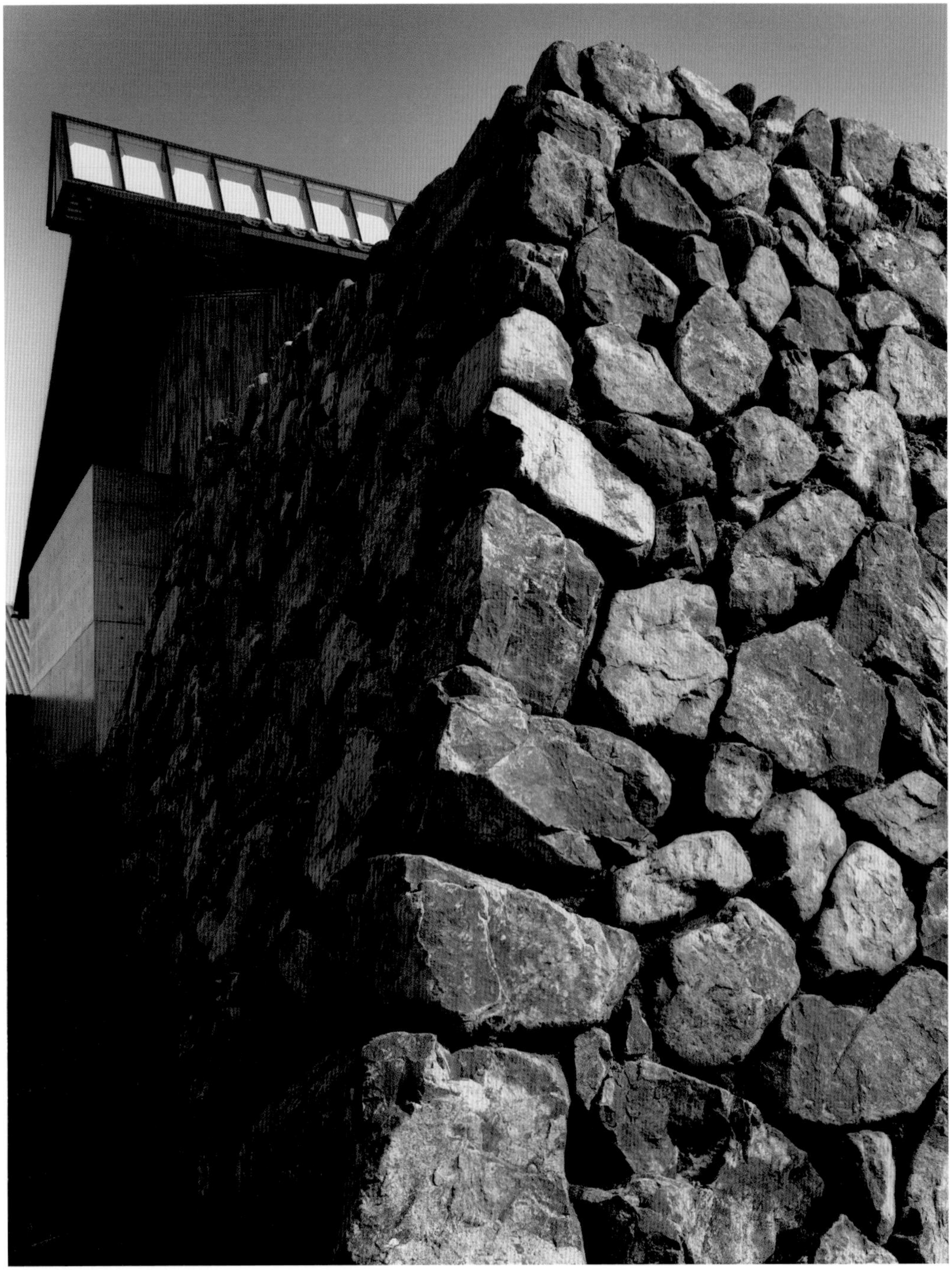

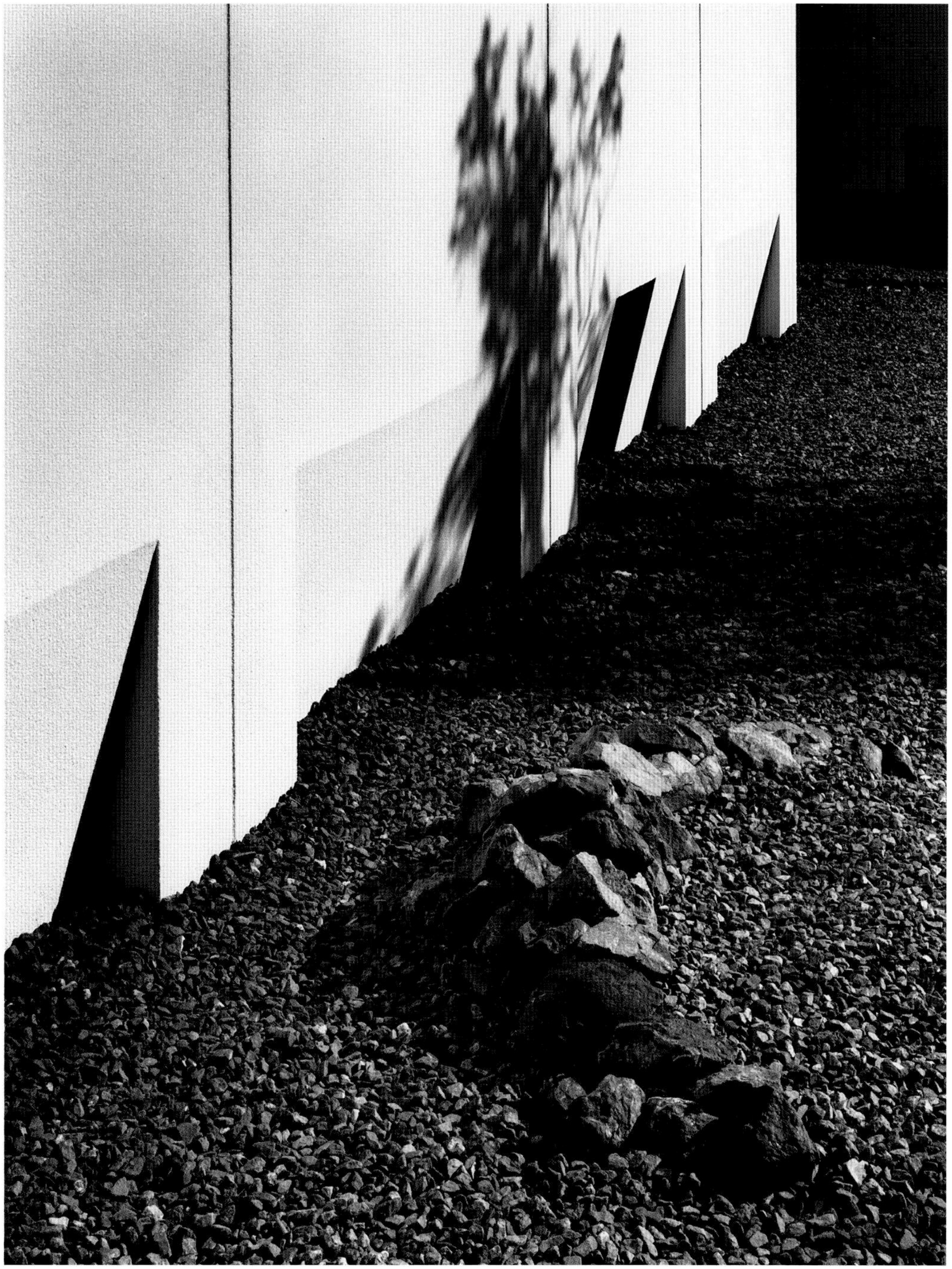

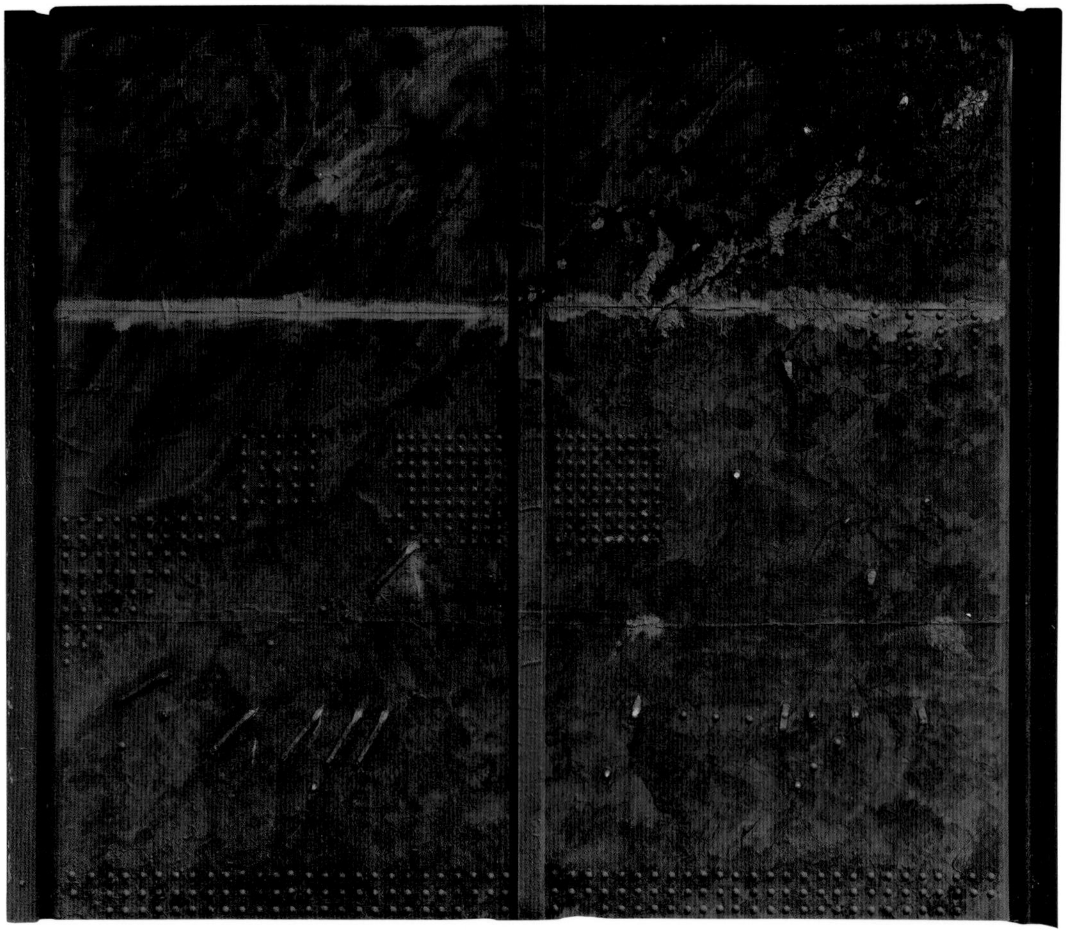

展 示 棟

■

Exhibition Hall

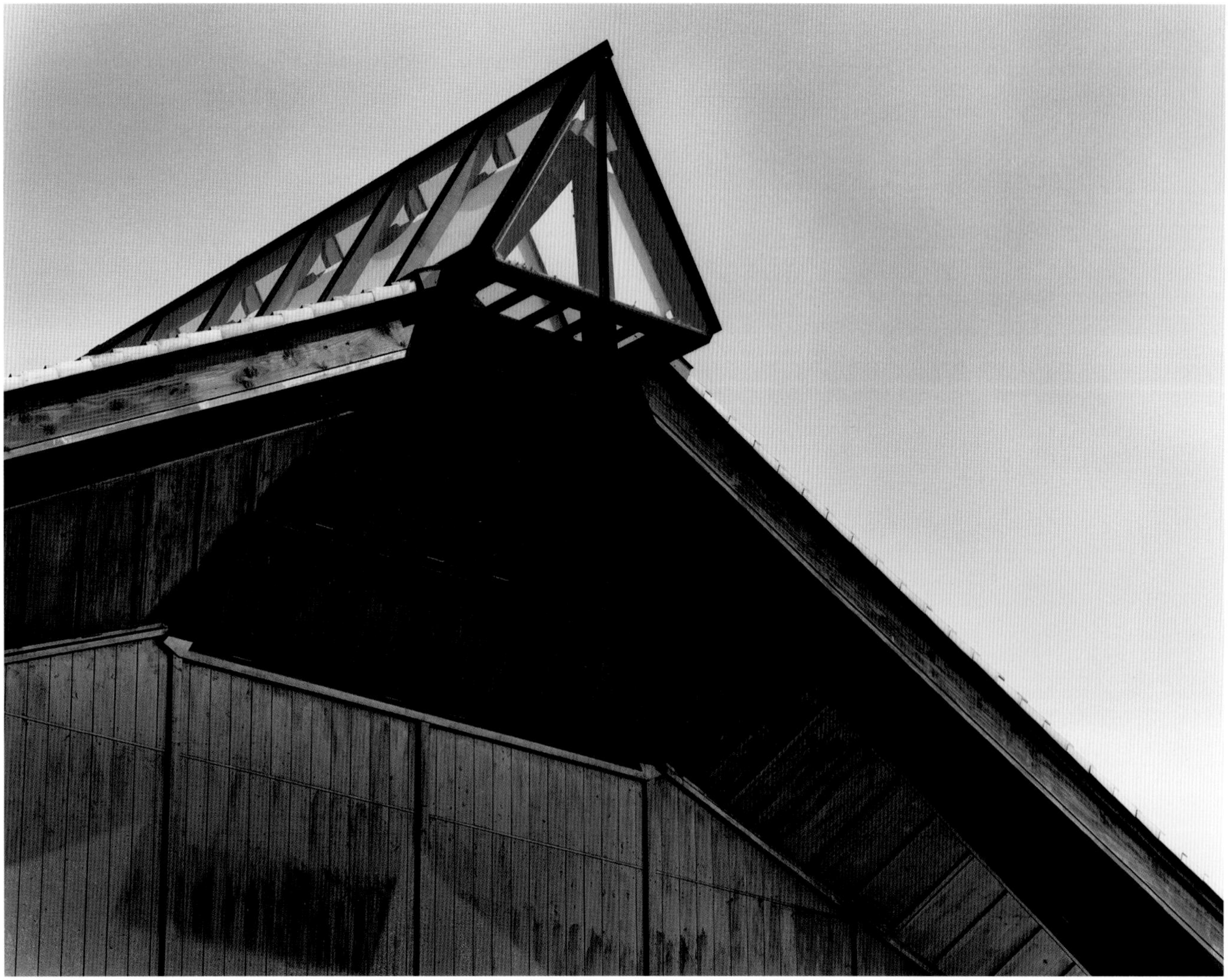

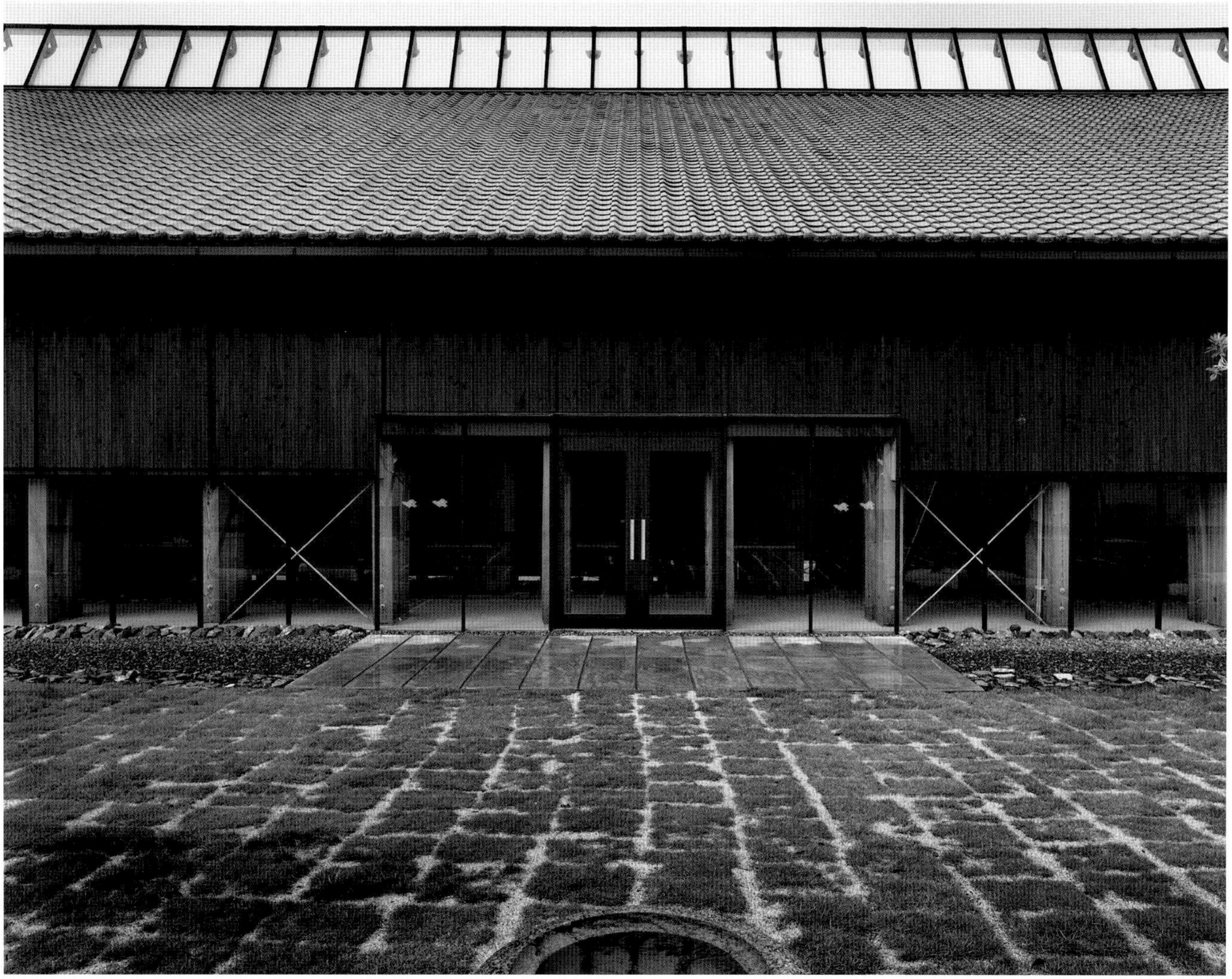

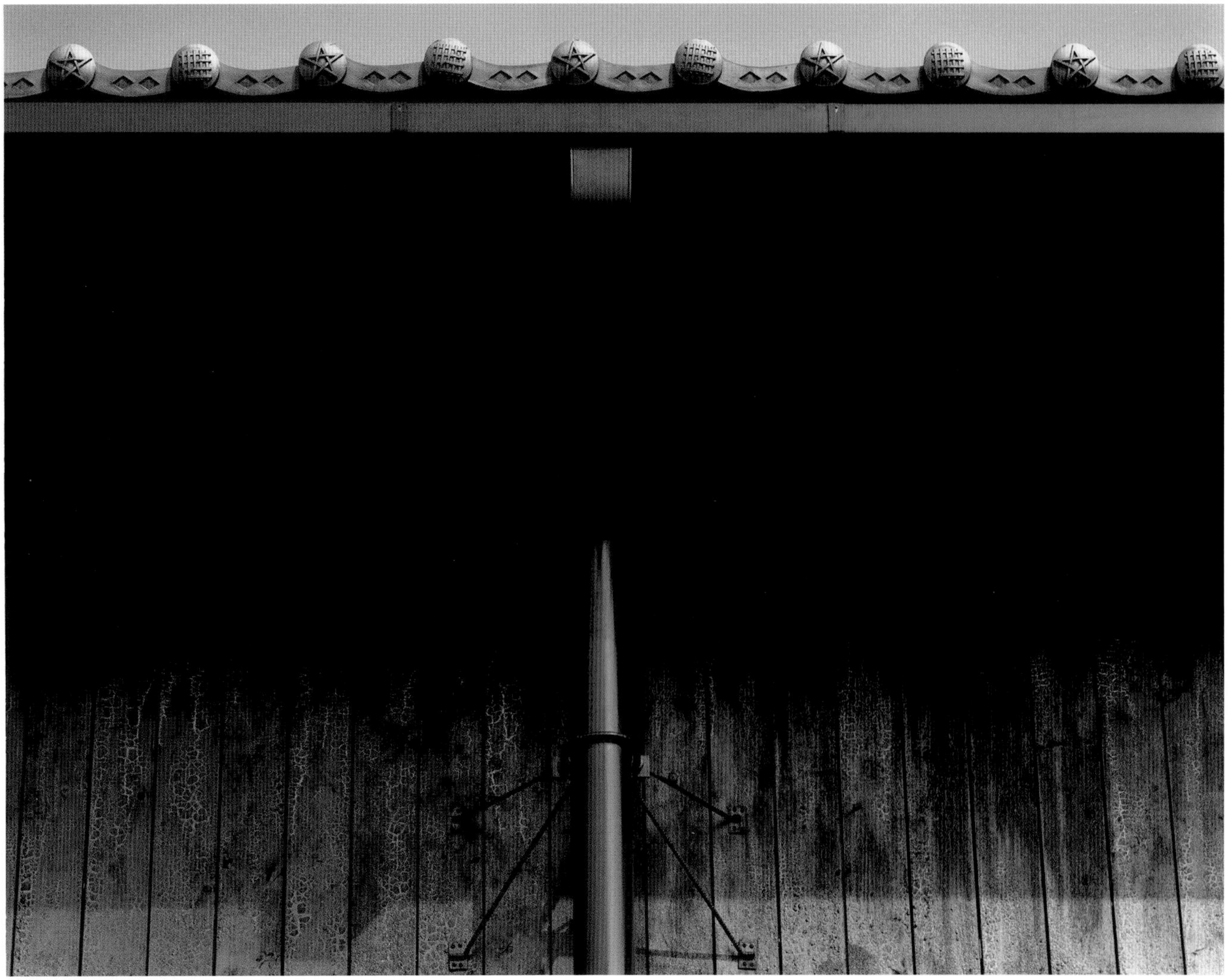

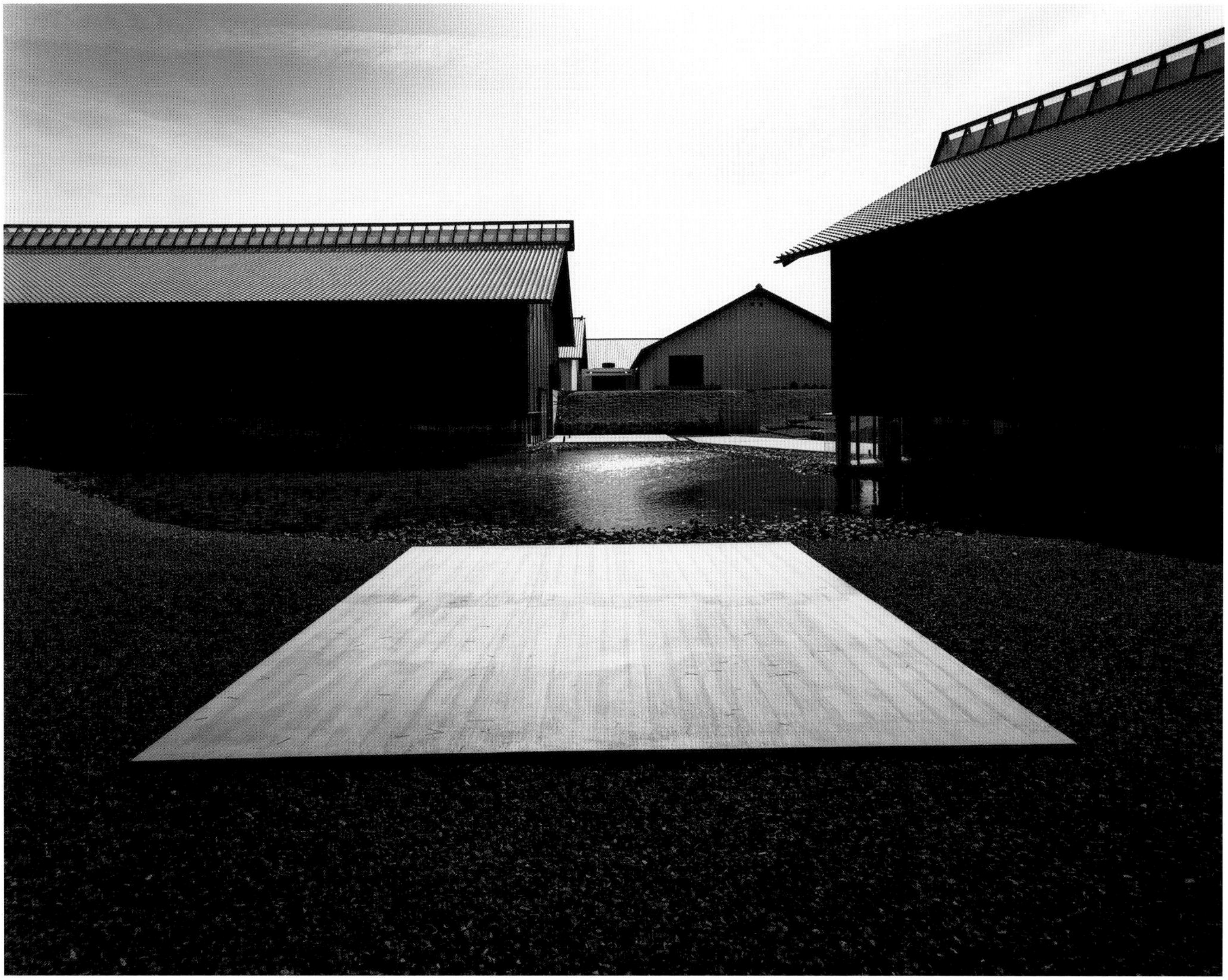

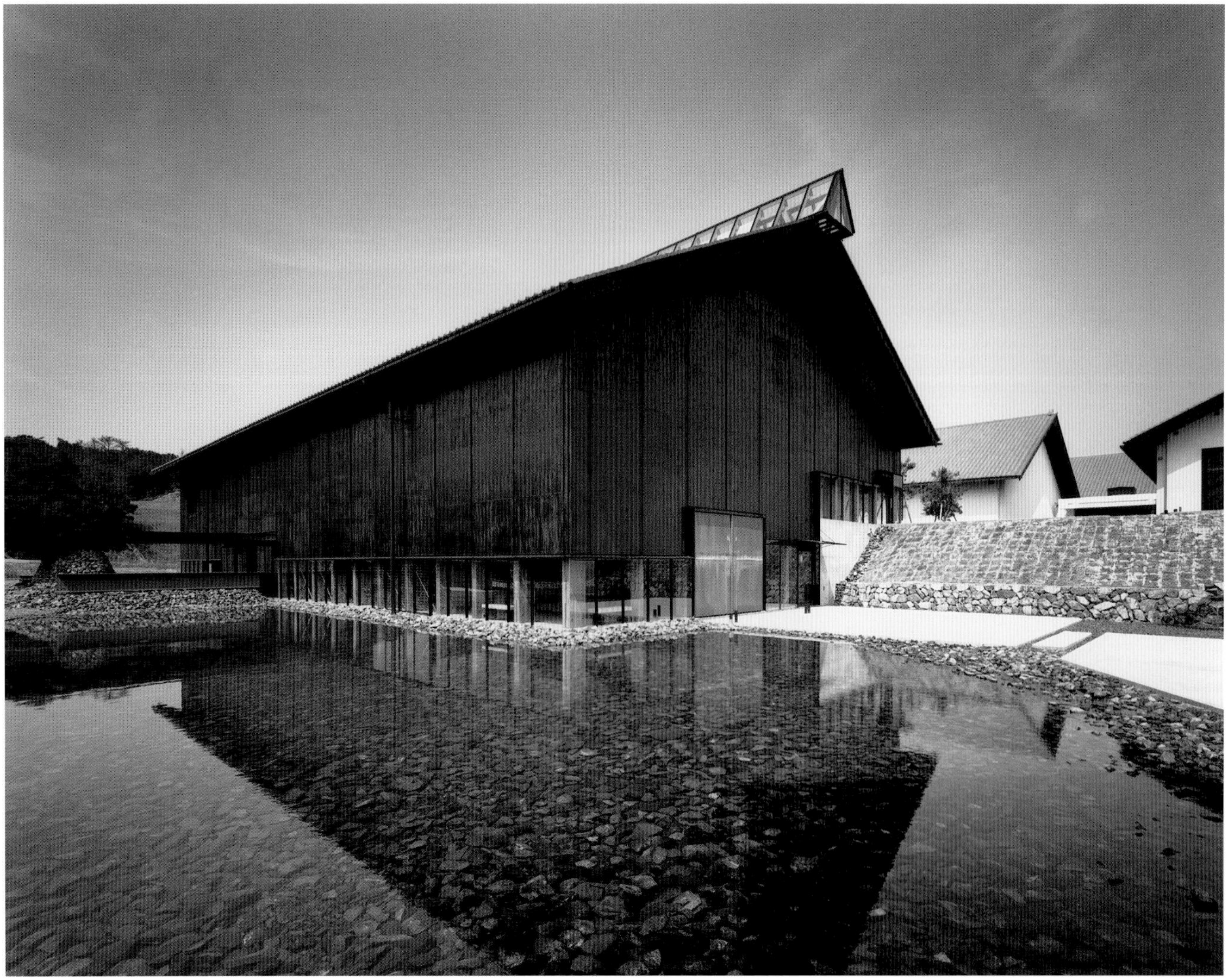

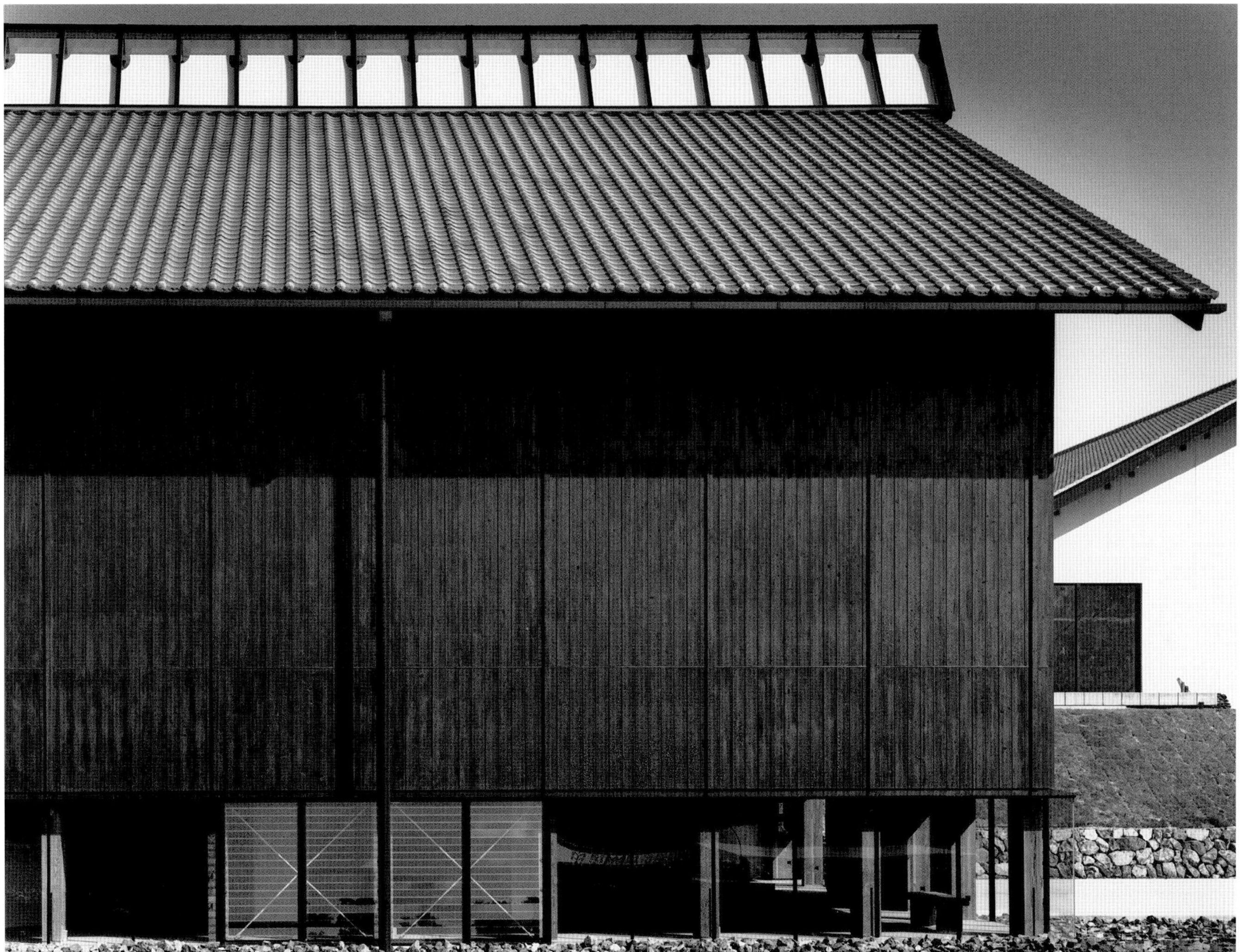

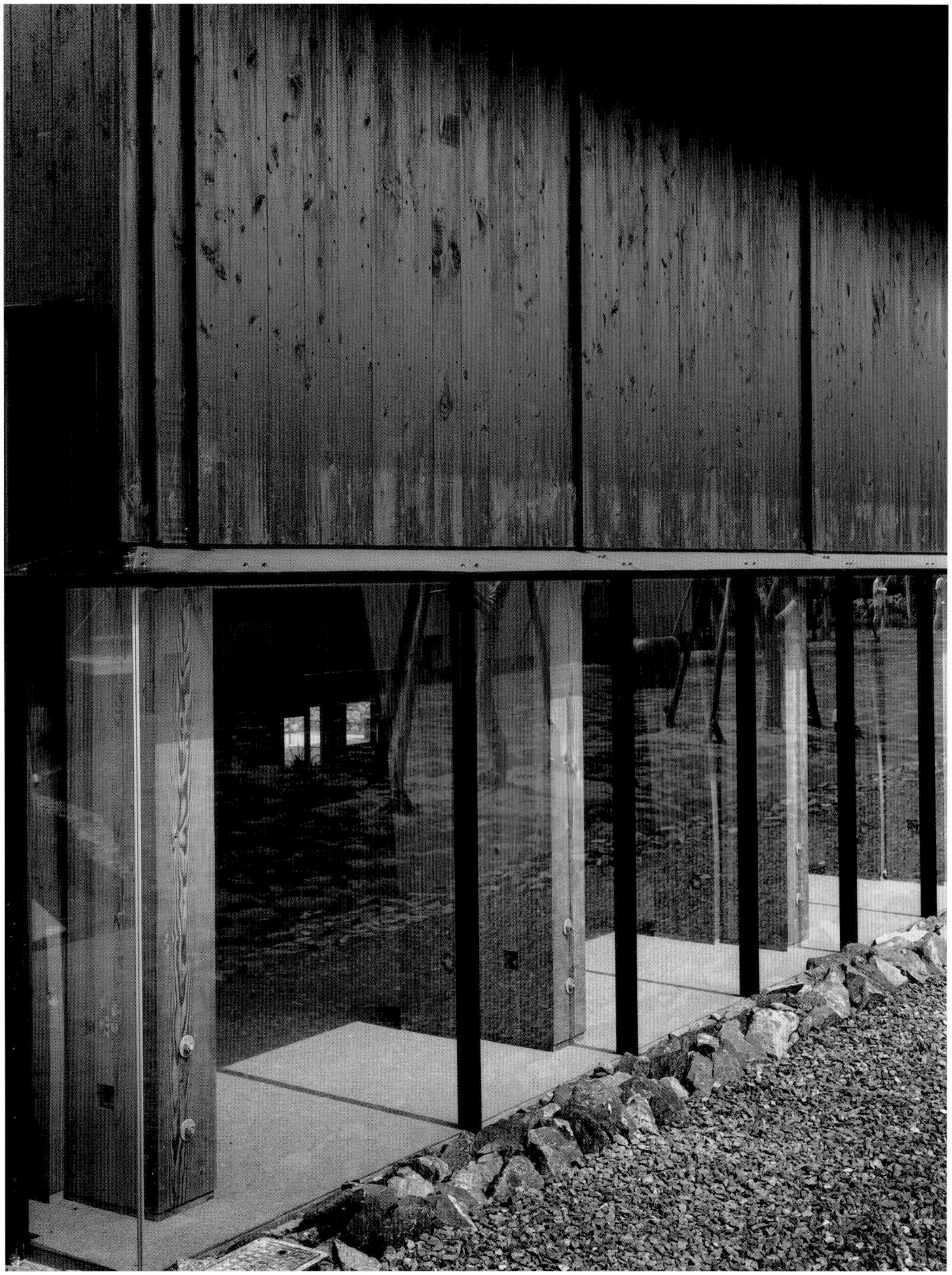

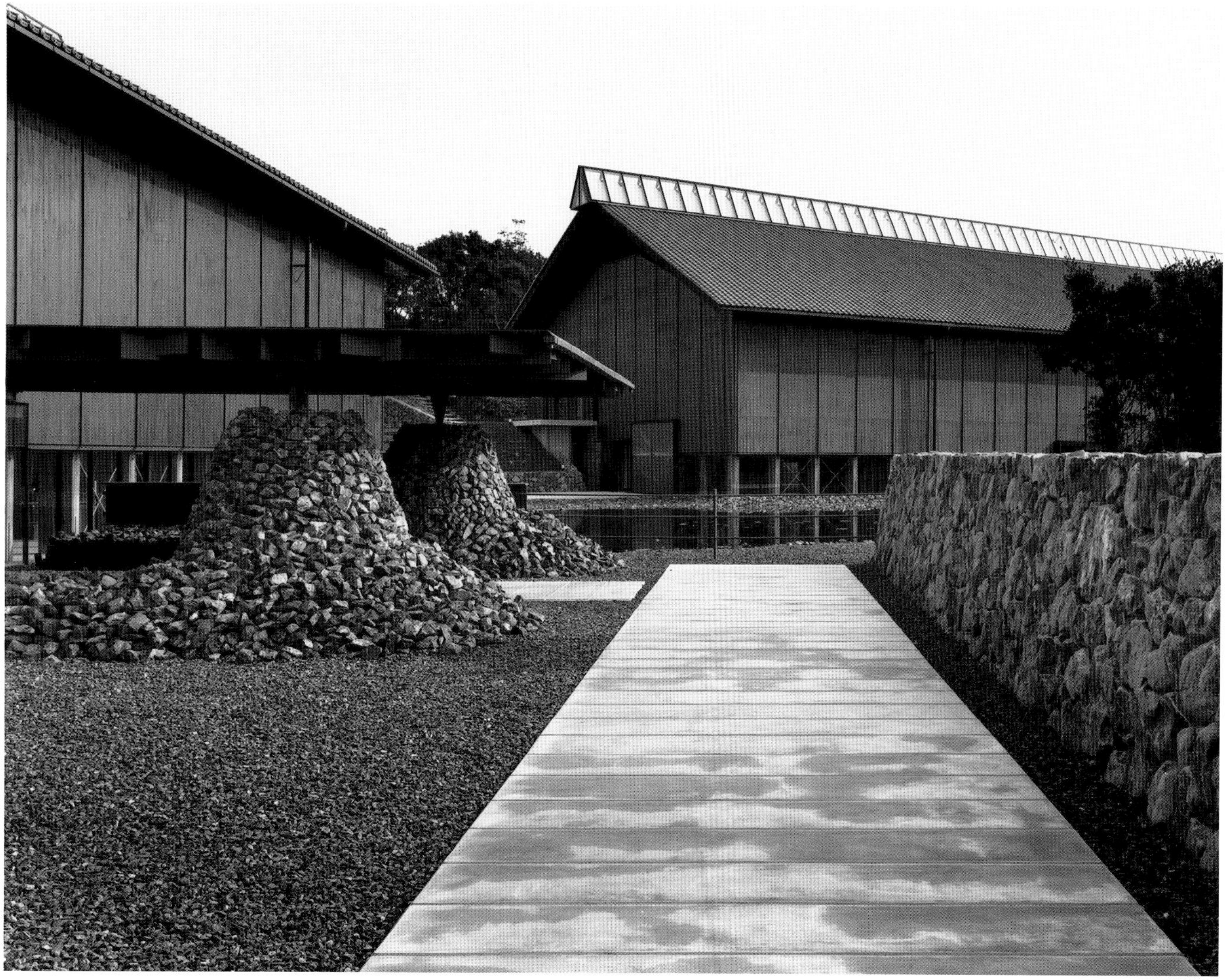

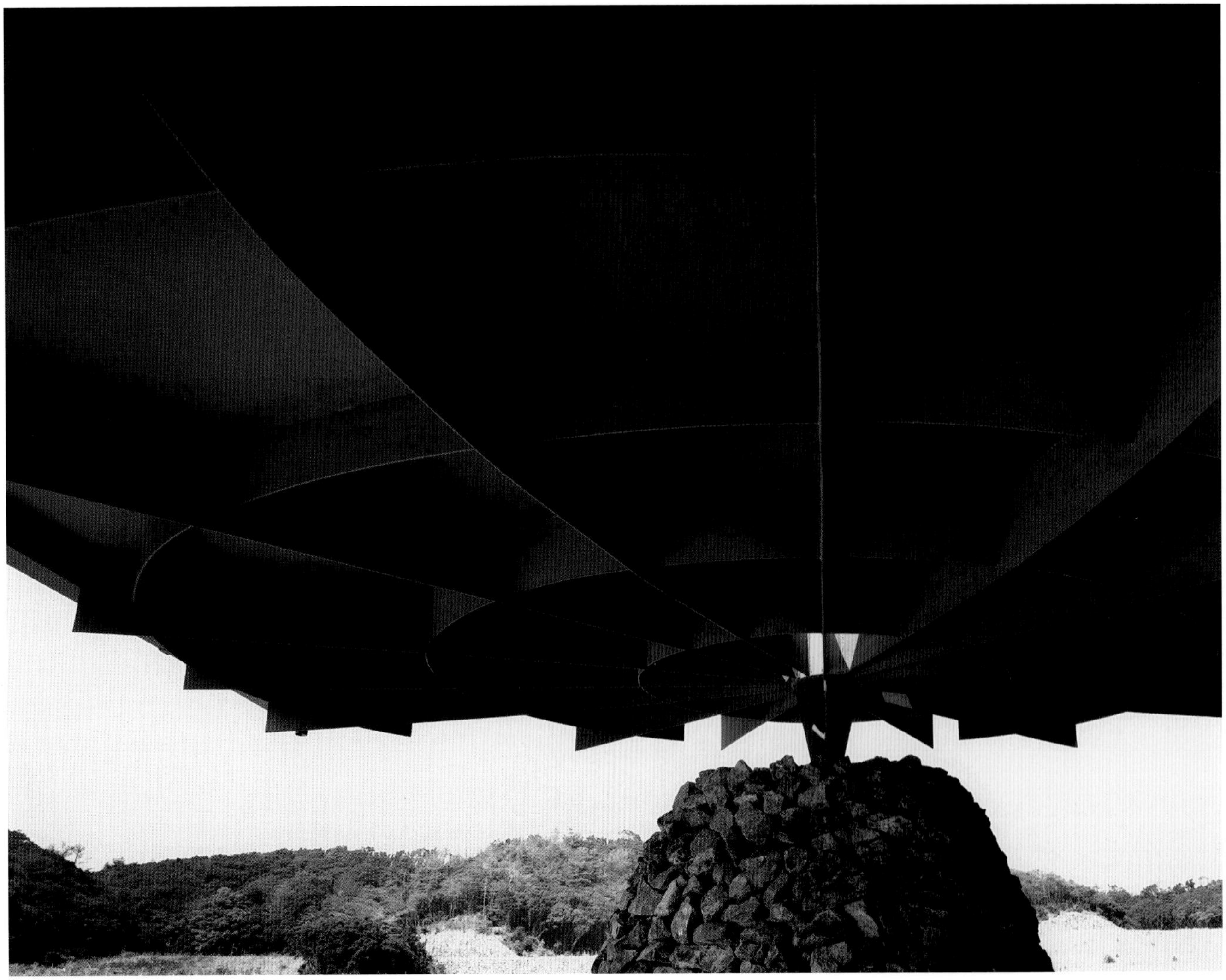

031

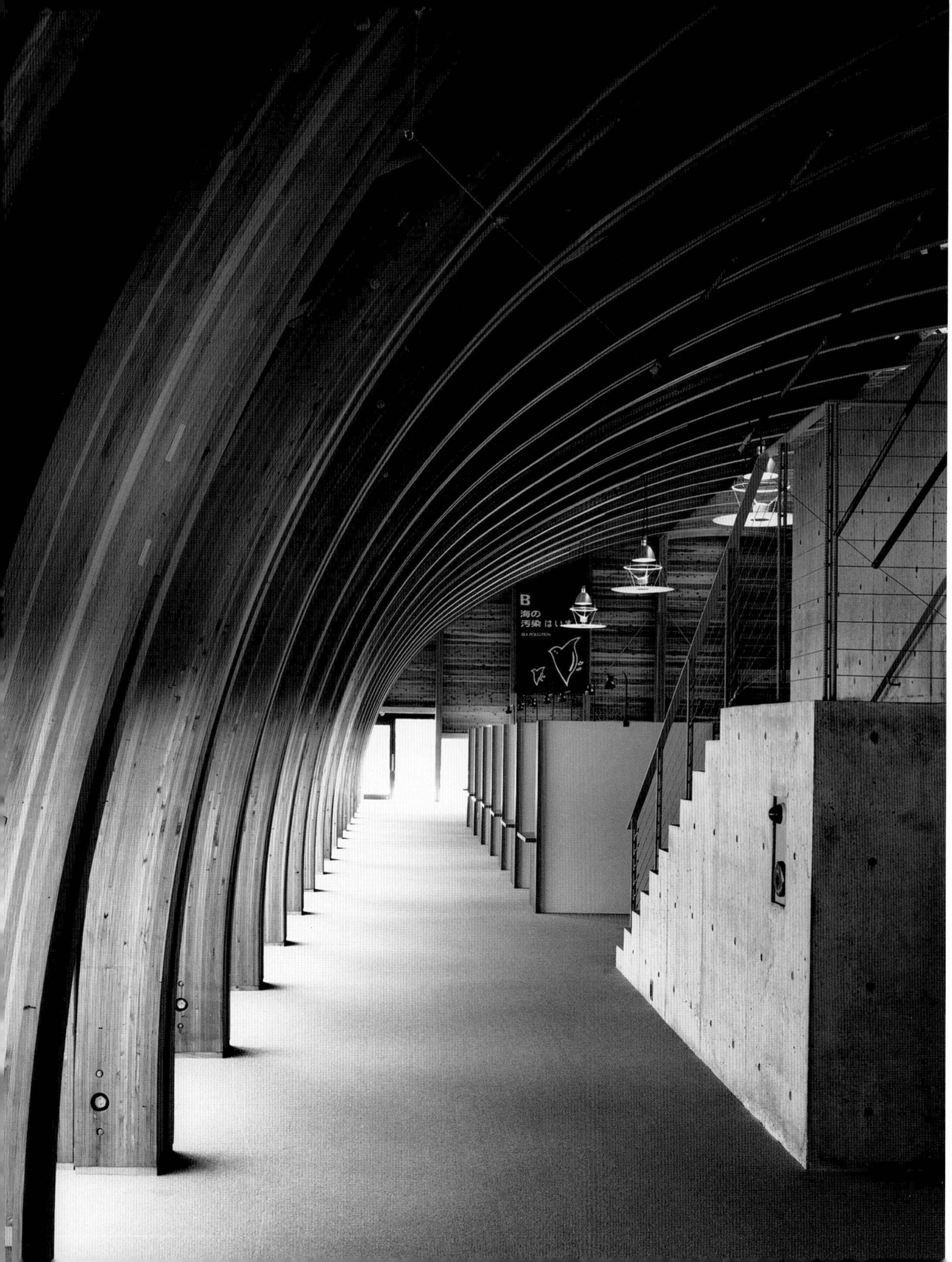
B
海の
汚染 はい
SEA POLLUTION

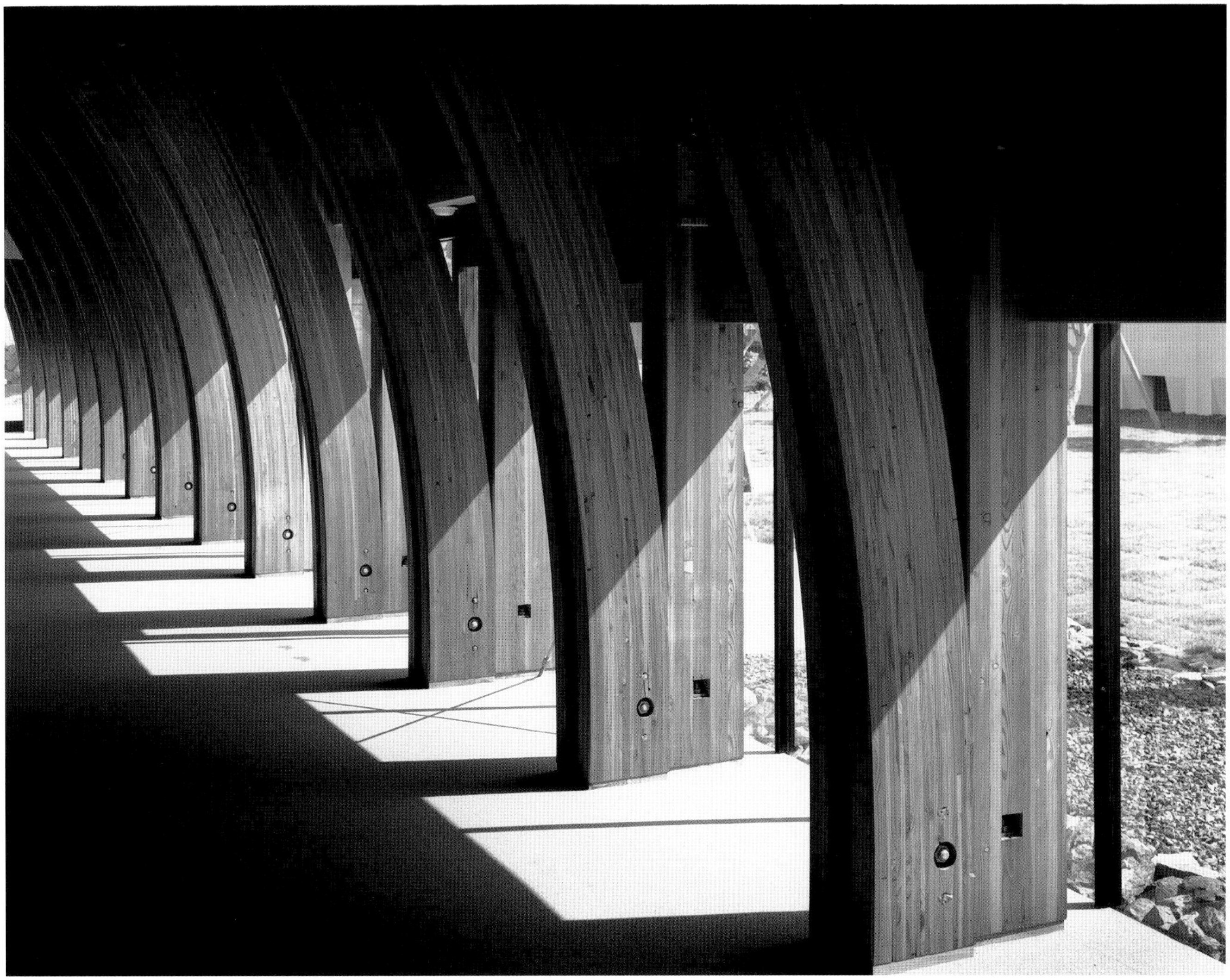

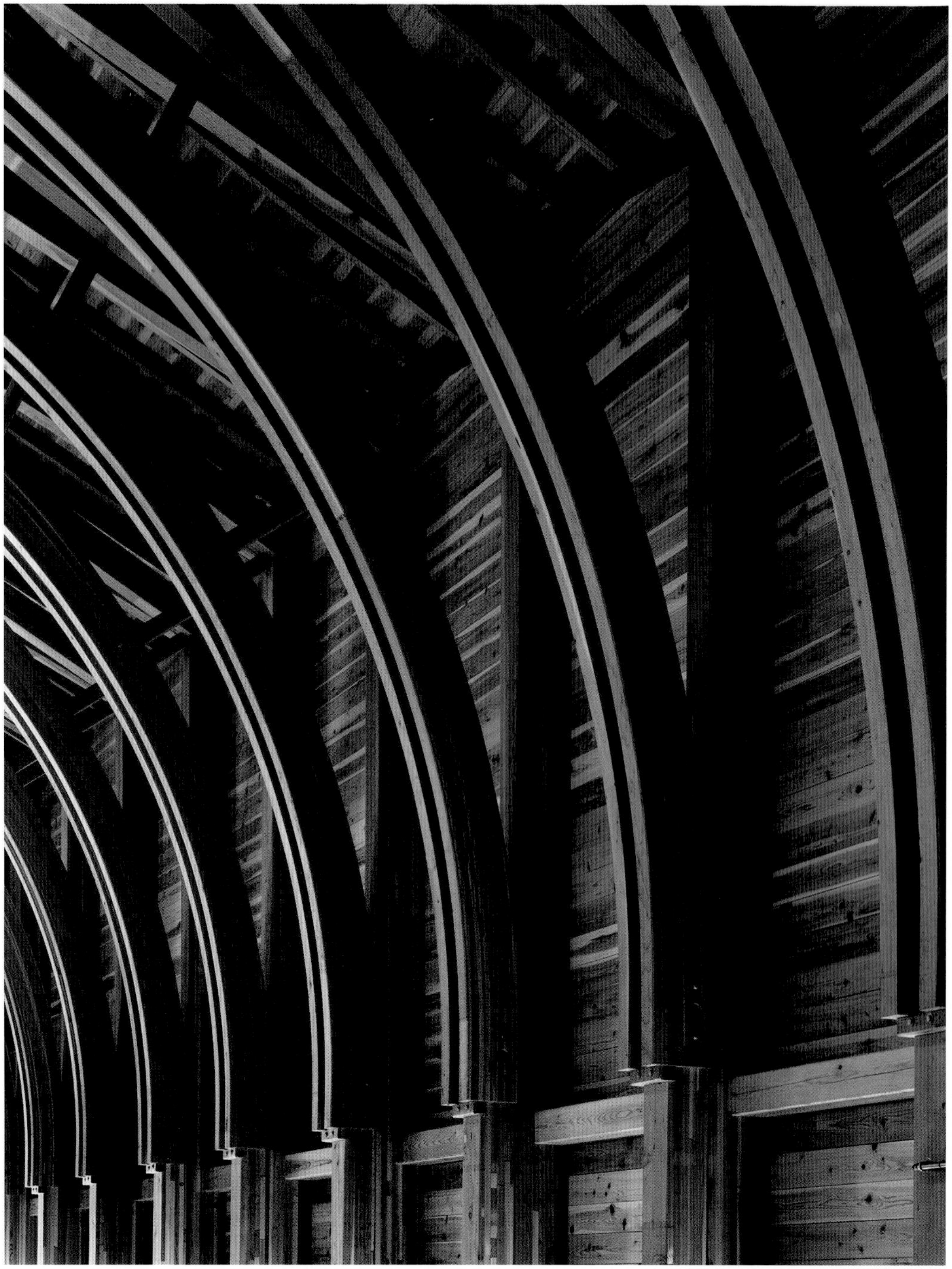

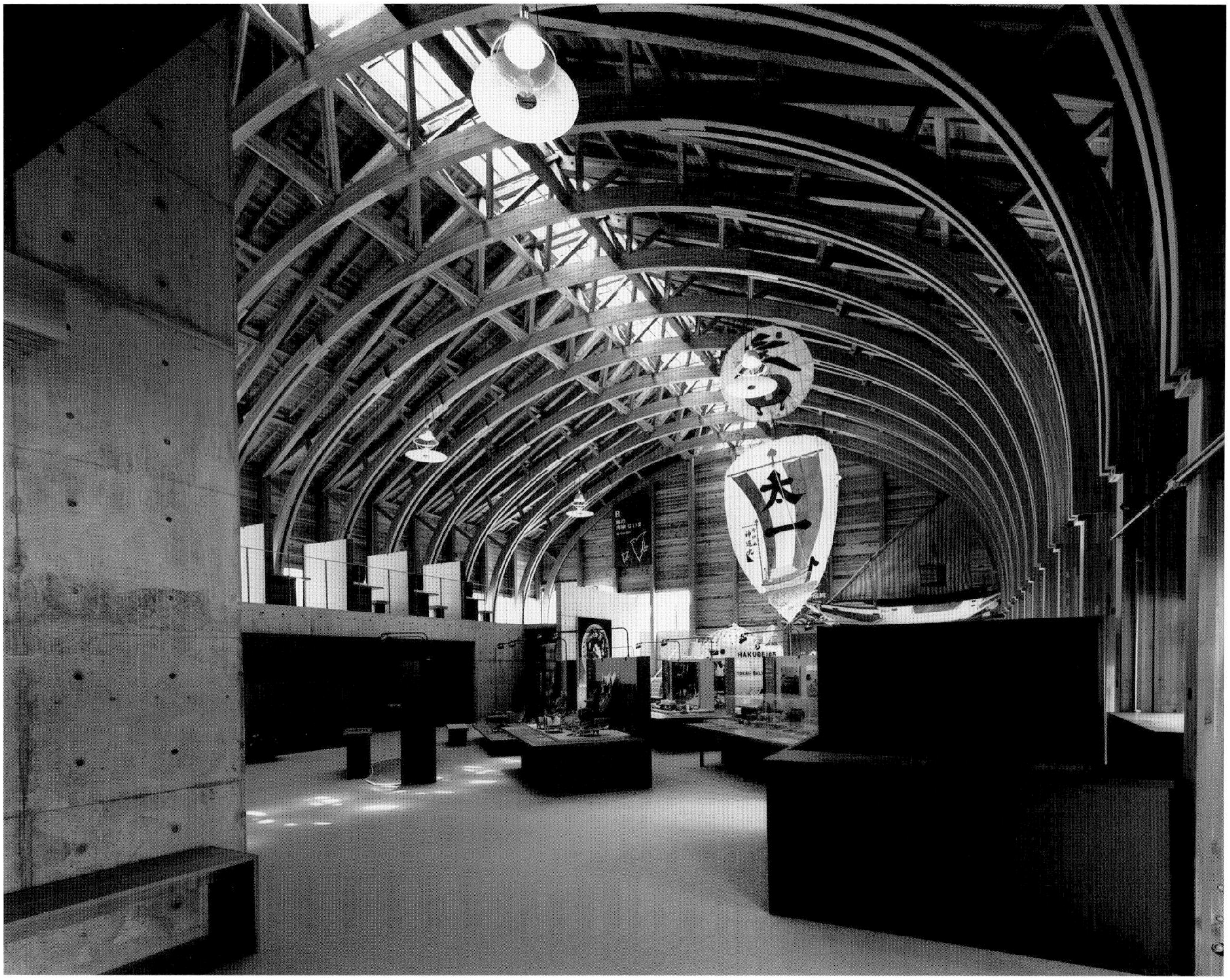
太一

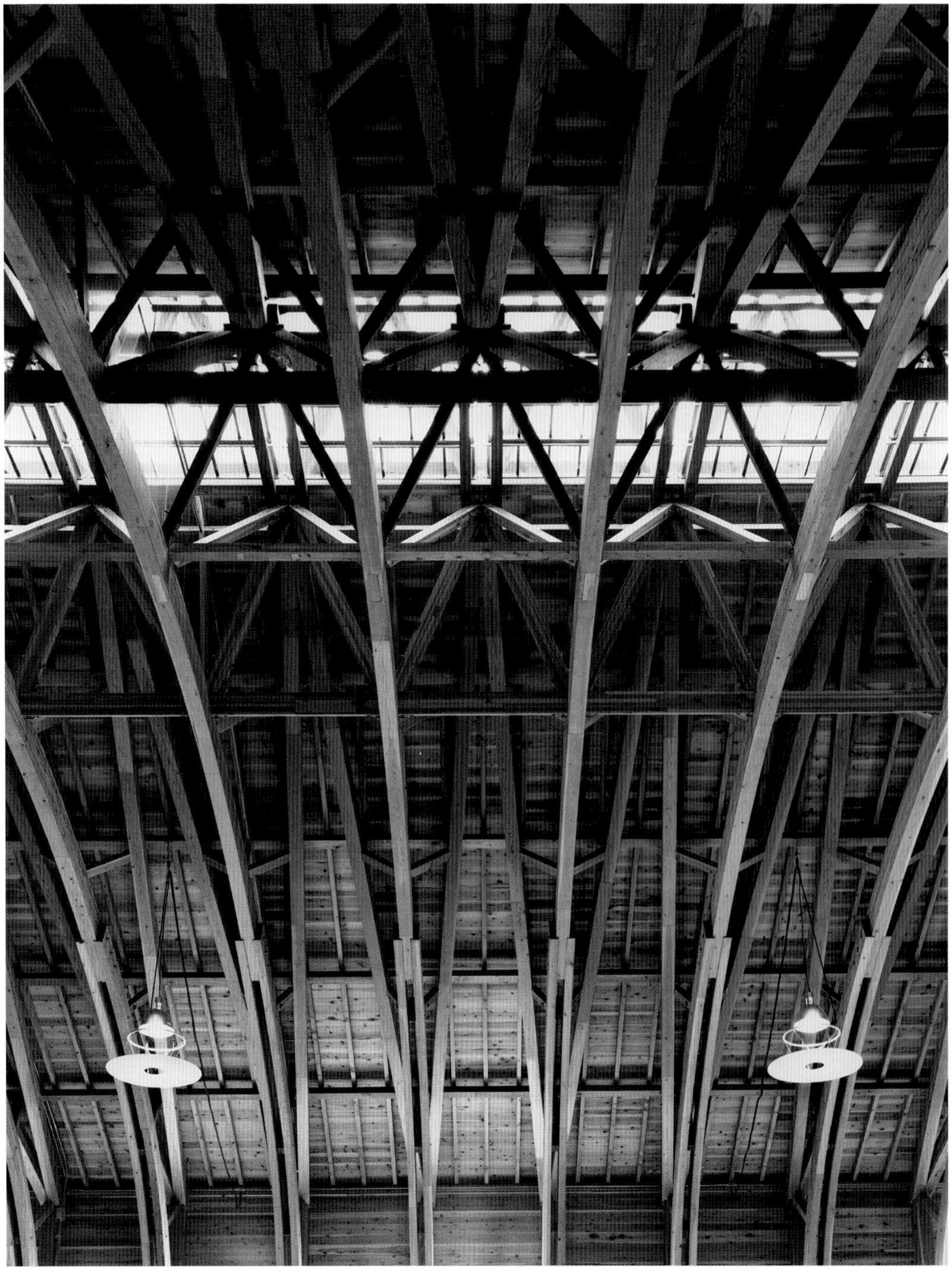

037

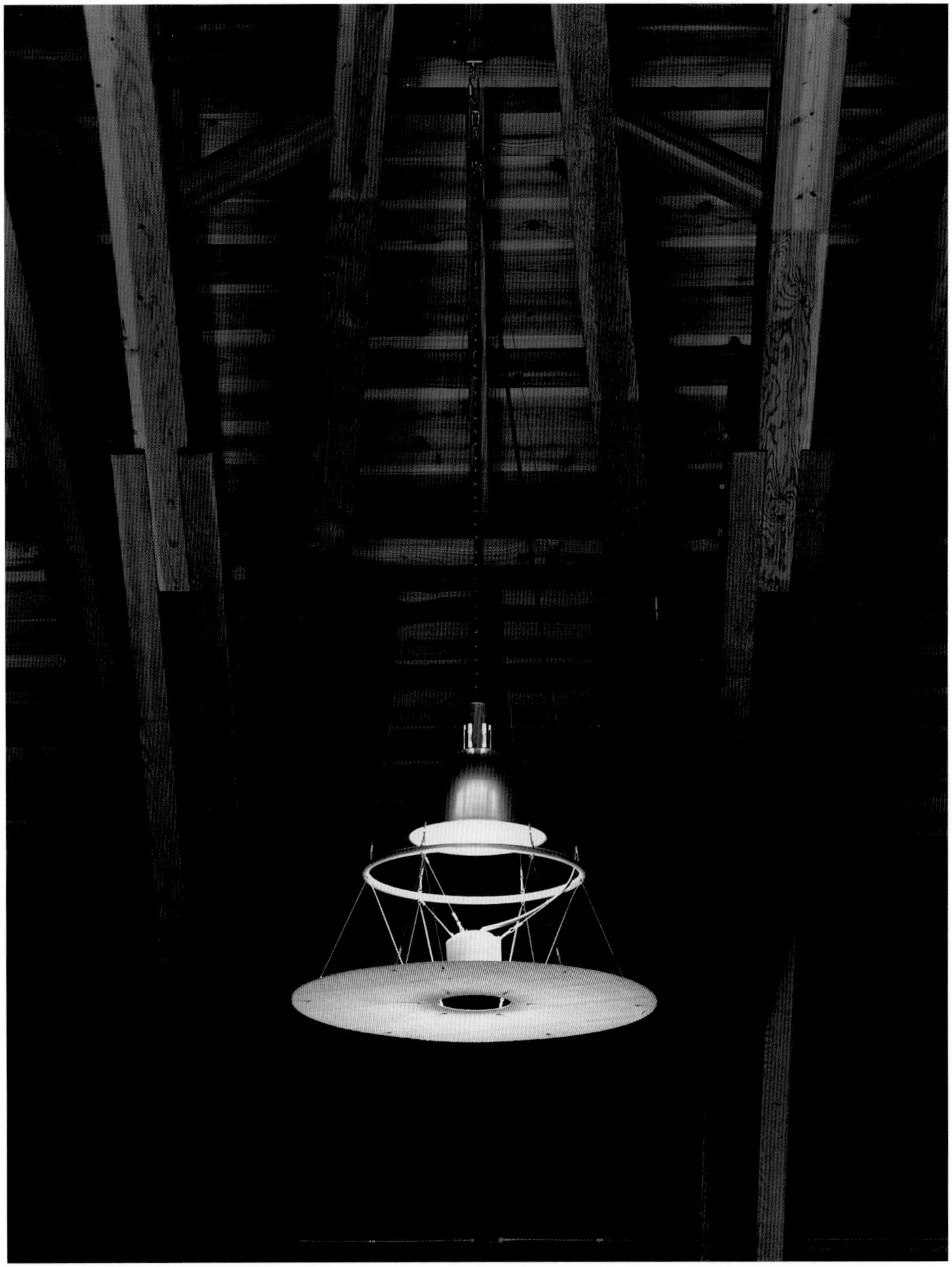

重要有形民俗文化財
収 蔵 庫

■

Repository

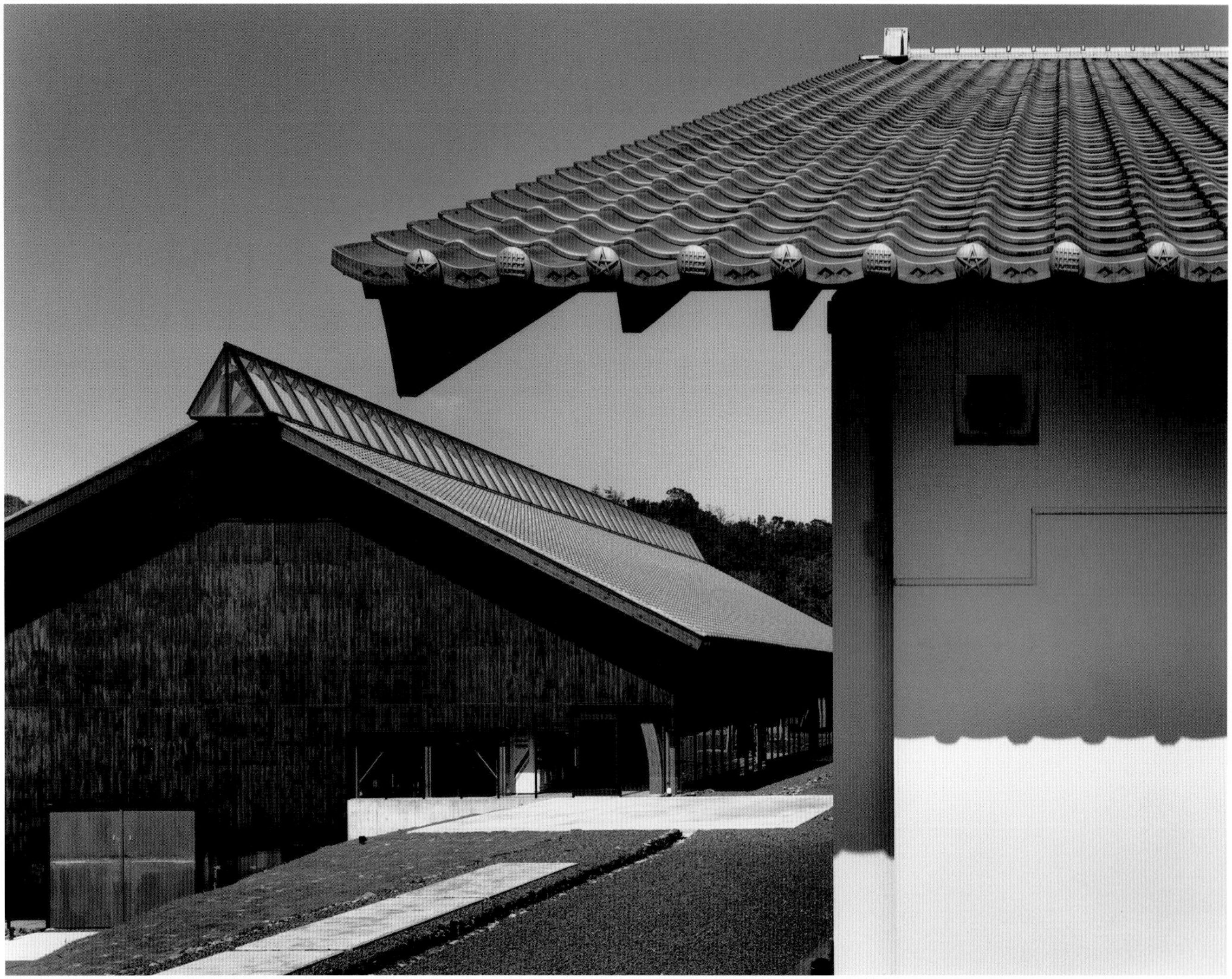

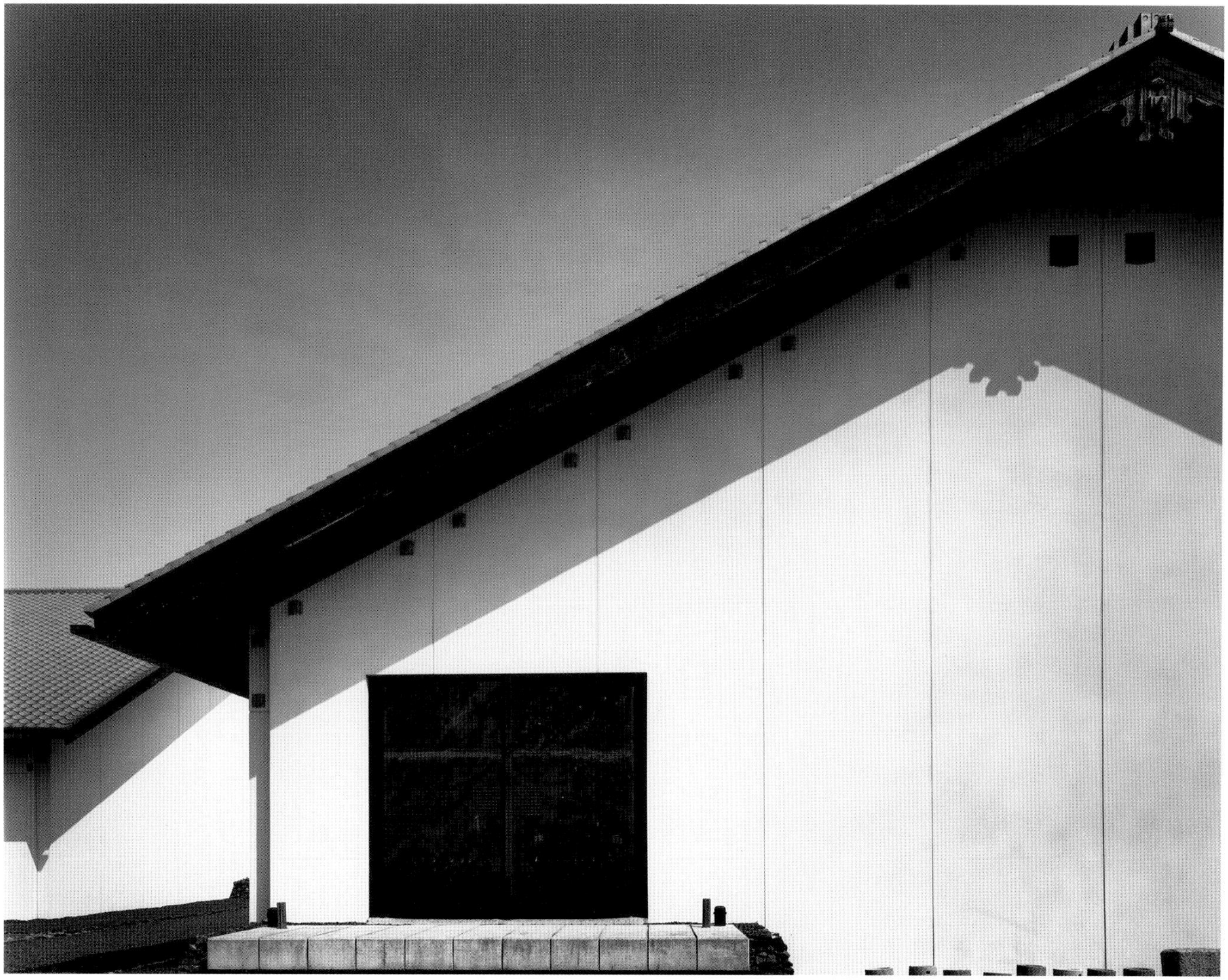

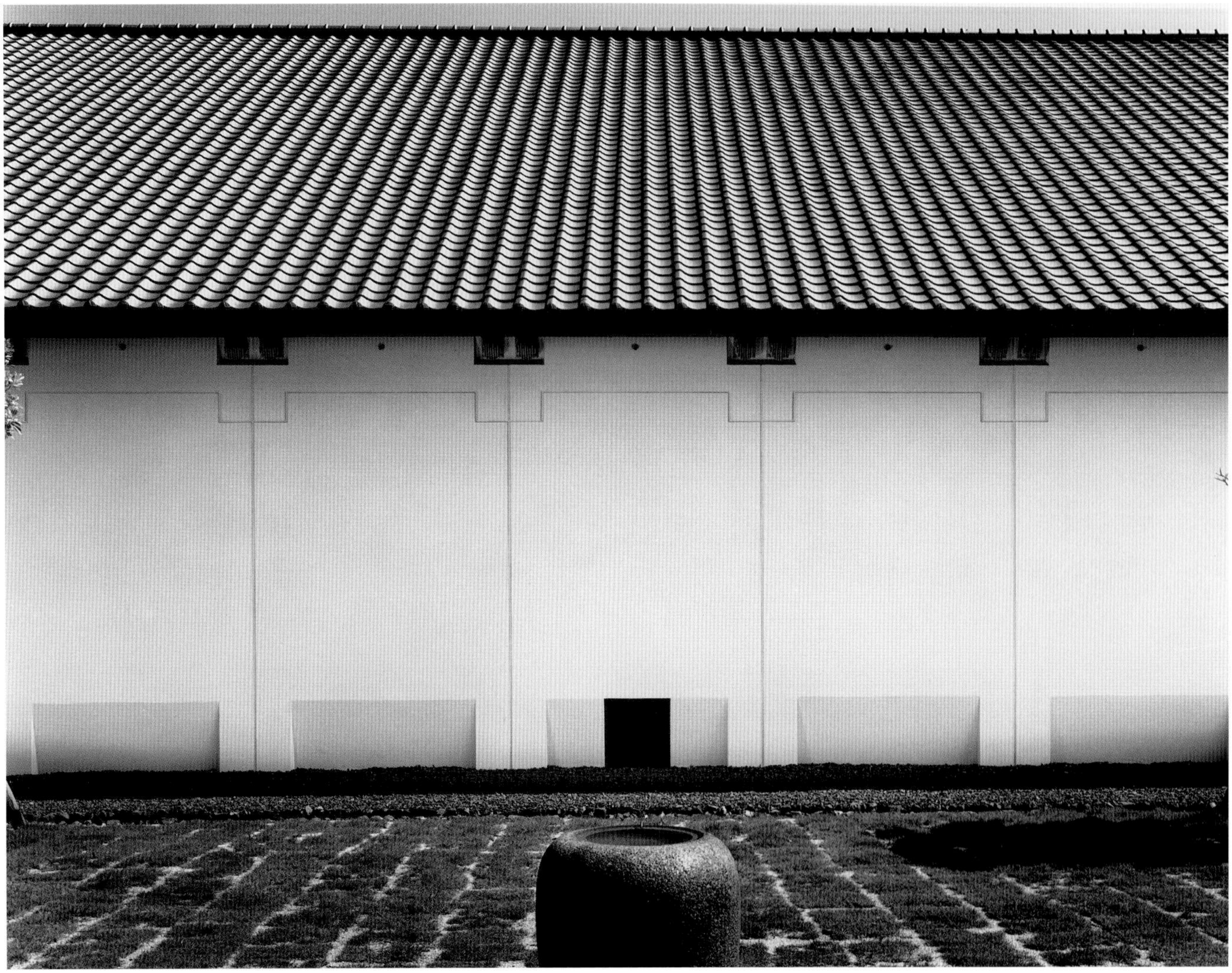

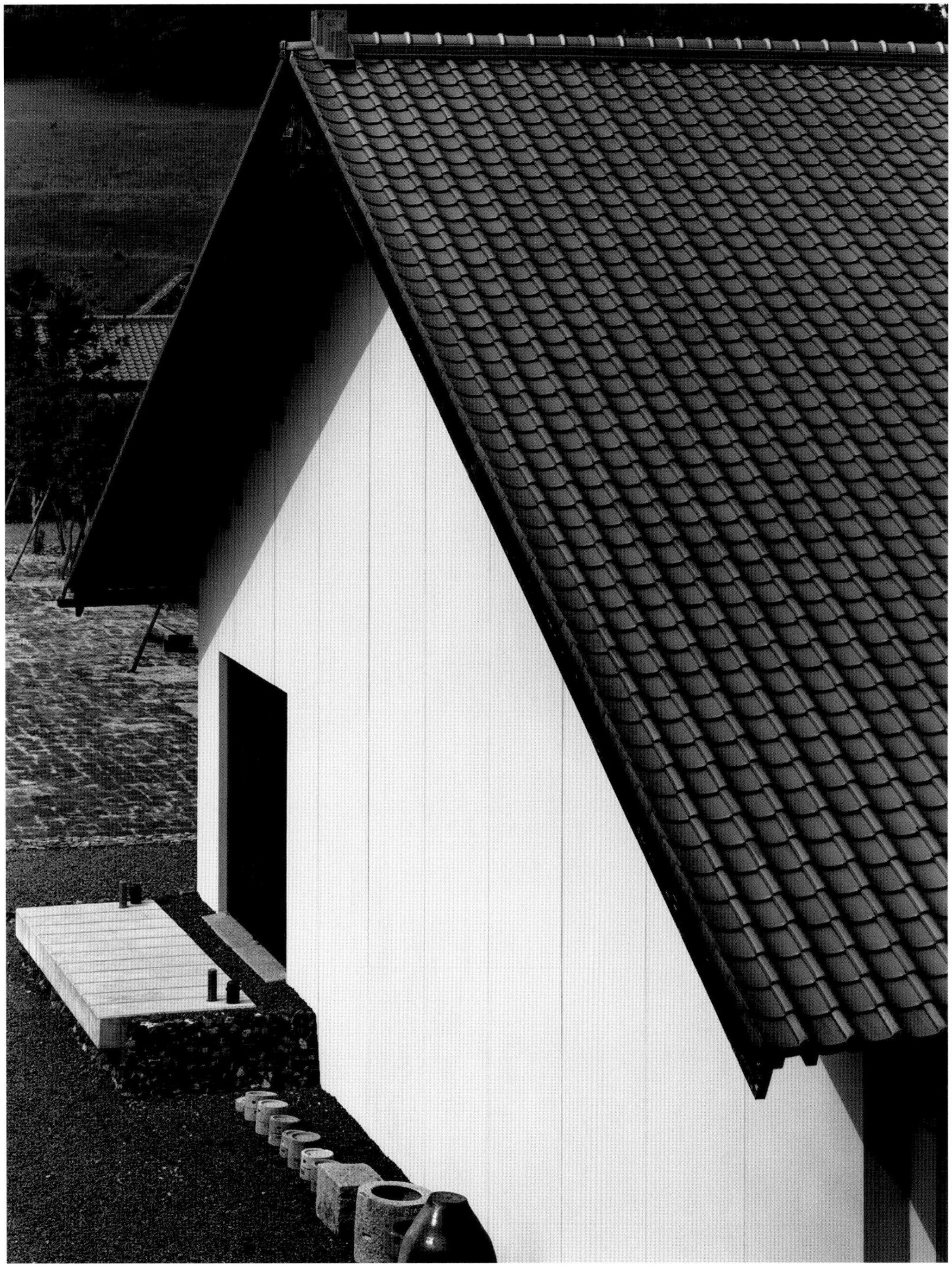

044

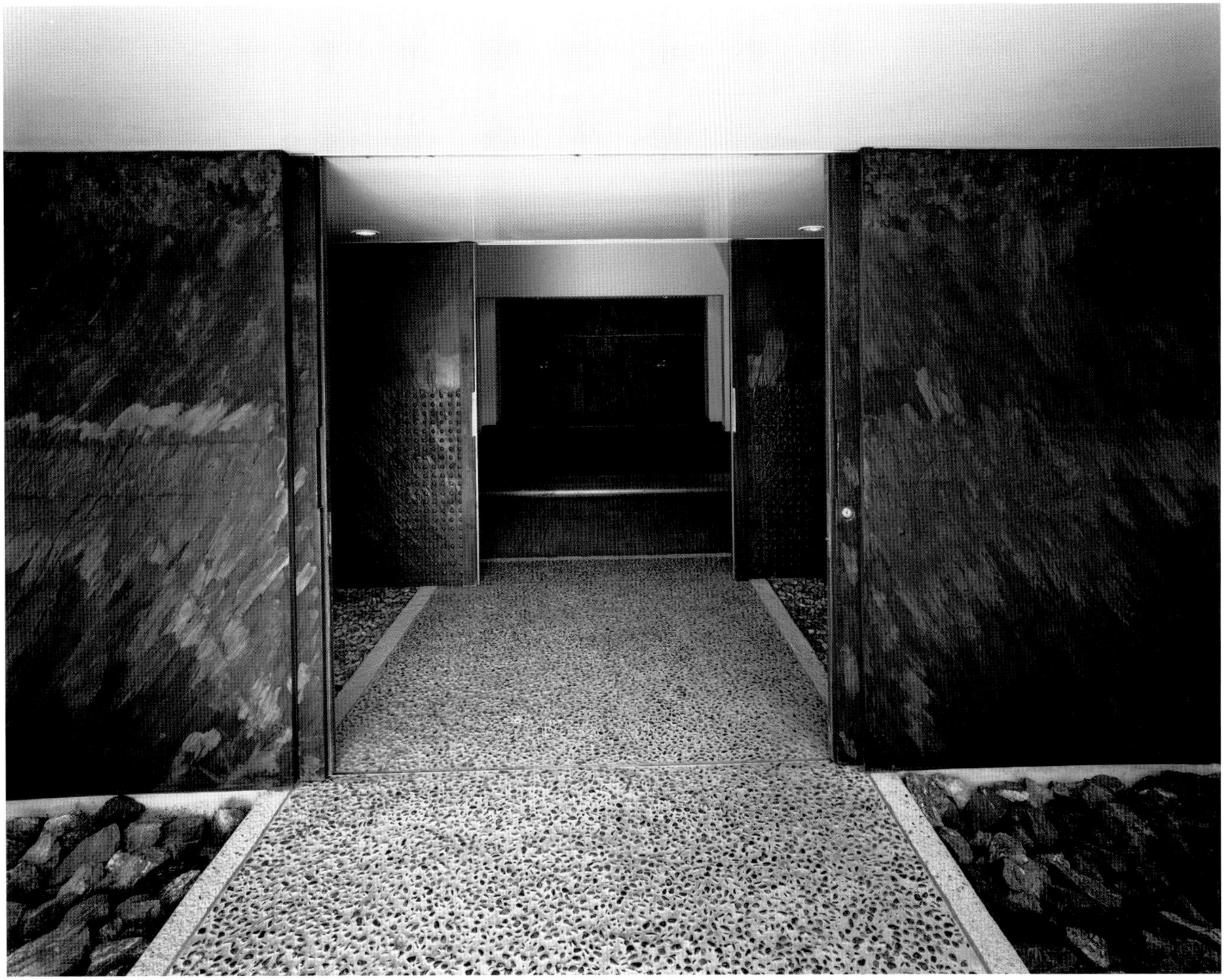

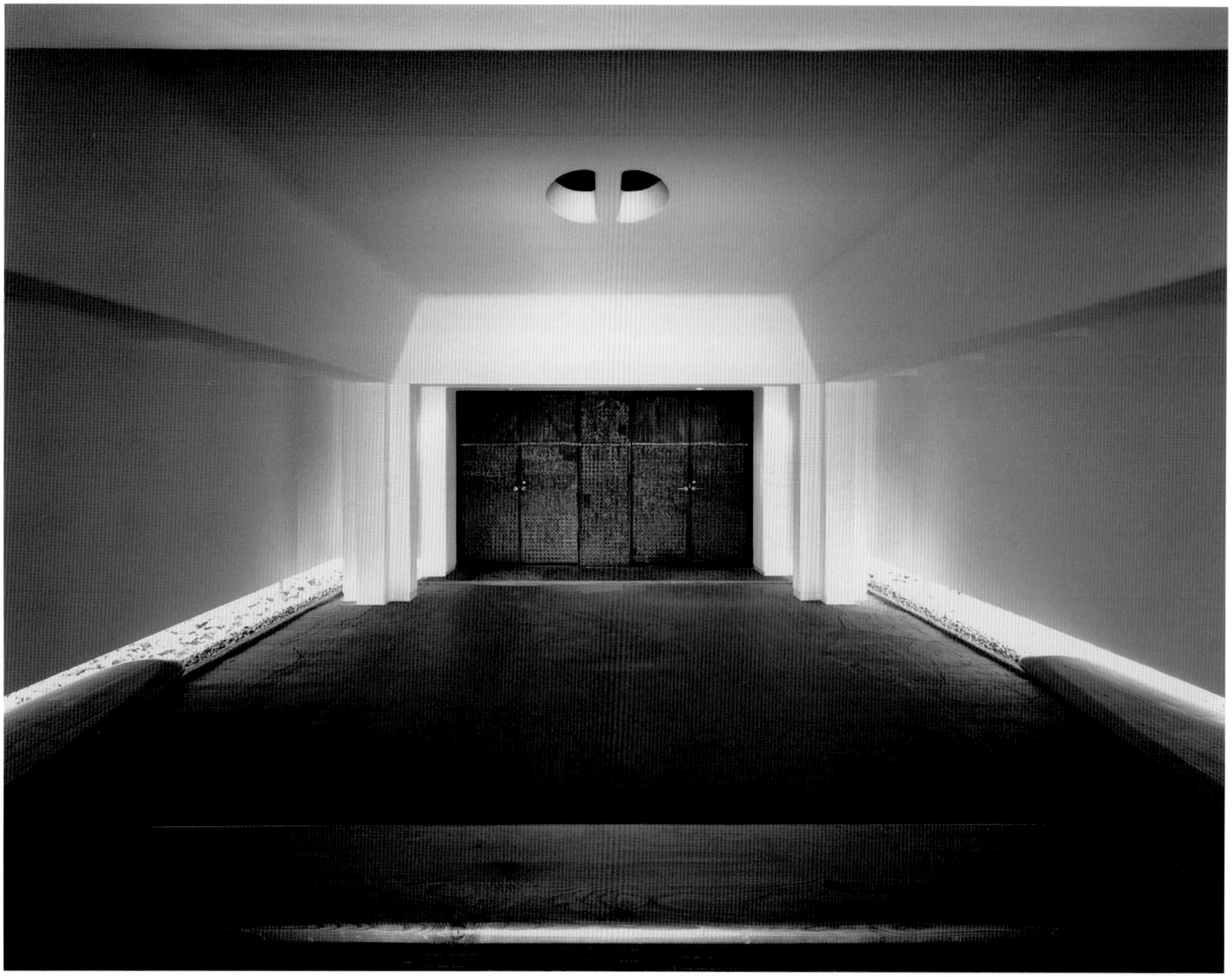

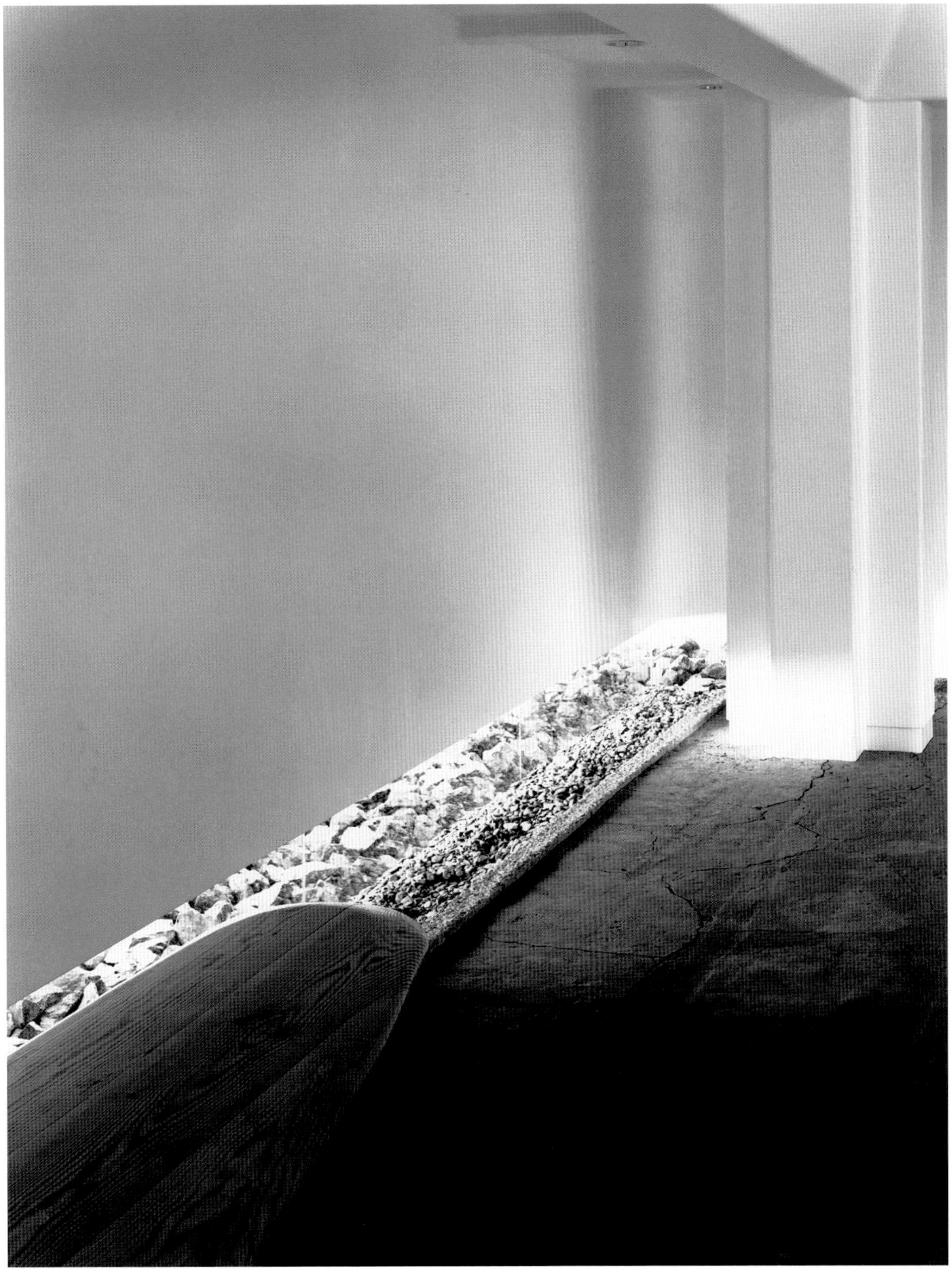

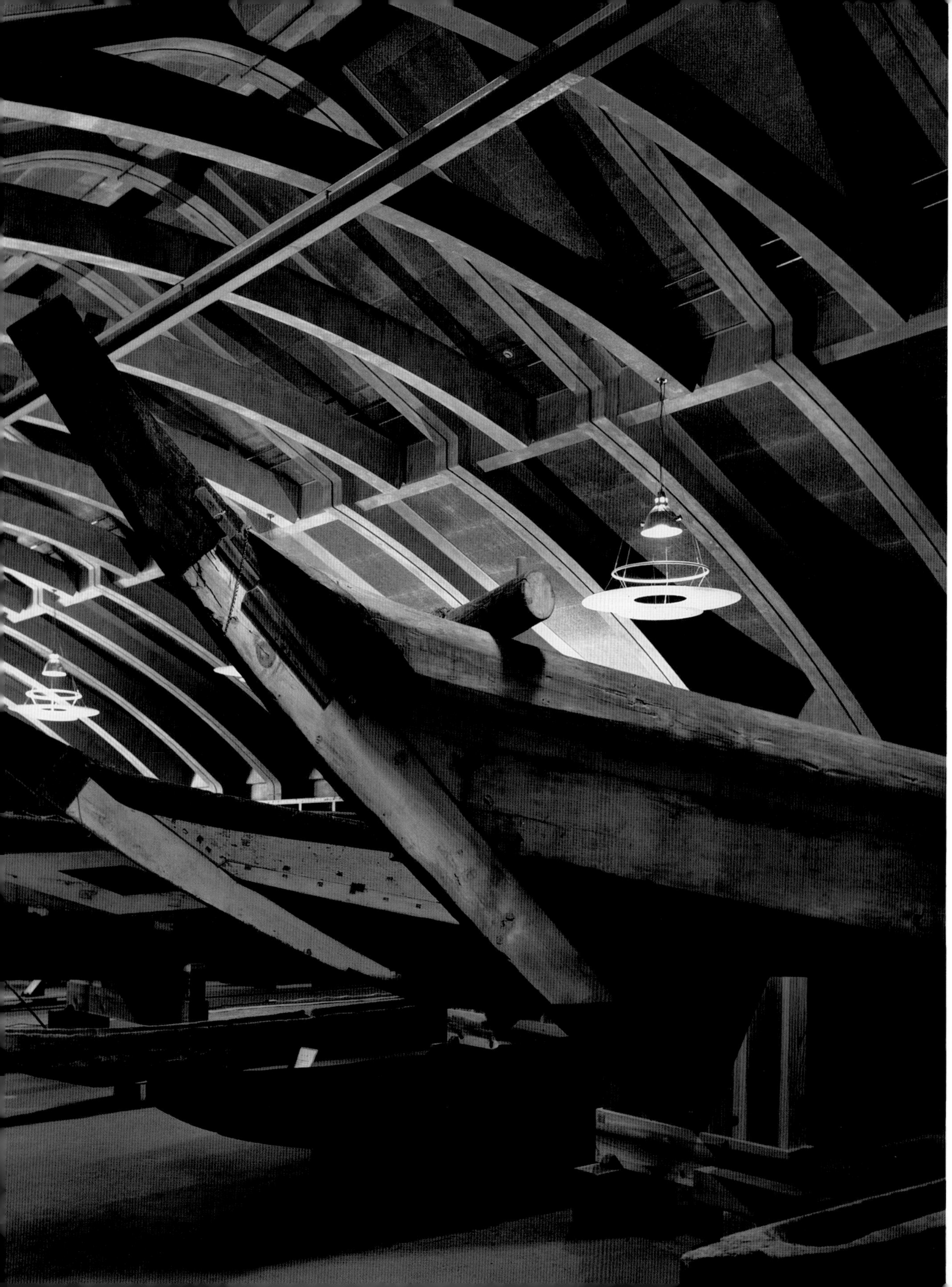

049

050

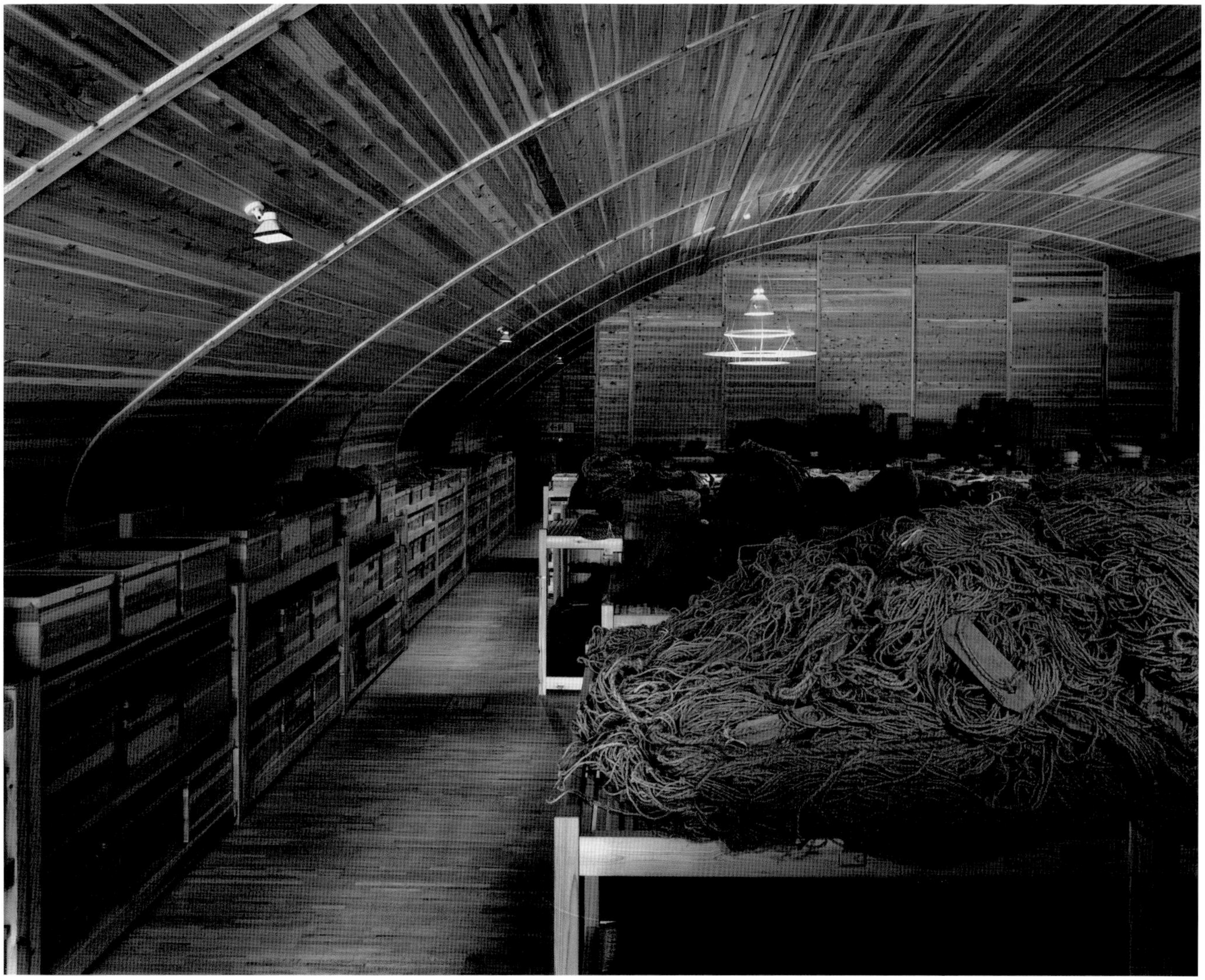

052

Chihiro Art Museum Azumino

安曇野ちひろ美術館　撮影■1998

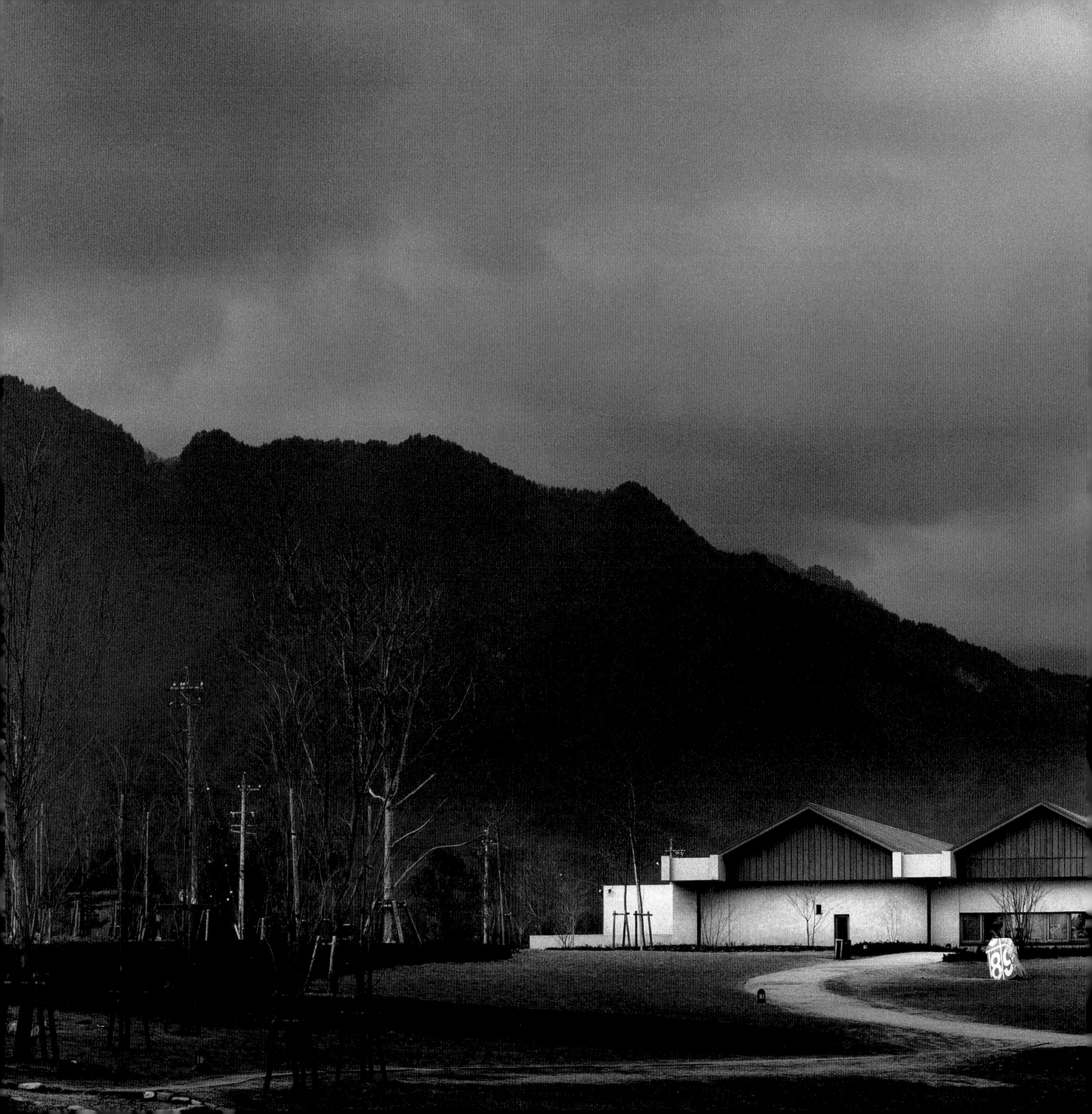

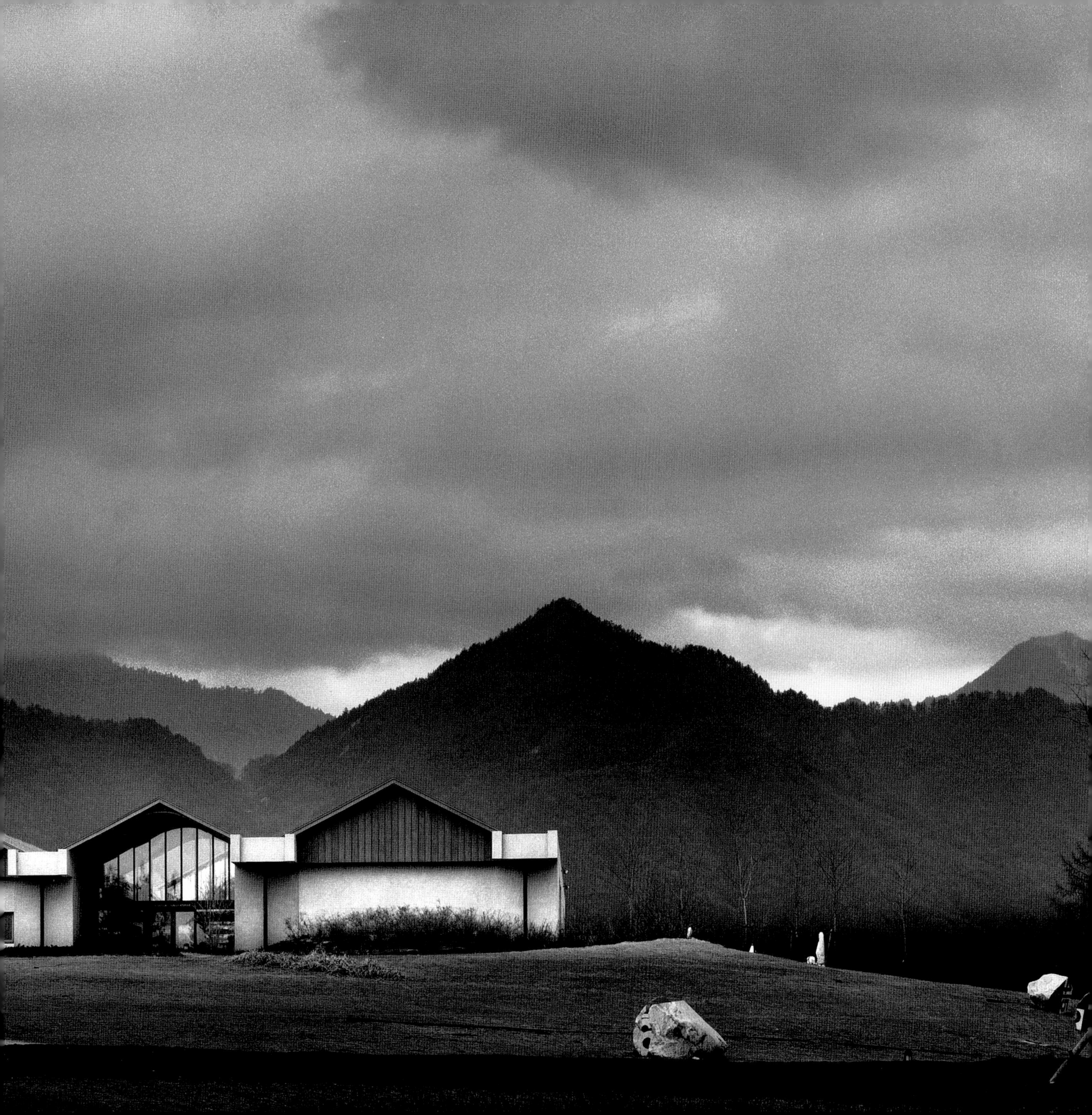

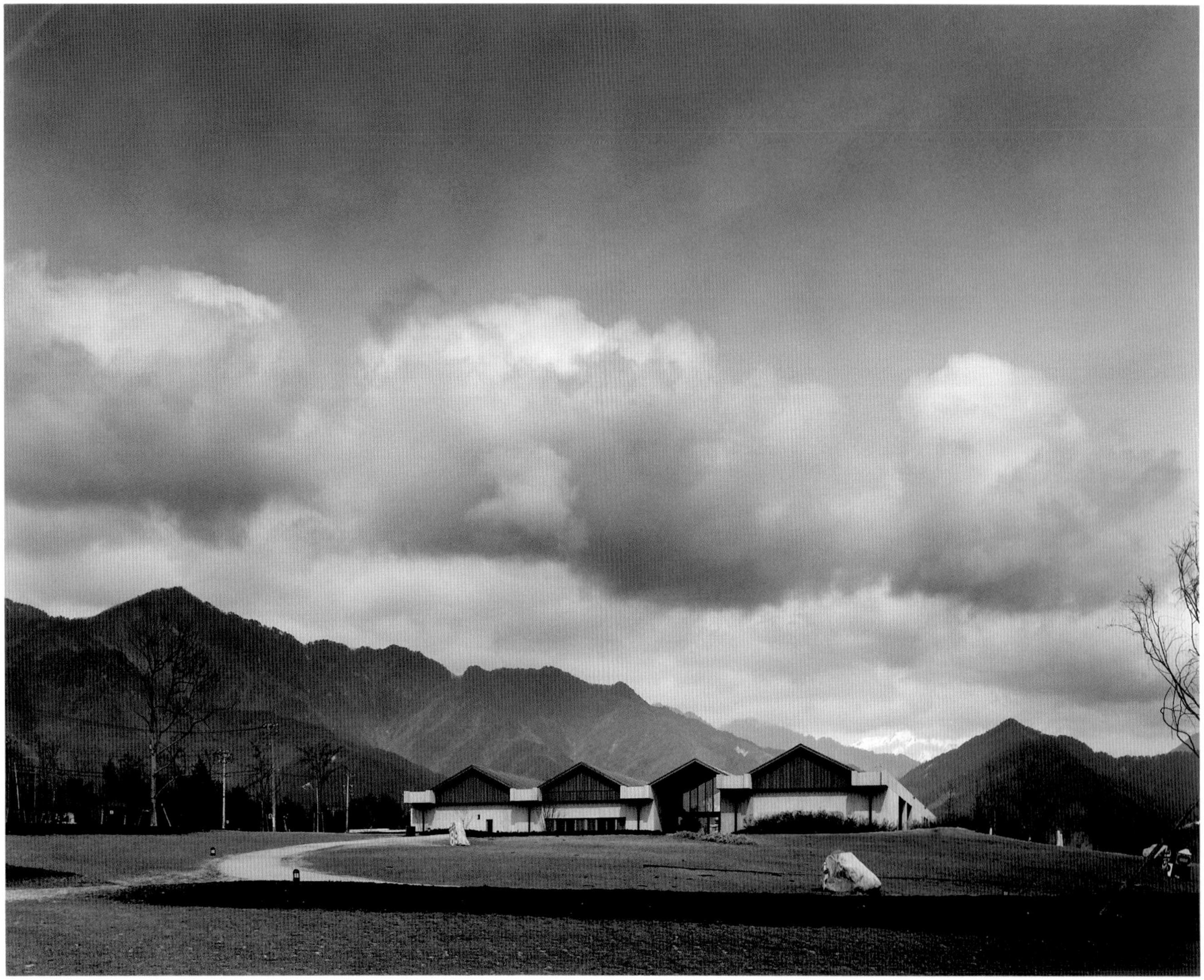

057

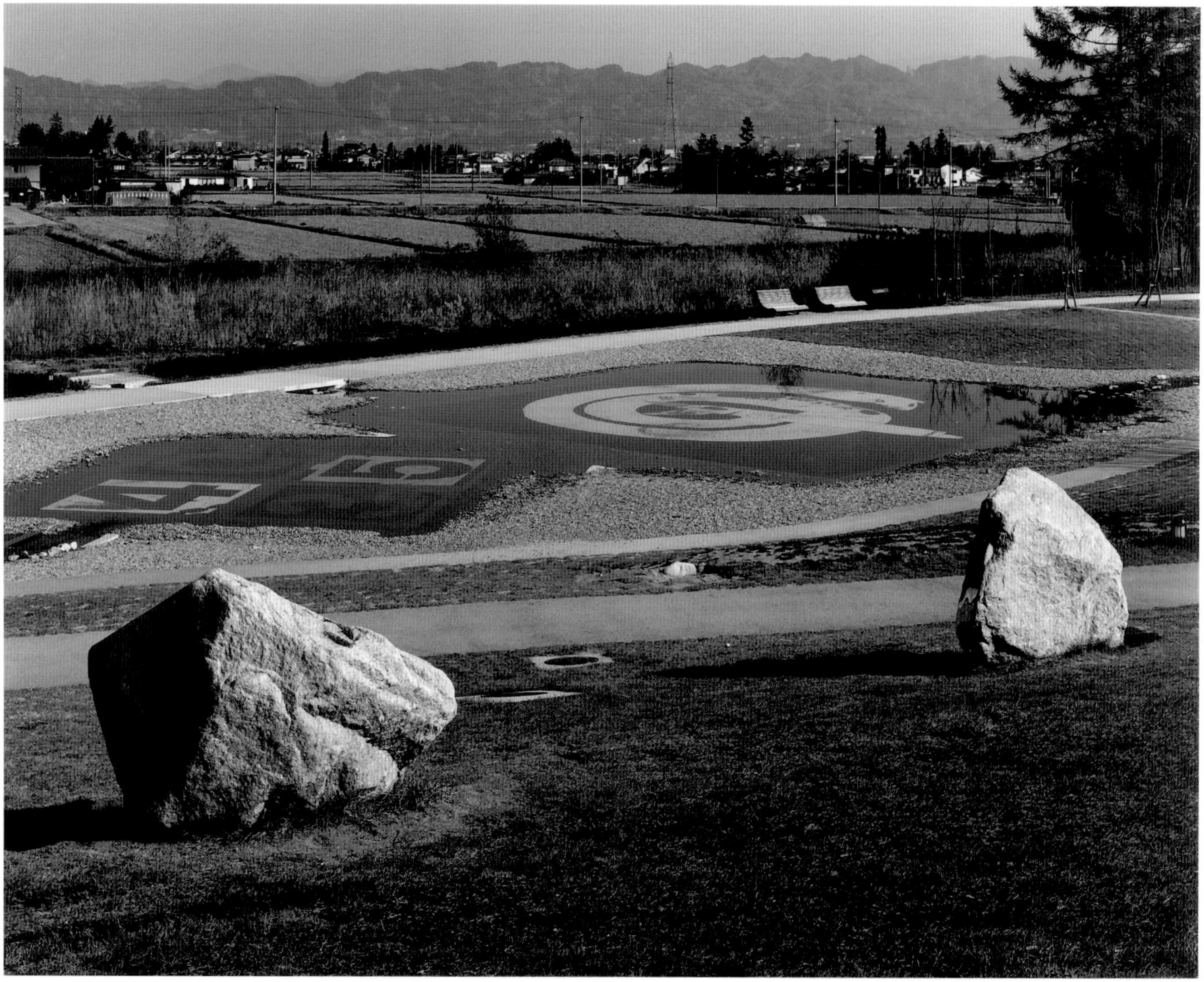

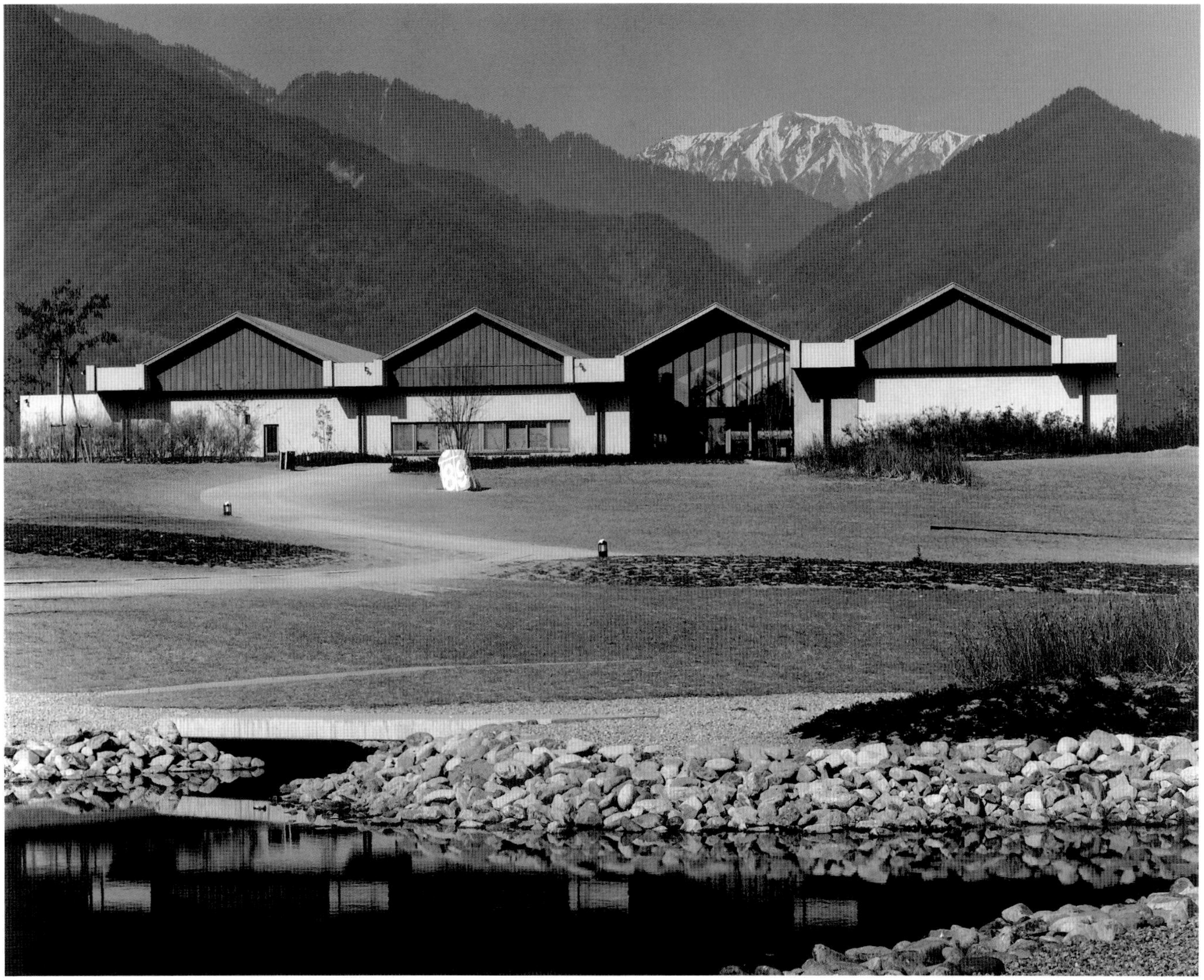

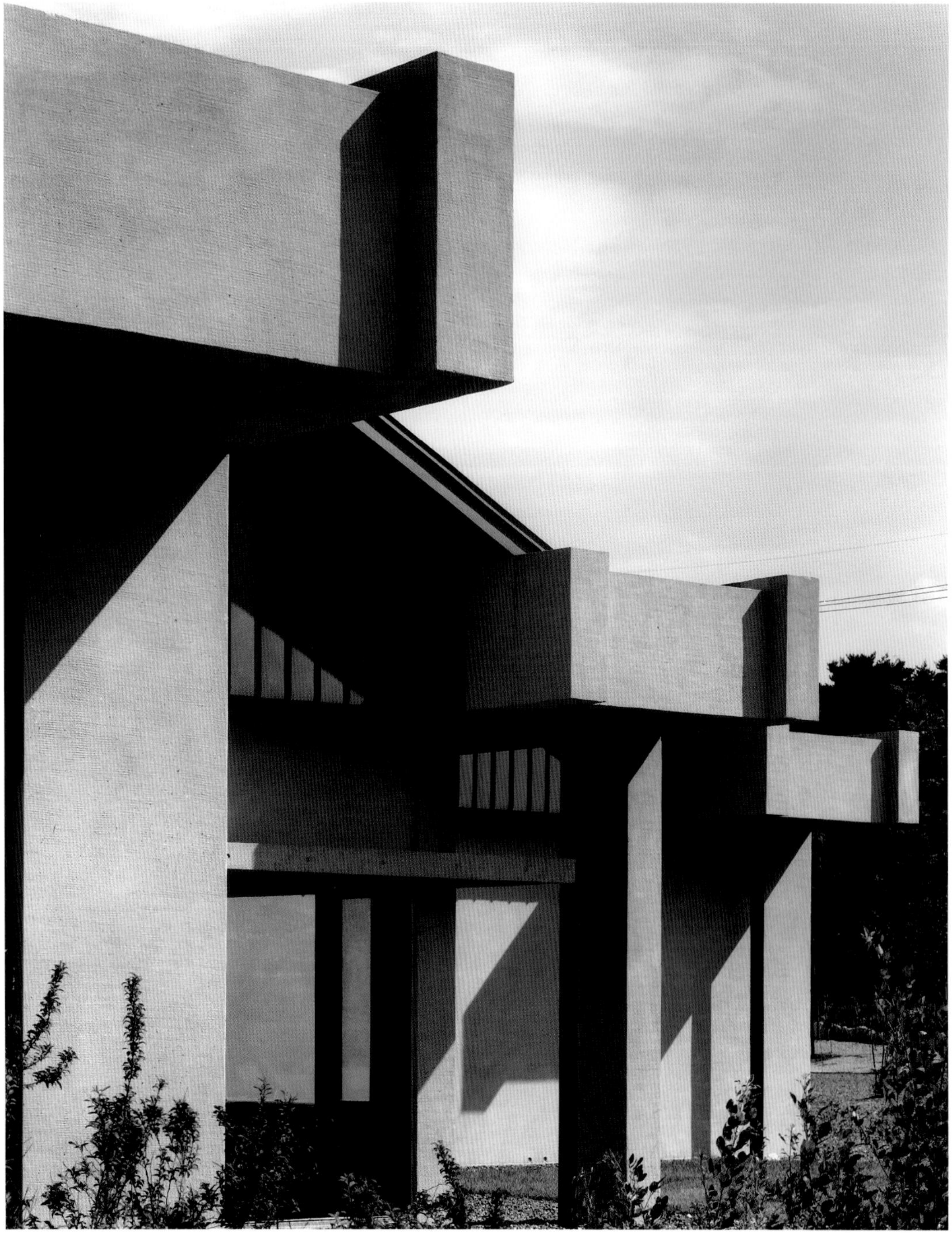

061

062

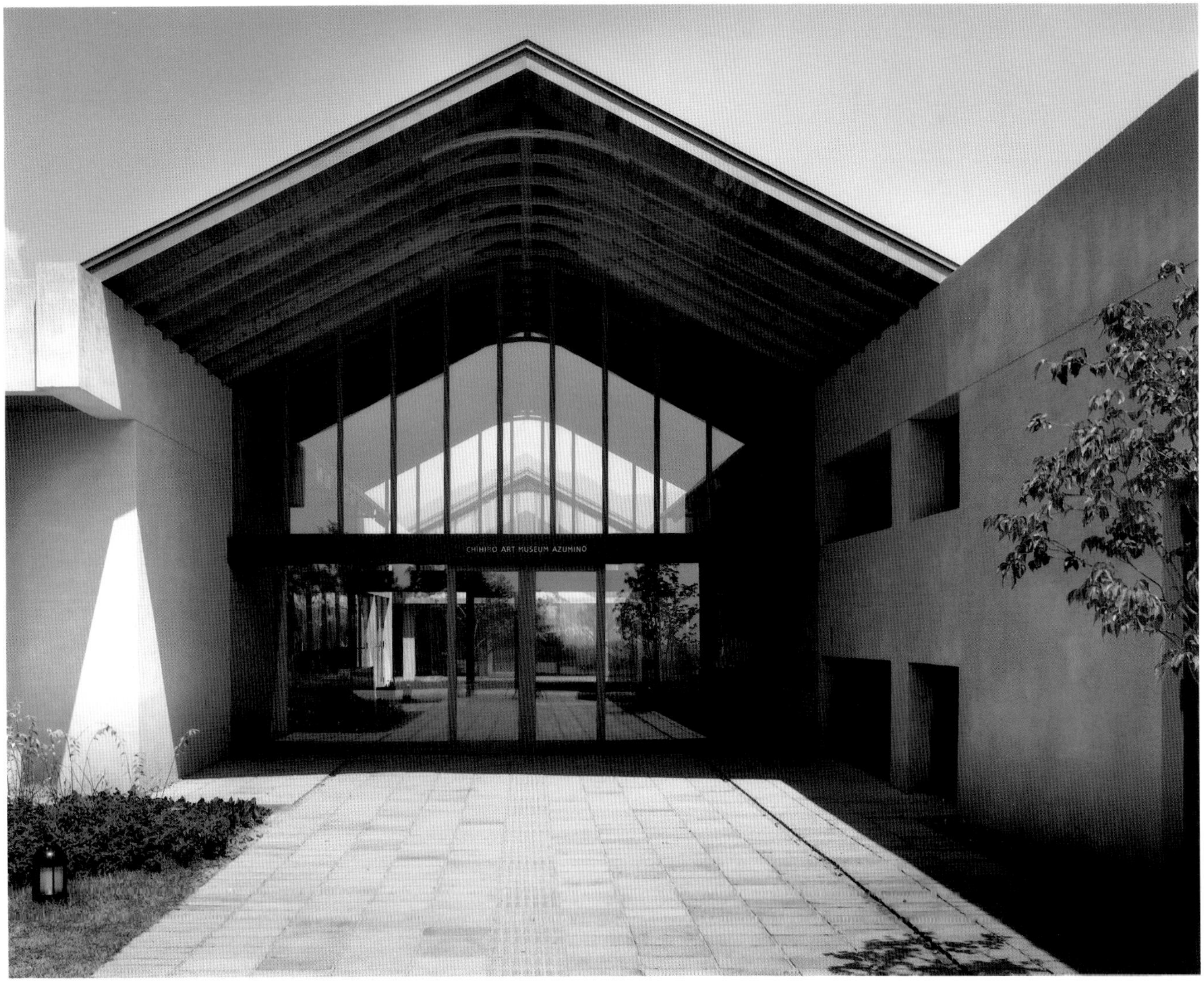
CHIHIRO ART MUSEUM AZUMINO

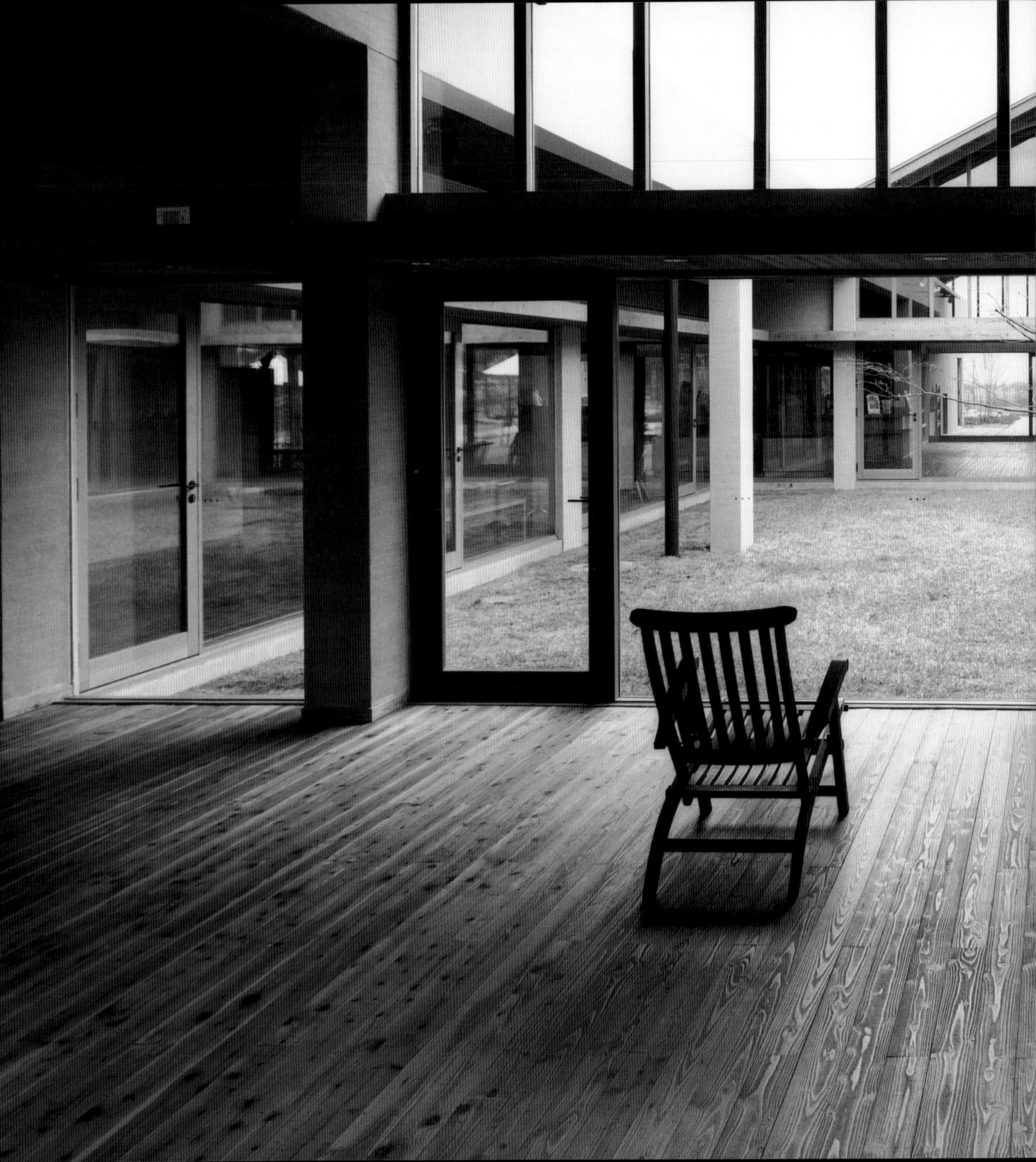

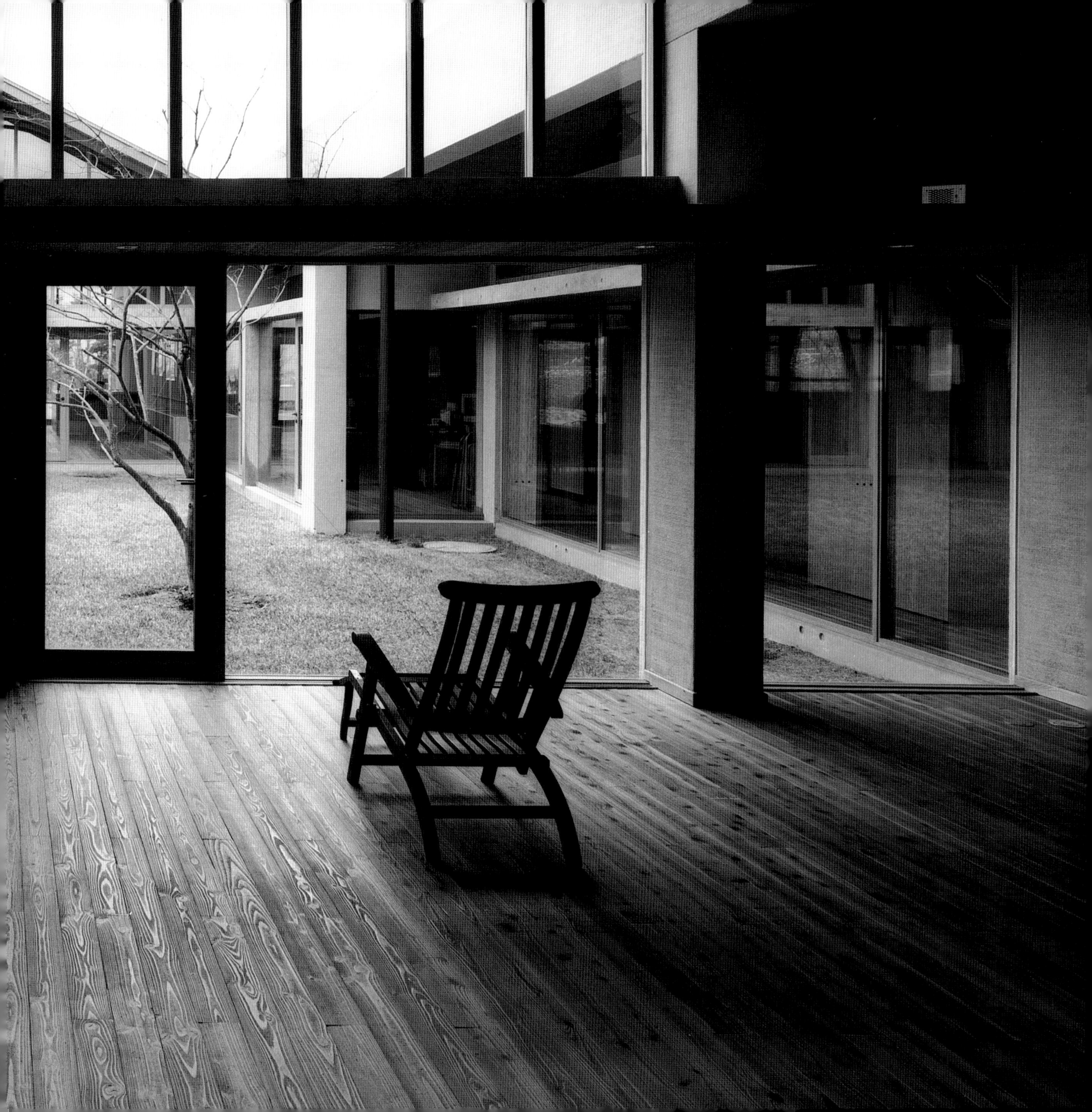

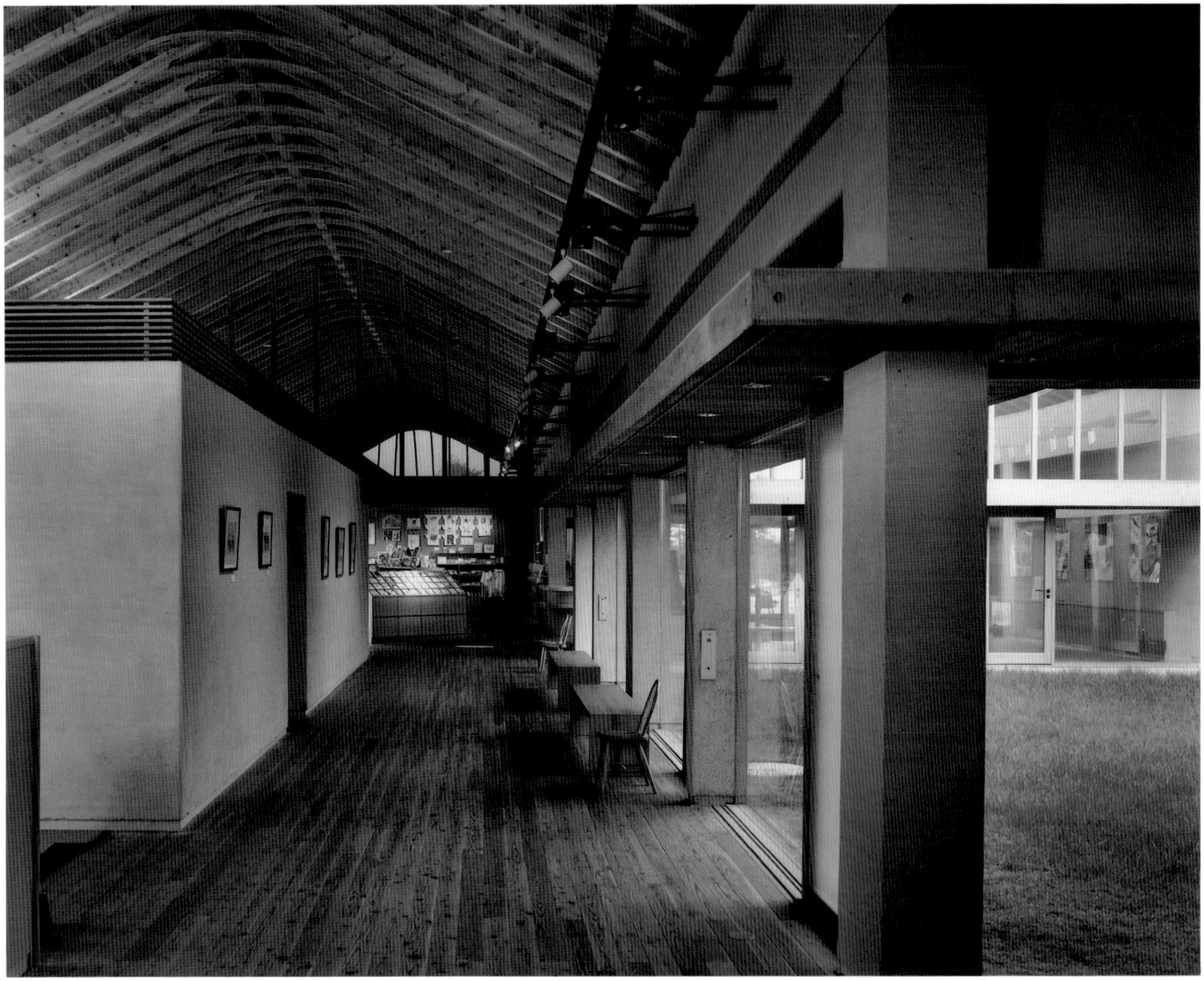

067

068

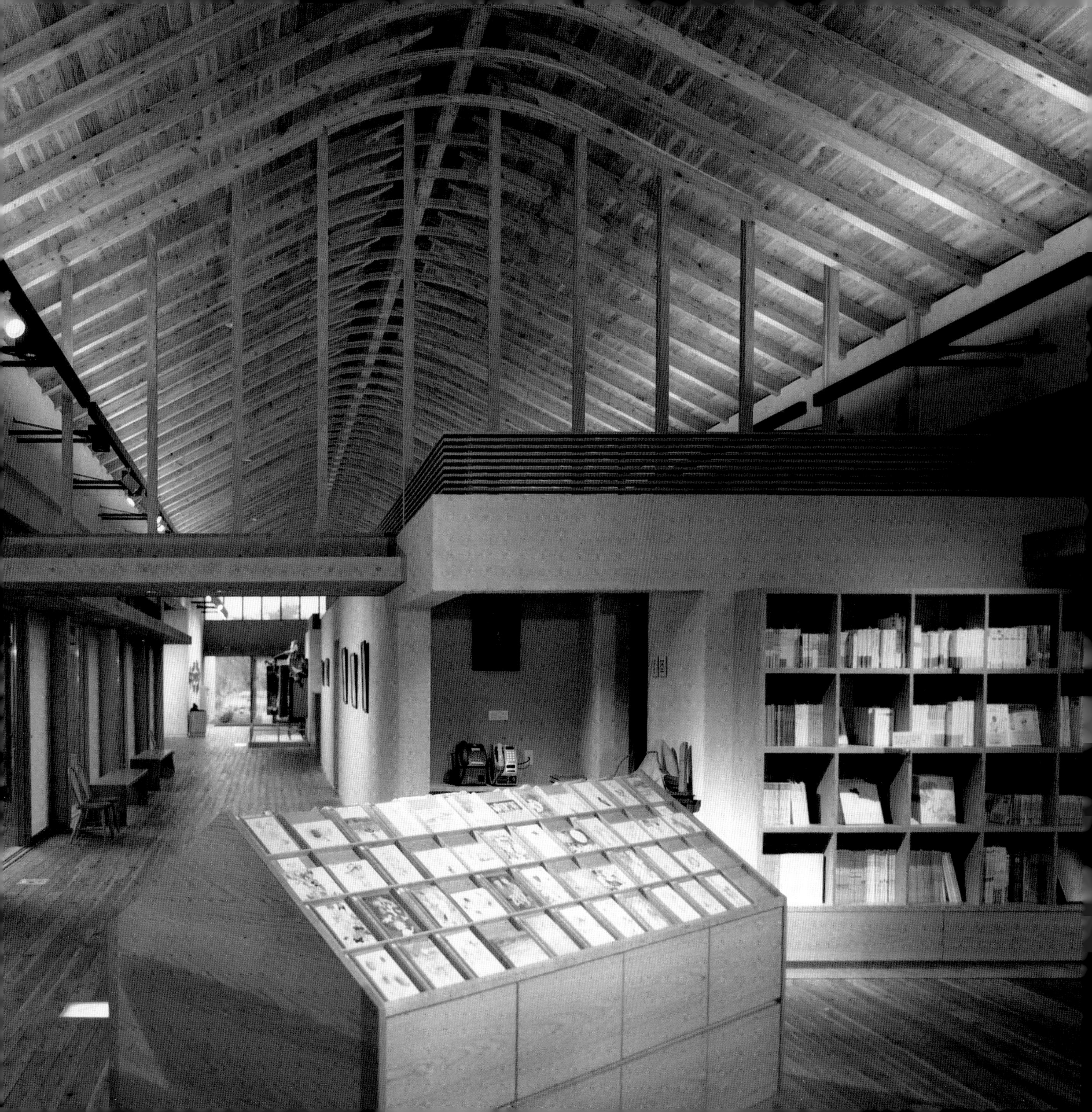

070

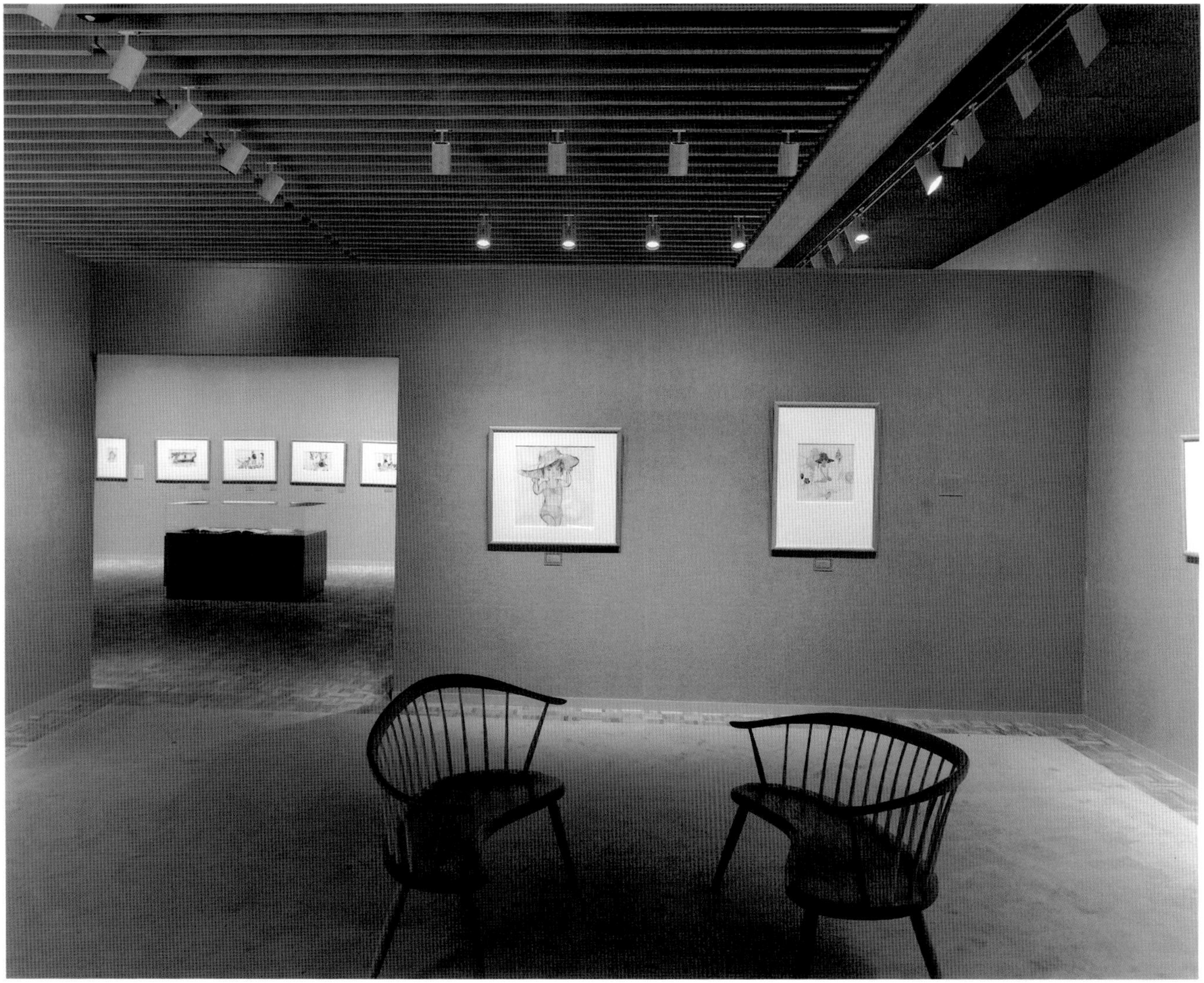

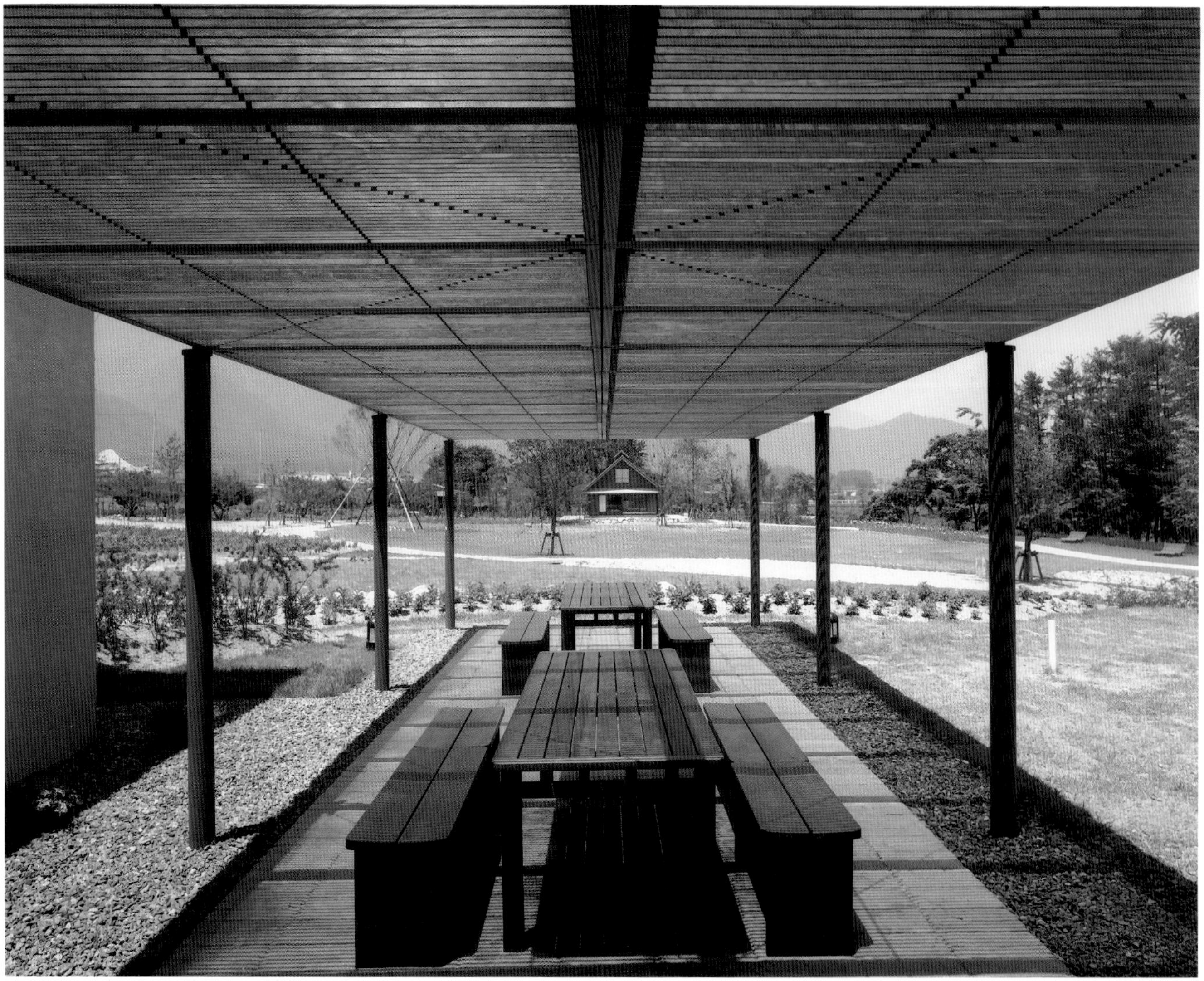

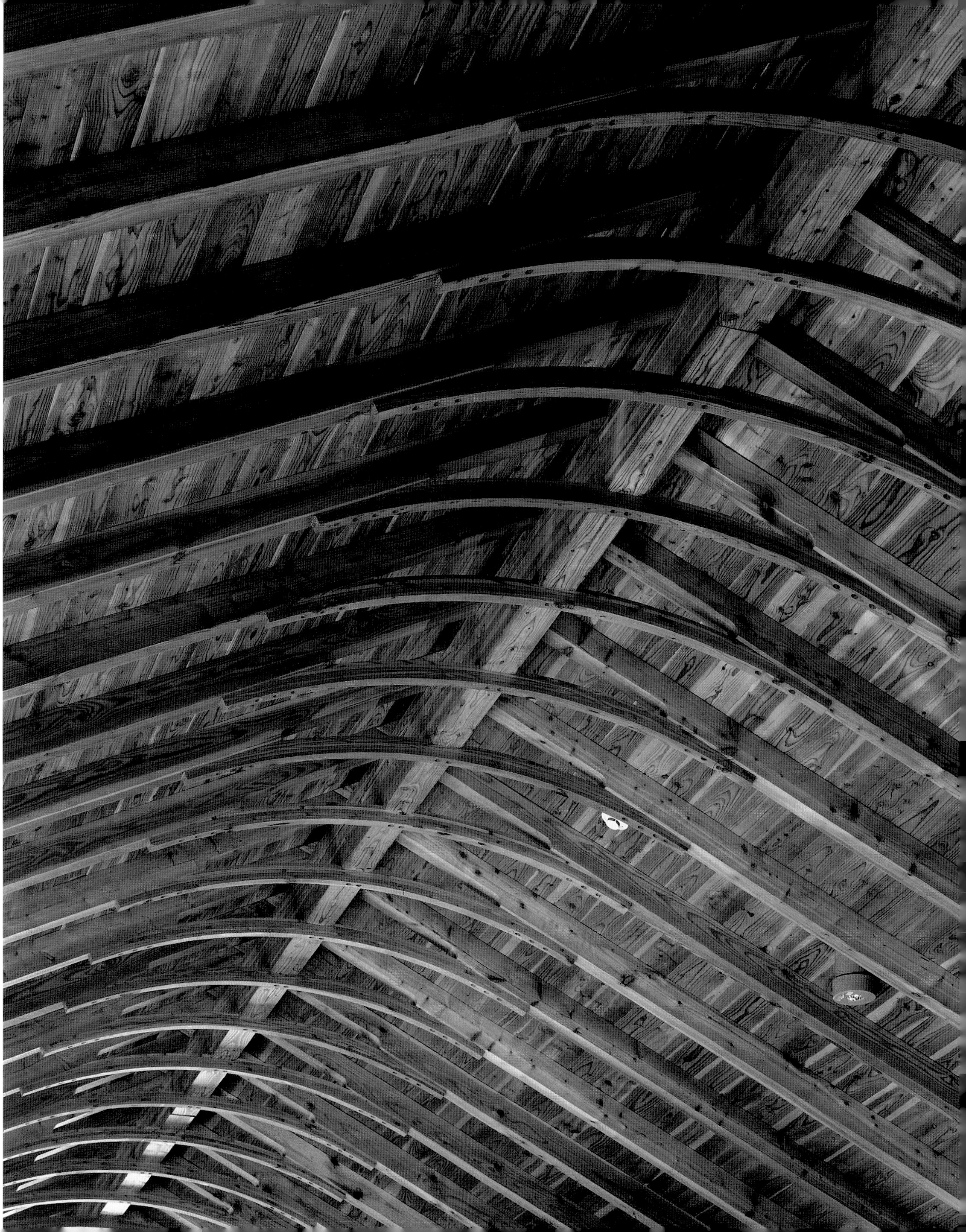

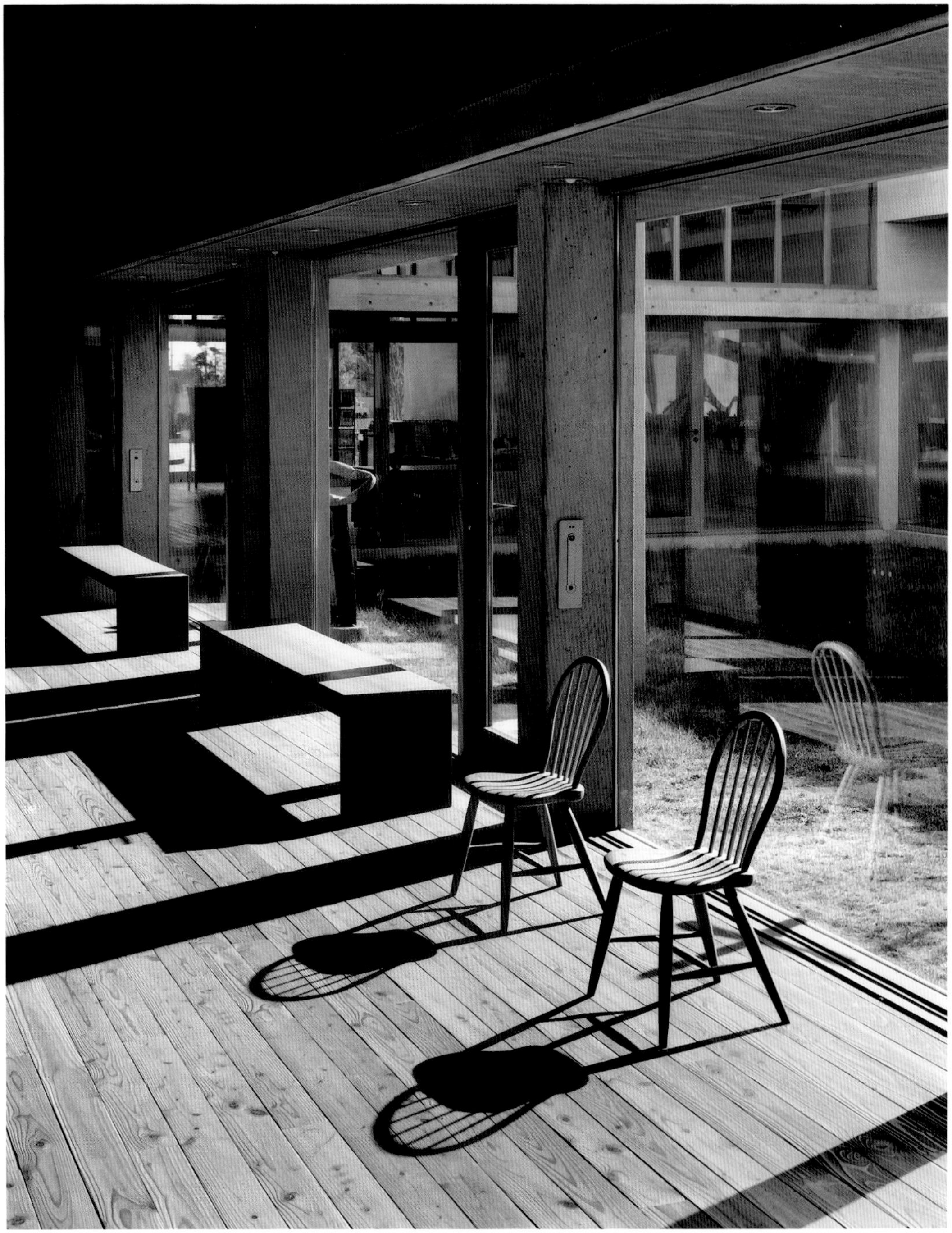

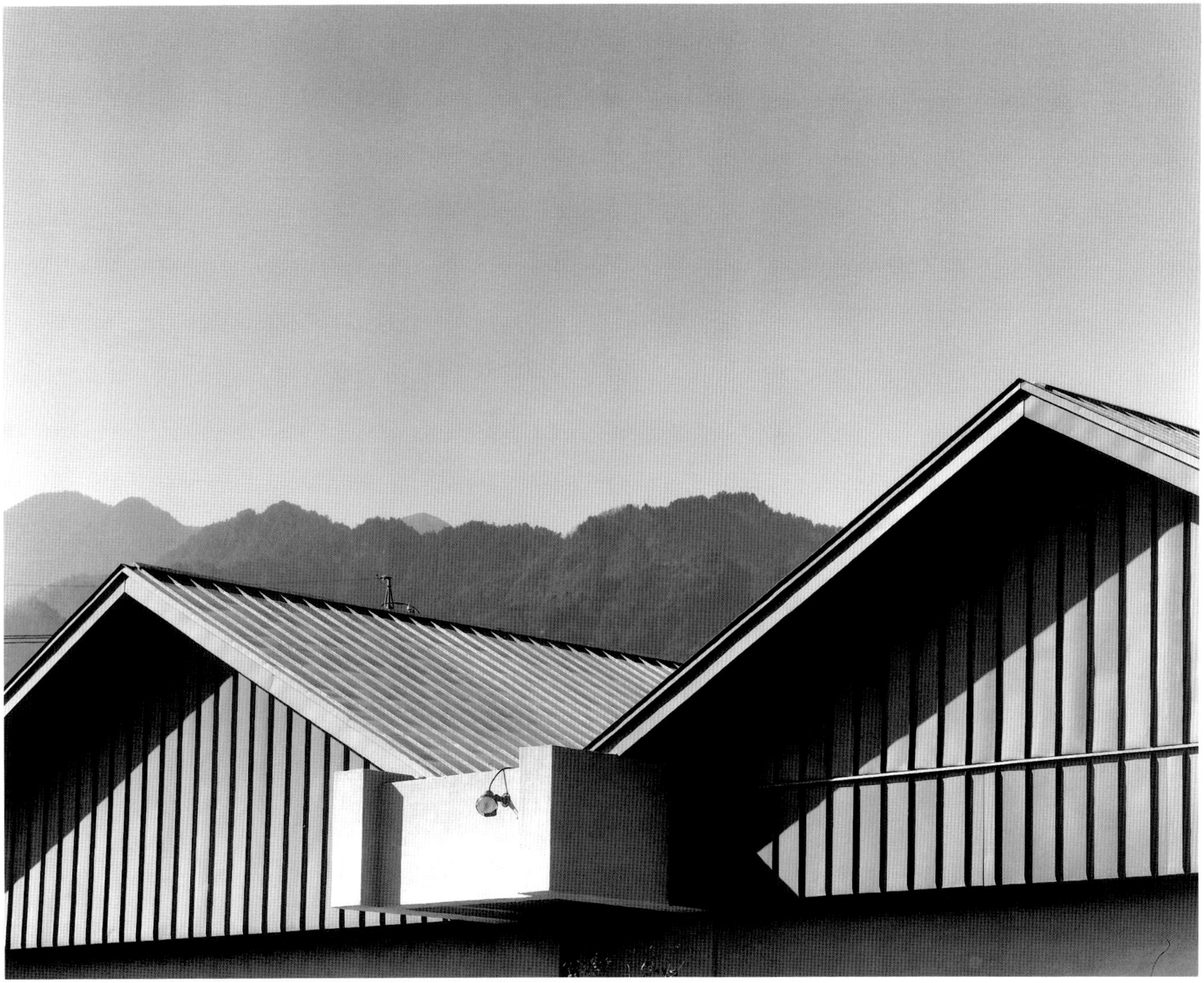

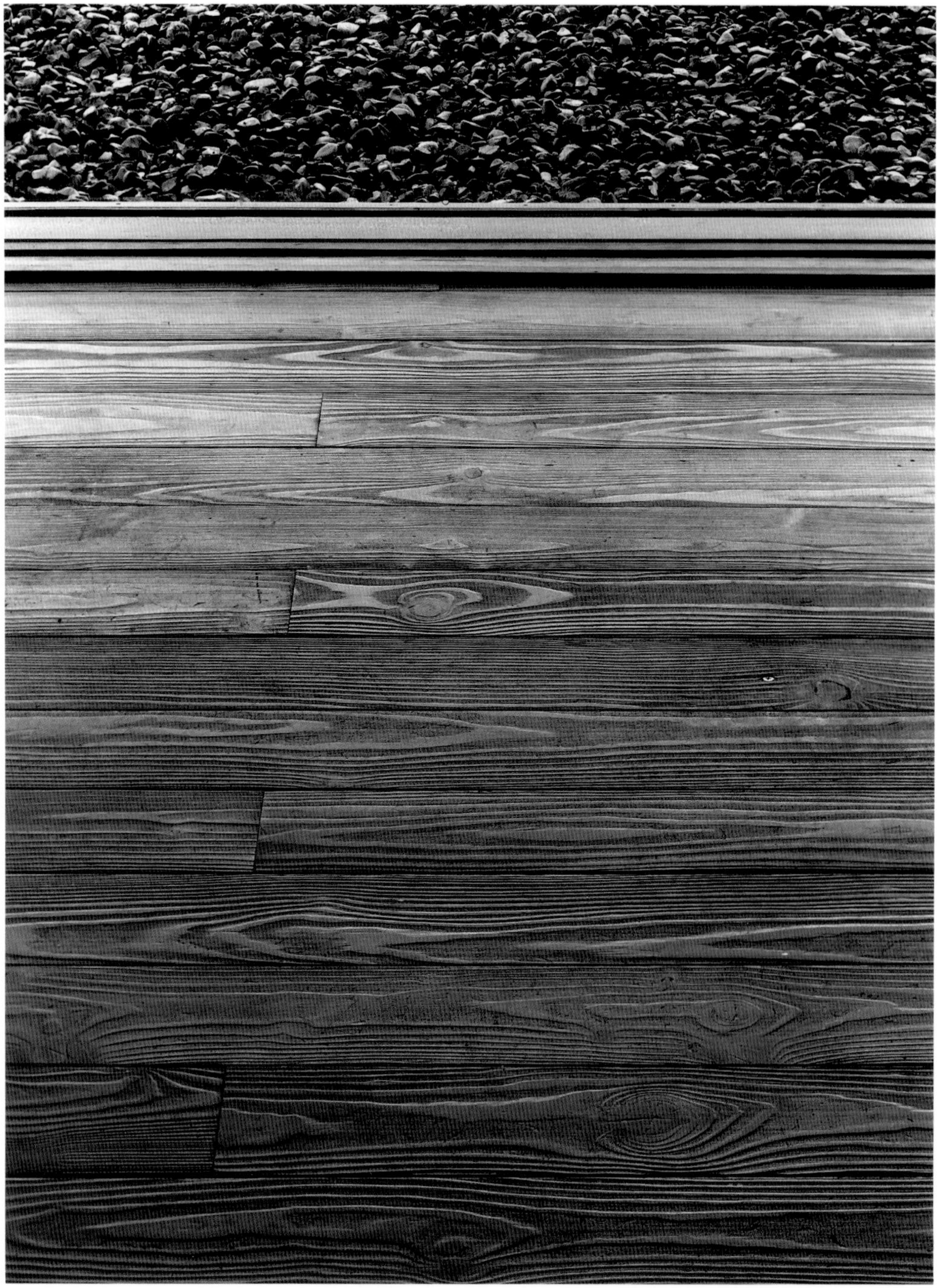

Makino Museum of Plants and People

牧野富太郎記念館　撮影■1999

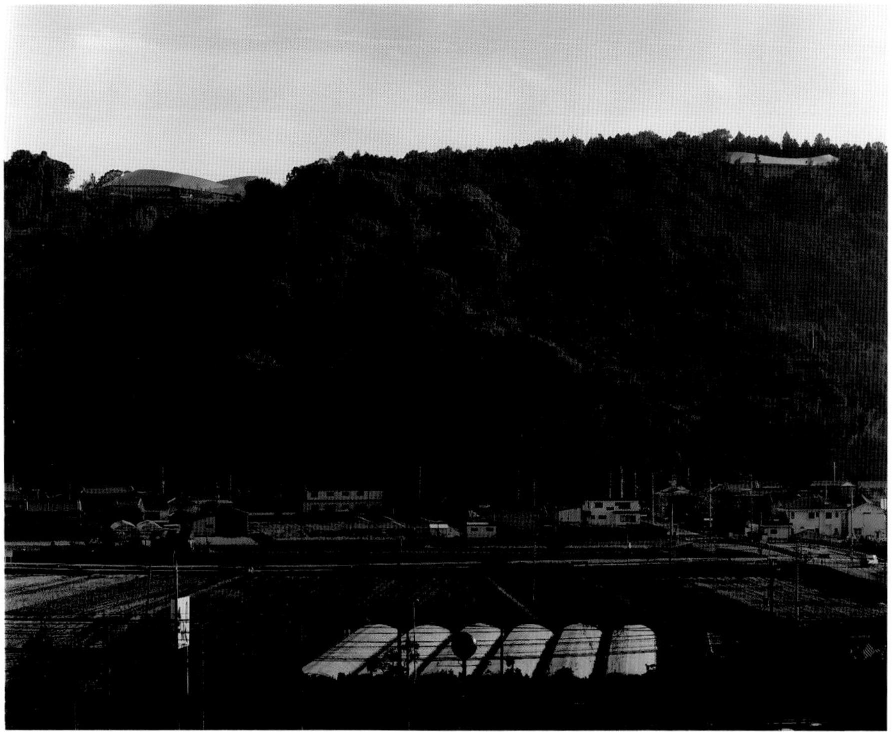

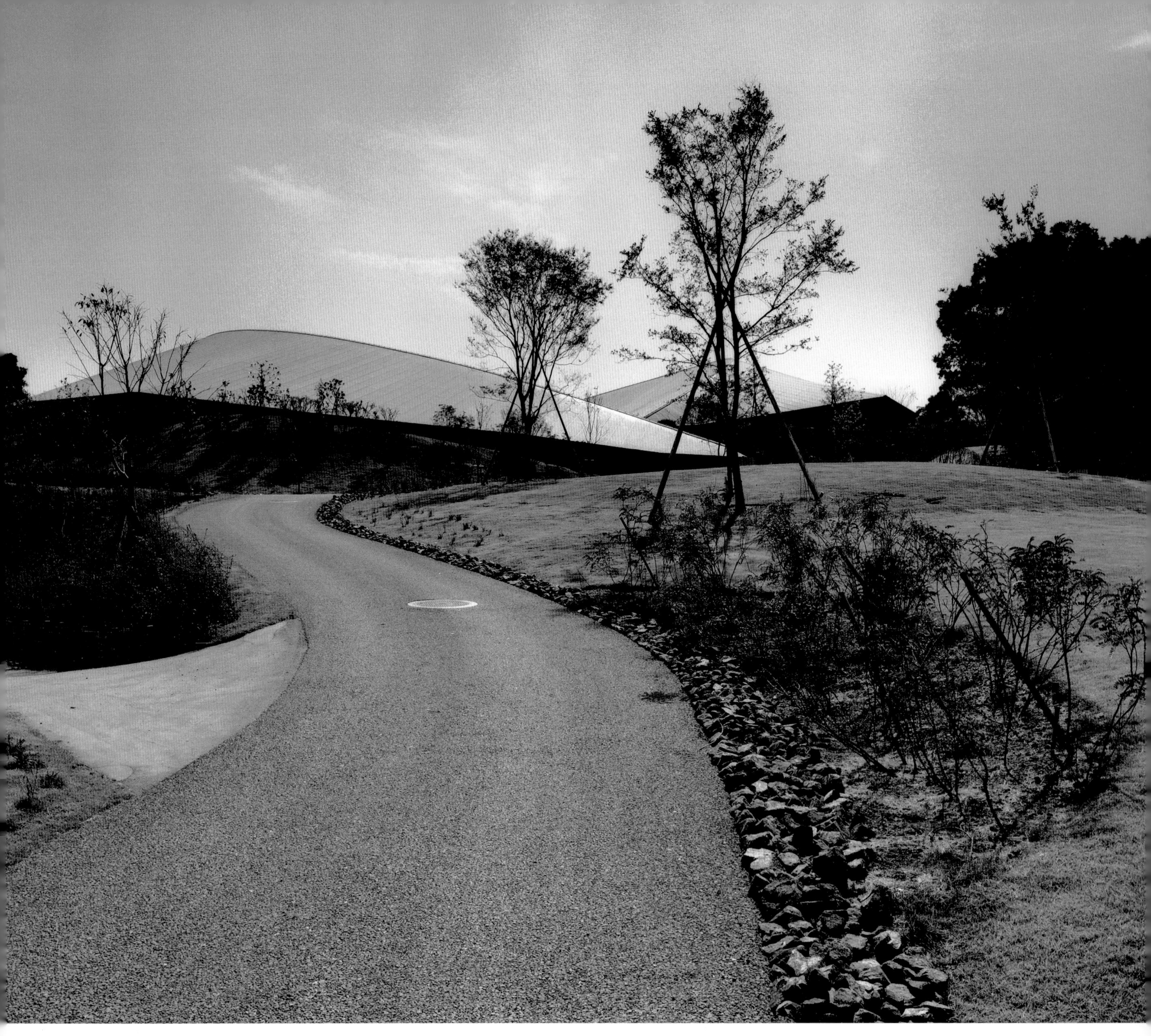

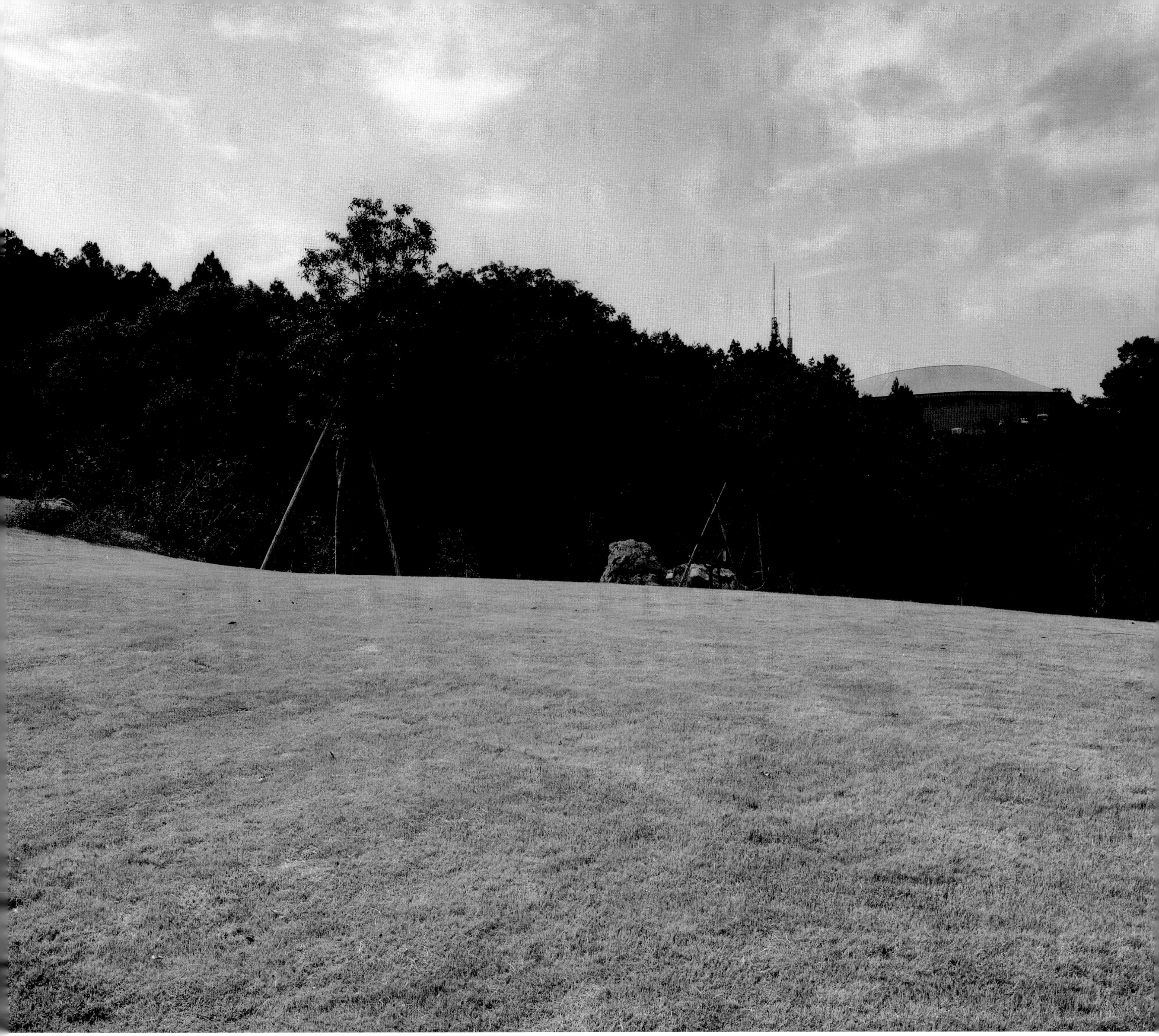

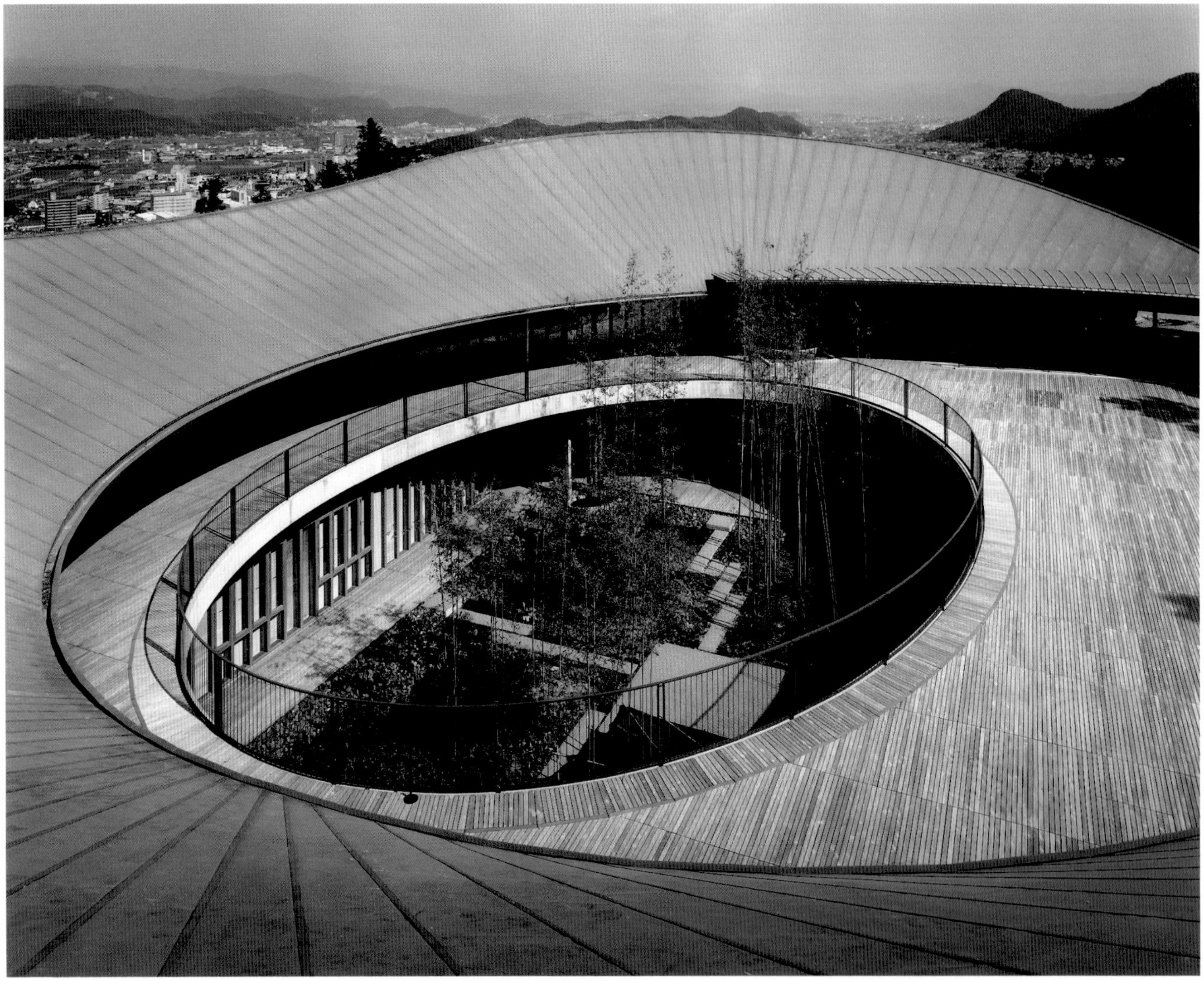

本　館

■

Museum Building

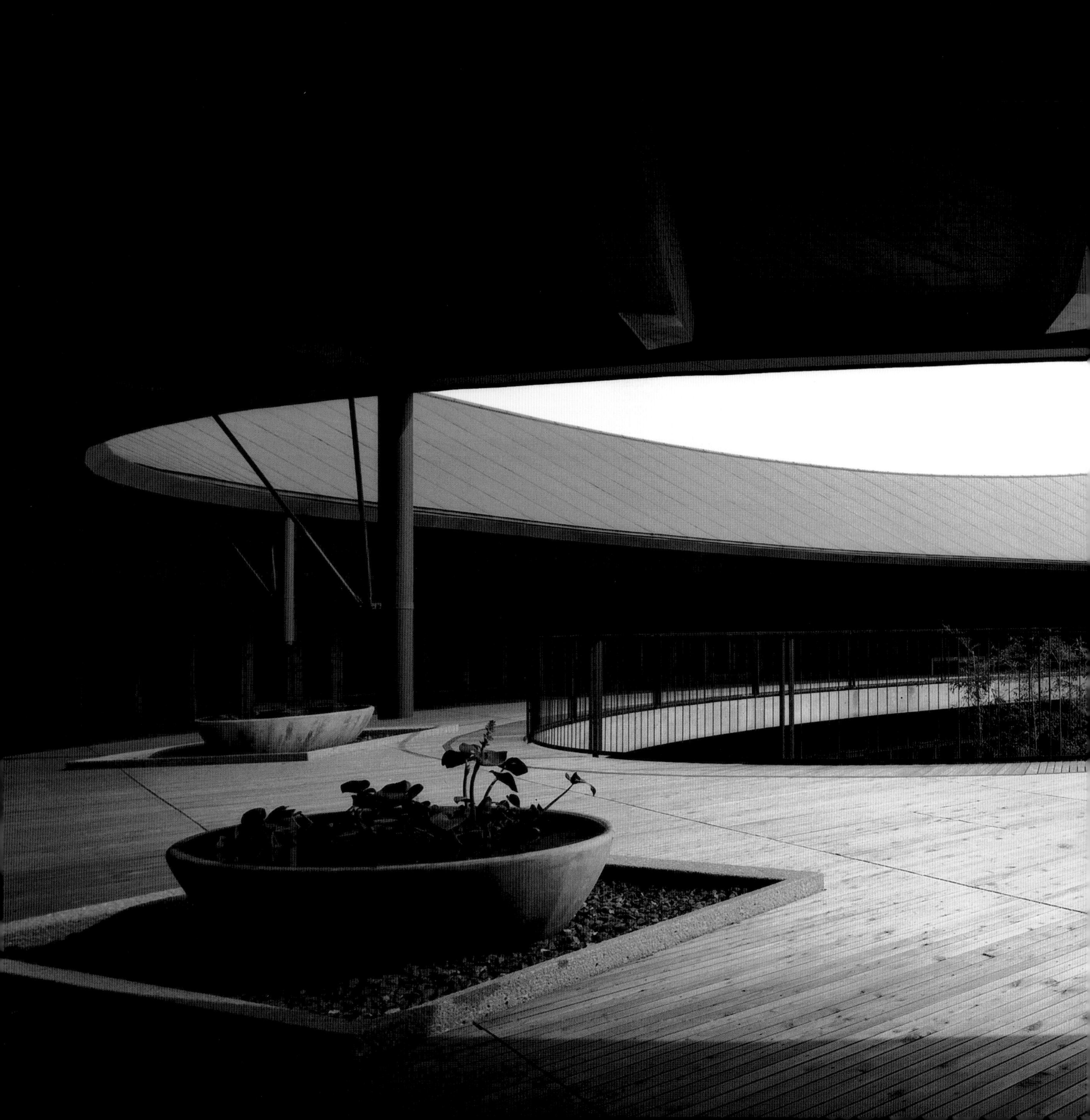

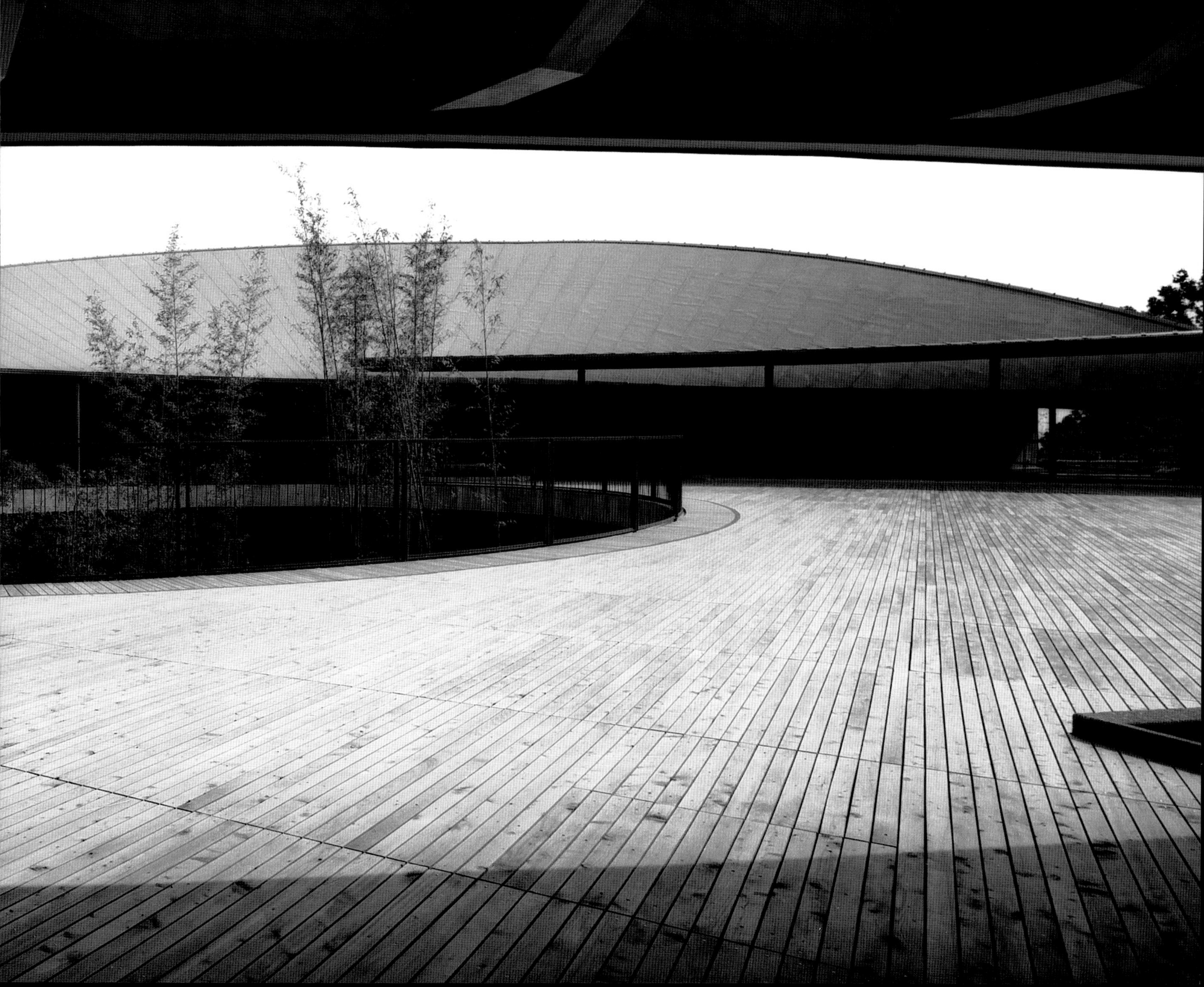

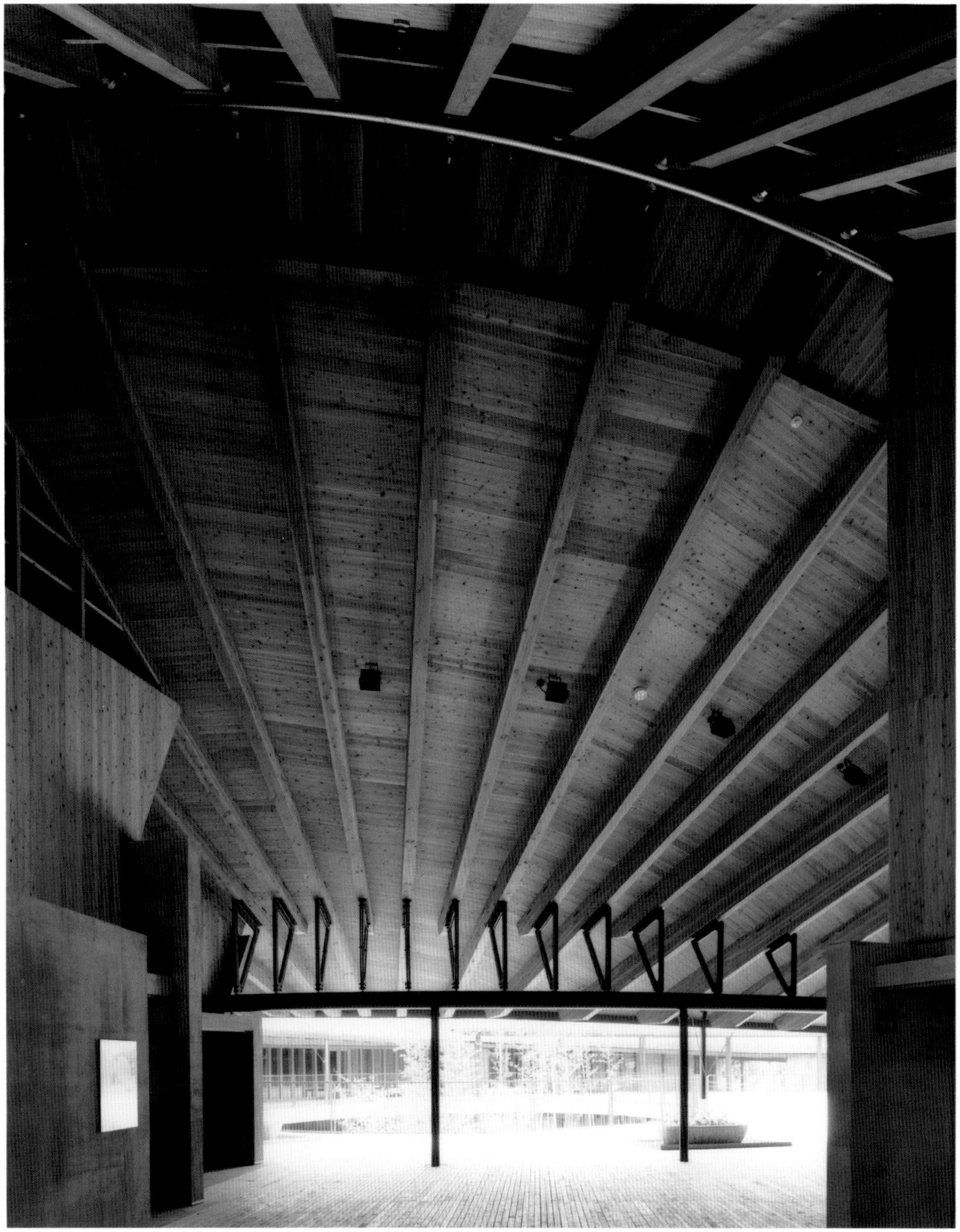

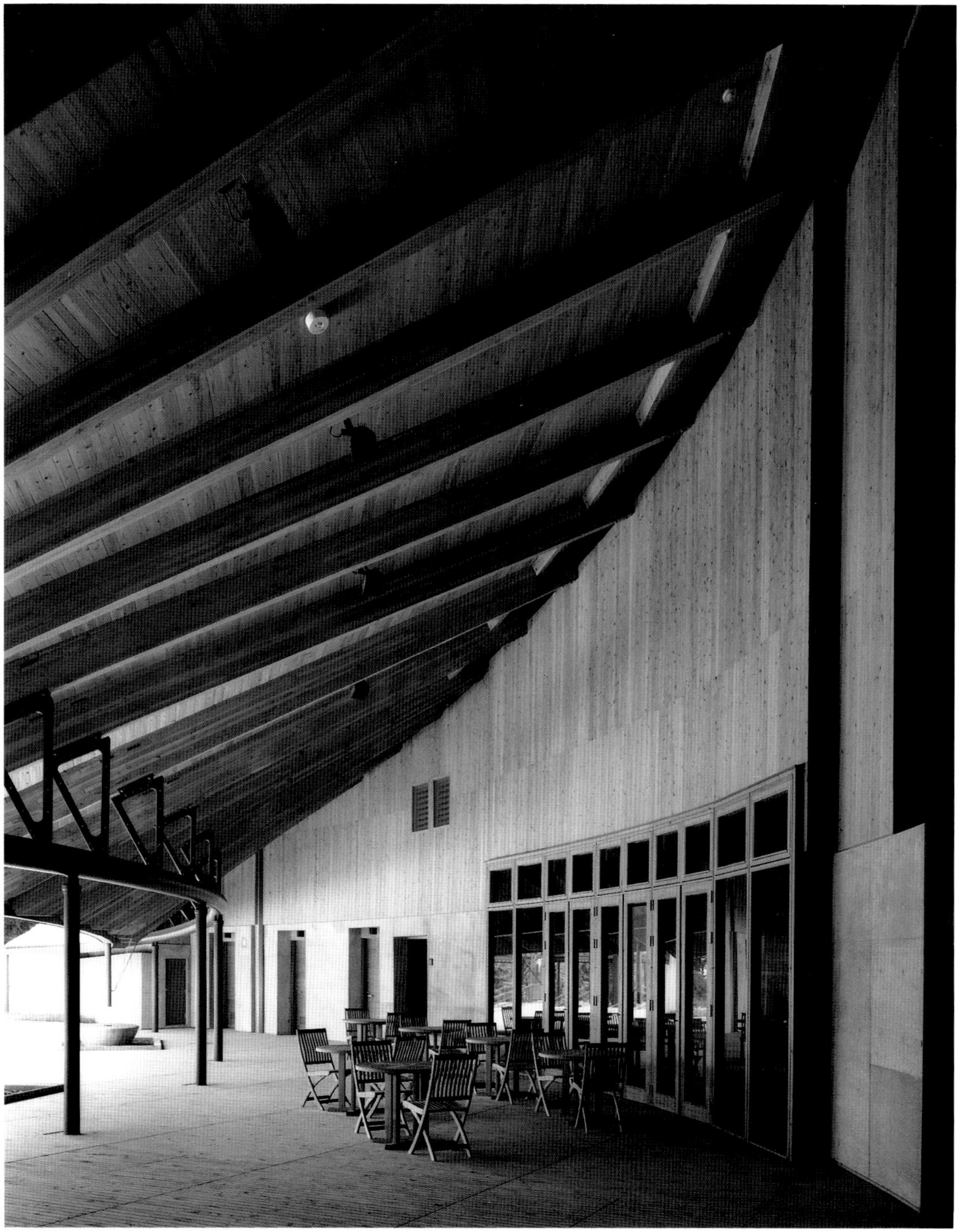

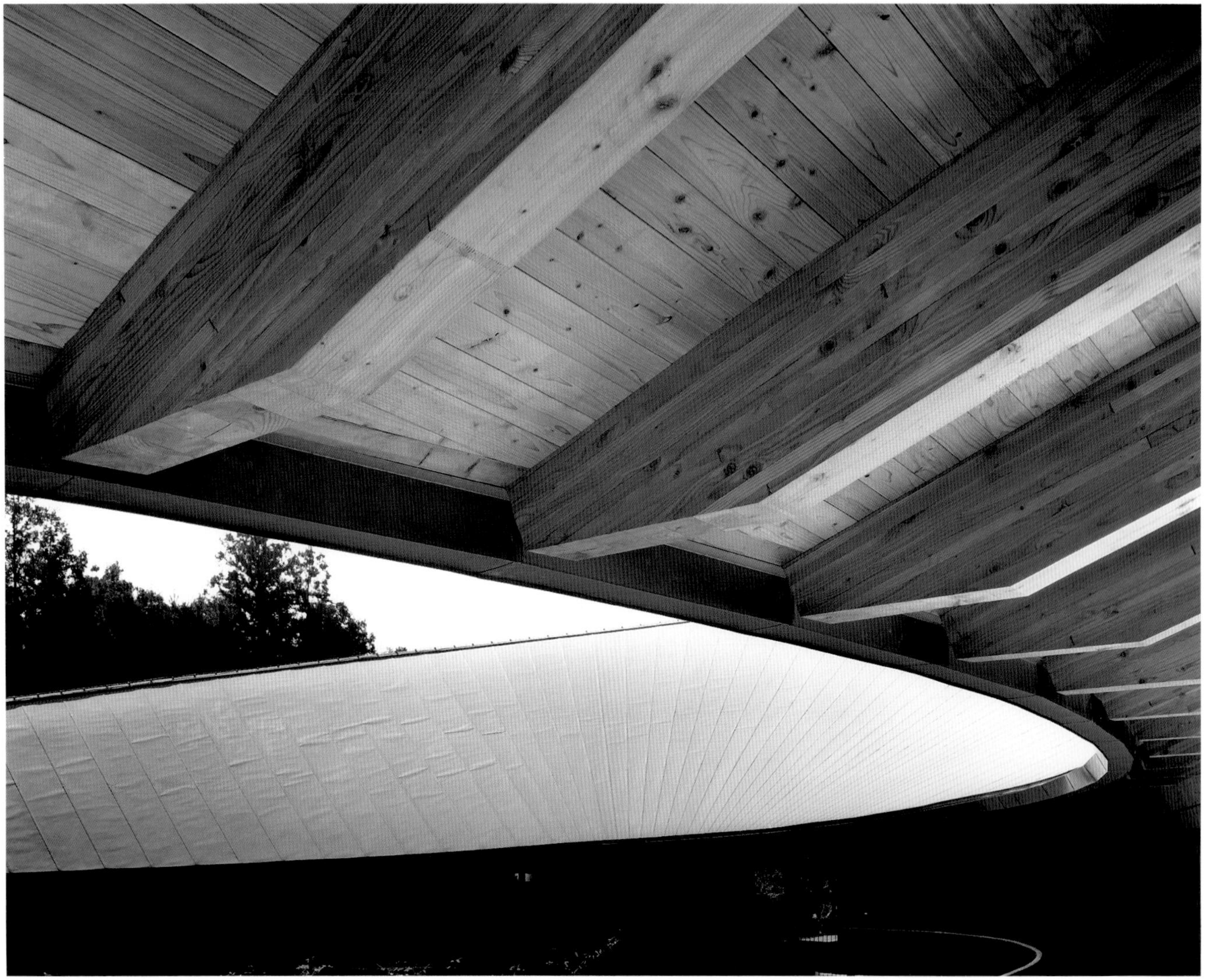

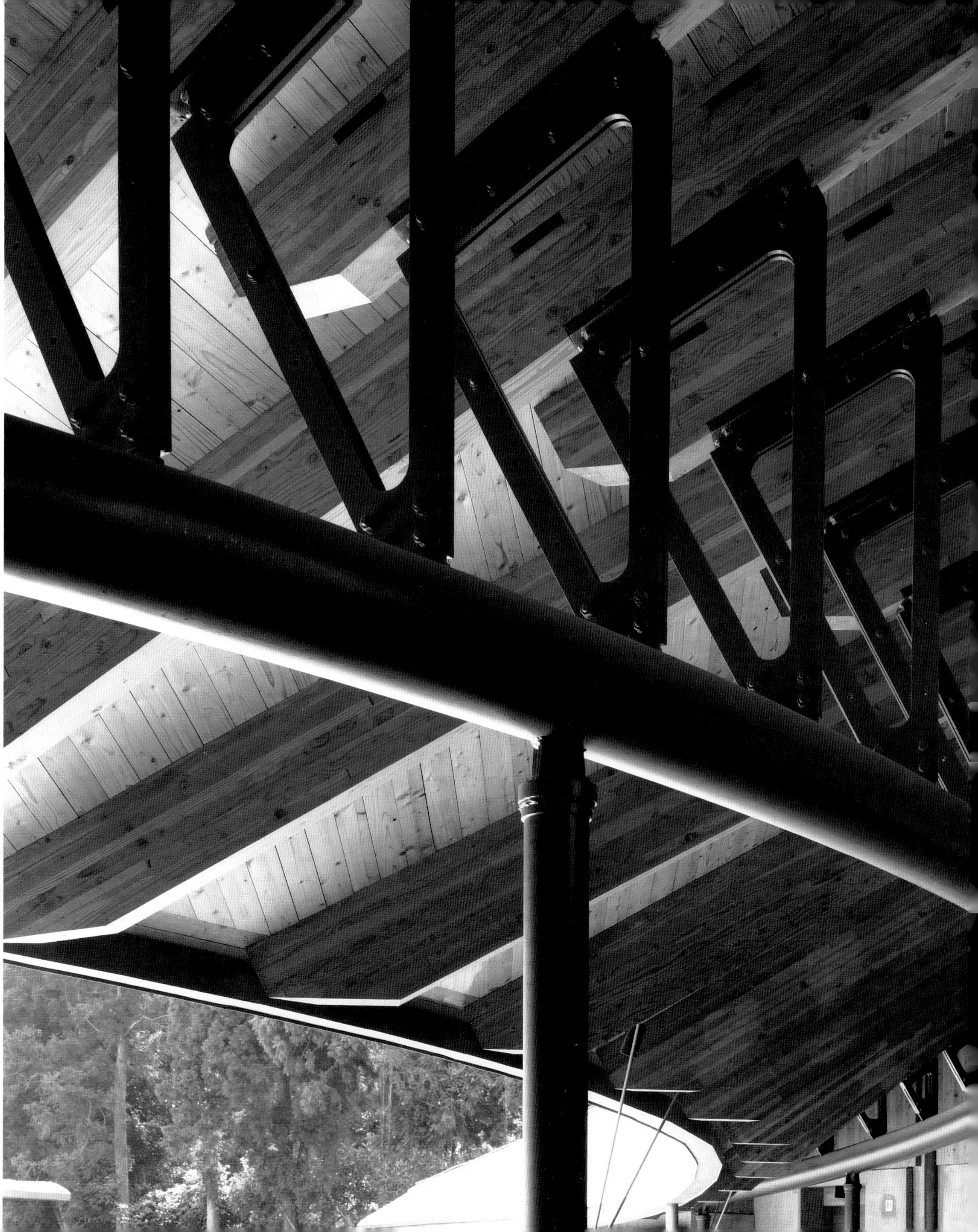

090

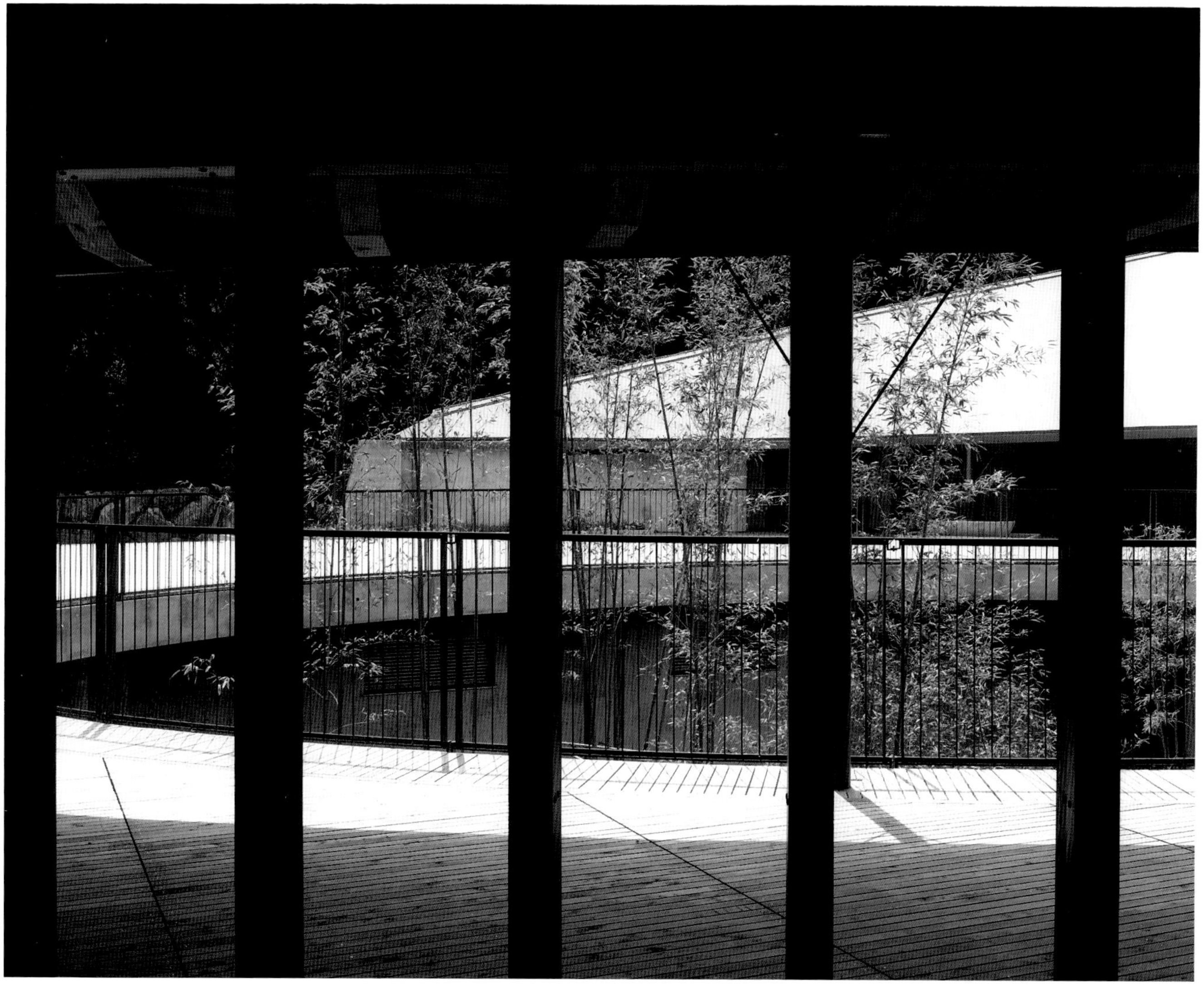

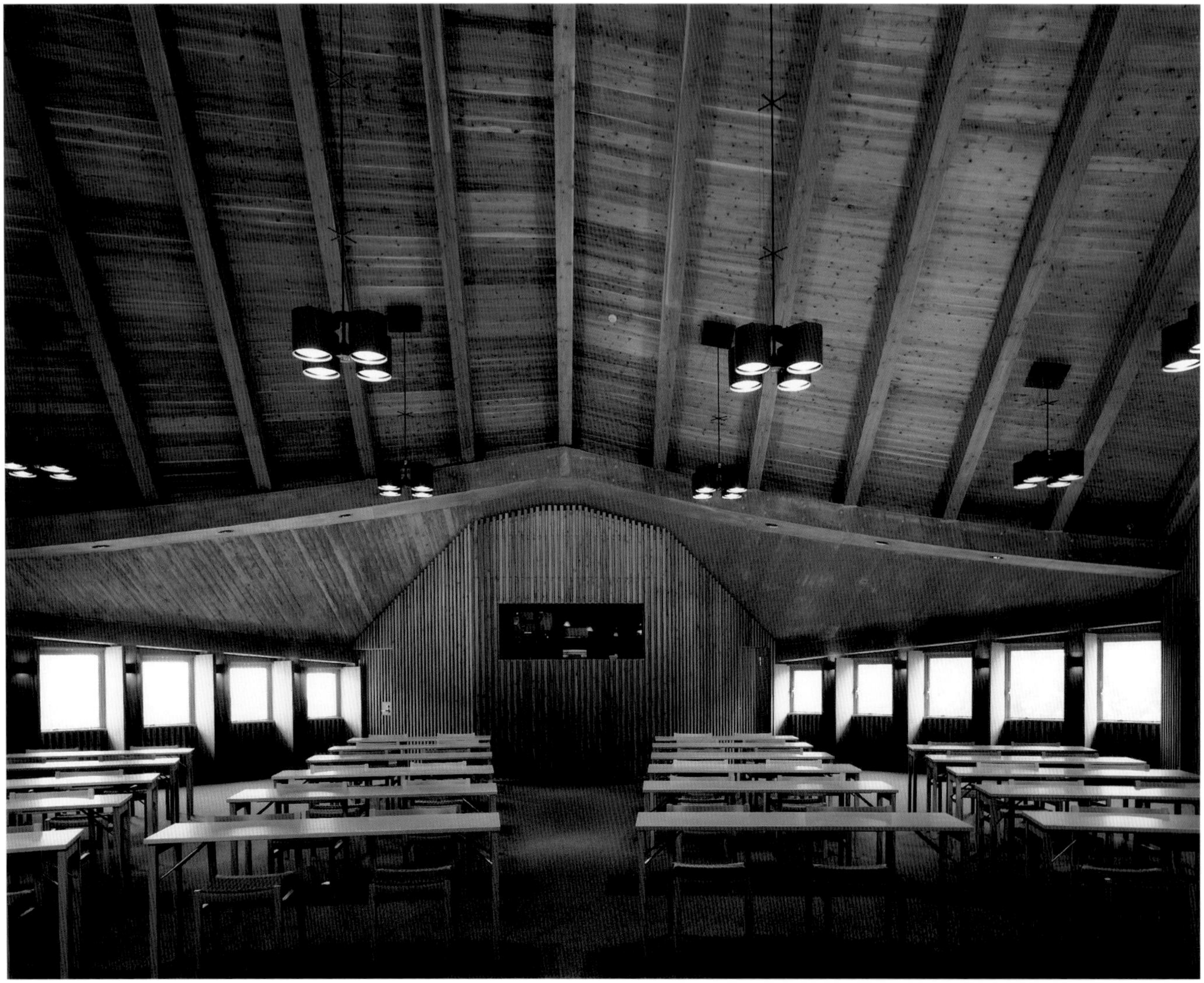

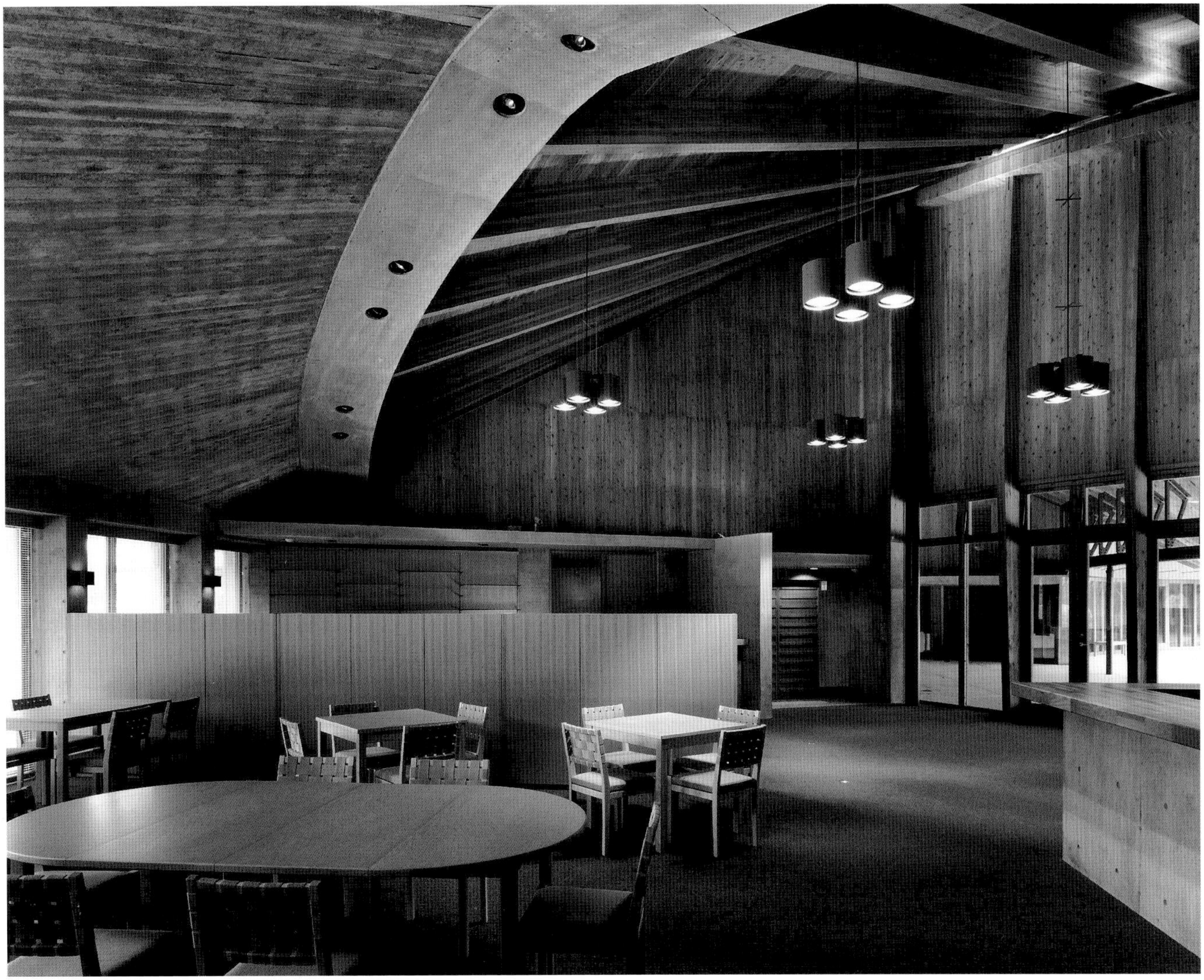

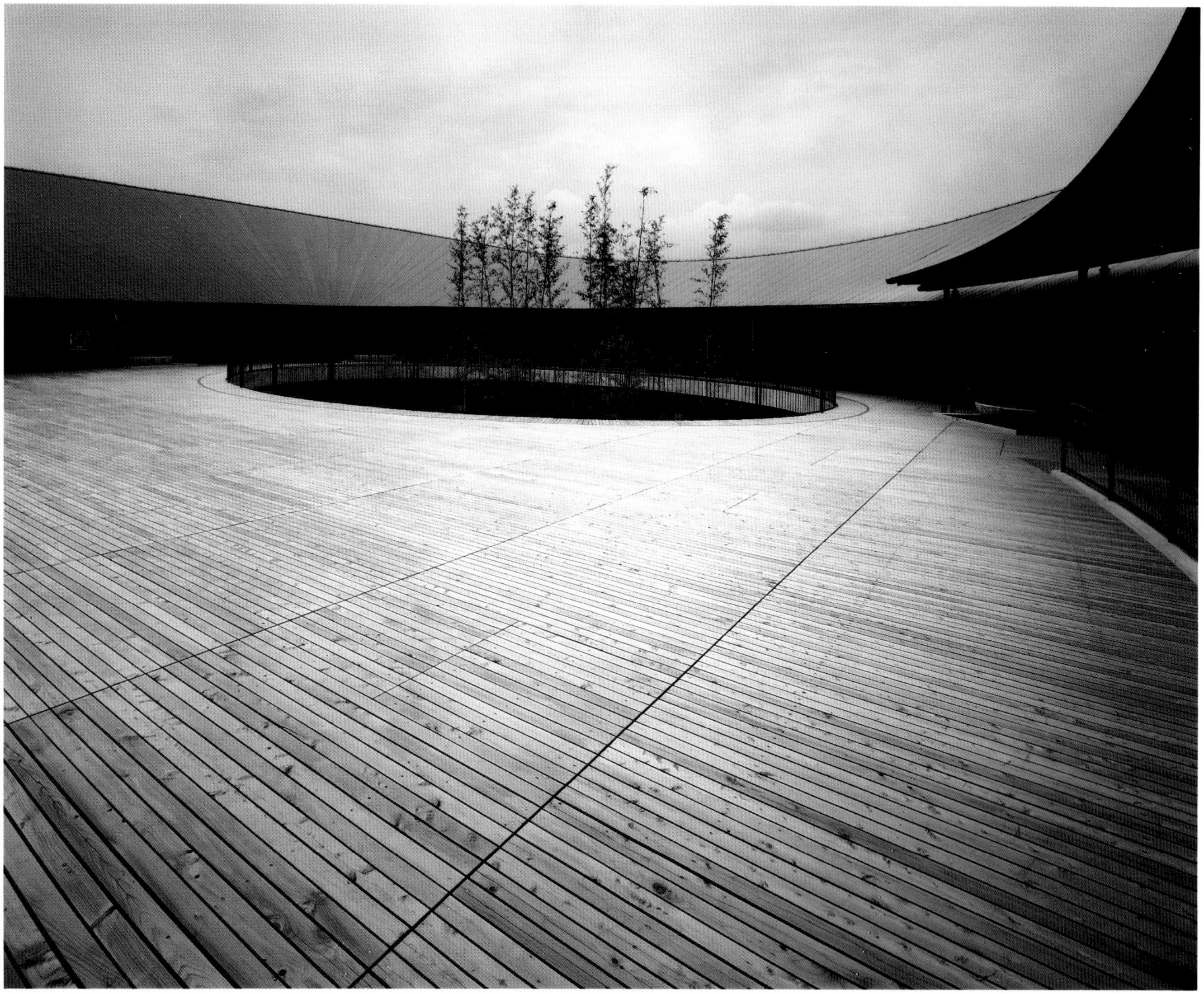

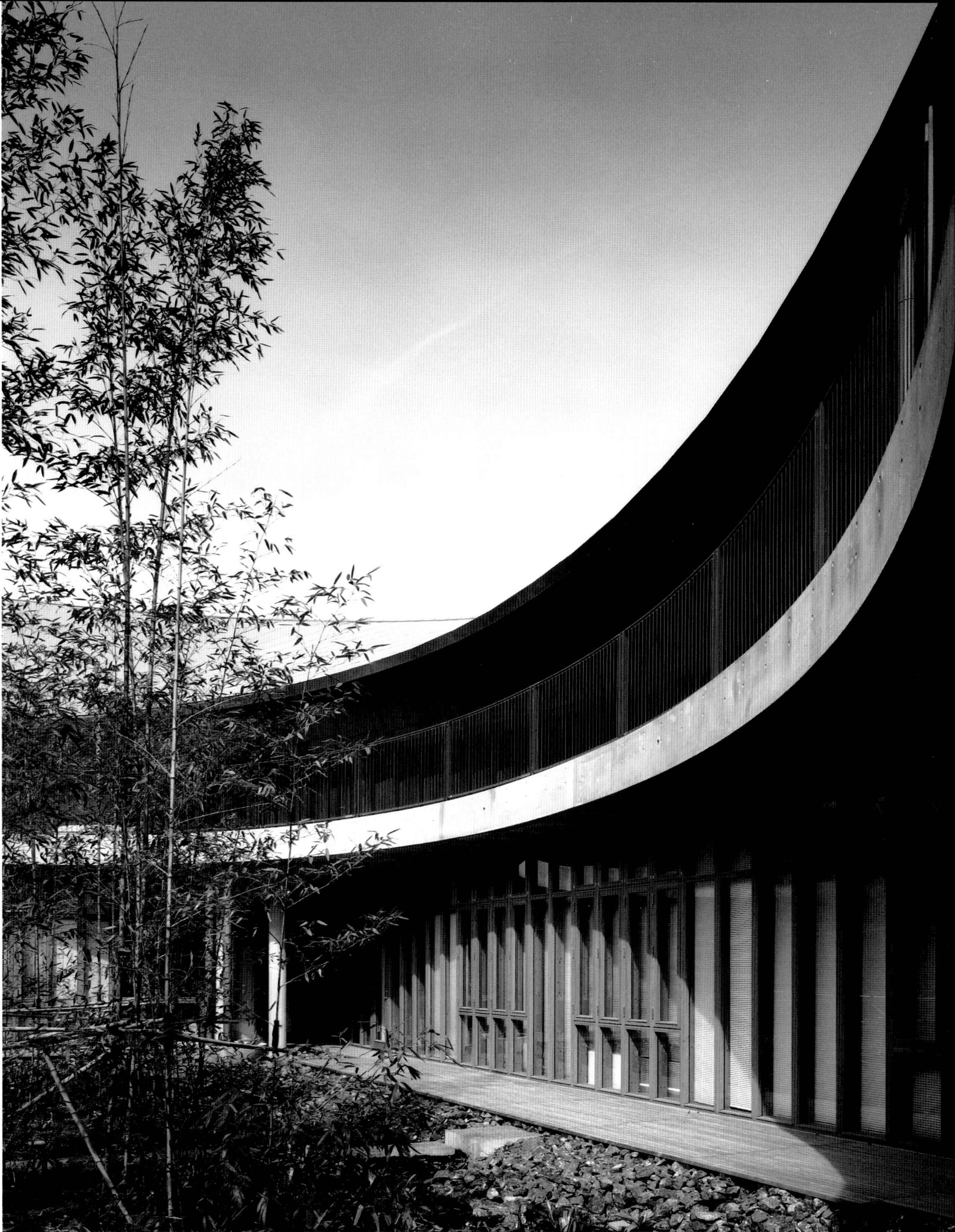

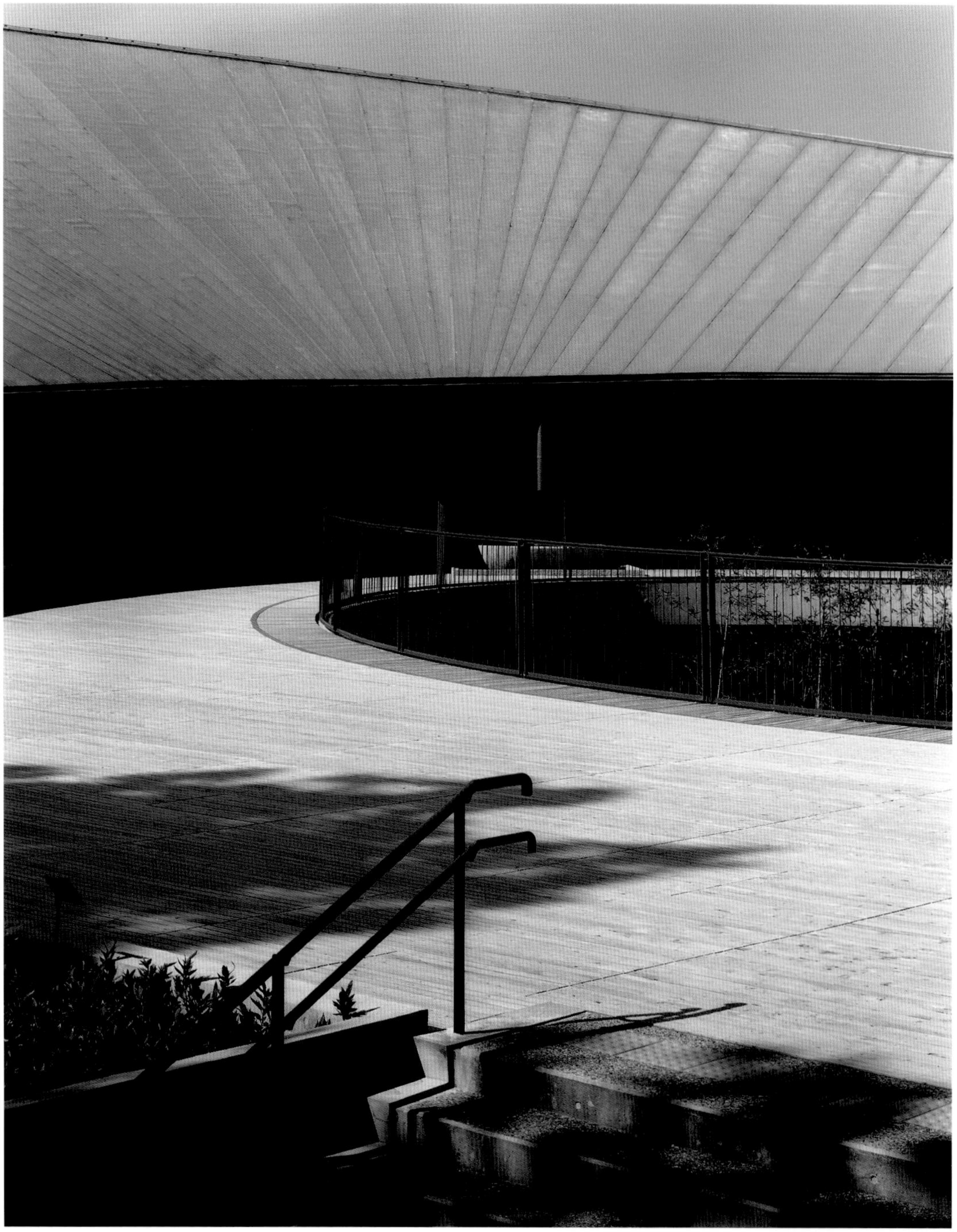

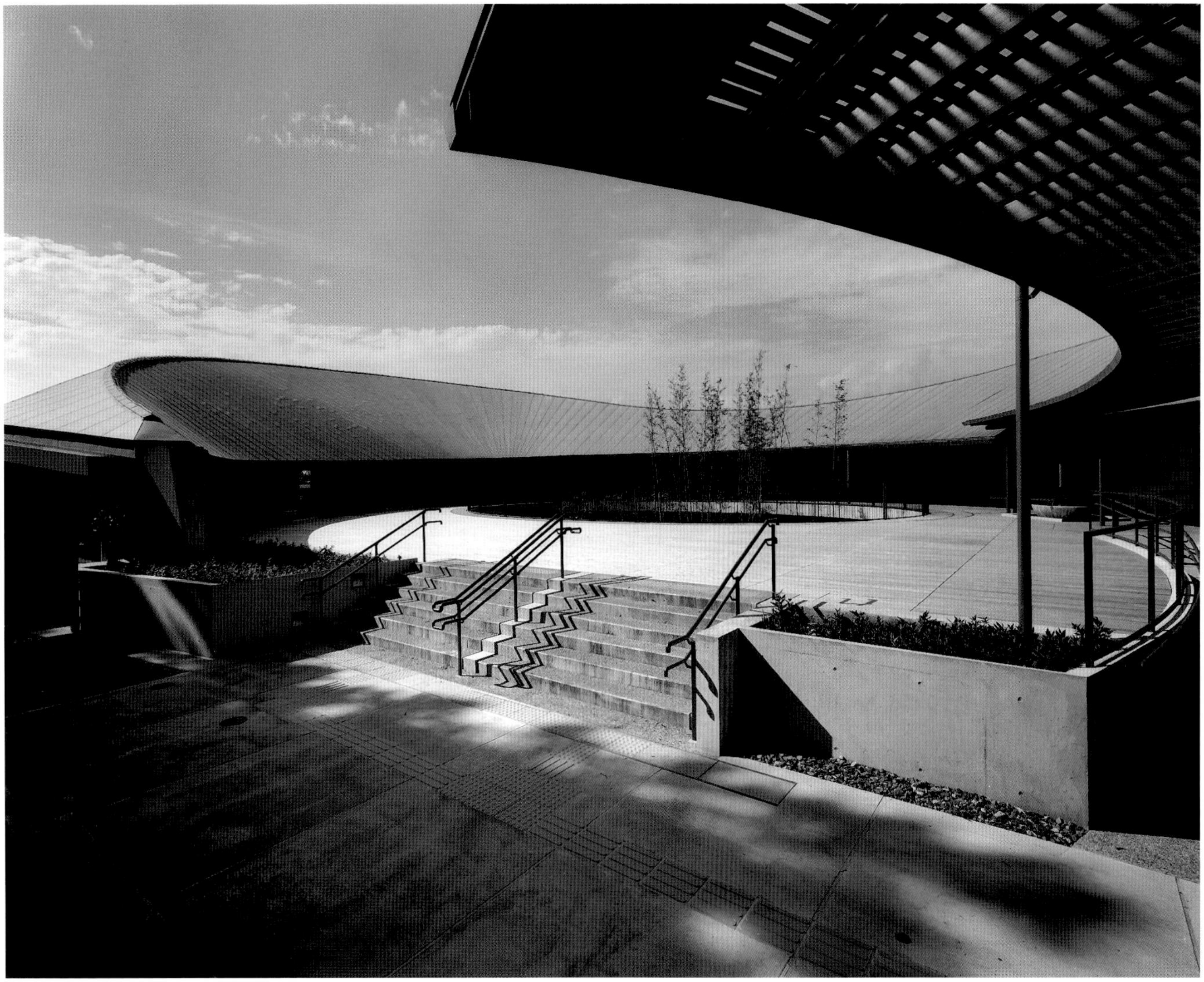

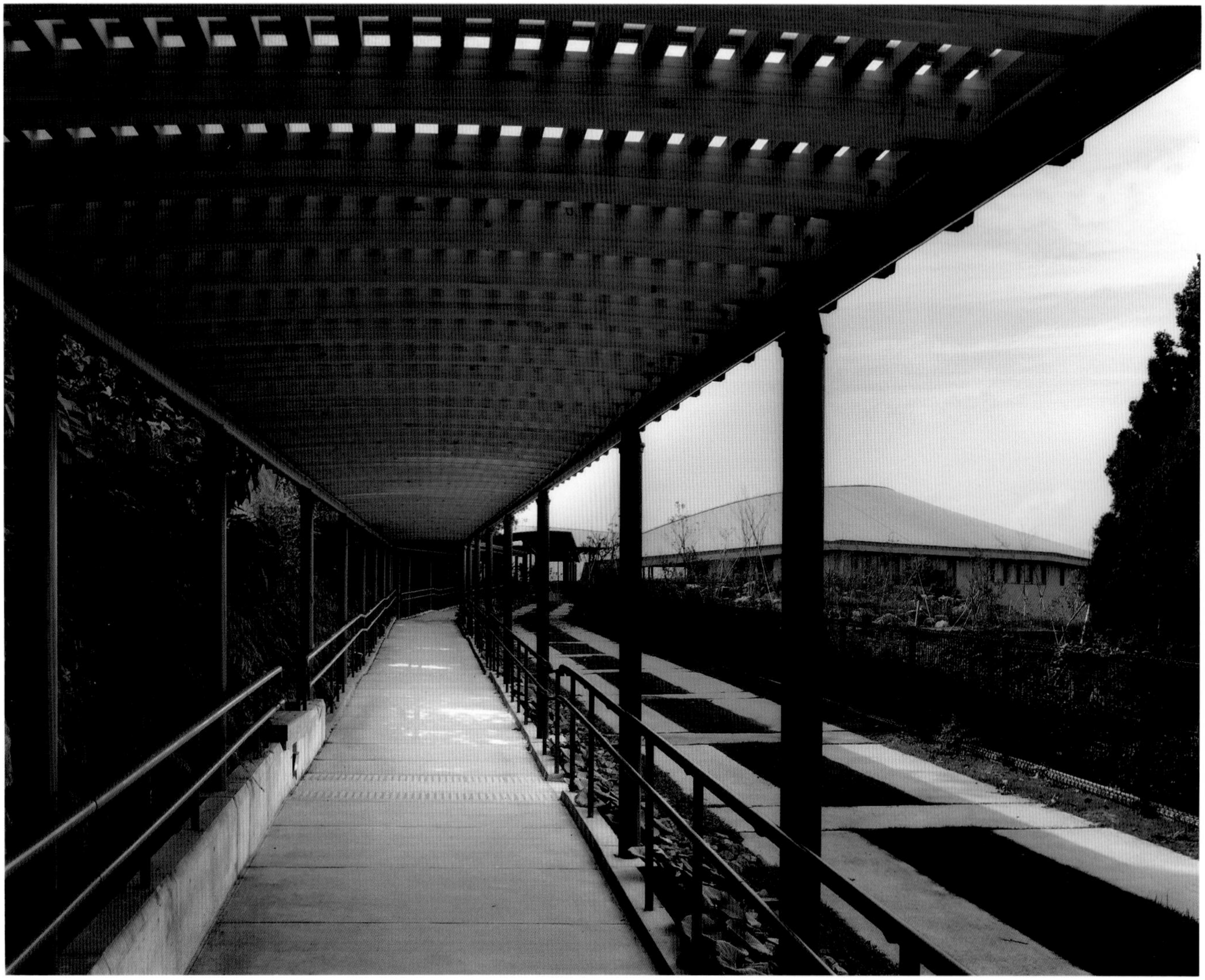

展 示 館

■

Exhibition Hall

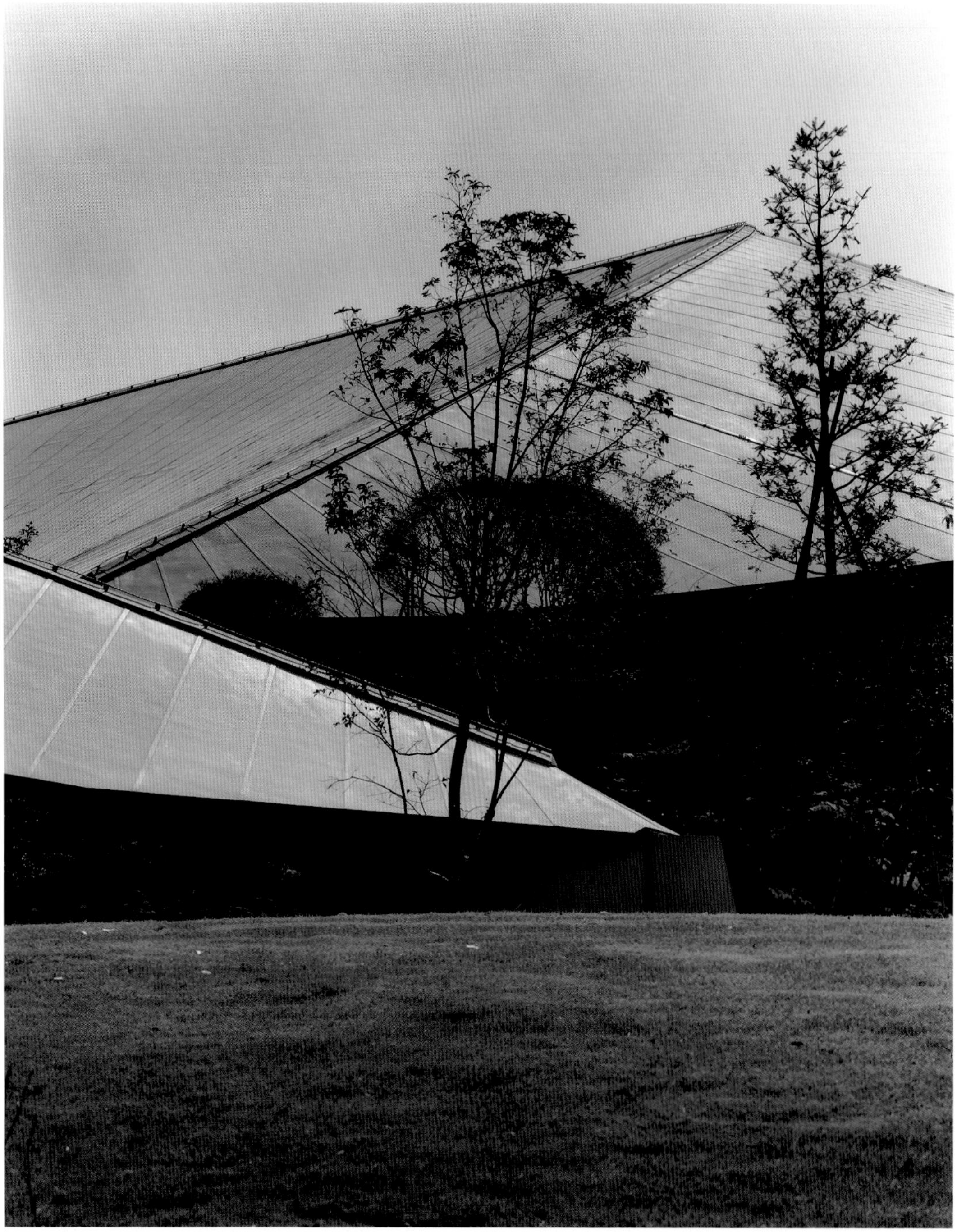

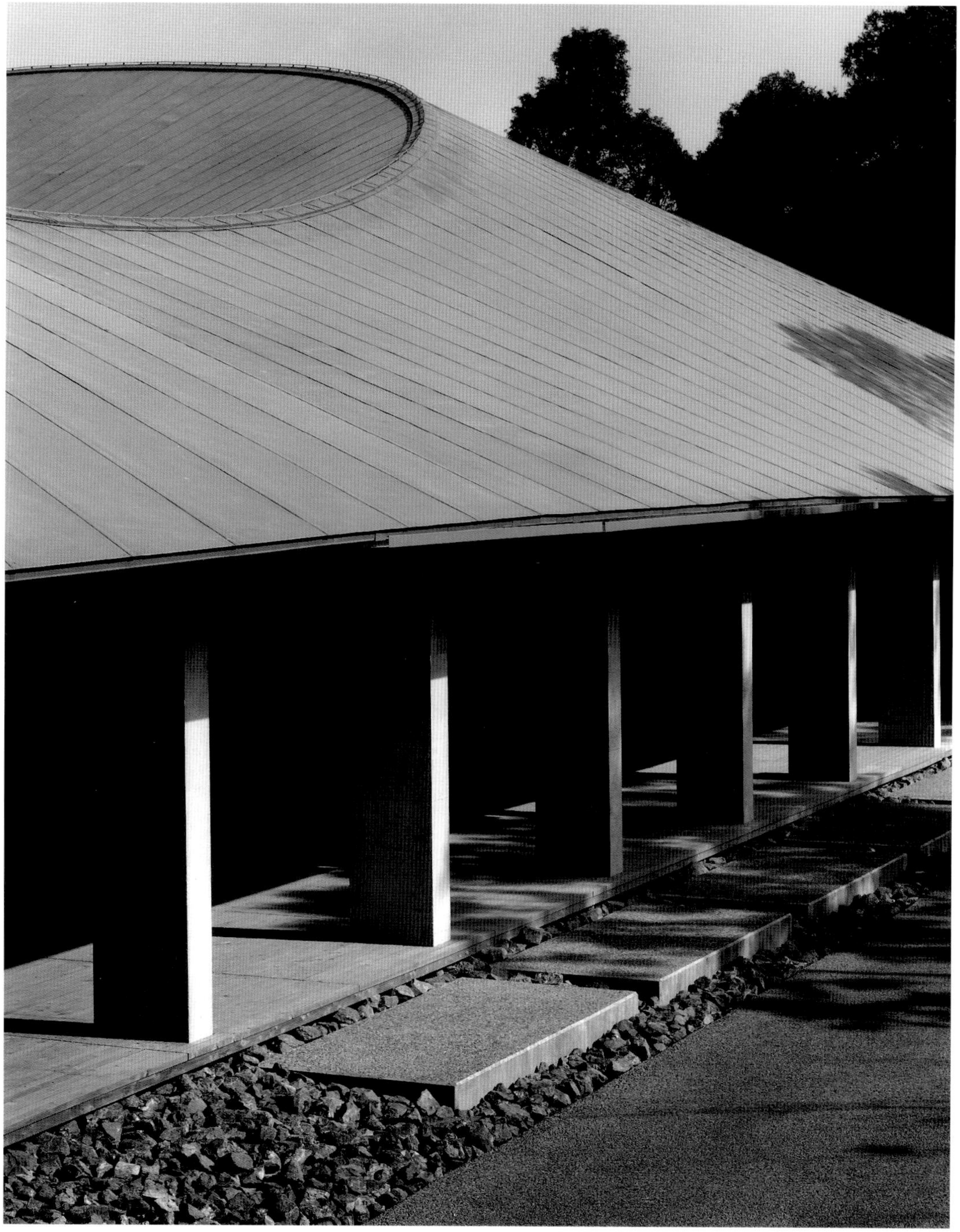

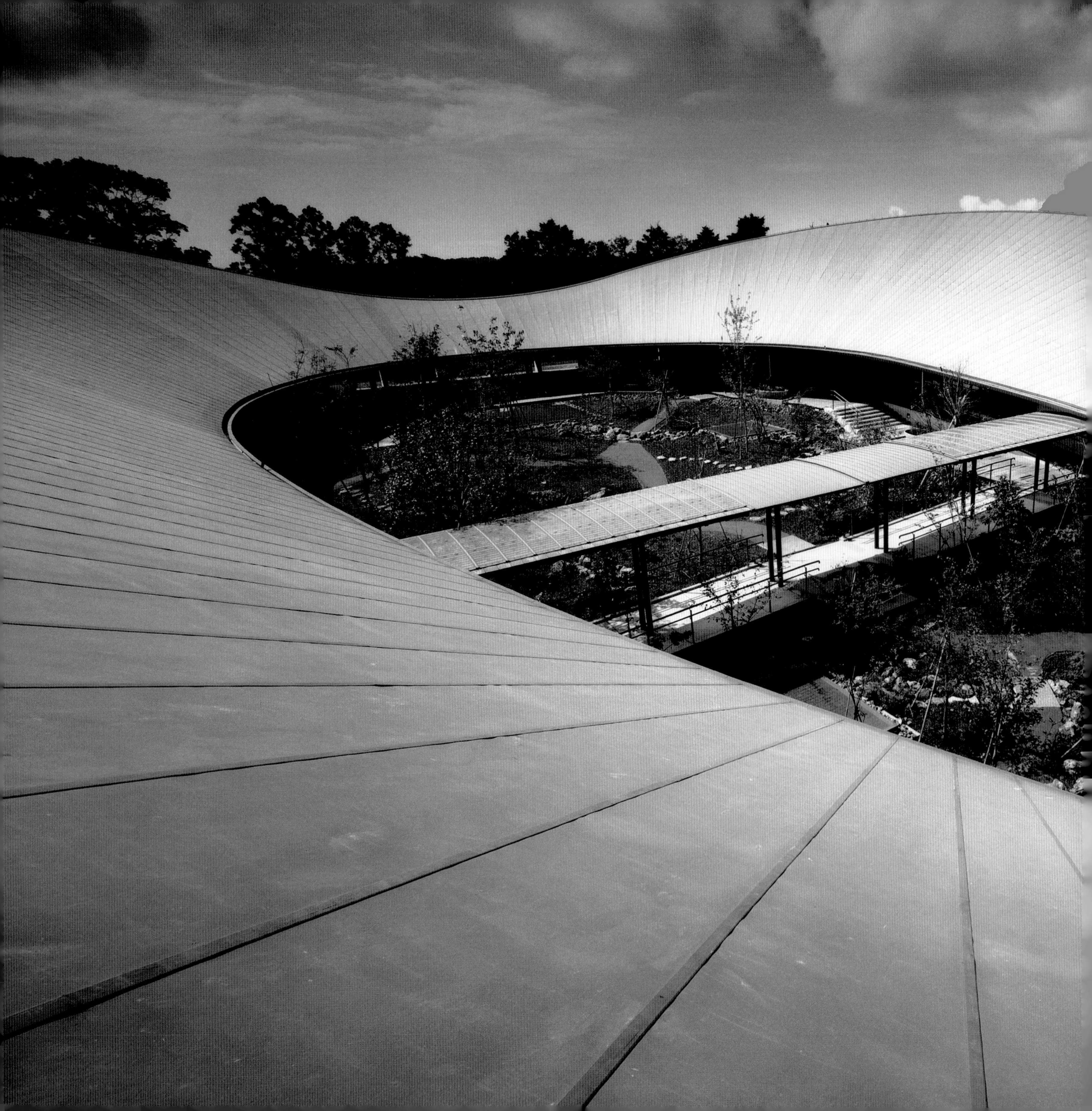

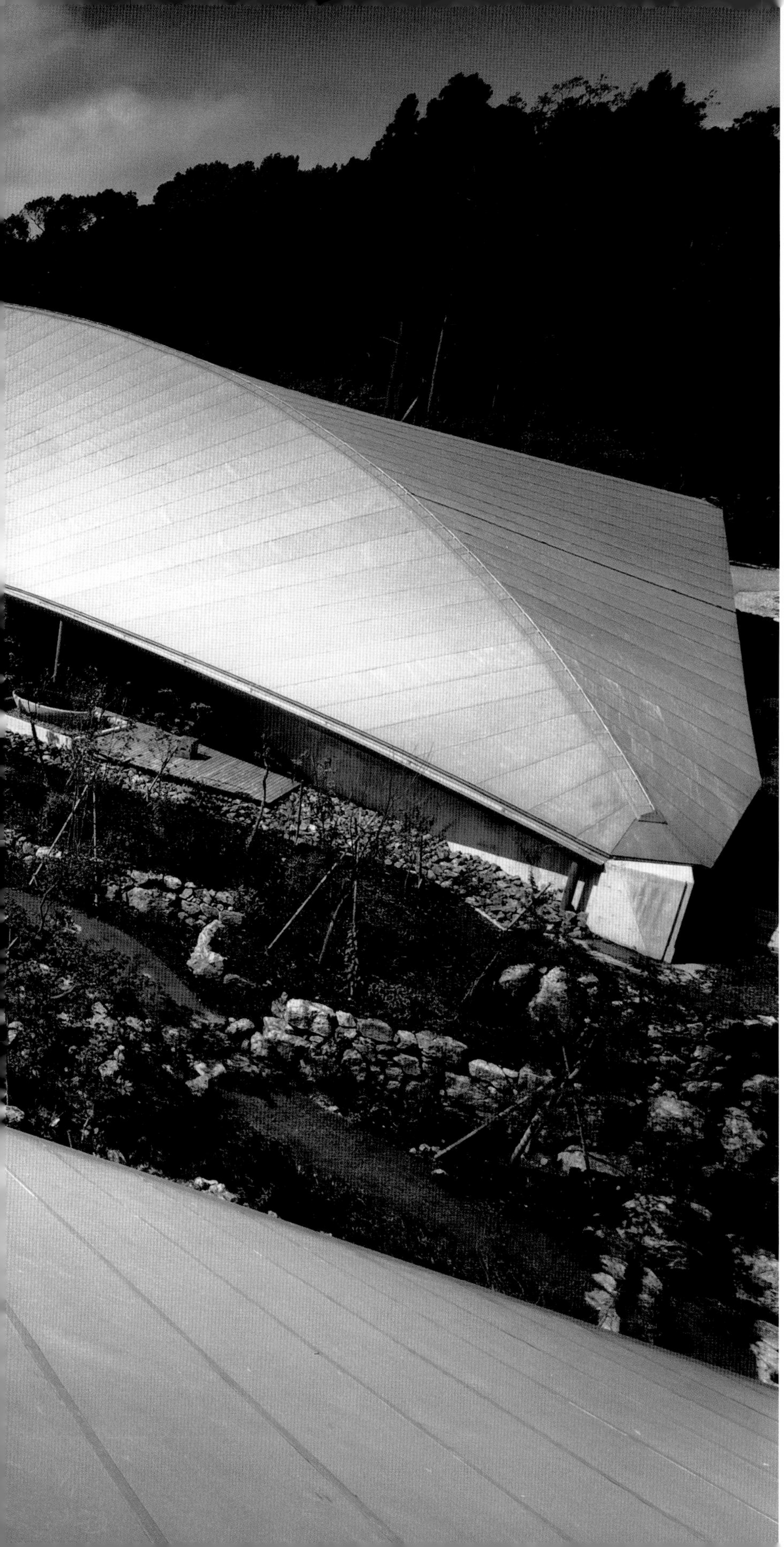

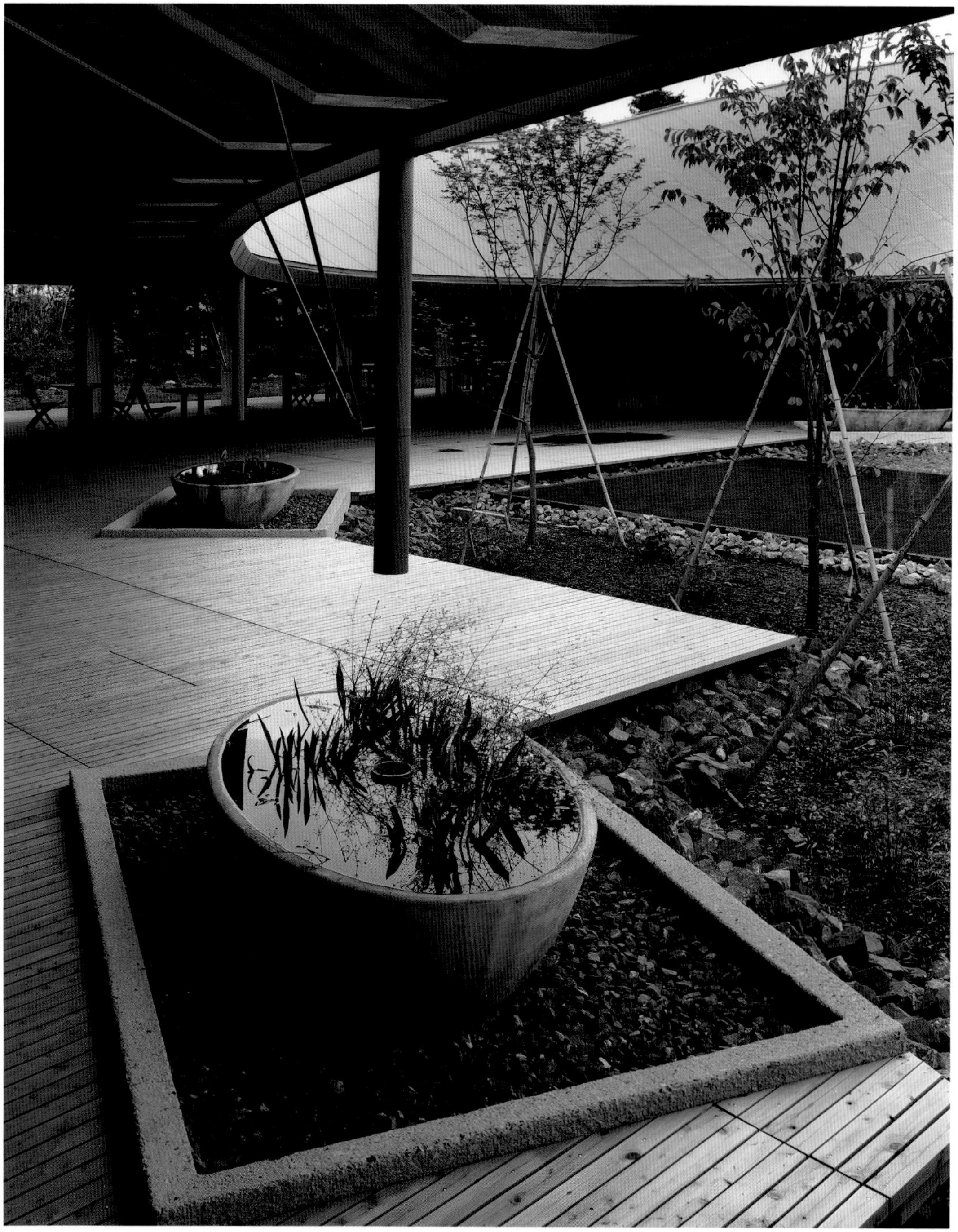

105

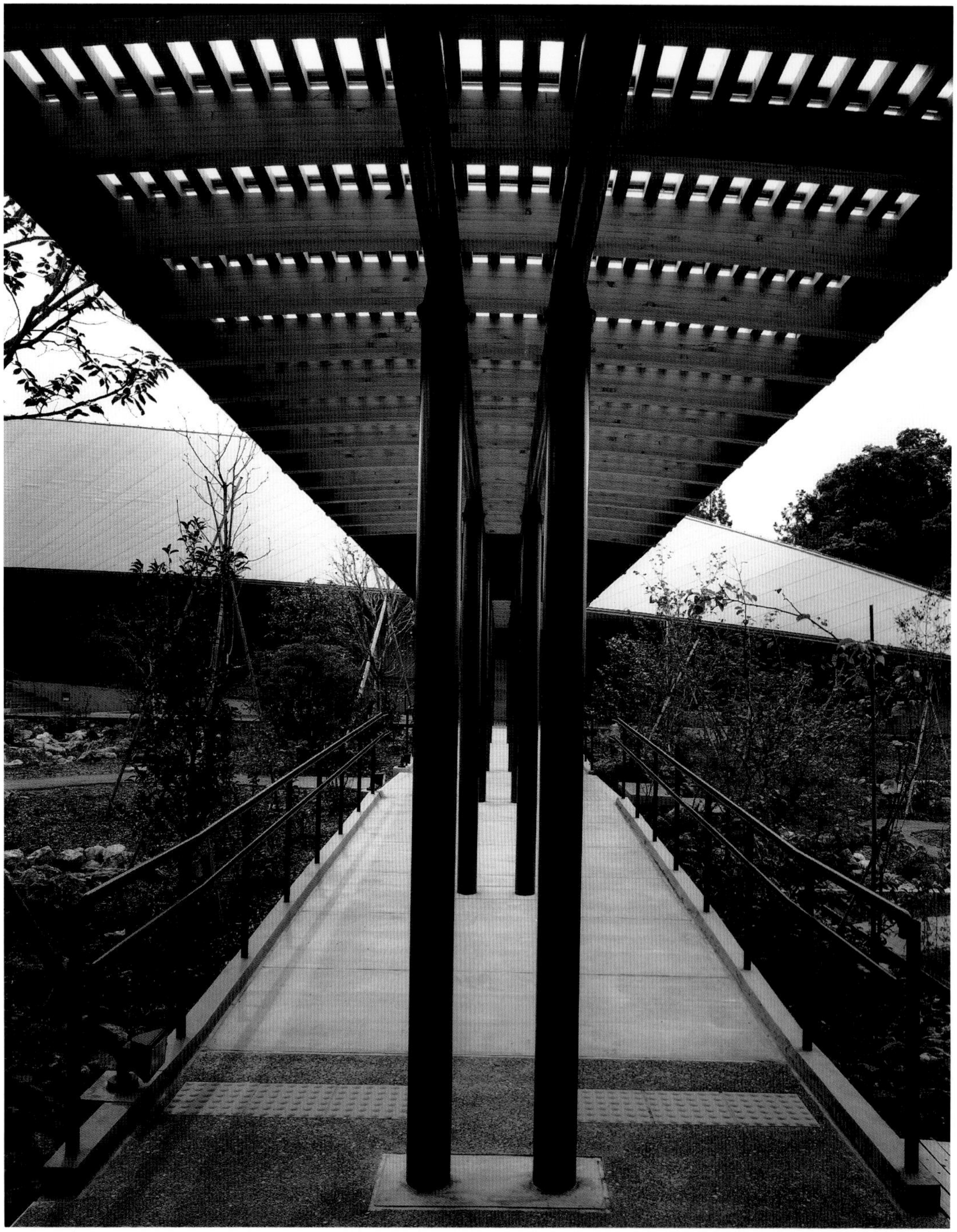

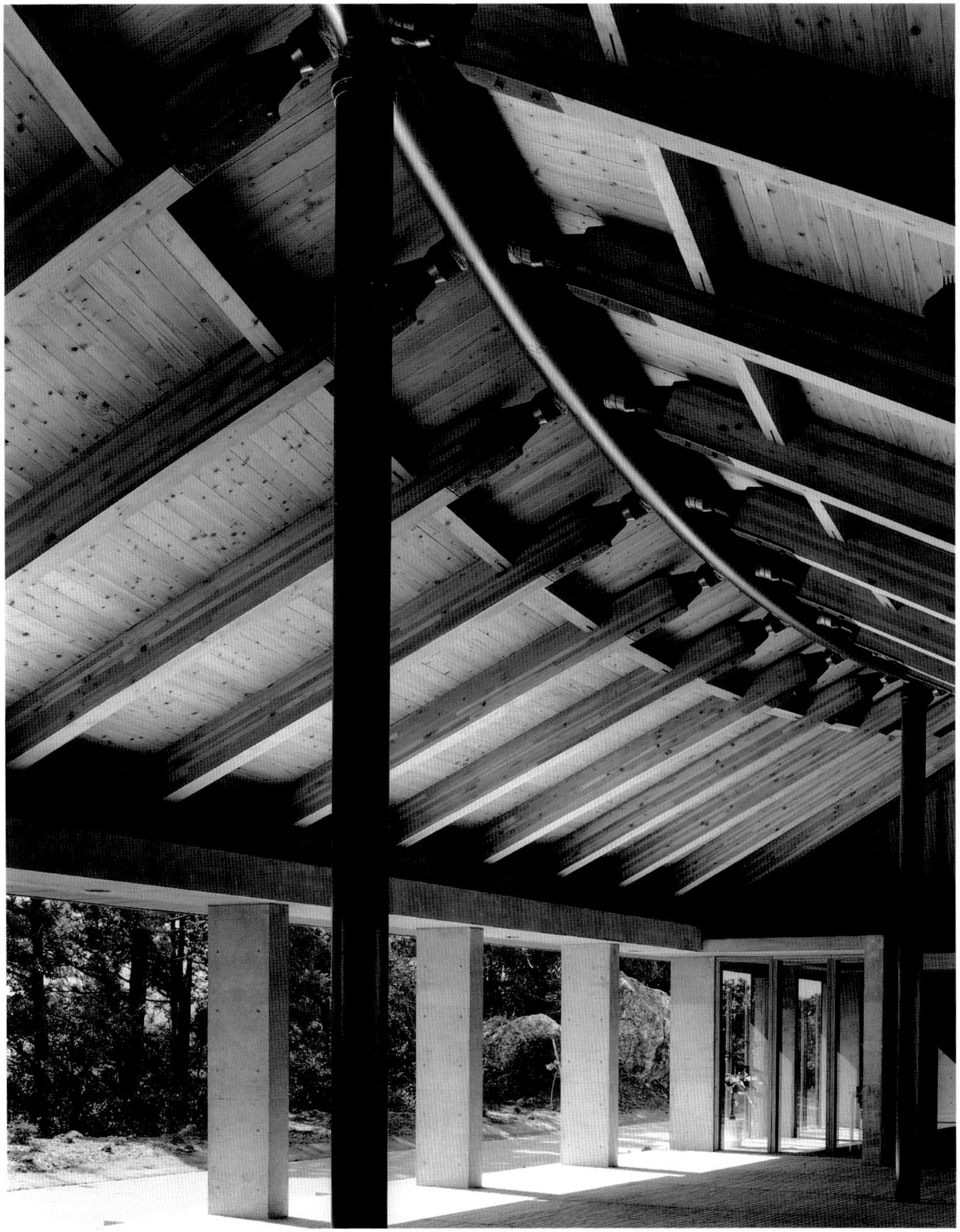

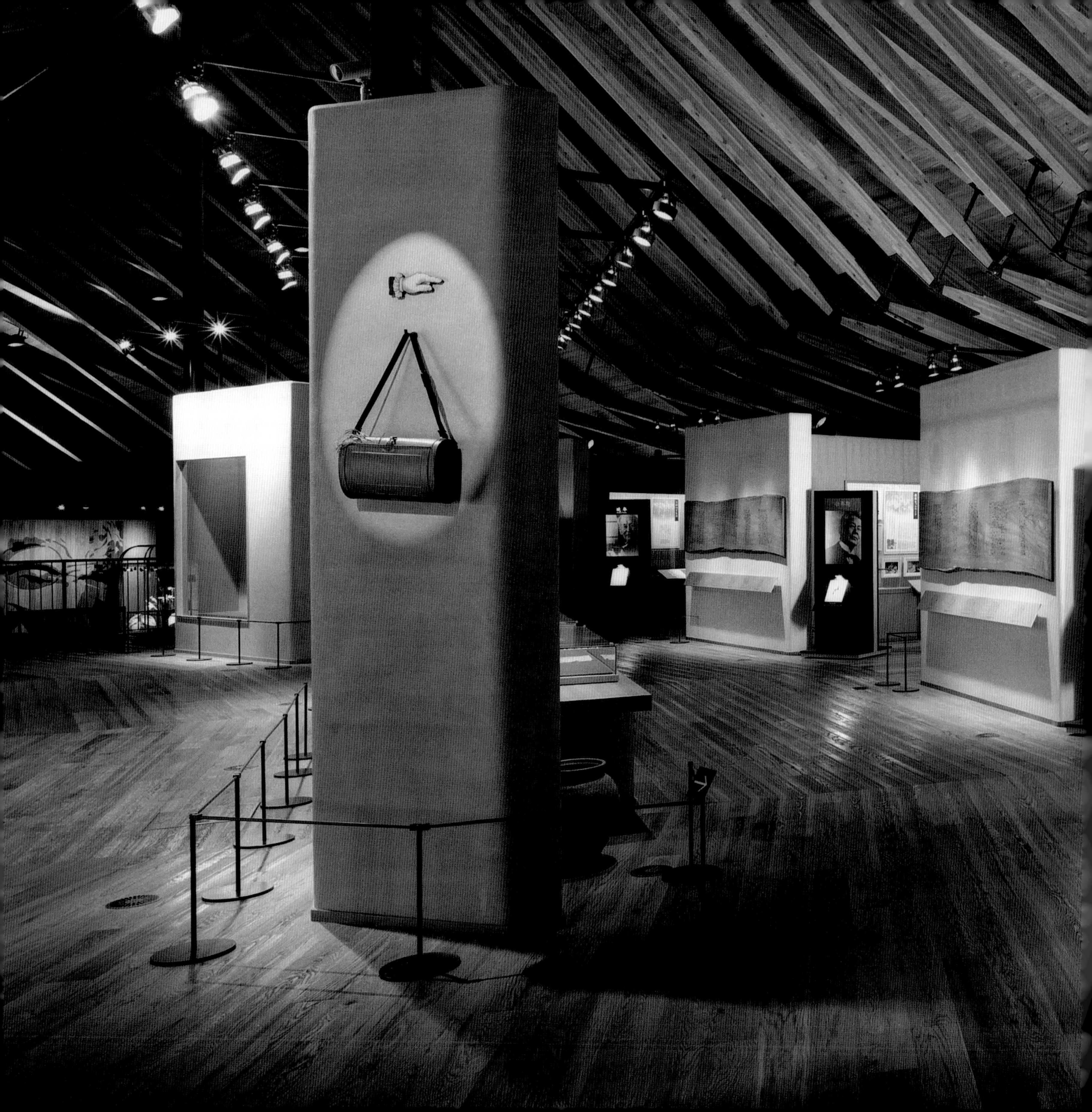

少年期
Early Years

バイカオウレン

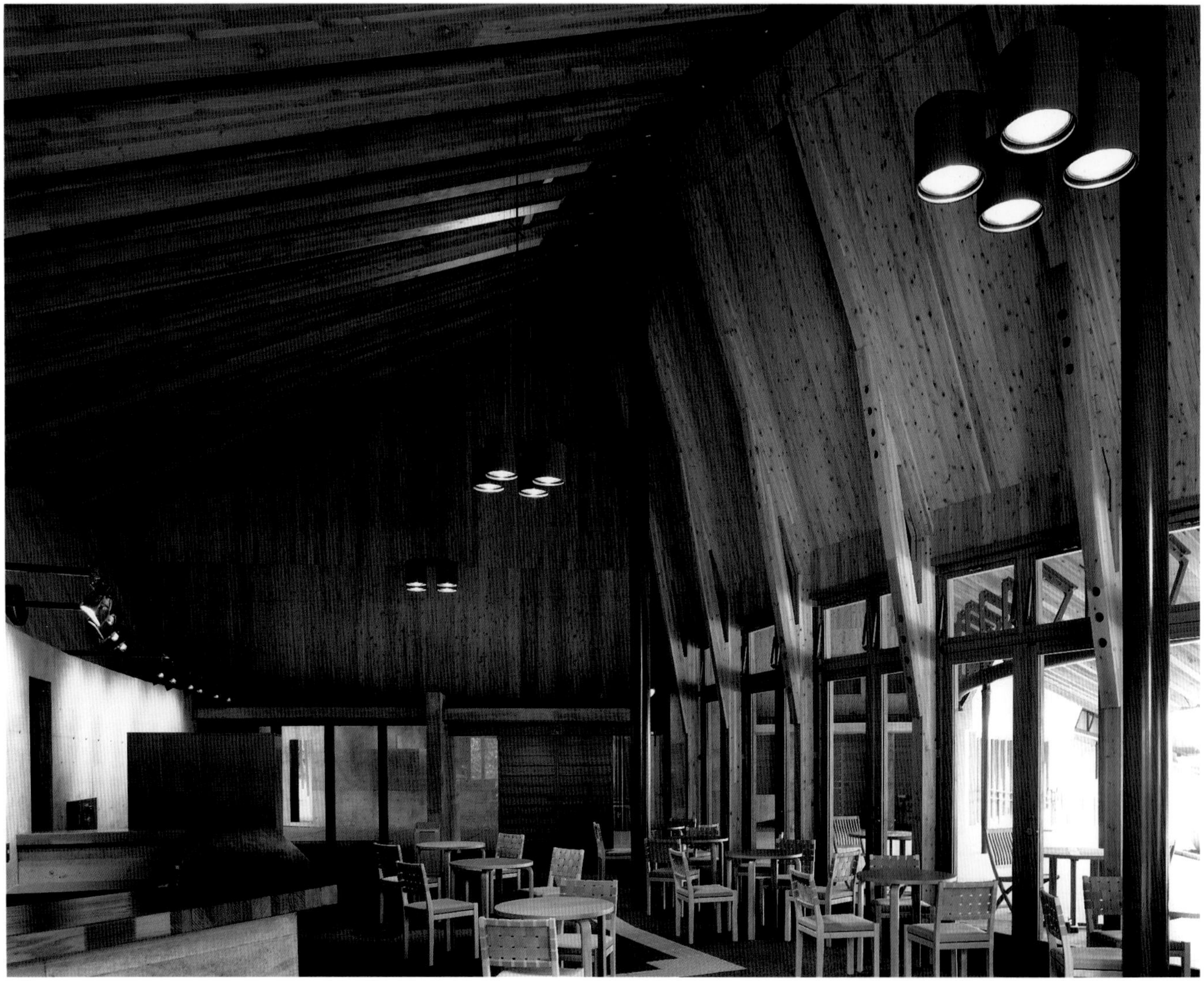

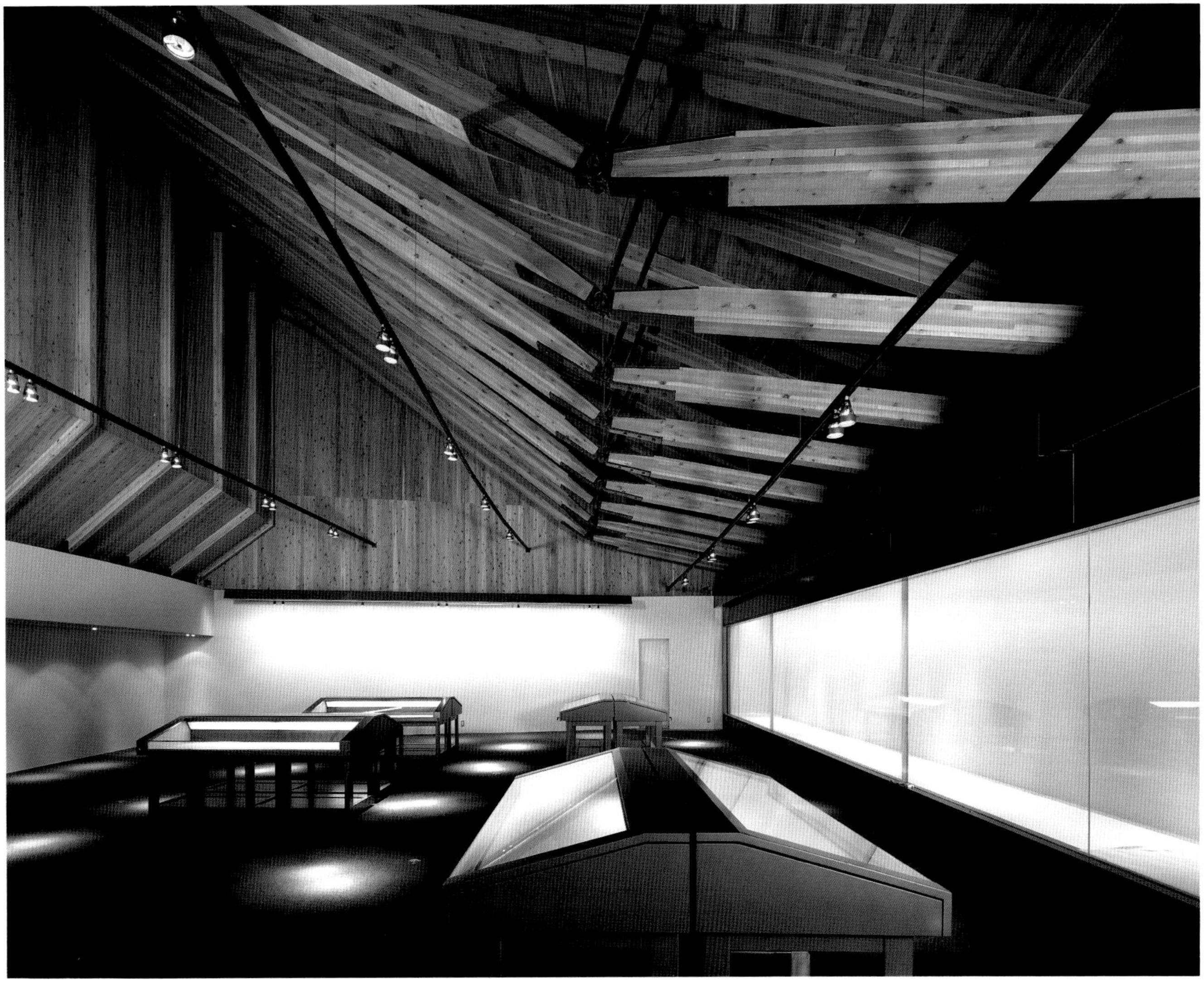

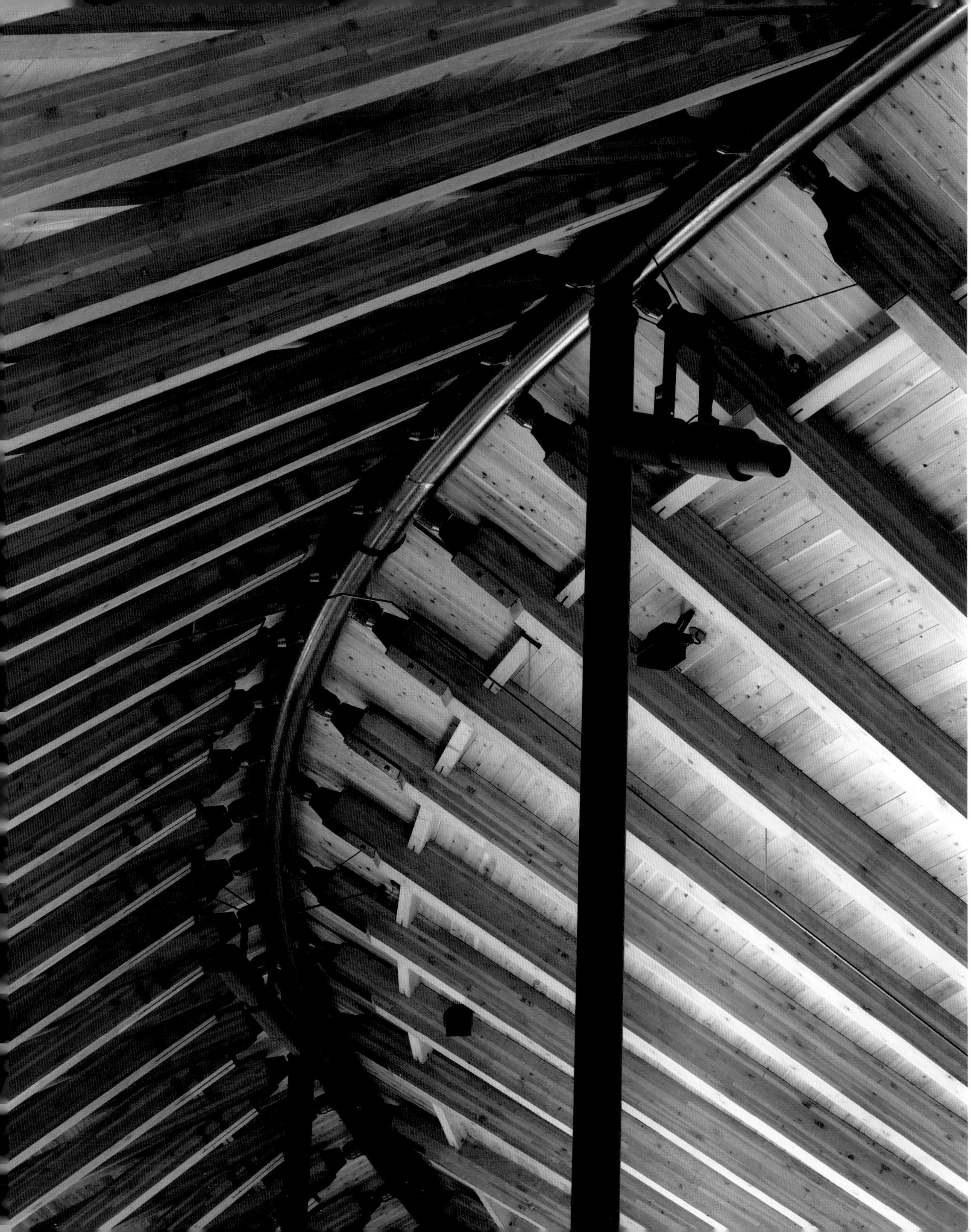

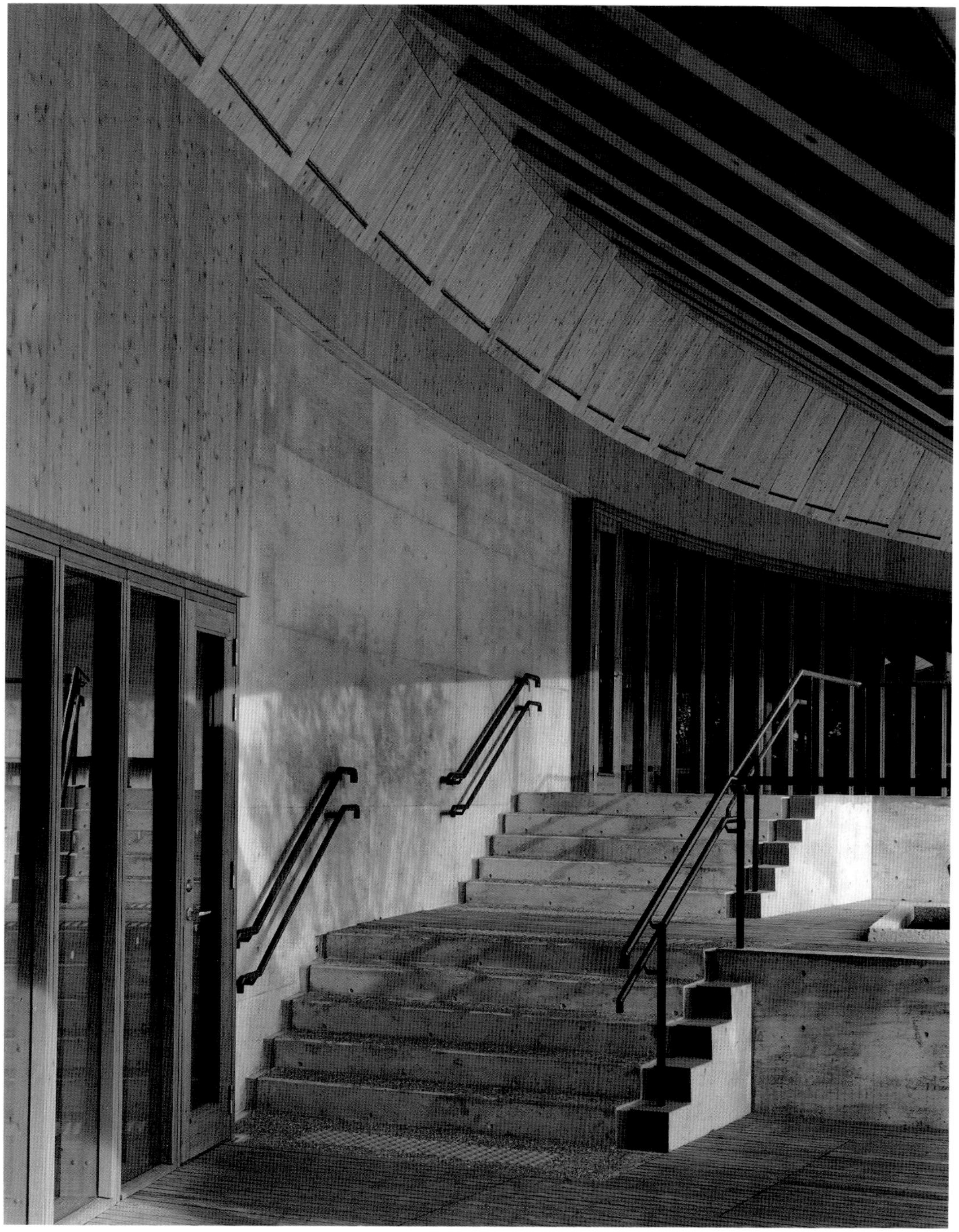

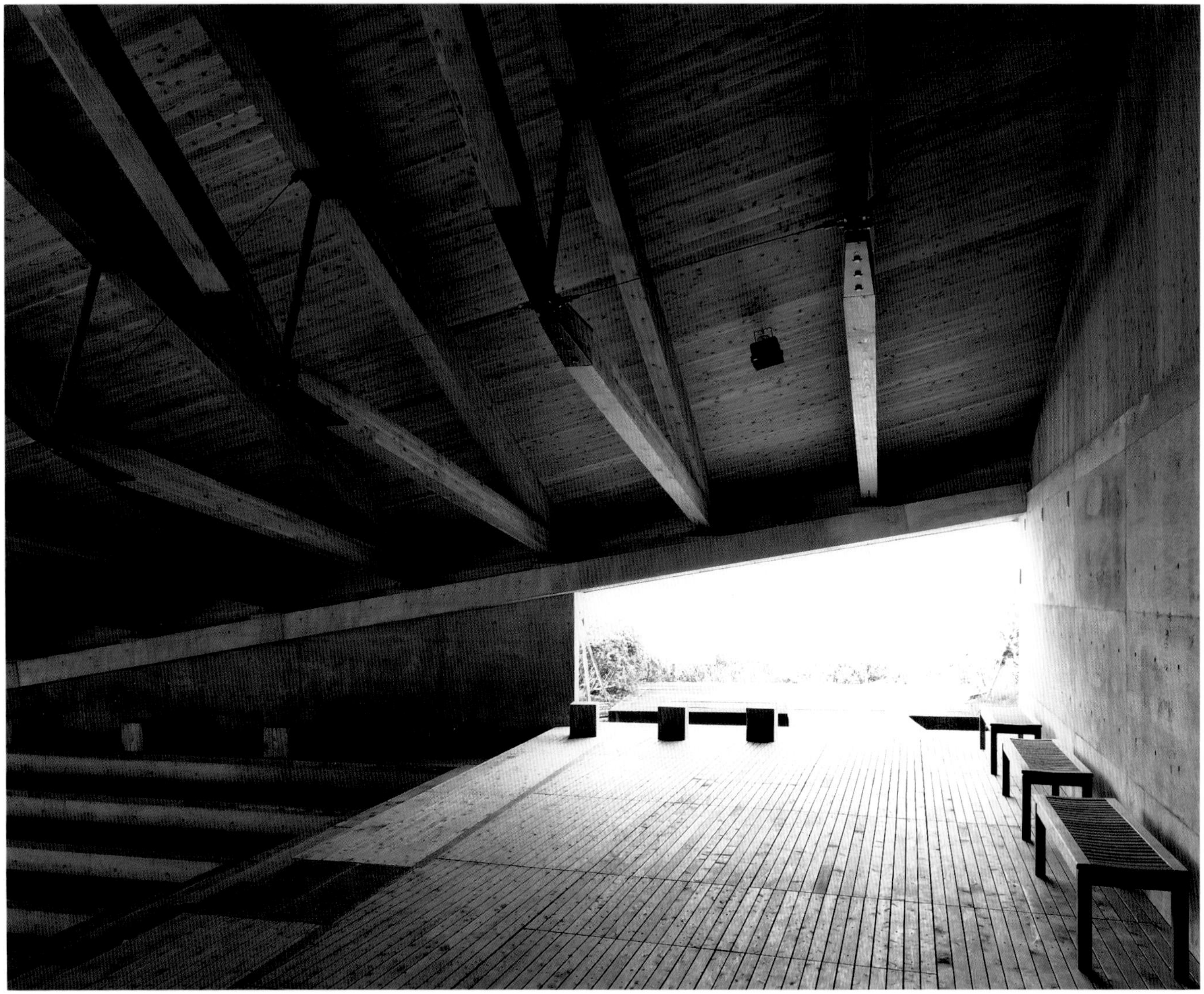

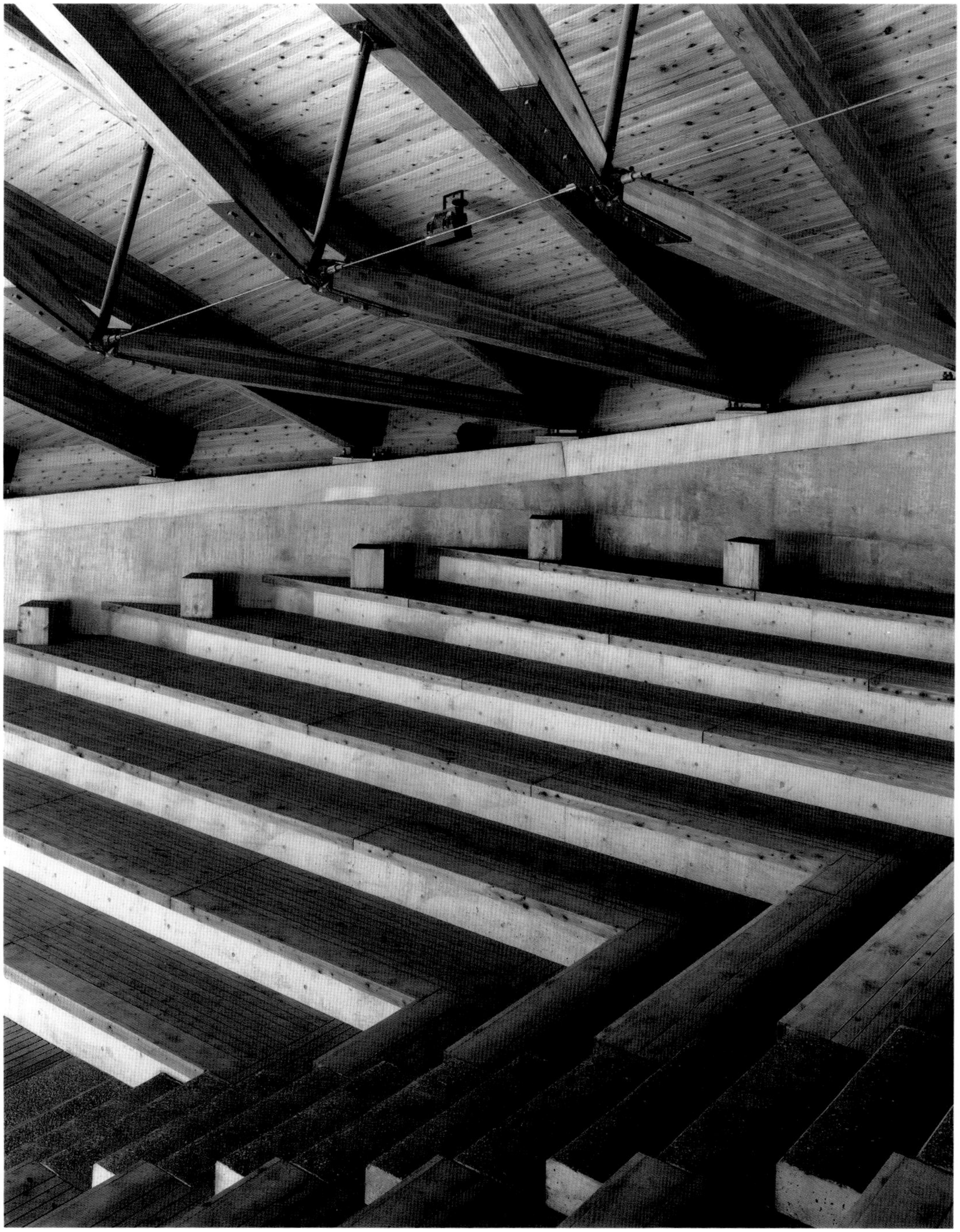

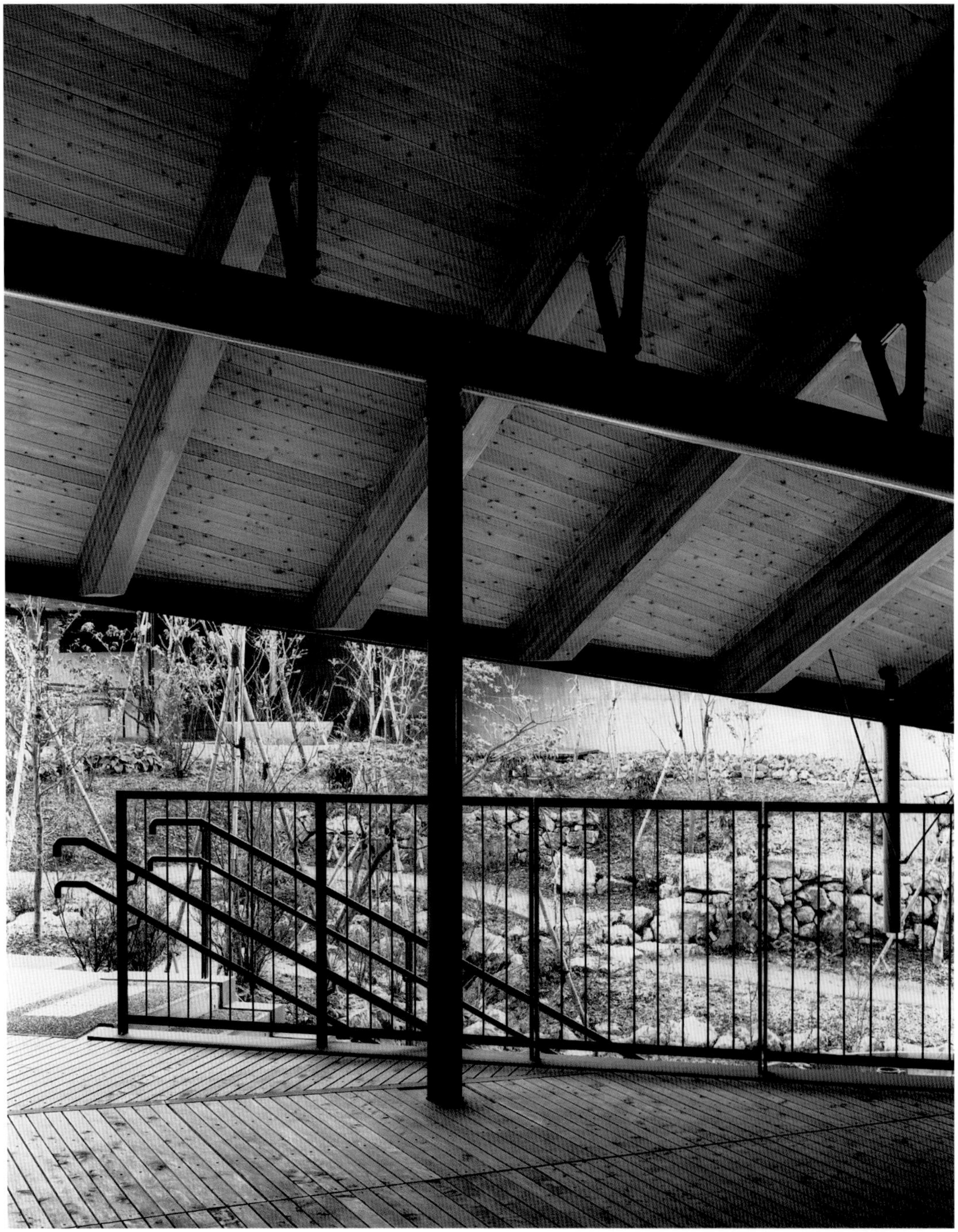

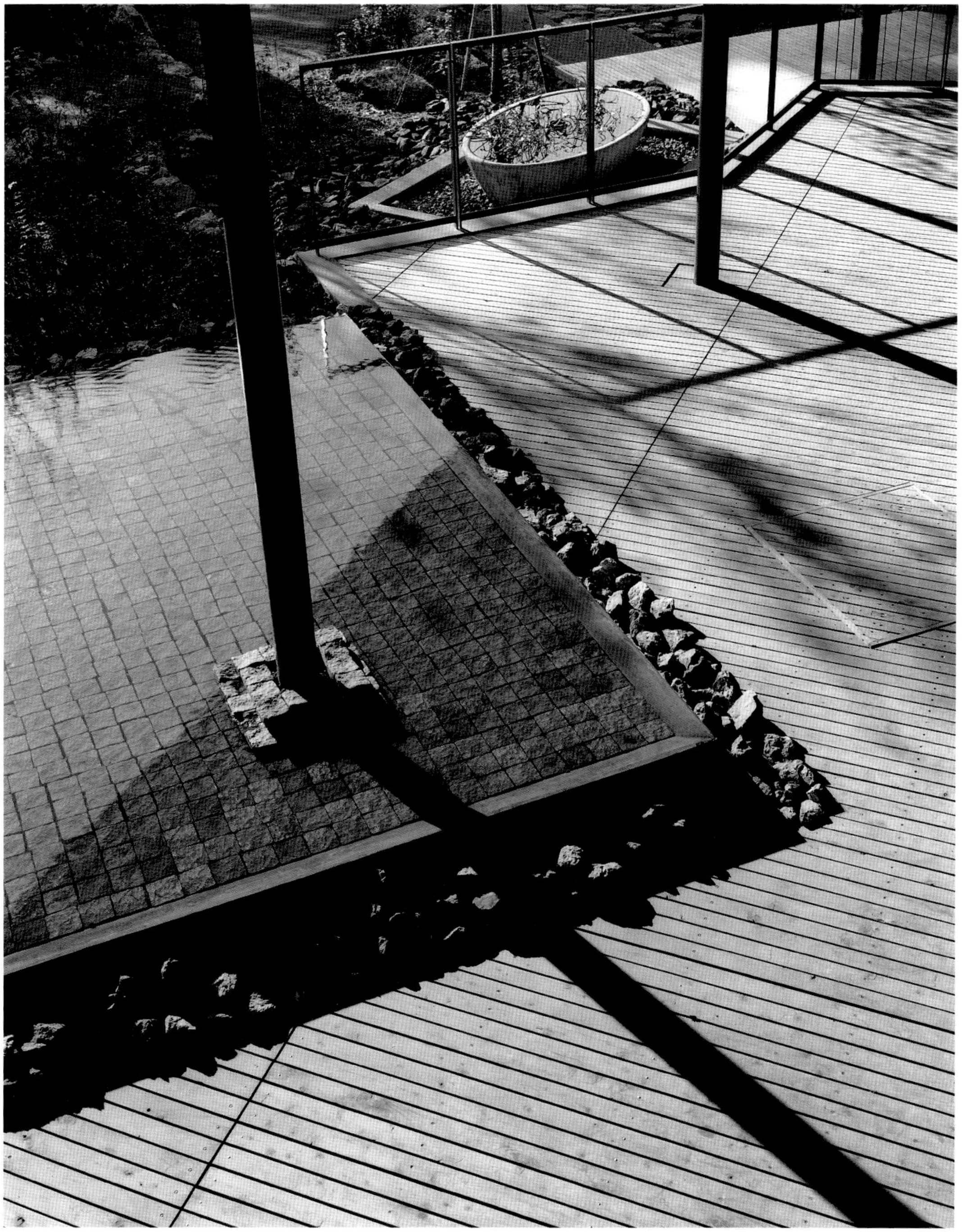

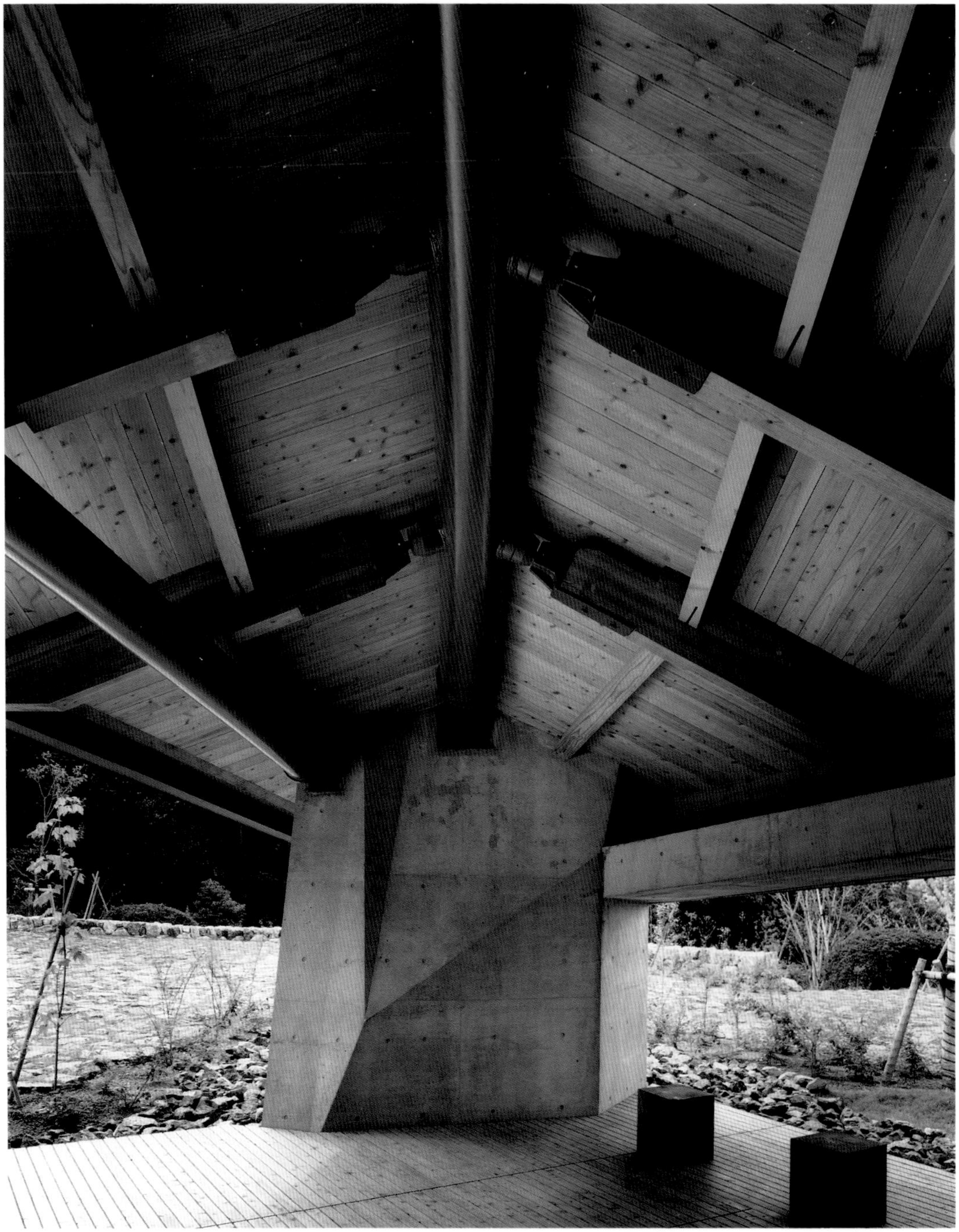

Fuji RINRI Seminar House

倫理研究所富士高原研修所　撮影■2001

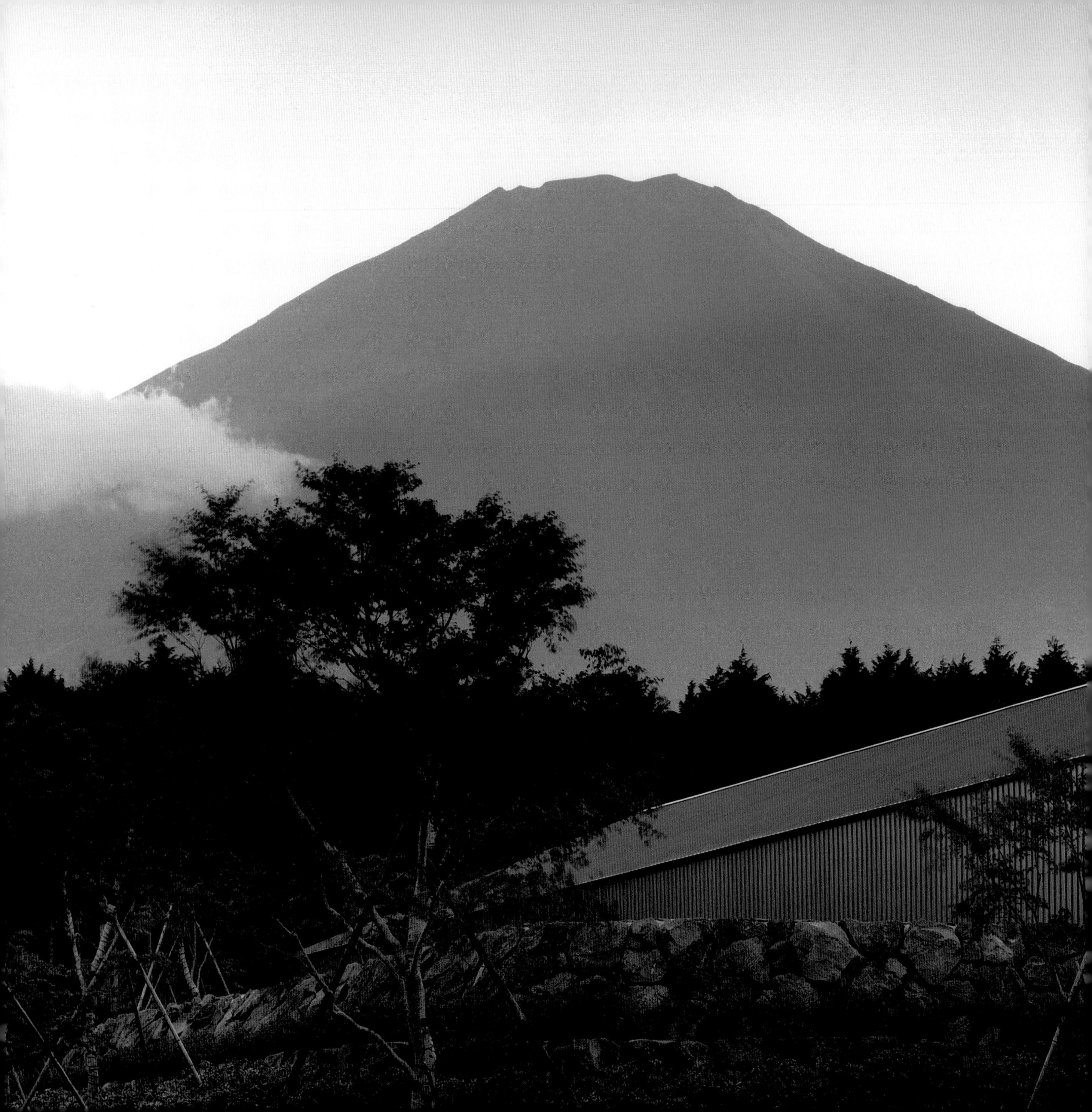

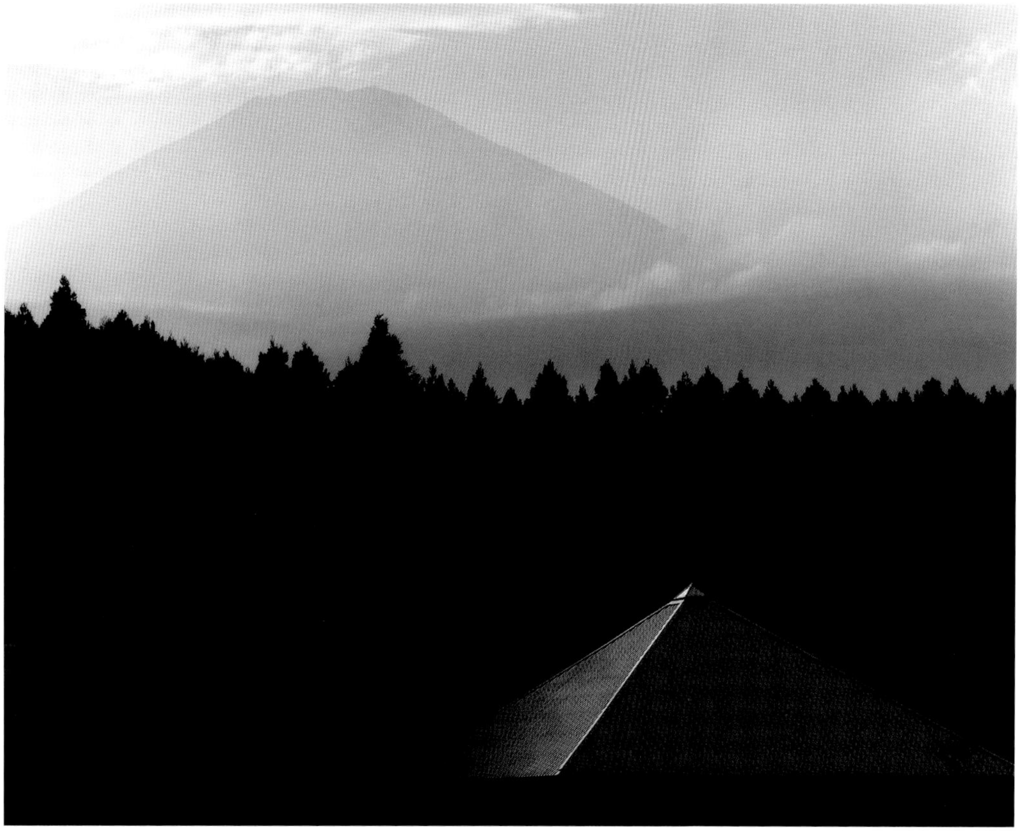

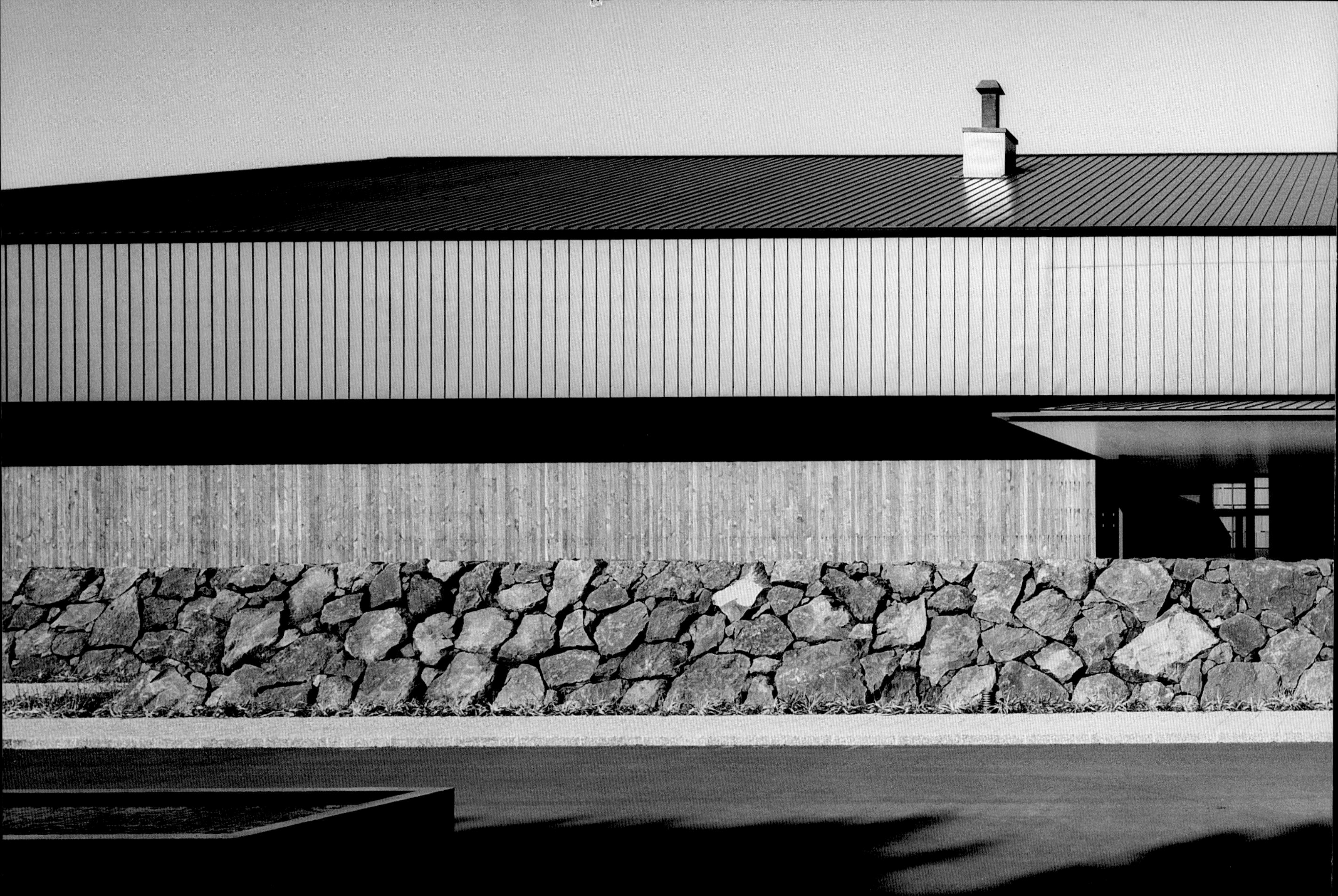

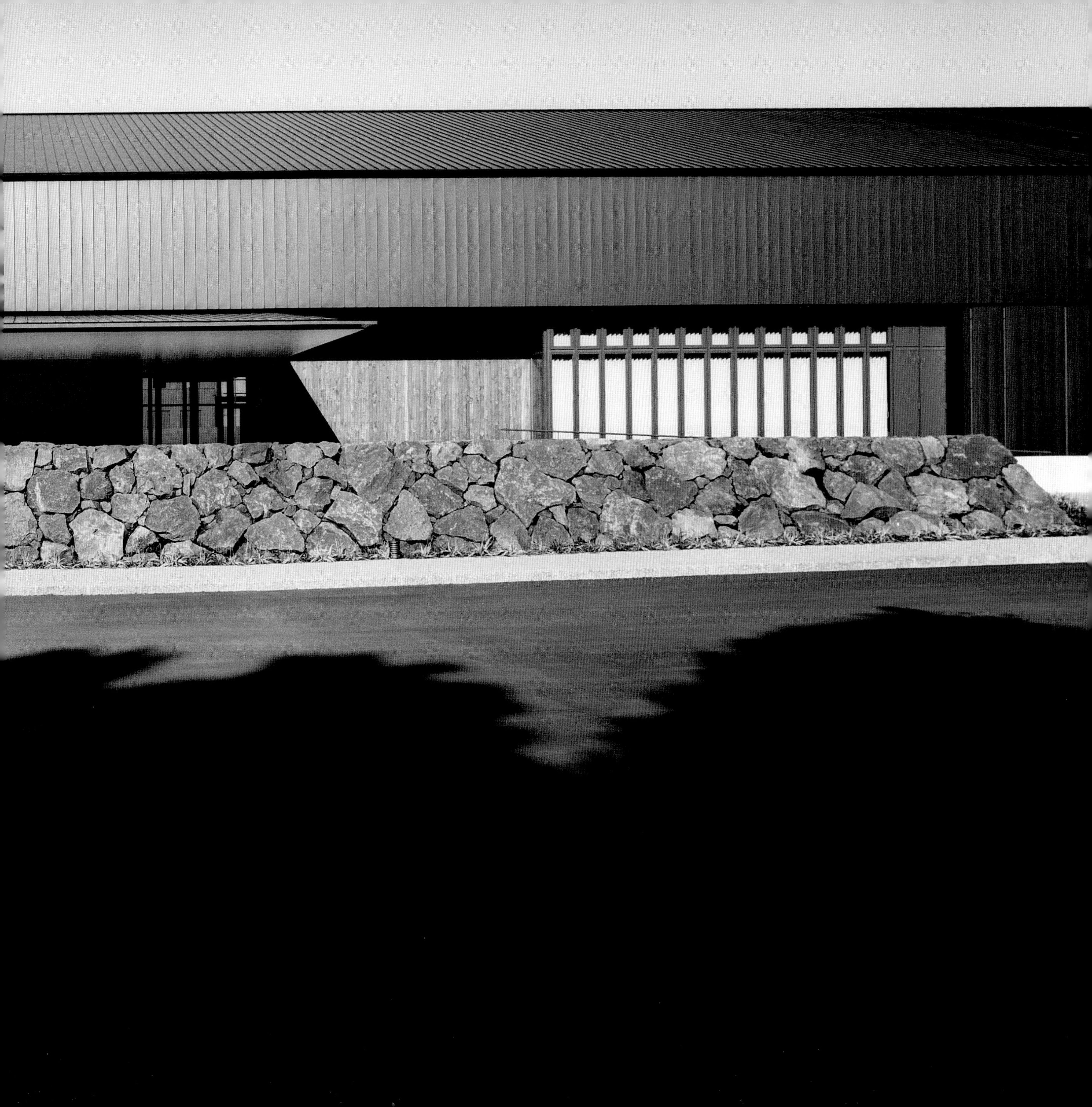

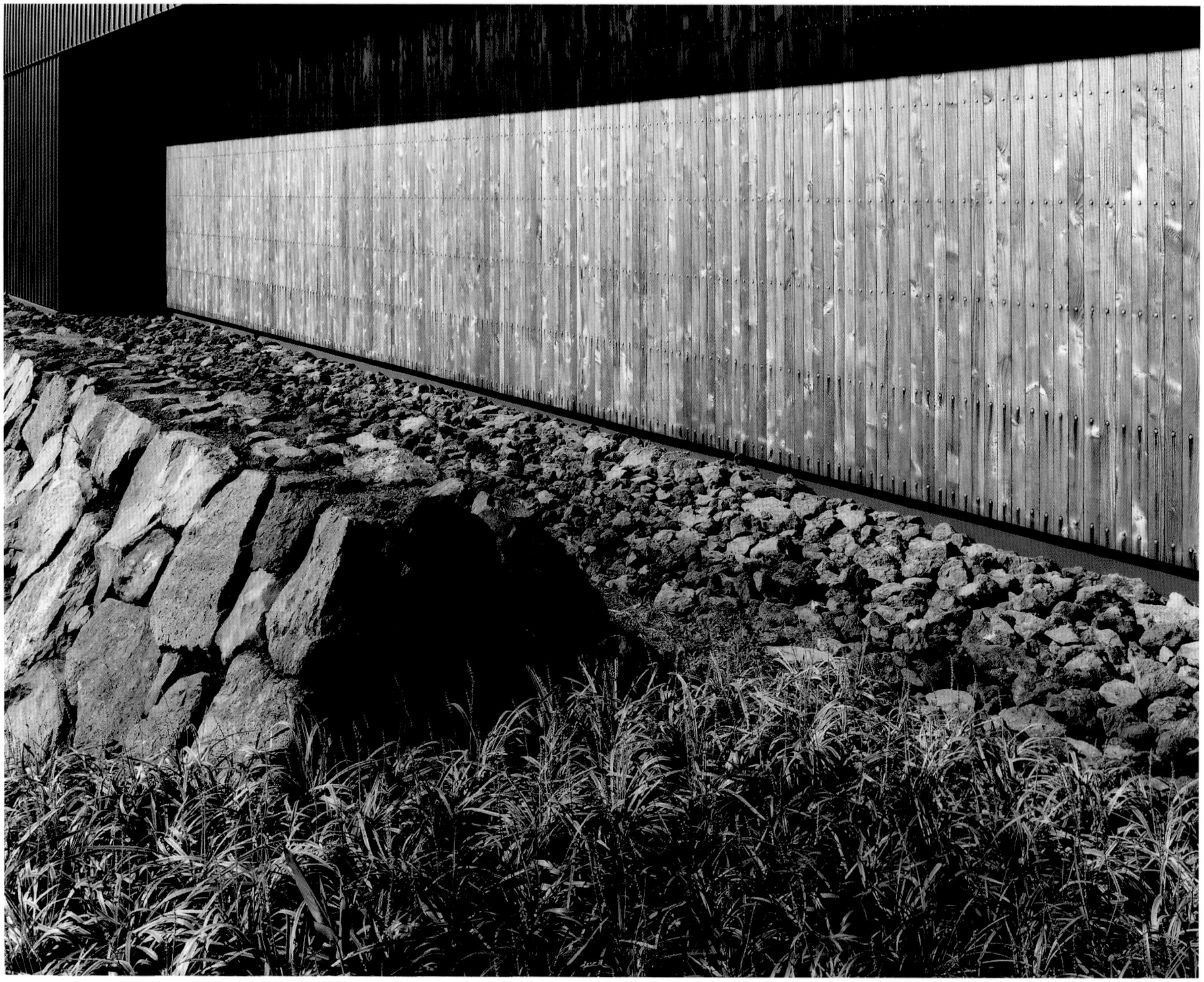

127

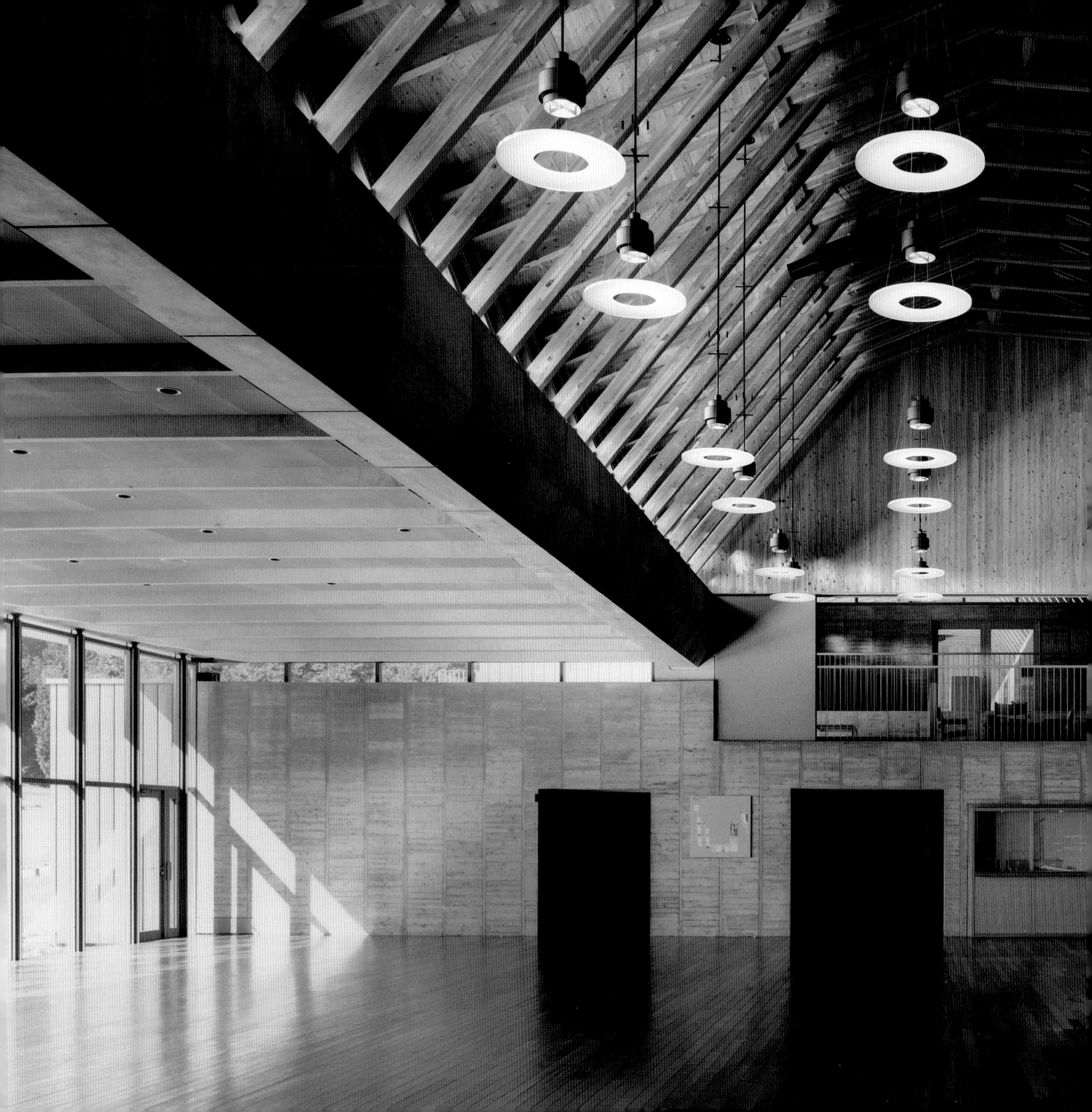

129

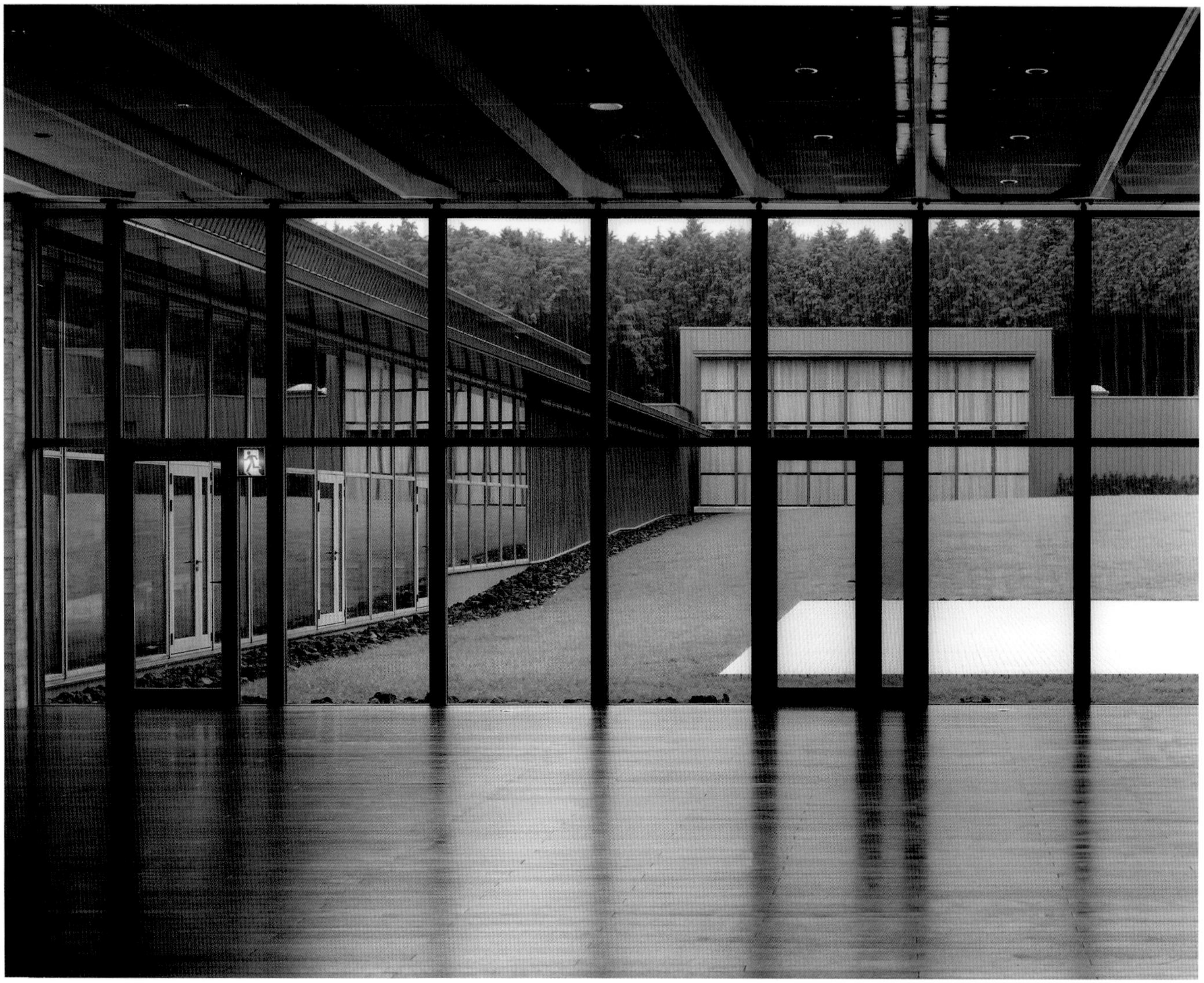

131

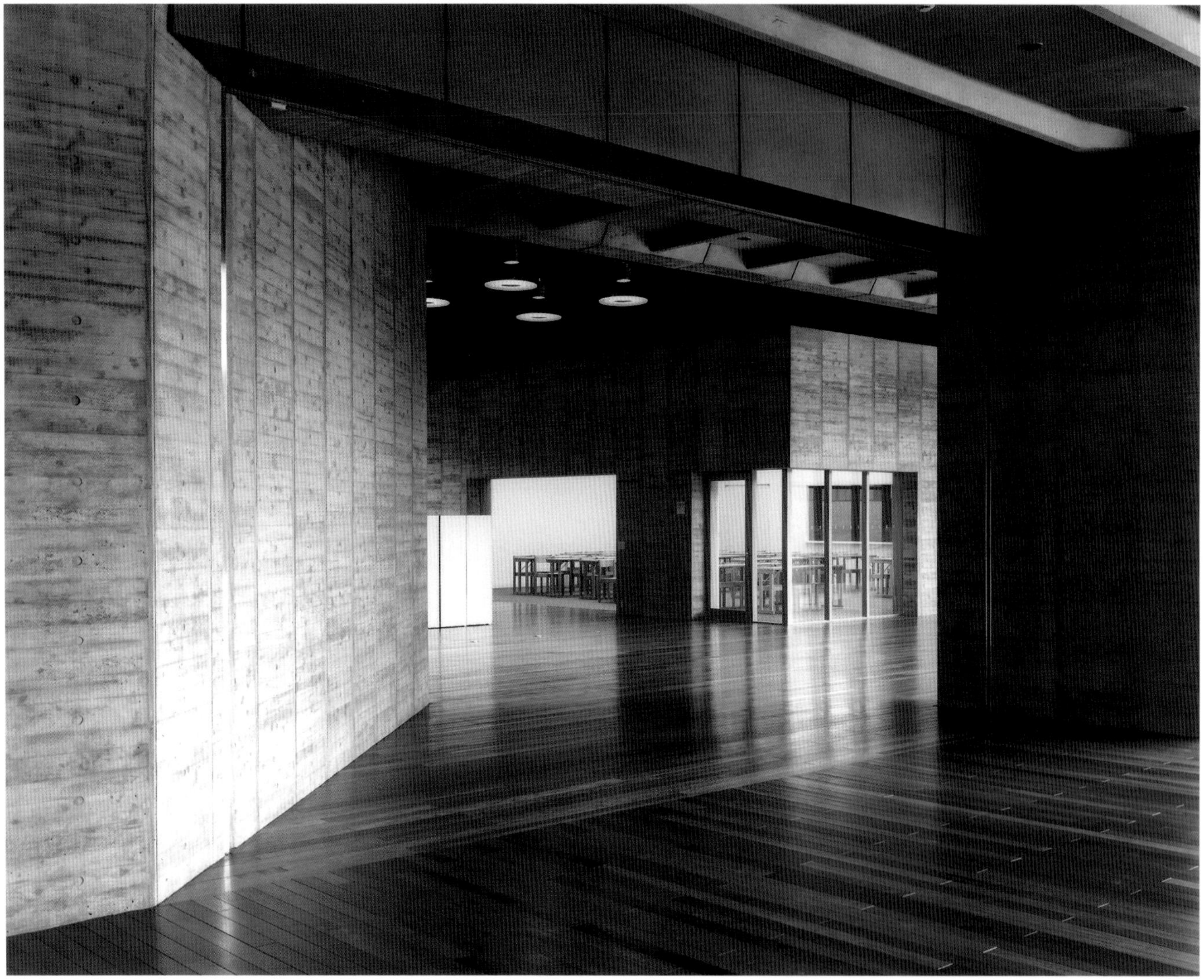

133

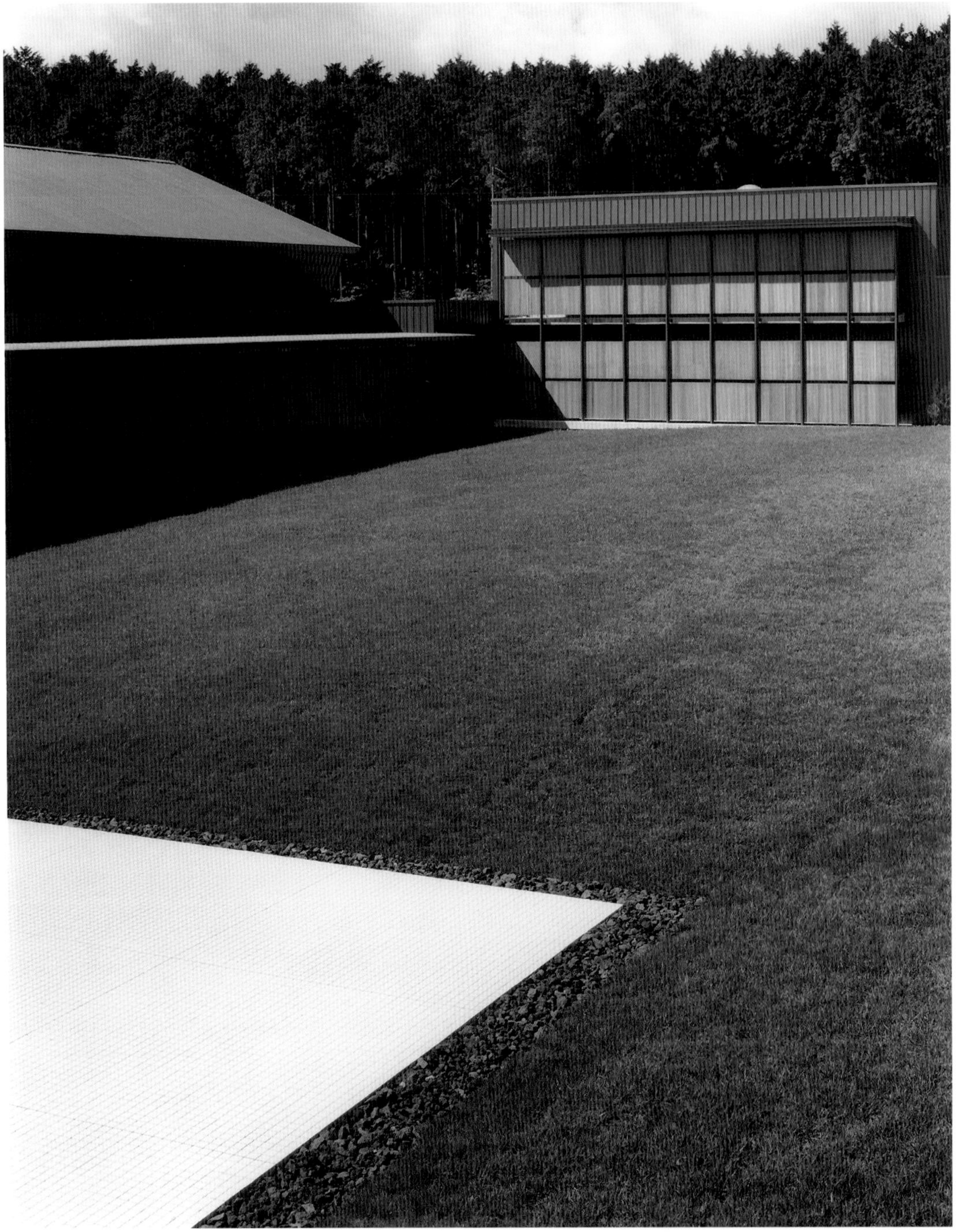

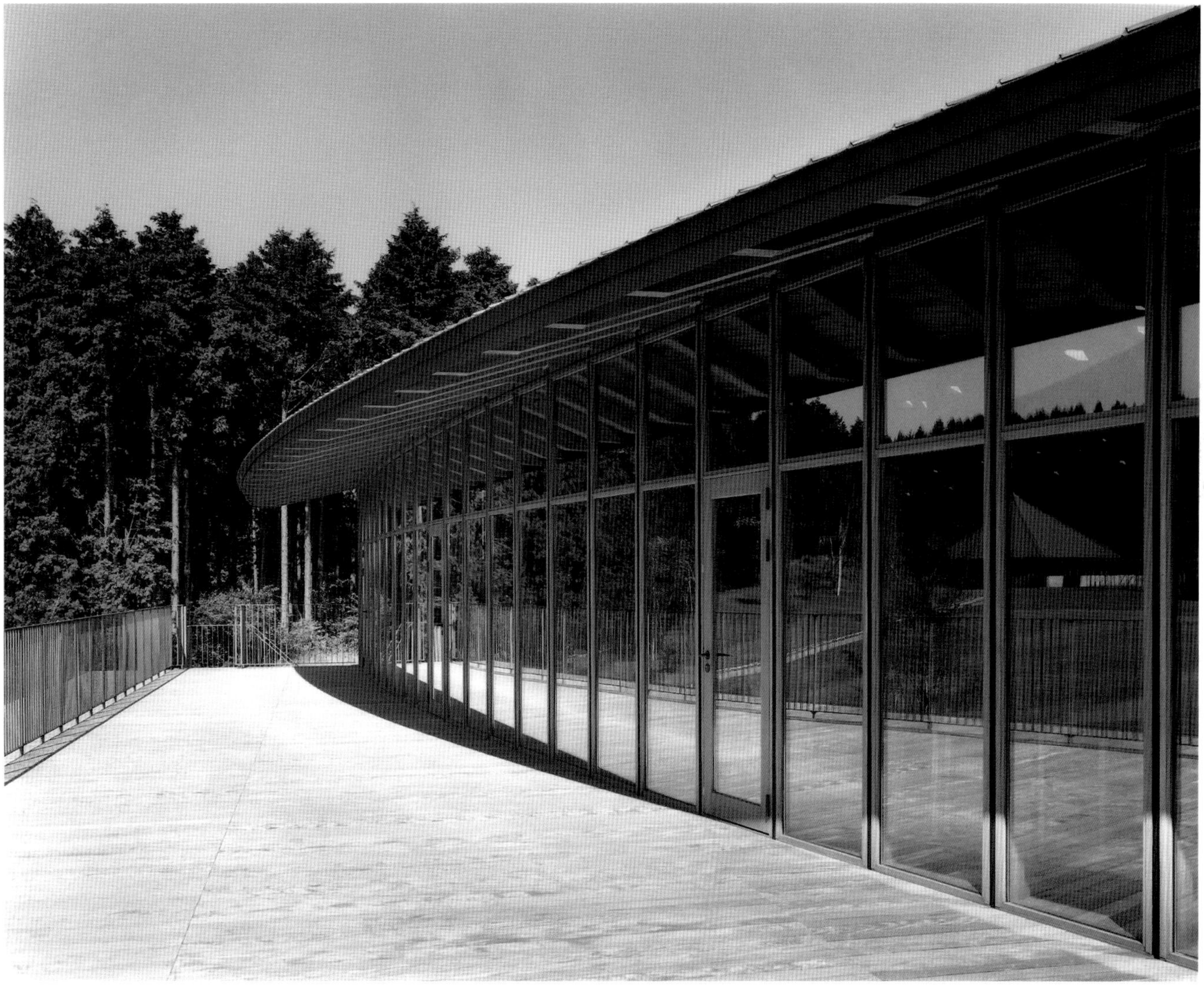

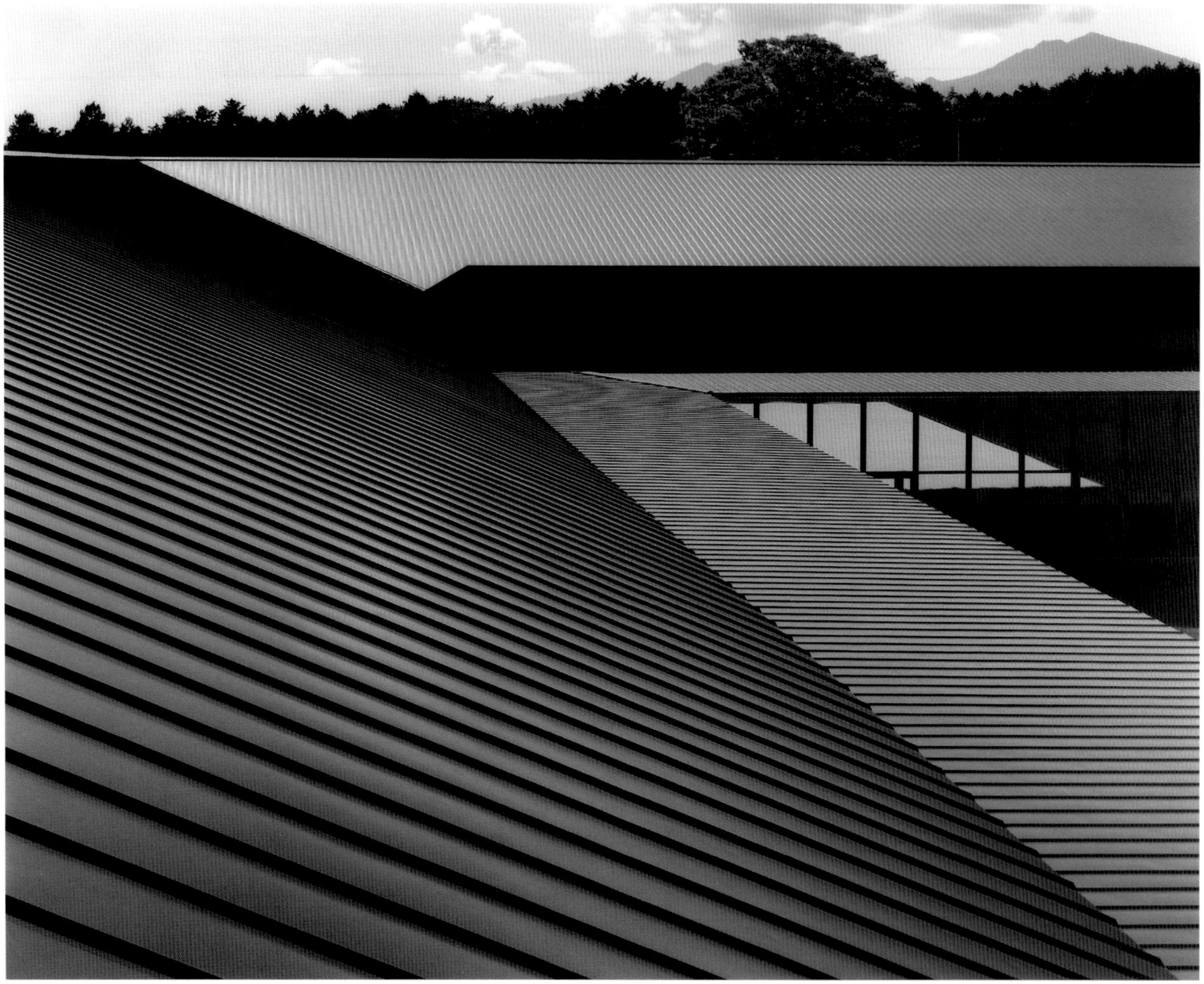

137

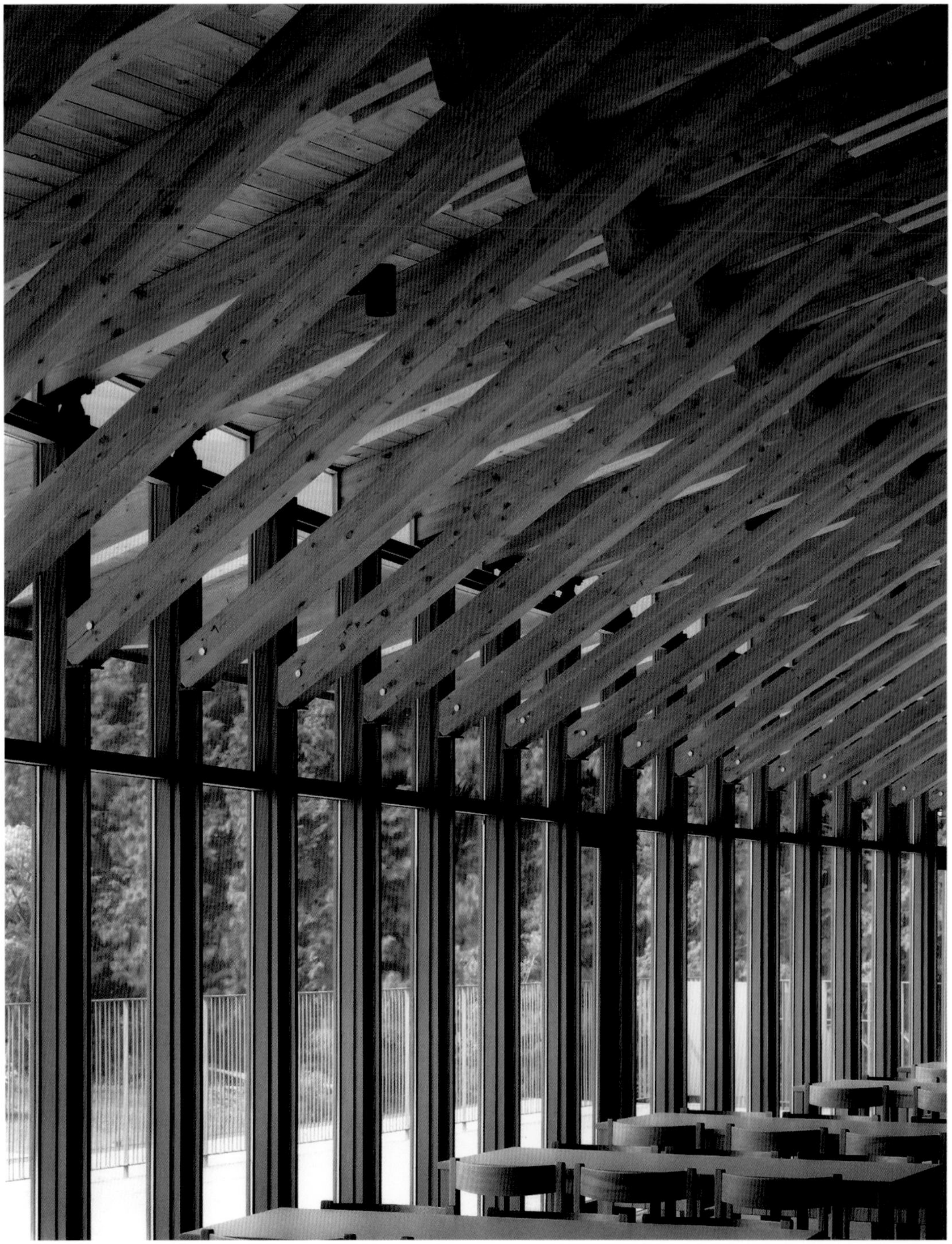

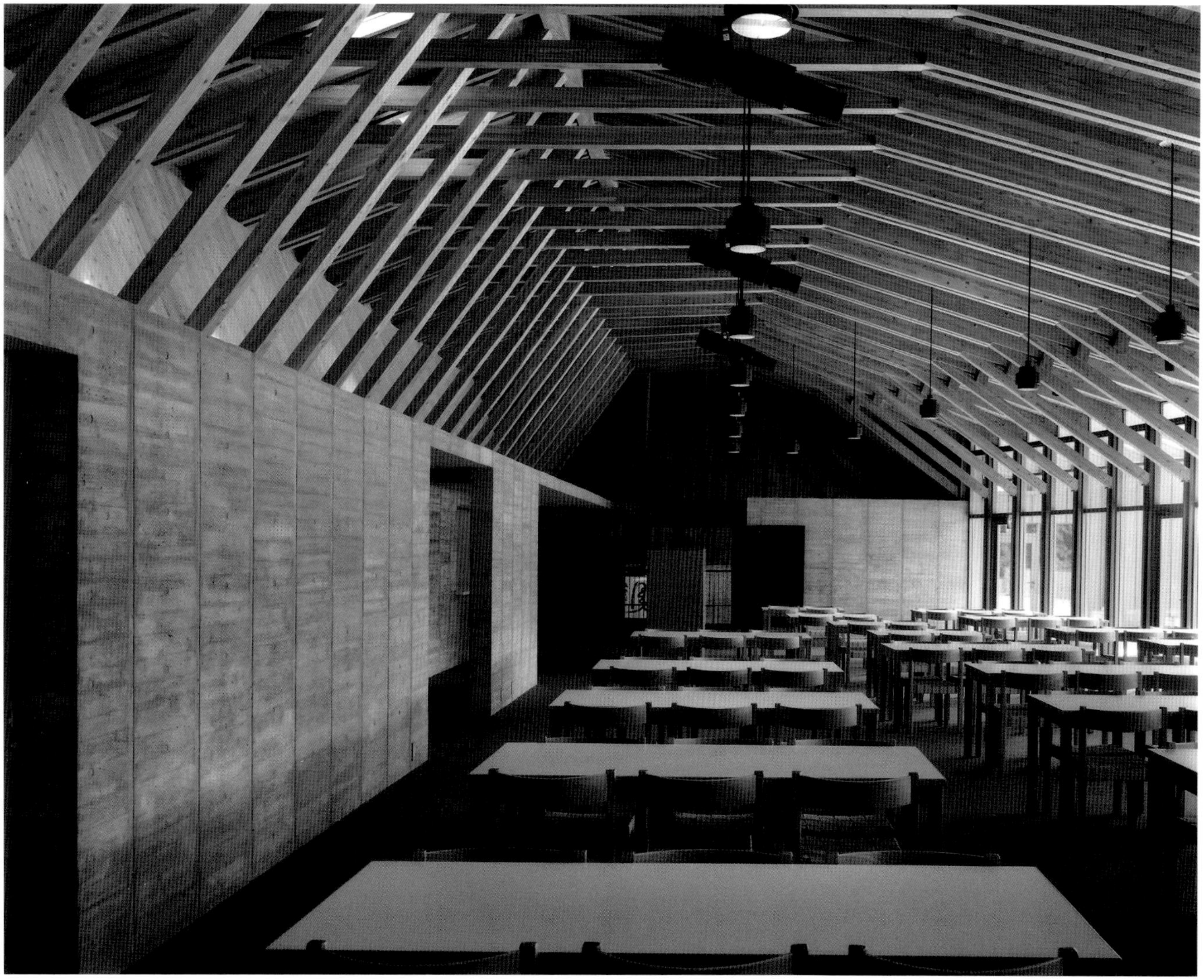

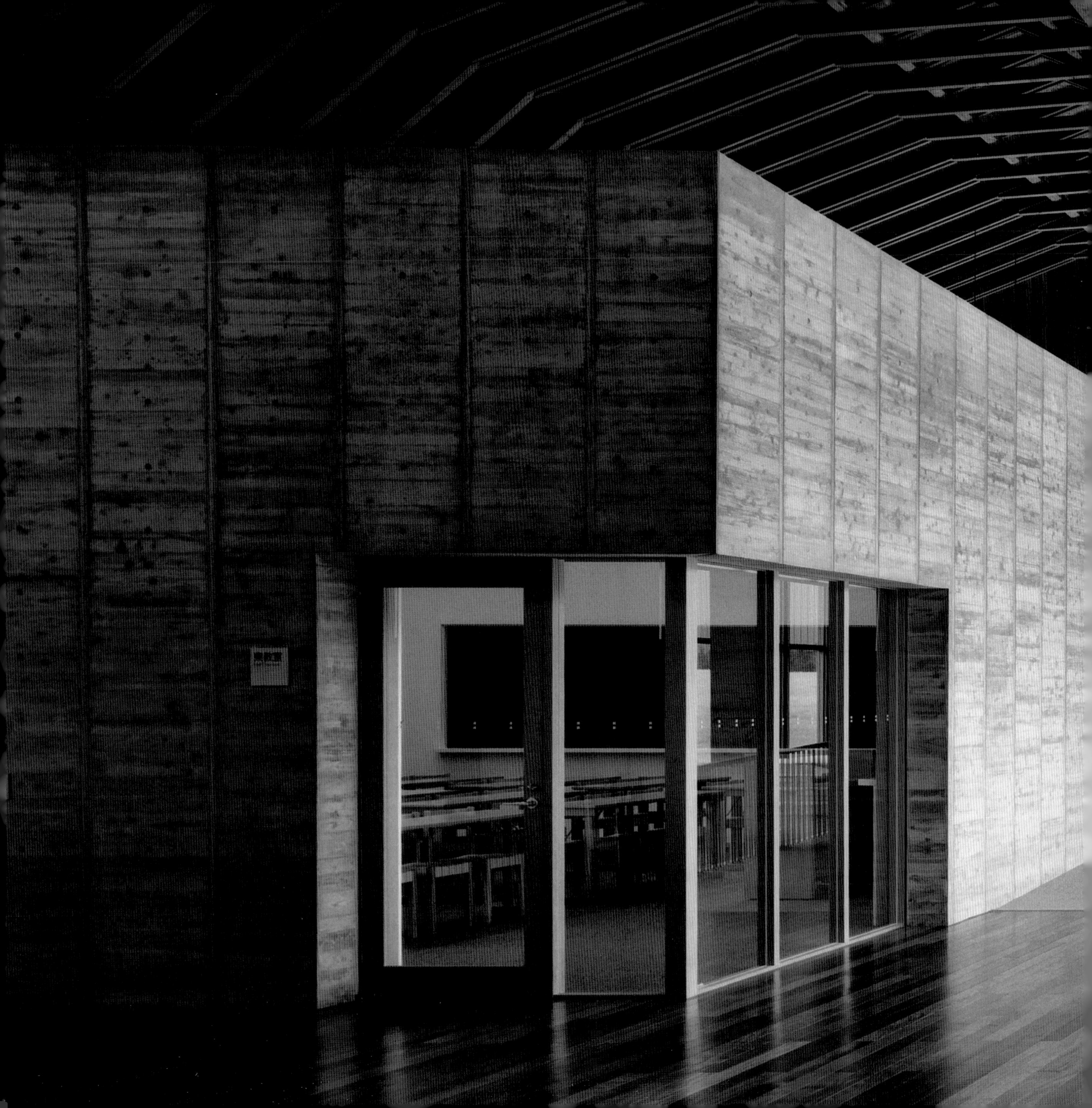

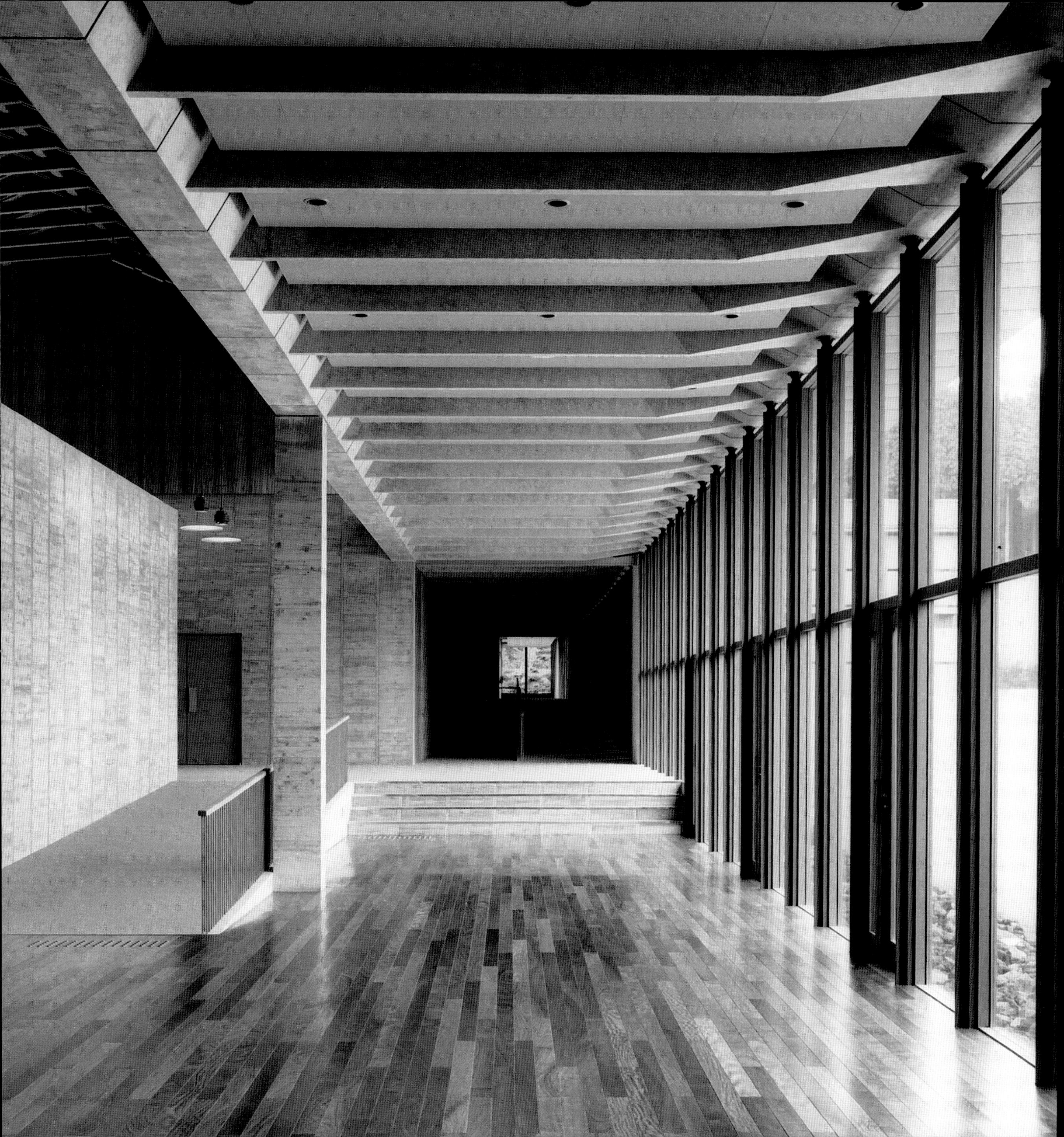

142

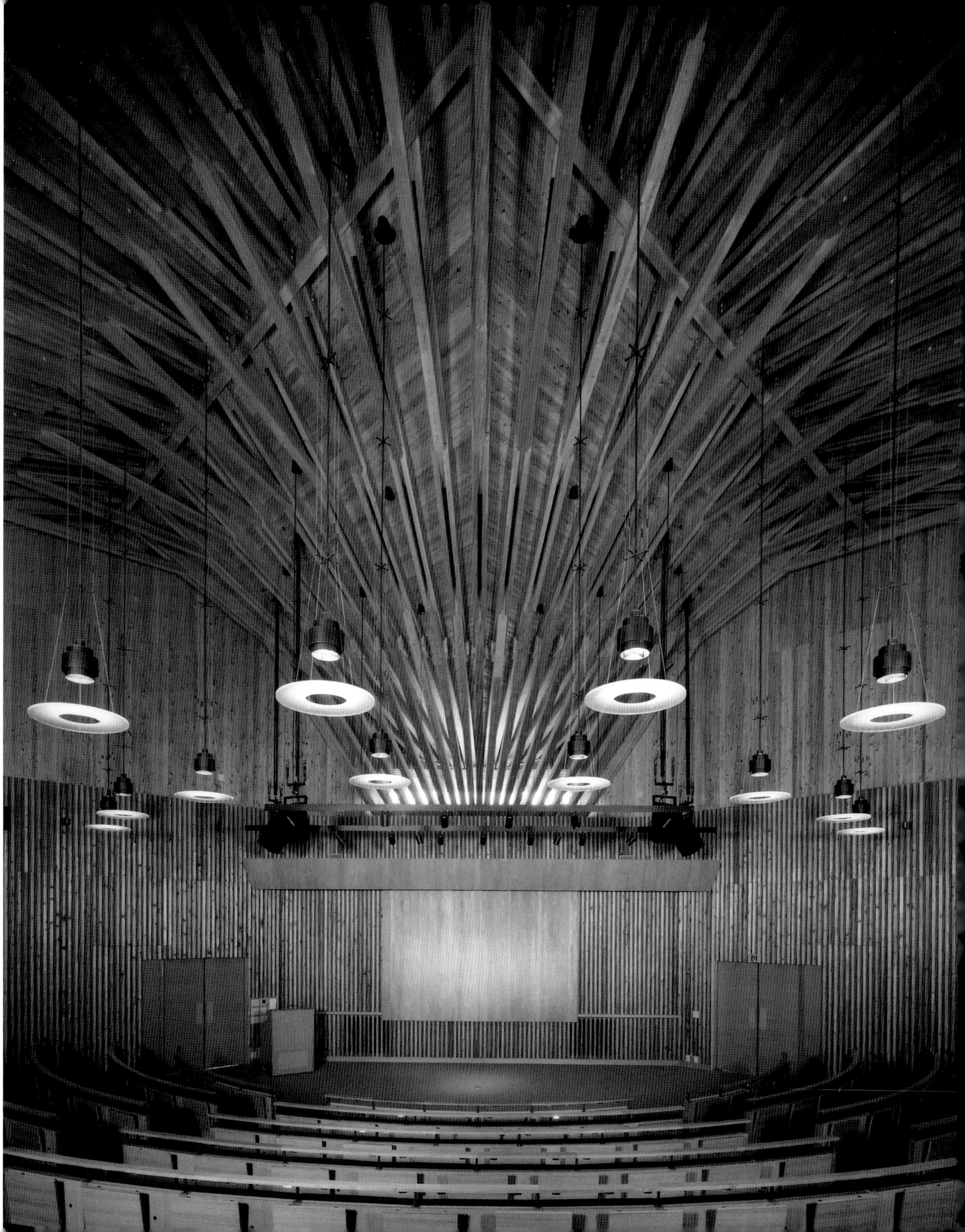

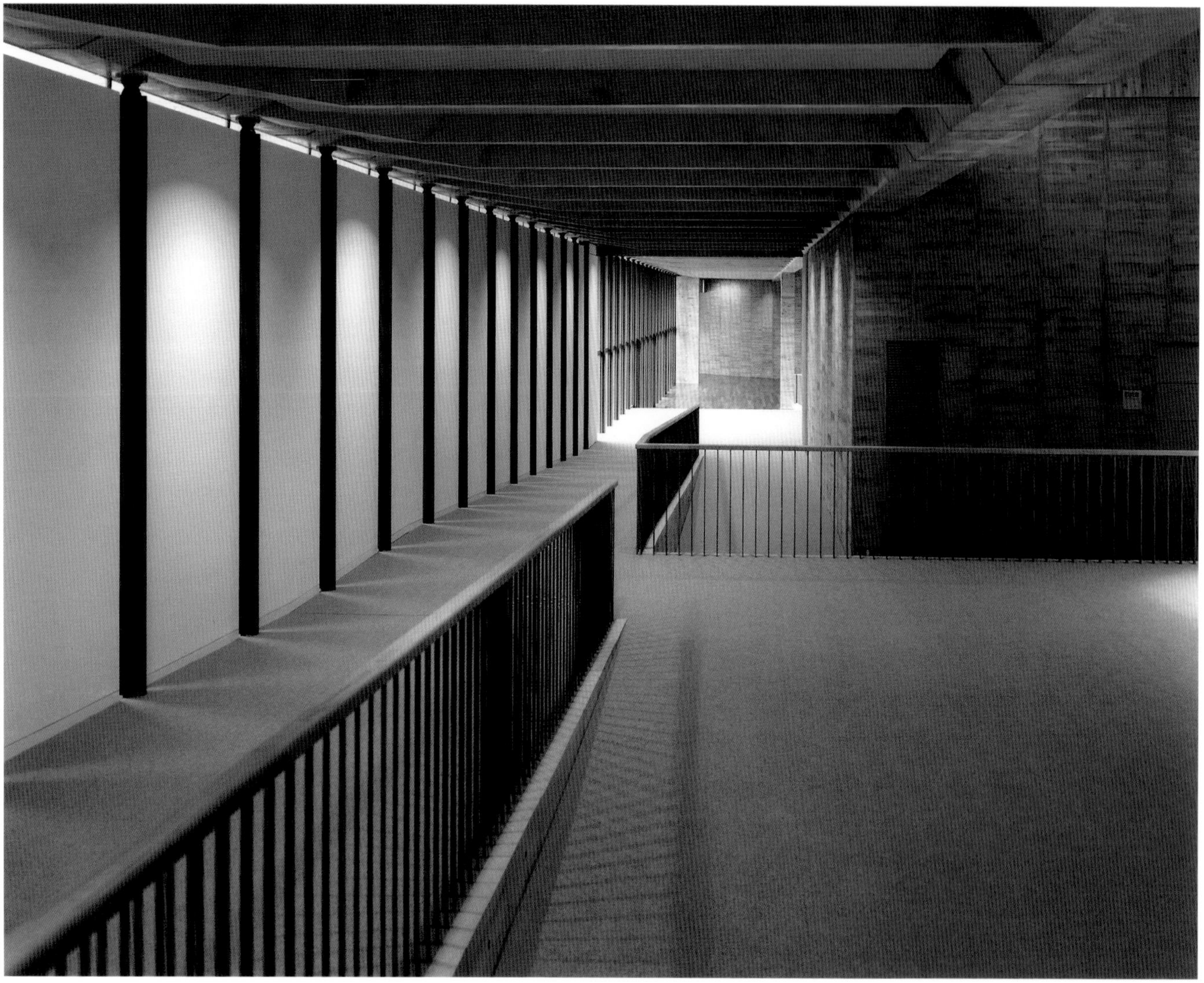

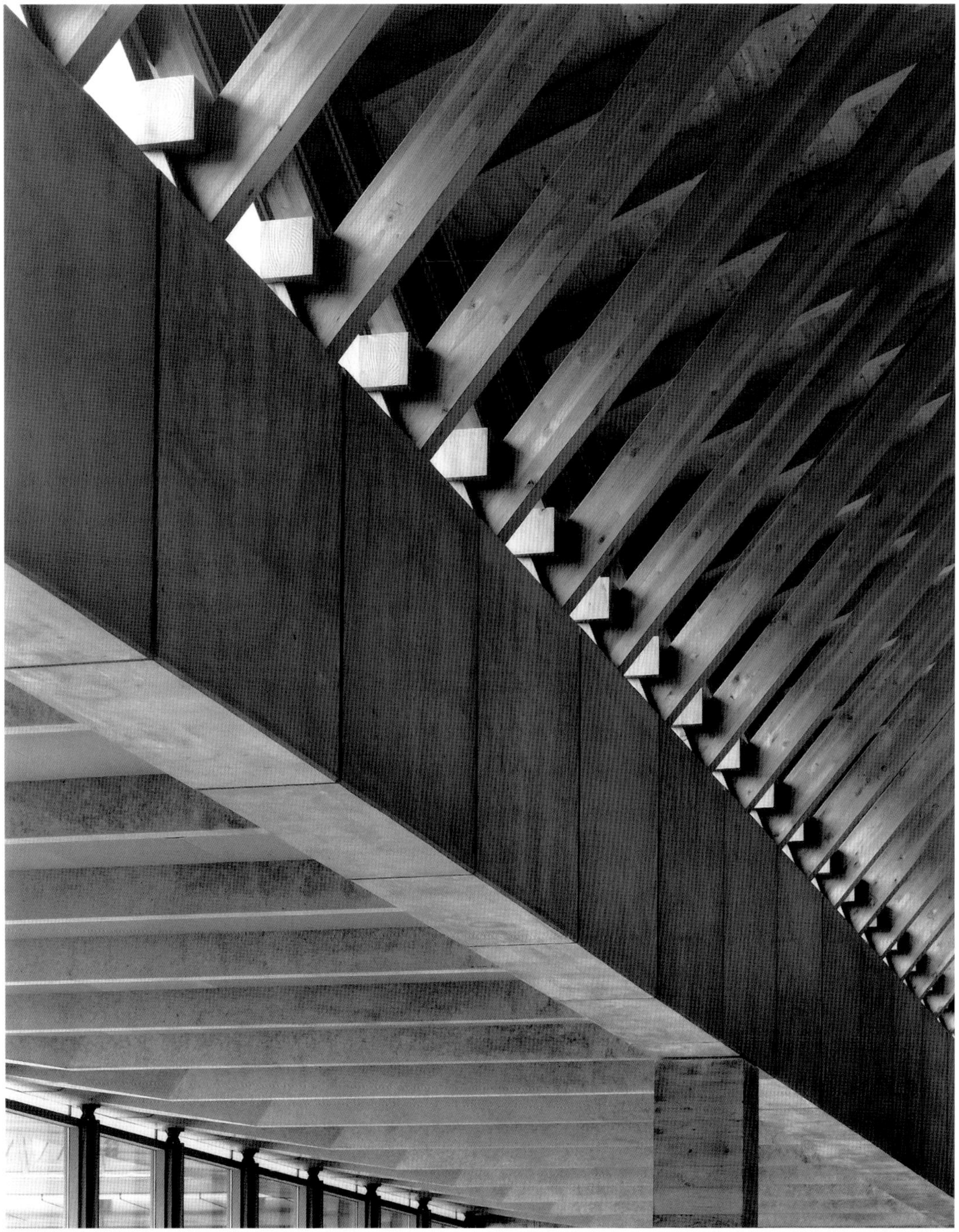

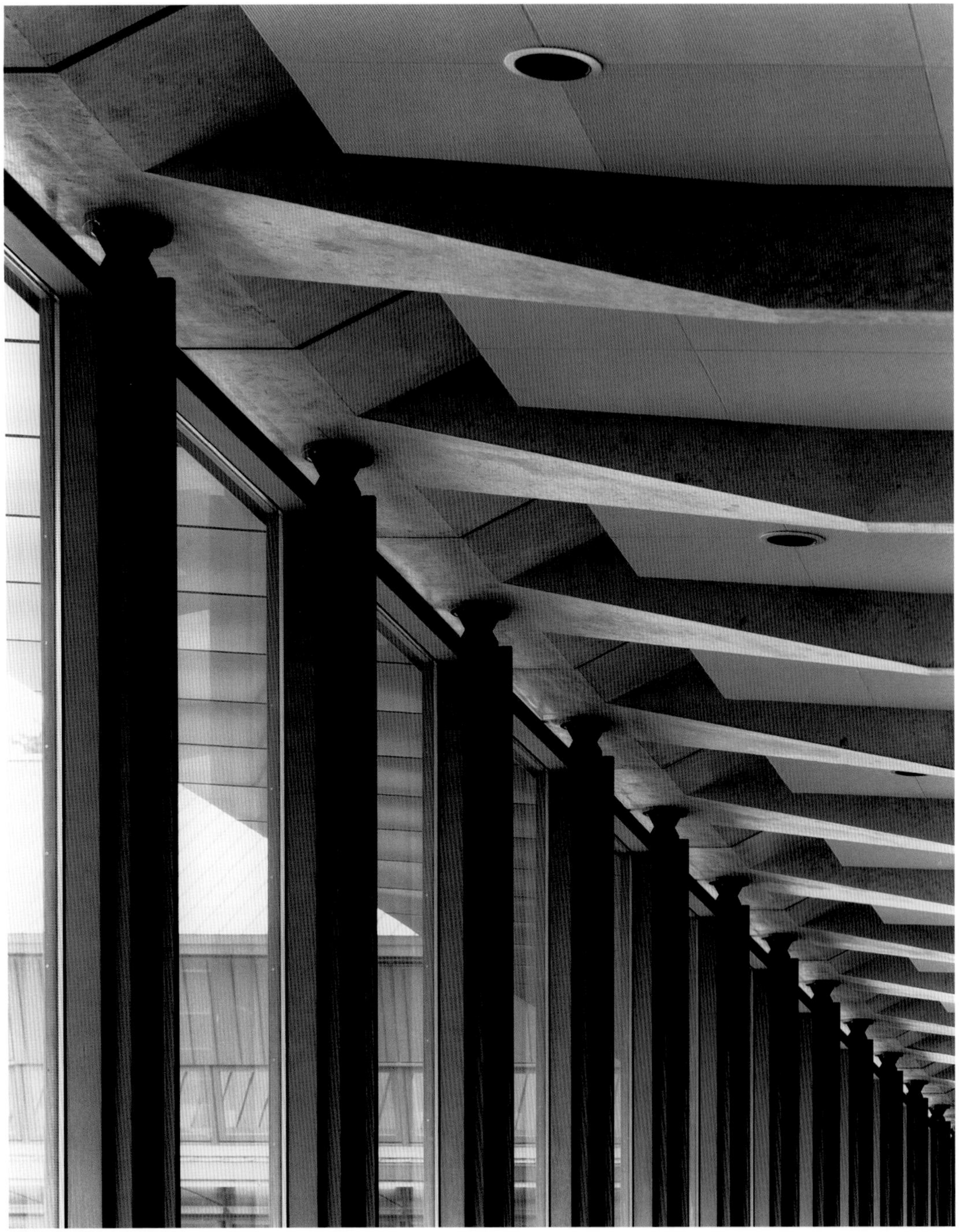

147

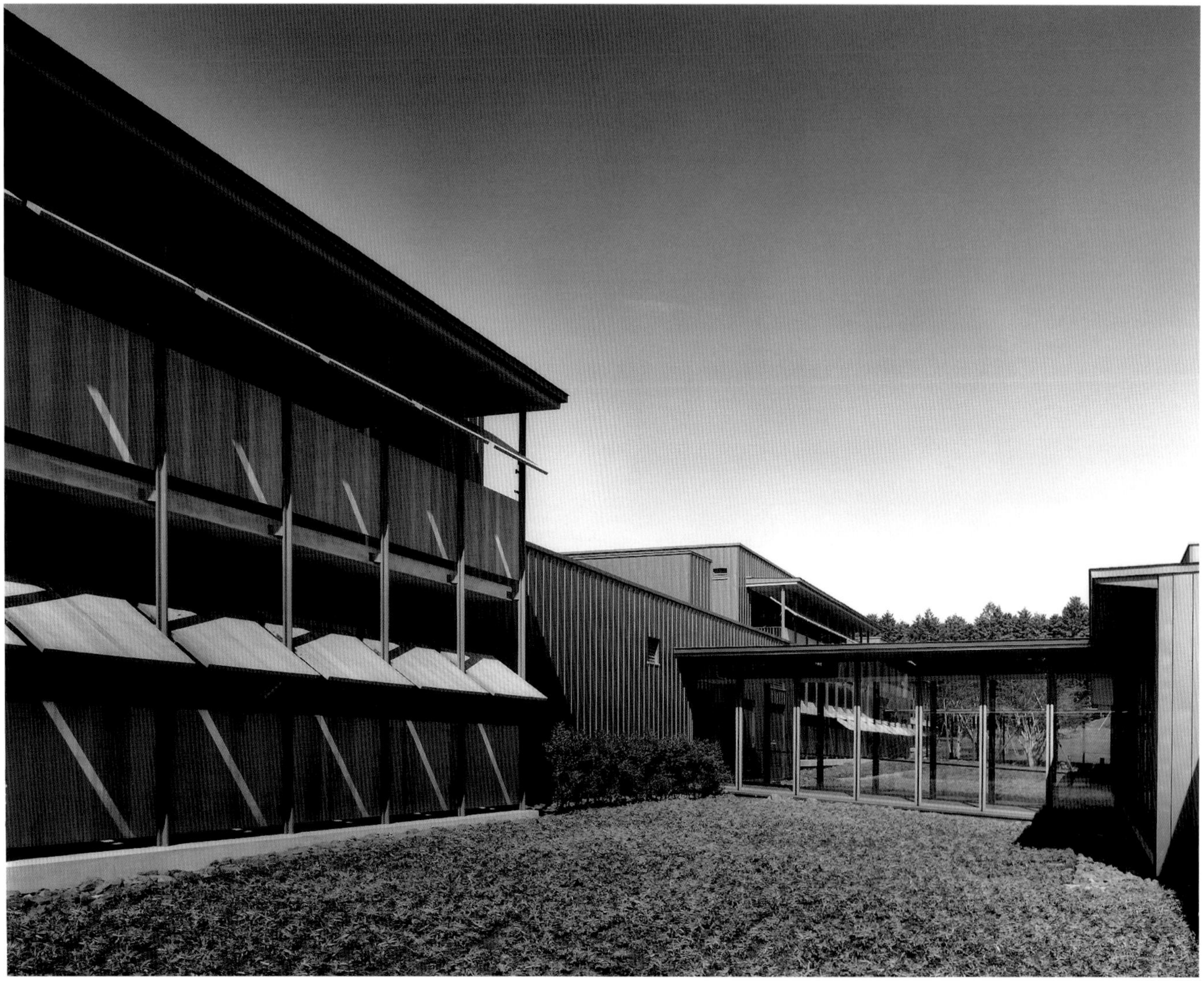

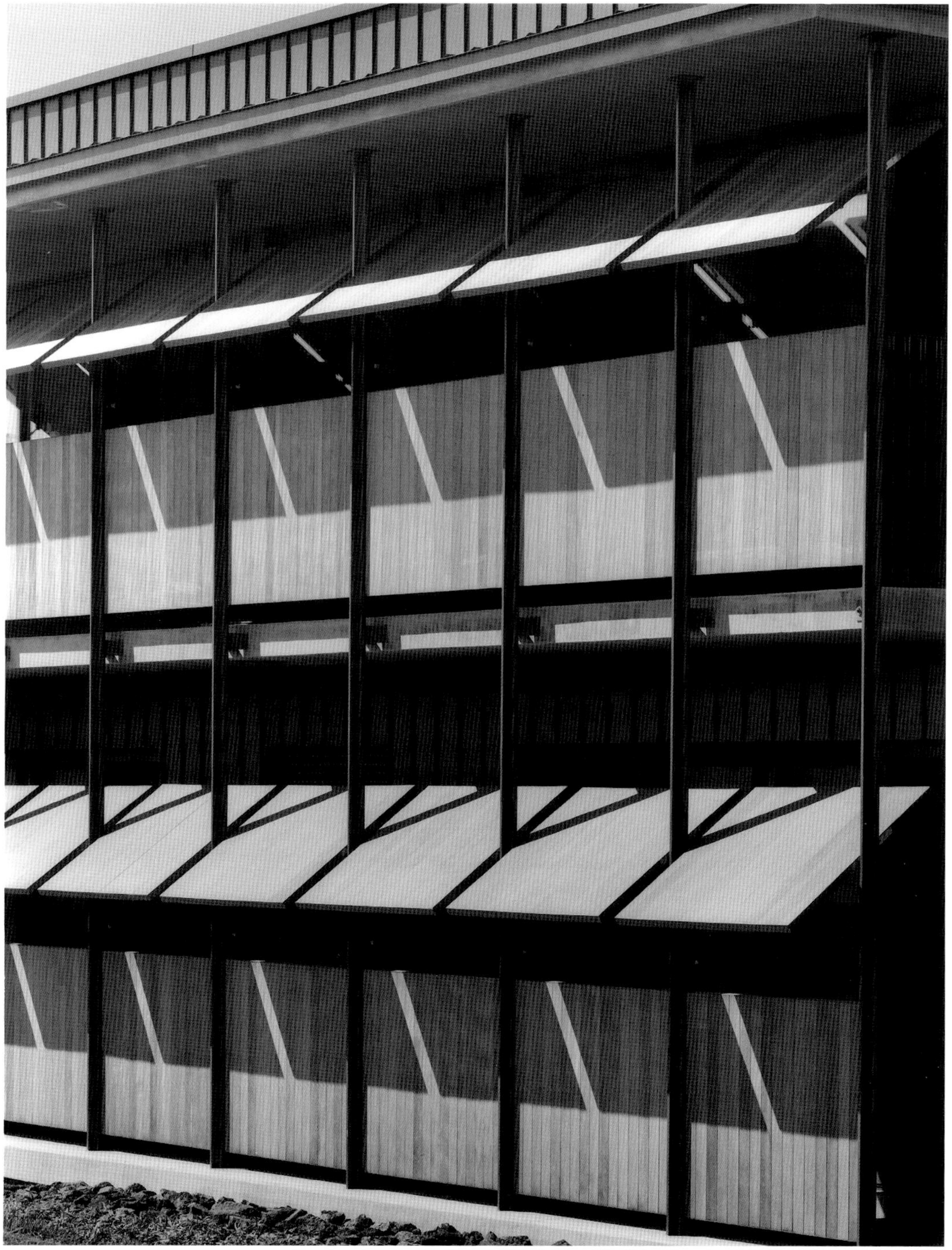

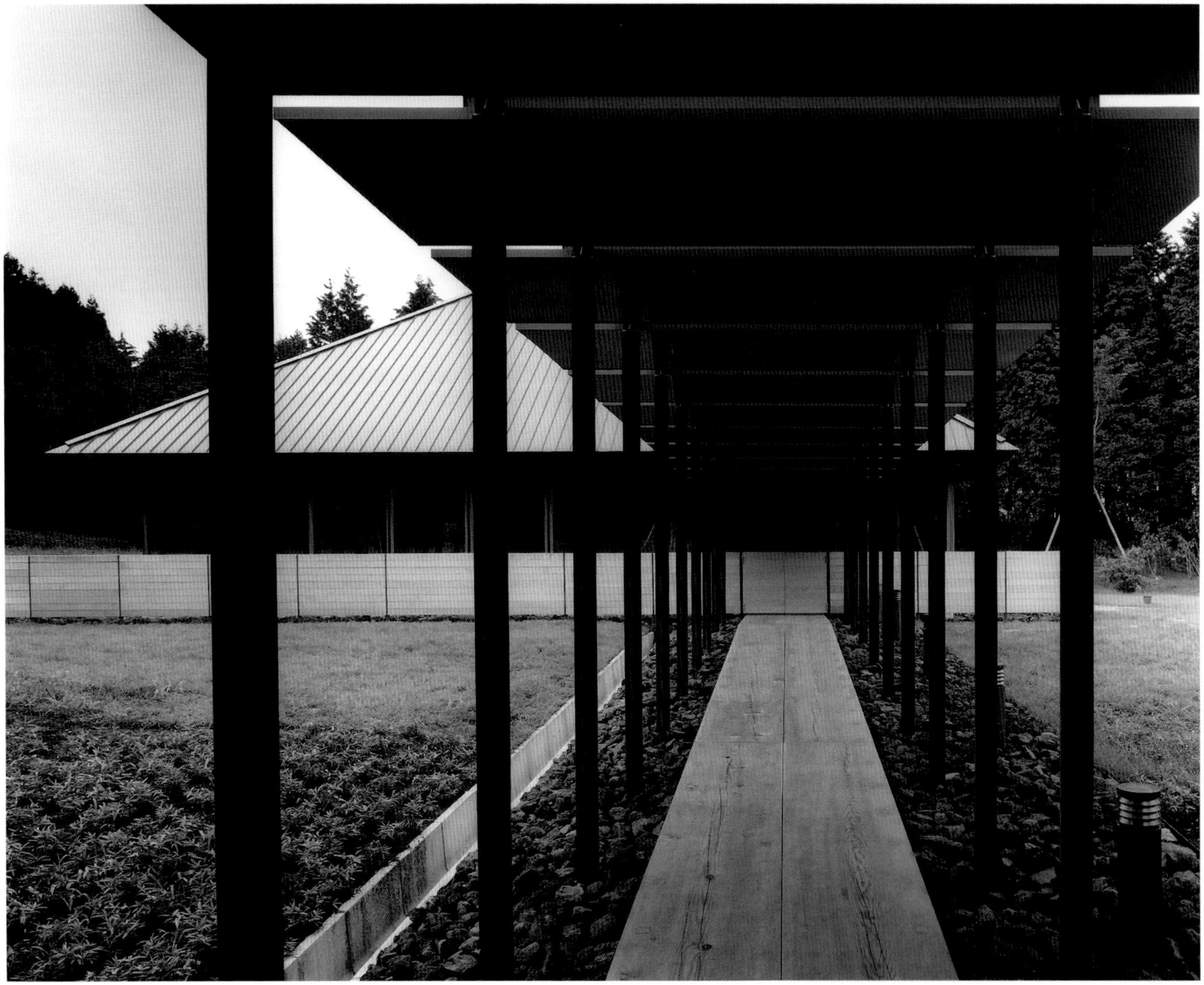

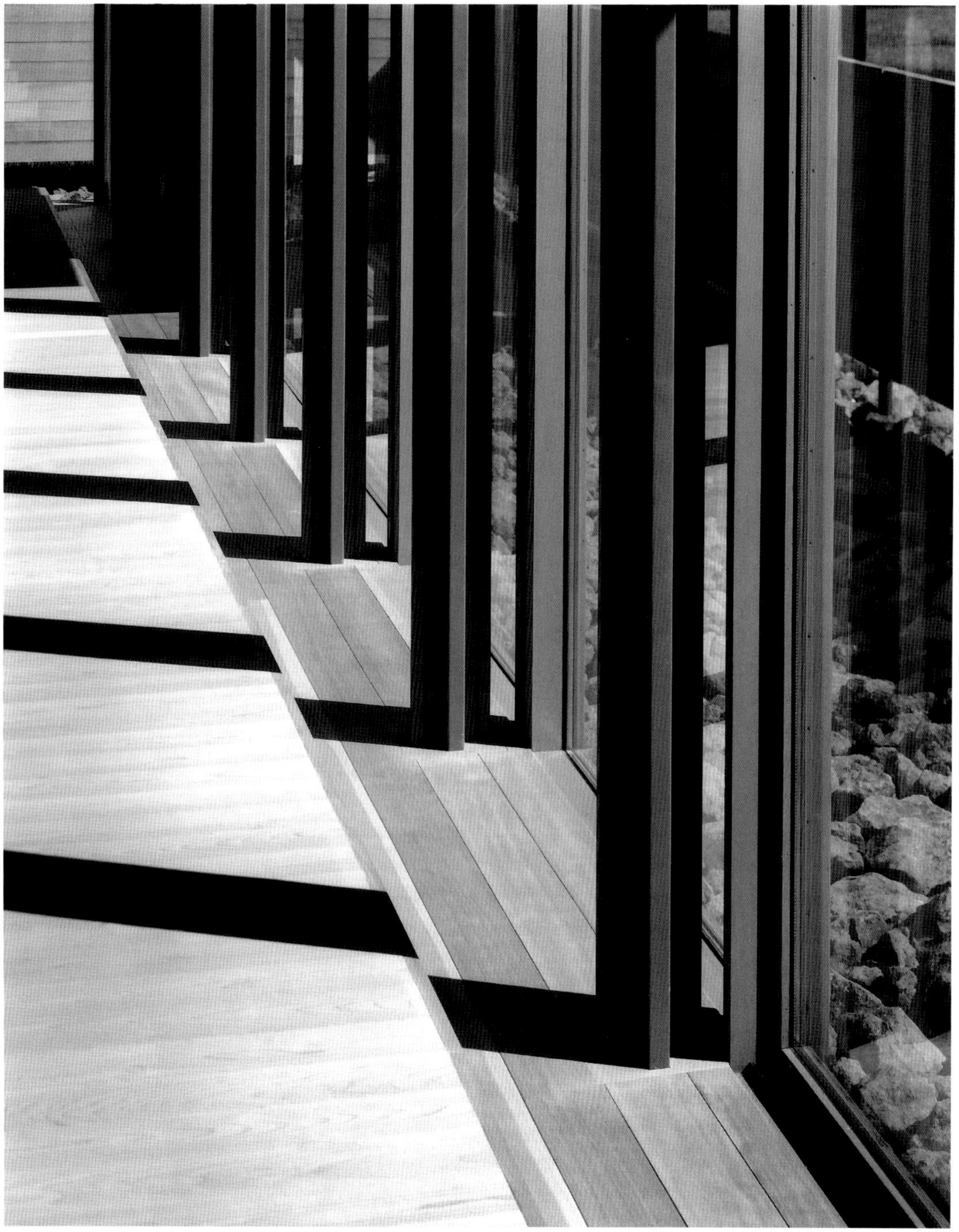

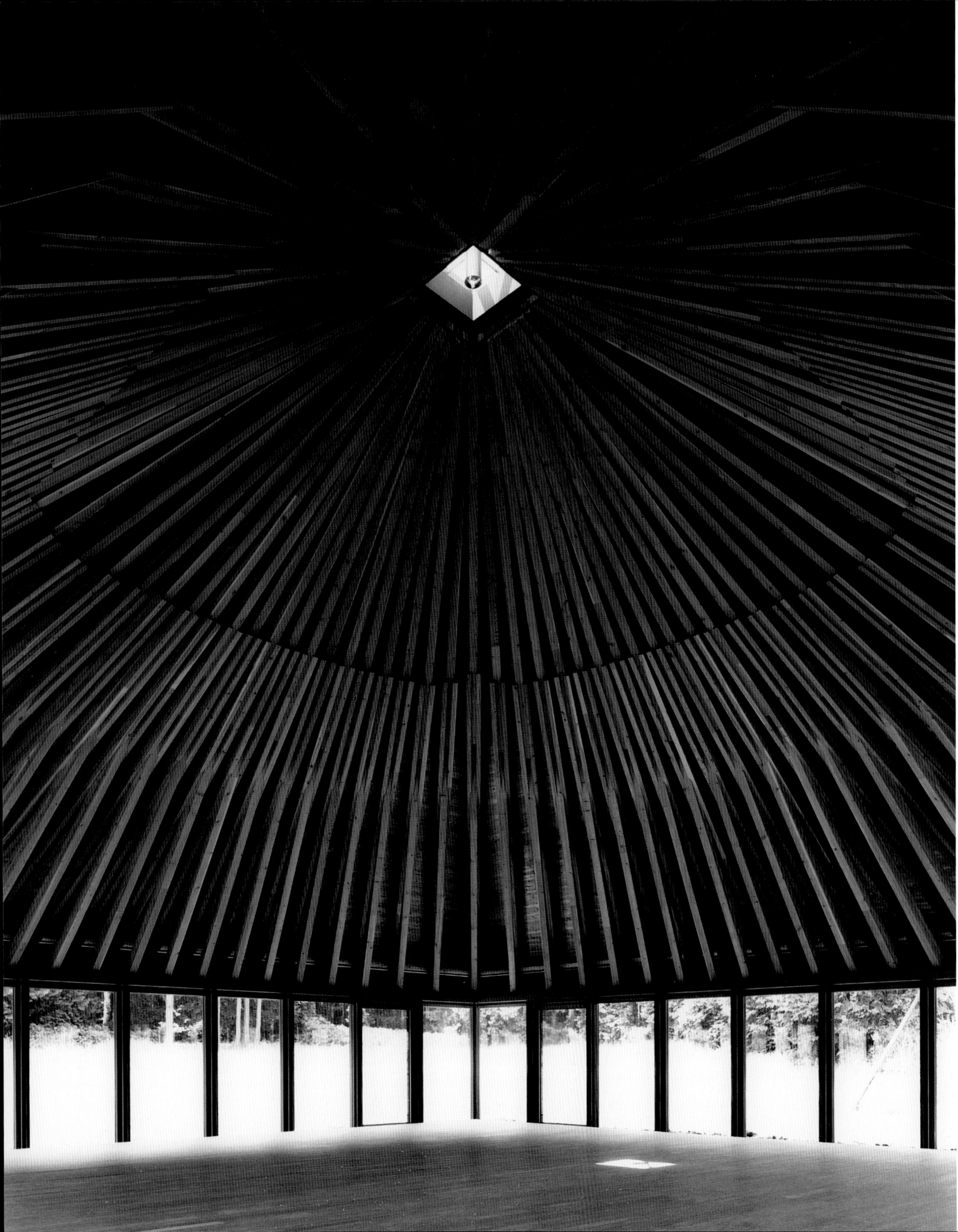

153

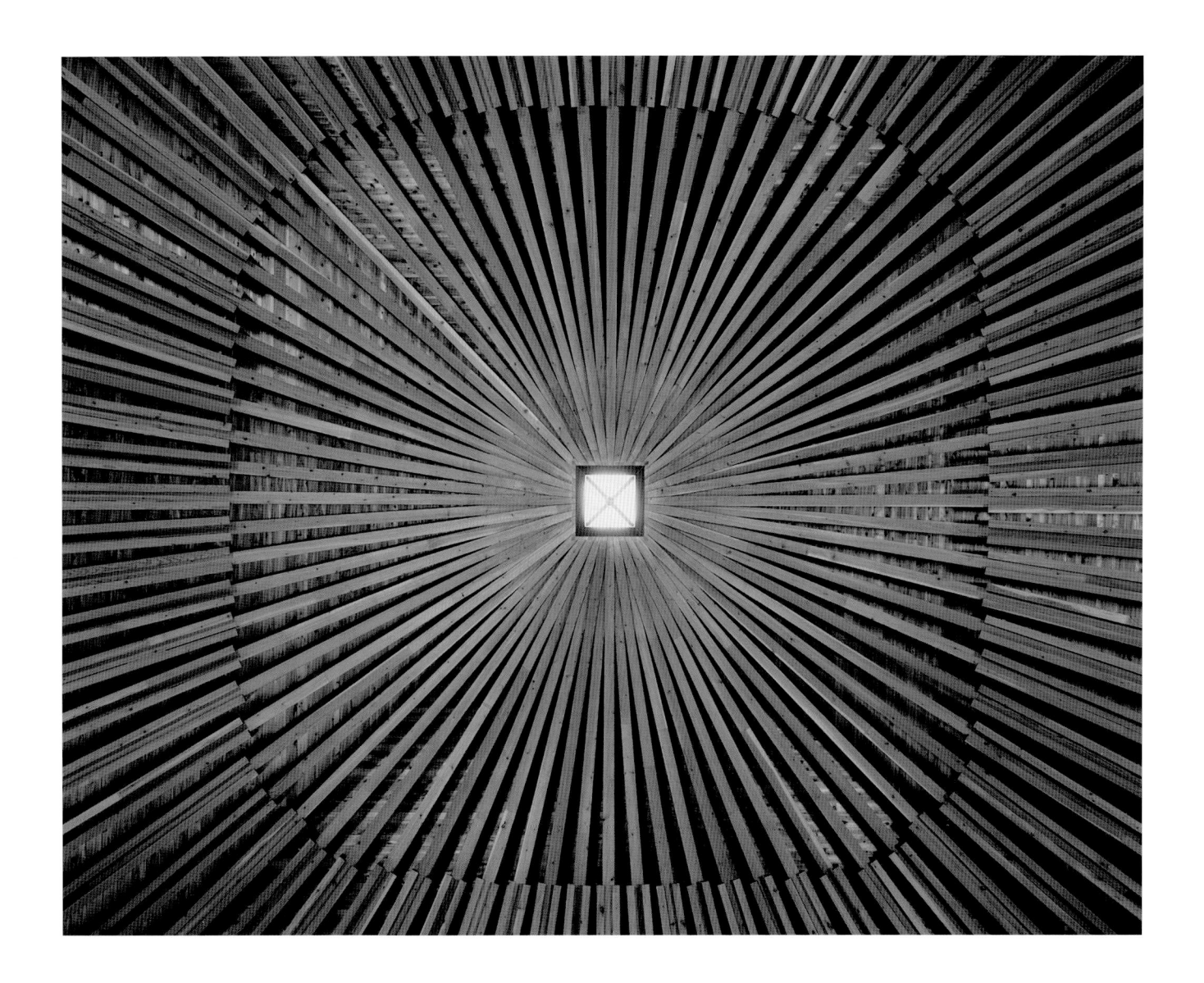

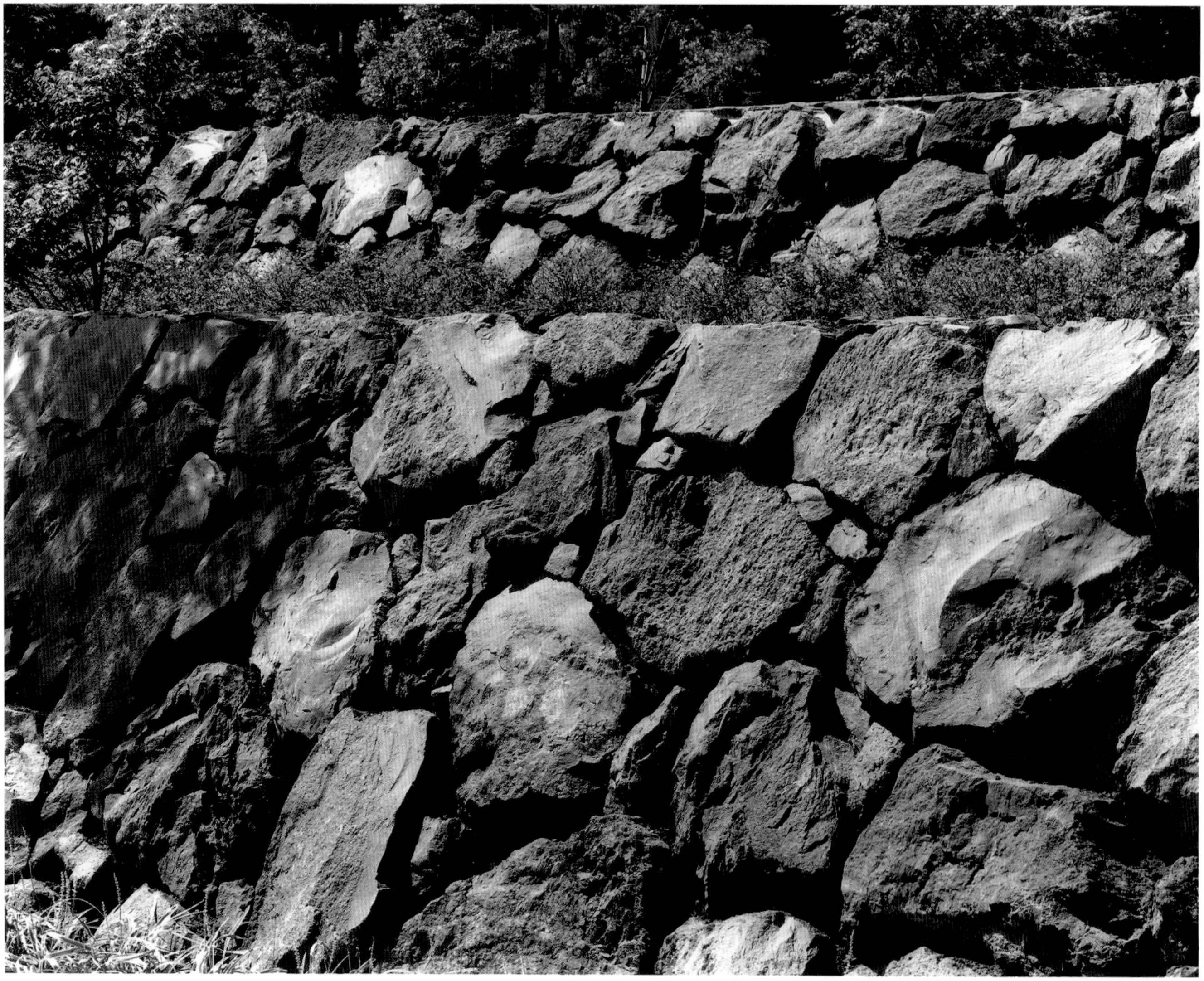

155

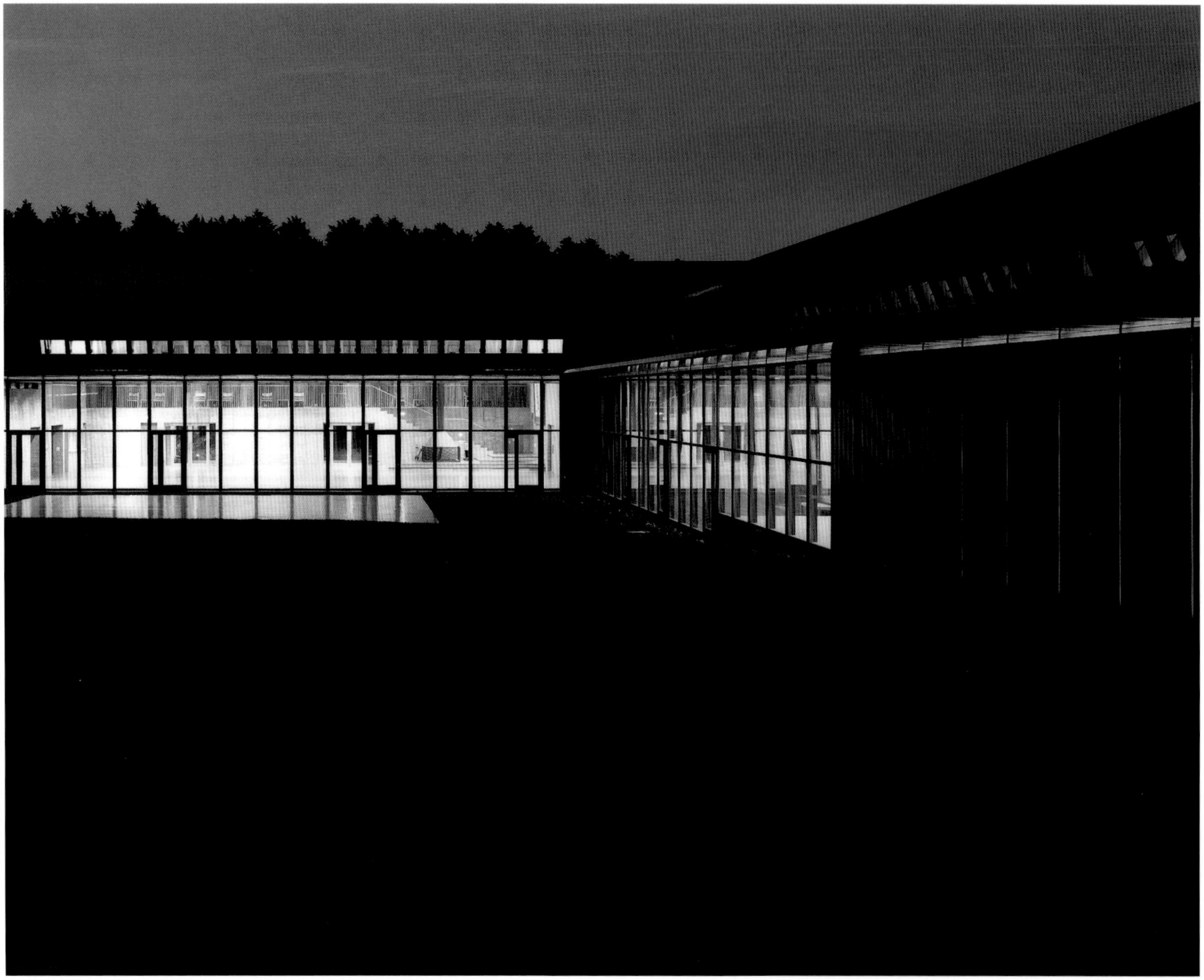

PROCESS

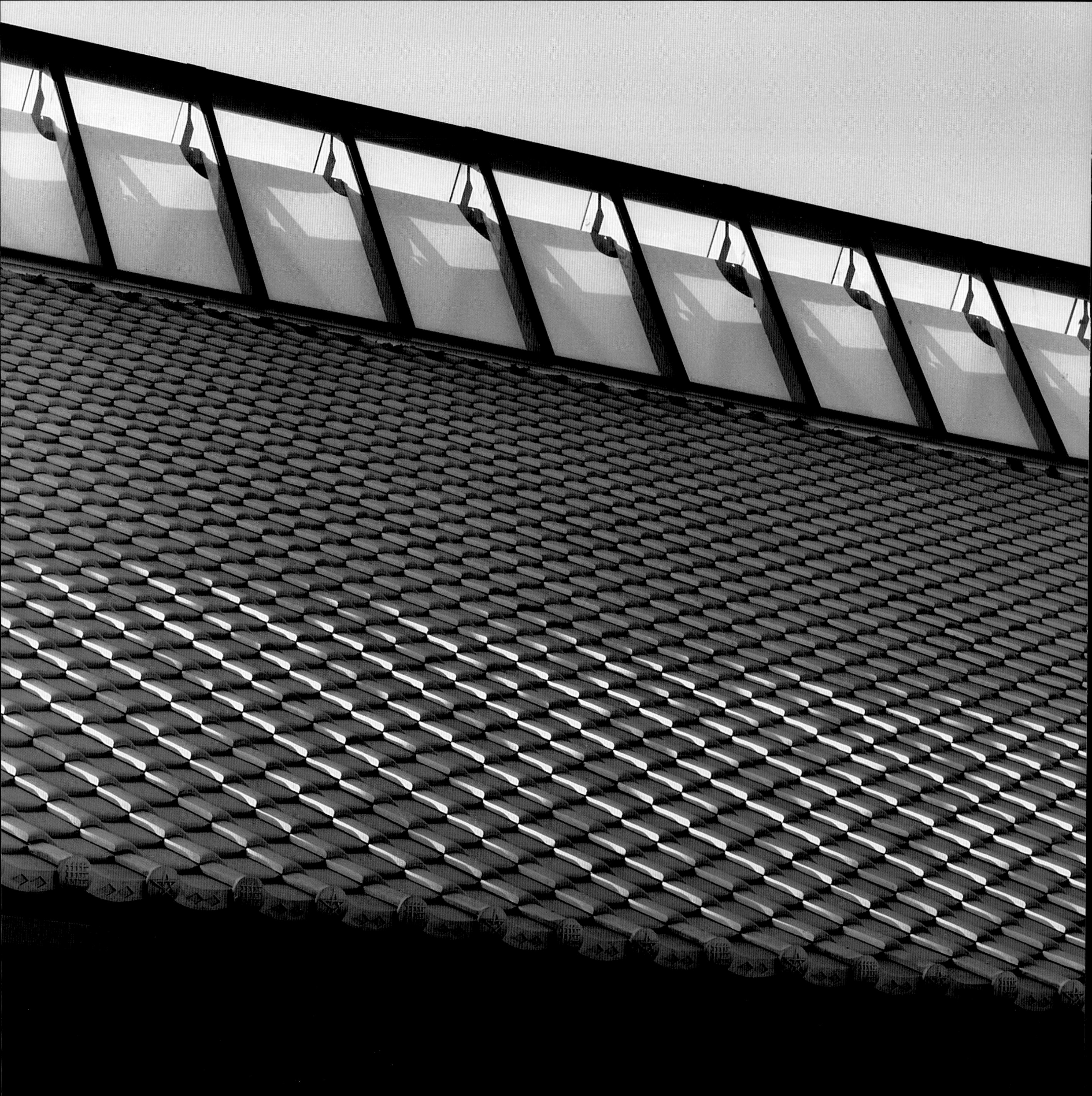

Sea-Folk Museum
海 の 博 物 館

PROCESS
1985-1992

Photo : NAITO ARCHITECT & ASSOCIATES

Structural Model

Elevation

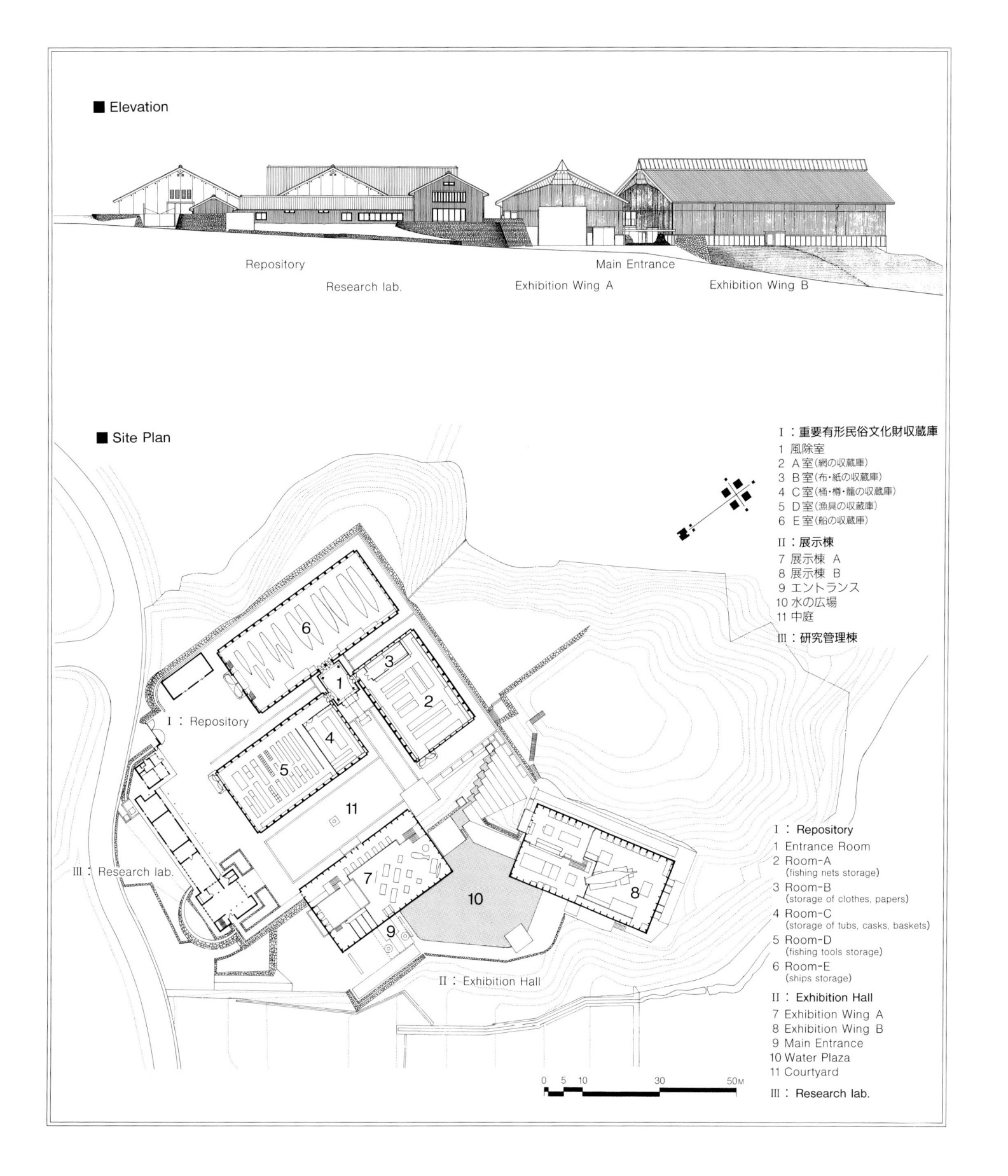

Repository
Research lab.
Main Entrance
Exhibition Wing A
Exhibition Wing B

Site Plan

Ⅰ：重要有形民俗文化財収蔵庫
1 風除室
2 A室（網の収蔵庫）
3 B室（布・紙の収蔵庫）
4 C室（桶・樽・籠の収蔵庫）
5 D室（漁具の収蔵庫）
6 E室（船の収蔵庫）

Ⅱ：展示棟
7 展示棟 A
8 展示棟 B
9 エントランス
10 水の広場
11 中庭

Ⅲ：研究管理棟

Ⅰ：Repository
1 Entrance Room
2 Room-A (fishing nets storage)
3 Room-B (storage of clothes, papers)
4 Room-C (storage of tubs, casks, baskets)
5 Room-D (fishing tools storage)
6 Room-E (ships storage)

Ⅱ：Exhibition Hall
7 Exhibition Wing A
8 Exhibition Wing B
9 Main Entrance
10 Water Plaza
11 Courtyard

Ⅲ：Research lab.

Erection

重要有形民俗文化財収蔵庫｜1985-1989｜Repository

収蔵庫は1985年に設計が始まった。

保存が目的の収蔵庫には，耐久性に細心最大の注意を払った。海の近くでひどい塩害が予想されるため，屋根には金属系の材料ではなく瓦を選んだ。瓦は建築の形態を強く拘束する。ここではメンテナンス上，スタンダードな規格サイズを使い，瓦に最も適した勾配の単純な屋根を作った。

コンクリートの架構は，桑名の工場でトレーラーで運べる大きさに作り，現場で組み立てる方法をとった。組み上げてからポスト・テンションをかけ，応力補正をすると同時に一体化する。この方法をとると，通常の二倍の強度の高品質のコンクリートで建物を作ることができ，基本的には圧縮力だけで構成されるので，クラックが発生しないなど，利点が多い。ふつう，コンクリートに含まれる残余水分もほとんどなく，収蔵物にとっては大敵の大気中のアルカリイオンも，この建物ではまったく観測されなかった。

■

Designing of the repository began in 1985. Utmost attention was paid to the durability of the structure whose purpose was preservation. Japanese roofing tiles were chosen instead of metal materials since it was anticipated that the museum being located near the sea would suffer severe salt damage. Roofing tiles place intensive restraints on architectural form. Therefore, standard sized tiles were used for maintenance purposes and a simple roof was designed with the most appropriate pitch for the tiles.

The site assembly method was adopted for the concrete framework. The framework was divided into sections which were made in a size transportable by truck from the factory in Kuwana. After the setting up, the framework was integrated at the same time the post-tension was applied in order to make the stress correction. This method enables construction of a high quality concrete structure with twice the conventional strength. There are a number of advantages in this method such as the non-occurrence of cracks, for the framework basically consists only of compressive stress. Also, as there is very little of the residual moisture normally found in concrete, absolutely no release of alkaline ion, the worst enemy for the items stored here, was observed within the building.

Erection

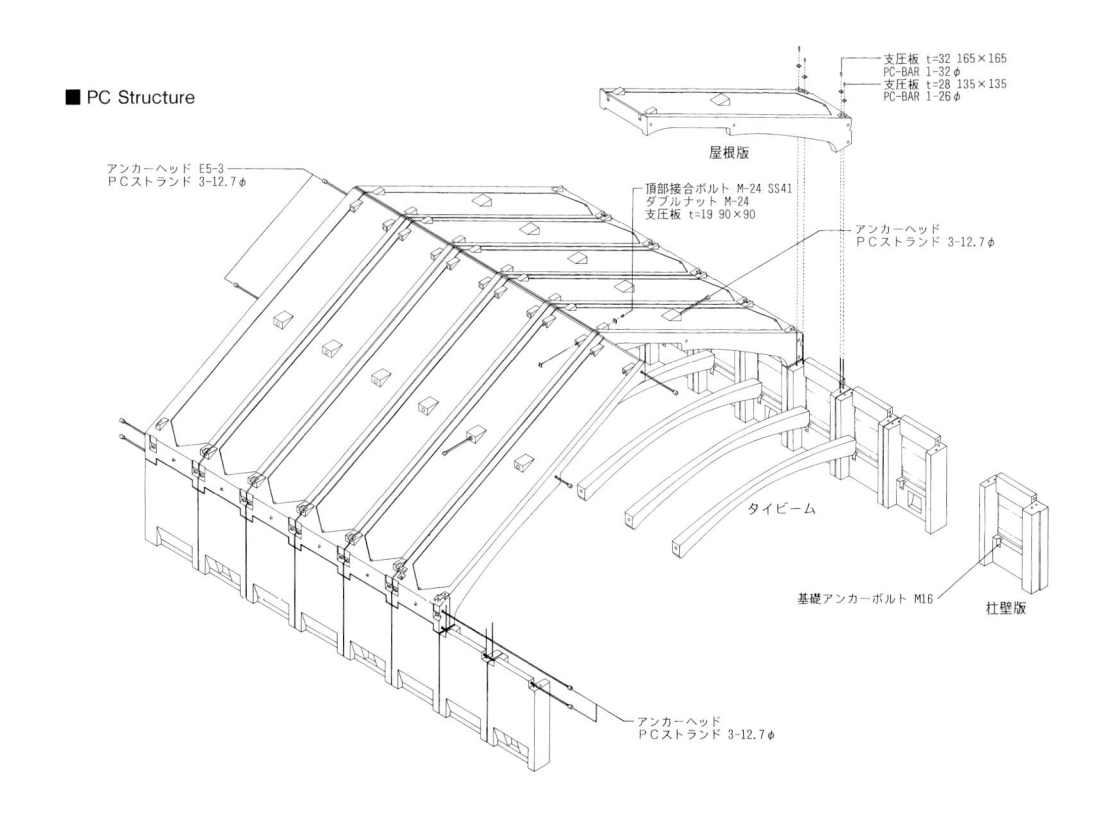

■ PC Structure

支圧板 t=32 165×165
PC-BAR 1-32φ
支圧板 t=28 135×135
PC-BAR 1-26φ

屋根版

アンカーヘッド E5-3
PCストランド 3-12.7φ

頂部接合ボルト M-24 SS41
ダブルナット M-24
支圧板 t=19 90×90

アンカーヘッド
PCストランド 3-12.7φ

タイビーム

基礎アンカーボルト M16

柱壁版

アンカーヘッド
PCストランド 3-12.7φ

Carpentry

収蔵庫は規模が大きいので，機械による温湿度調整をしていない。収蔵物は，紙，布，木，鉄，それぞれ材料によって適性湿度が違う。従って，それらをブロックに分け，湿度が多いほうが良い場合は床を土間，乾燥が好ましい場合は内壁と床を板張にして対応している。壁の板張は，湿度調整作用と防虫作用のある杉板を使った。全体として，保存に関しては極めて良い結果が得られている。

■

Owing to the extensive scale of the repository, the temperature and humidity are not mechanically controlled. Each stored item requires a different humidity suited to the material such as paper, fabric, wood, or ferric metal. Therefore, the items are divided into different blocks. Those which required greater humidity were placed in an area with a hammered soil floor, and for those items requiring dryness, the interior walls and floor were accommodated with wood panels. Japanese cedar panels were used for the interior walls for their insect control properties. As a whole, an exceptionally fine result was achieved with regard to preservation.

PC Structure

■ Details

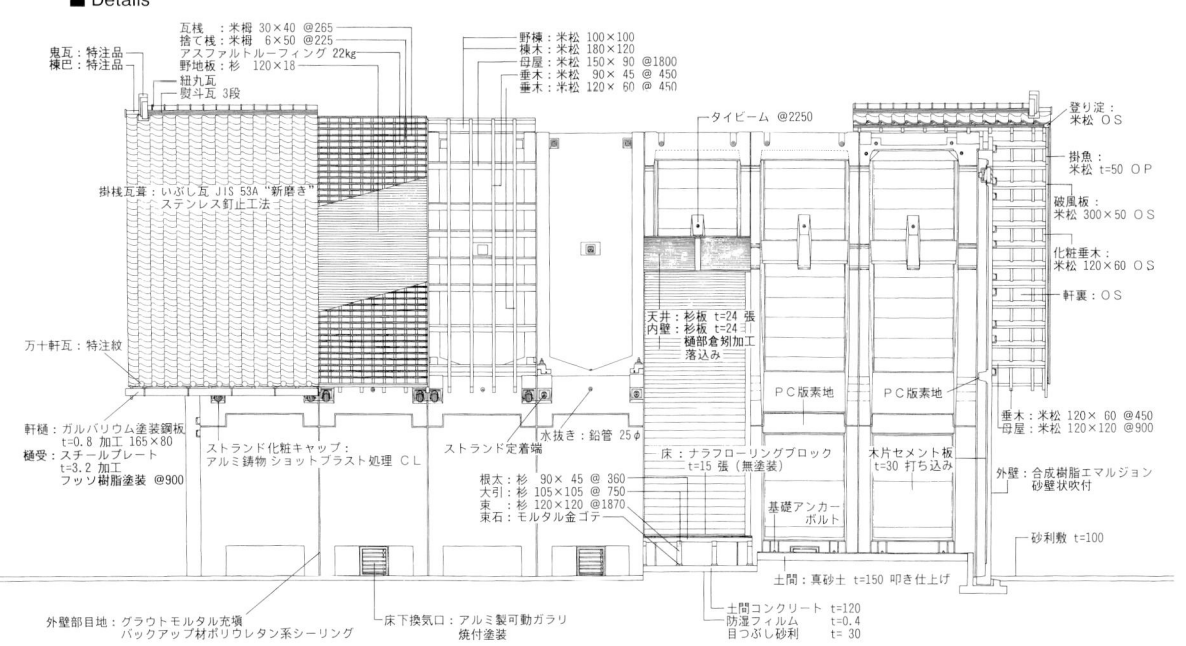

瓦桟	米栂 30×40 @265
捨て桟	米栂 6×50 @225
	アスファルトルーフィング 22kg
野地板	杉 120×18
野棟	米松 100×100
棟木	米松 180×120
母屋	米松 150×90 @1800
垂木	米松 90×45 @450
垂木	米松 120×60 @450

鬼瓦：特注品
棟巴：特注品
紐丸瓦
熨斗瓦 3段

掛桟瓦葺：いぶし瓦 JIS 53A "新磨き"
ステンレス釘止工法

万十軒瓦：特注紋

軒樋：ガルバリウム塗装鋼板
t=0.8 加工 165×80
樋受：スチールプレート
t=3.2 加工
フッソ樹脂塗装 @900

ストランド化粧キャップ：
アルミ鋳物 ショットブラスト処理 CL

ストランド定着端

水抜き：鉛管 25φ

根太：杉 90×45 @360
大引：杉 105×105 @750
束：杉 120×120 @1870
束石：モルタル金ゴテ

外壁部目地：グラウトモルタル充填
バックアップ材ポリウレタン系シーリング

床下換気口：アルミ製可動ガラリ
焼付塗装

タイビーム @2250

天井：杉板 t=24 張
内壁：杉板 t=24
樋部倉別加工
落込み

PC版素地

床：ナラフローリングブロック
t=15 張（無塗装）

木片セメント板
t=30 打ち込み

基礎アンカー
ボルト

土間：真砂土 t=150 叩き仕上げ
土間コンクリート t=120
防湿フィルム t=0.4
目つぶし砂利 t=30

登り淀：
米松 OS

掛魚：
米松 t=50 OP

破風板：
米松 300×50 OS

化粧垂木：
米松 120×60 OS

軒裏：OS

垂木：米松 120×60 @450
母屋：米松 120×120 @900

外壁：合成樹脂エマルジョン
砂壁状吹付

砂利敷 t=100

Erection

展示棟|1988-1992|Exhibition Hall

　博物館建設の最終段階である展示棟は，1988年に設計が始まった。
　収蔵庫は防災や保存の観点からコンクリートにした。これに対して，人の多く関与する展示棟は，かねて博物館の要望でもあった木造の大架構とした。展示は，独立型の展示台が中心で壁面をあまり使わないことから，建物の足元をできるだけ開放的にし，外部とつながった広がりのあるスペースを作ろうとした。来館者が閉塞感なしに展示物に親しめるような空間にすることが大きな目的だった。
　円筒状で一方向に均質な蛇の骨のような有機的構造をイメージした。屋根の頂部に背骨のような応力が集中するタイトな部分があって，そこから徐々に力が分散されて地面に伝わっている。屋根面の斜材とアーチ状の部材が相互に助け合って力を伝え，架構全体が成り立っている。曲線の部材が作れる岐阜の集成材工場で柱梁を作って，それを現場で組み立てる方法をとった。

■

Designing of the exhibition hall, the final stage in the construction of the museum, began in 1988.
　The repository, in consideration of fire prevention and to assure the preservation of the stored items, was built of concrete. In contrast, the exhibition hall, which in many ways involves people, has large wooden frameworks, a requirement previously set forth by the museum. The exhibits are mainly placed on independent platforms, and as there is little of use the wall surfaces, the structure's floor is kept unobstructed as much as possible. The intention was to create an open space linked with the surroundings exterior, something unthinkalbe in a conventional museum. A major objective was to create a space where visitors could enjoy the exhibition without a feeling of being hemmed in.
　The image envisaged for the exhibition hall was an organic structure similar to the bones of a snake, cylindrical, and a horizontal repetition of a single bone shape. The stress converges onto a crowded spot like a spine on the highest point of the roof, and is gradually dispersed and conveyed to the ground. A diagonal member of the roof's surface and an arch member interdependently convey the stress to form an overall structure. The curved arch members were made by a glue-laminated timber manufacturer in Gifu and the site assembly method was adopted.

Carpentry

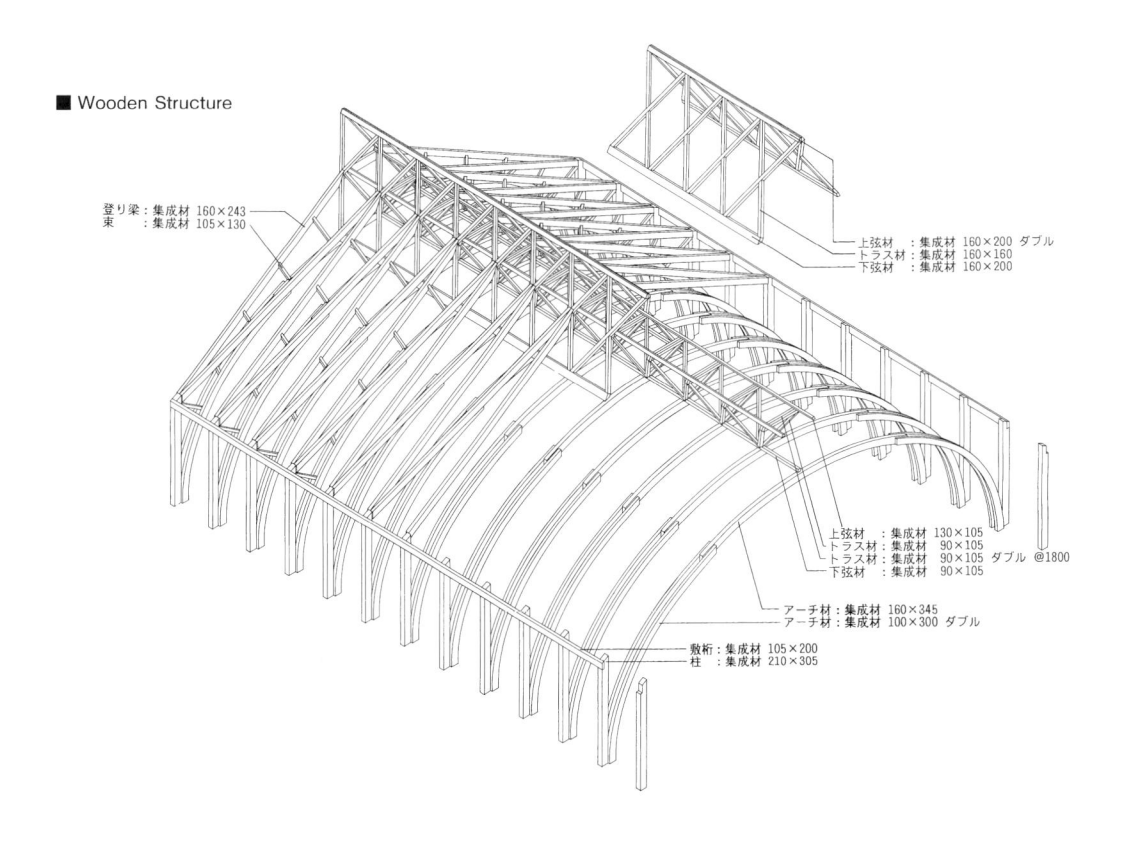

■ Wooden Structure

登り梁：集成材 160×243
束　　：集成材 105×130

上弦材　：集成材 160×200 ダブル
トラス材：集成材 160×160
下弦材　：集成材 160×200

上弦材　：集成材 130×105
トラス材：集成材 90×105
トラス材：集成材 90×105 ダブル @1800
下弦材　：集成材 90×105

アーチ材：集成材 160×345
アーチ材：集成材 100×300 ダブル

敷桁：集成材 105×200
柱　：集成材 210×305

Structural Details

　たくさんの部材が集中する背骨のジョイント部分はもっとも苦労したところで，在来木造の仕口の知恵をできるだけ生かし，金属系の部材は補助的に使うようにした。屋根から突出したこの部分をトップライトとし，展示棟全体に光が降り注ぐようにした。屋根は収蔵庫でよい結果が得られた瓦葺きとし，外壁は杉板の二重張りのうえにタールにカーボンを混ぜた塗装を施してある。
　エントランスのキャノピーは，応力線に沿ったリブを張りめぐらすことで軽量化を図った。運搬ができるように，工場で半分づつ作り，現場でジョイントした。
■

　The joint part of the spine where many members converge proved the most difficult in designing. To utilize as much as possible the knowledge concerning joints in traditional wooden structures, it was decided to use metal members in a supplementary role. This joint part which protrudes from the roof was employed as a skylight so that the entire exhibition hall would be illuminated from above. Japanese roofing tiles were chosen for their success with the repository, and the exterior walls were double-lined with Japanese cedar panels and painted with a tar-carbon mixture.
　The canopy at the entrance was designed to be lightweight by stretching ribs along the direction of stress. To facilitate transport, the canopy was made in two sections at the factory and jointed at the site.

Wooden Structure

■ Details

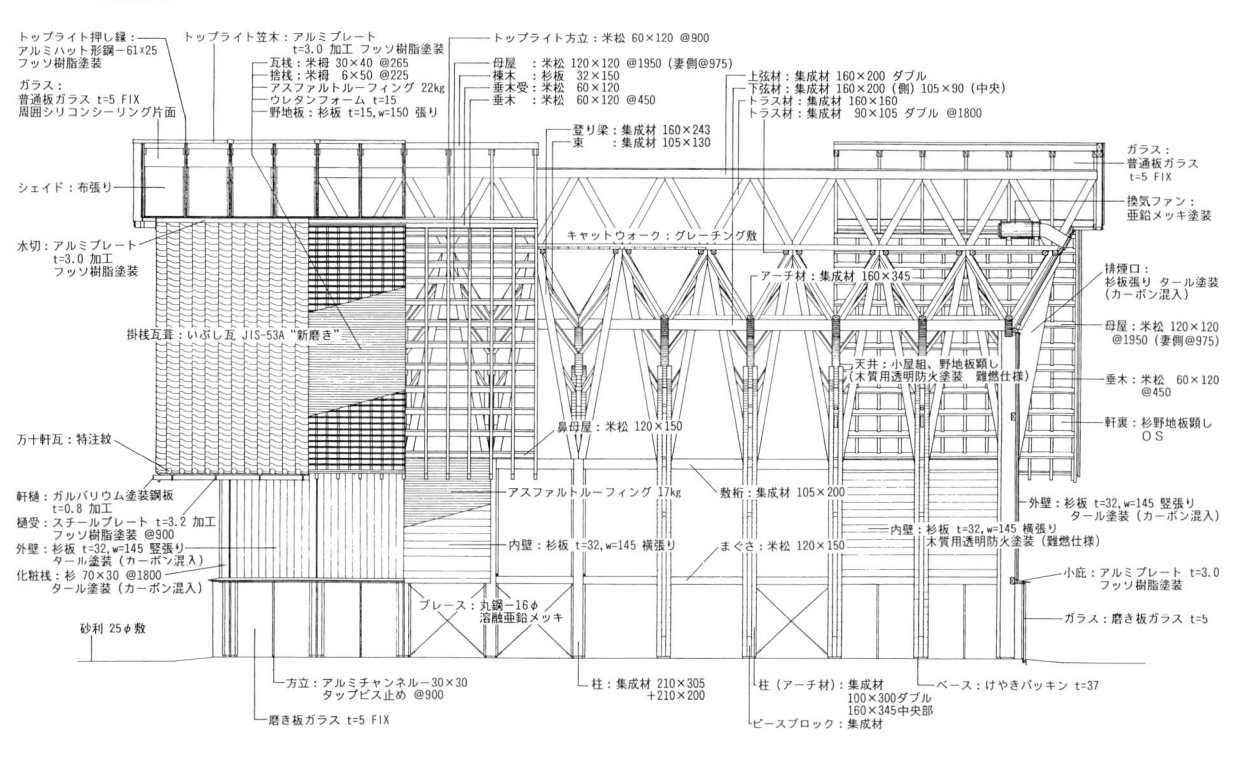

失われた時を求めて

内藤 廣

　この博物館に人を案内すると，それぞれ色々なことを思い浮かべるようだ。鯨のお腹のなか，船の竜骨。収蔵庫の外観は蔵，展示棟は大きな納屋。どの印象も間違ってはいない。スタディ模型や実際に立ち上がっていく建物を見て，そのどれもが頭の中をよぎった事があるからだ。結果として現れた類似性は興味深い。しかし，そういうものを思い浮べて，似せて作ったわけではない。

　実際，収蔵庫は蔵の作りに似ている。PCポストテンションで架構を作り，塩害で金属系の屋根材が使えないので，その上に土蔵のような置き屋根の形で瓦を乗せた。展示棟は，外壁を板張にしてタール状の塗装をかけたから，かつて真っ黒な鯨油を外壁に塗ったこの地方の民家や網小屋に似ている。竜骨のような構造体は，収蔵庫では，全体の力が曲げ応力なしに，自然に地盤まで伝わるように配慮した結果だ。展示棟の場合は，蛇の骨のように，背骨に応力の集中する場所があって，そこから細かい肋骨が地面に力を伝えていく，という新しい構造形式に挑戦した結果だ。それらが有機的なイメージを喚起するのは，ごく自然なことといえる。しかし，こうした選択の基準は，あくまでもその合理性であり経済性であった。

　不思議に思えたのは，ほとんど性能とコストしか問題にしないで作られたものなのに，懐かしいとか，どこかで見たことがあるとか言う人が居ることだ。その理由は漠然としたもので，瓦や壁の素材，架構，展示物といった具体的な個別の要素がそう言わしめているのではない。どうやら博物館全体が醸し出す空気が，日常的な眼差しの裏側にある既視観を誘い出しているようなのだ。

　ひとつの建物，それも手の内に入るほどのあまり大きくない建物に長い時間かかわっていると，自分の意識の底にあるものが次第に姿を現しはじめる。それは，容易に変わるような類の物ではなく，時代が変わっても意識を超えた脳髄の奥底にあって，変わらずに現れてくるある種の質のようなものなのだと思う。このプロジェクトの最初からのスケッチやメモを整理してみて，場当たり的に判断していると思っていた物が，意外にひとつの方向を向いていることが解った。博物館の建設が終盤にさしかかった一昨年あたりから，そうした諸々の行き着くであろう先を「素形」という言葉で，言い表わしてみようという気になった。

　博物館の収蔵物，とりわけ舟の形を見ていると「素形」の所在が明らかになる。ここに集められているのは，大木を刳貫いて作った丸木船から大型の鰹船まで，木造の漁船ばかりだ。大きいのから小さいのまで，

それぞれがその時代の技術で実現可能な範囲で考え抜かれた最適解だ。少しでも性能が劣れば仲間との競争に負けてしまう。波に対する配慮が足りなければ、船底一枚の下は地獄、海が荒れれば命も落とす。そのため、どの部分にも工夫がしてあり、ゆるがせにしていない。

こうした中に現れる形態は、たしかに人間が作ったものであるけれども、物理的な物の向う側に、かつてそれらが対していた手強い自然の像を結ばせる。これを見て懐かしいと思うのは、そこにある物を見て感じるのではなく、その背後にある自然とともに育まれた「失われた時」を想起させるからに他ならない。地中海の集落、かつての駅舎や工場、これら原初的な建築の形態の中に現れる素朴な美しさや強さもこの時間の中にある。

与えられた条件の中で最適解を求める設計作業は、舟を造るのに似ていたと言えなくもない。そこには全くといっていいほど、恣意的な形態操作の紛れ込む余地はなかった。幸か不幸か「素形」に向かって作業仮説を立てるしか建築を語る術がない状況に、ずっと置かれていたとも言える。

建築を考えるうえで、時間の枠組みを設定すると様々なことが明らかになる。建築を存在させようとする時間が短ければ短いほど、形の選択肢は限りなく増えていくし、逆に時間を引き伸ばしていくと、その幅はどんどん狭くなっていく。おそらく「素形」とは、この狭くなる選択肢の中で最後に残るもののことだ。空間を過剰に意識すれば、建築の形態は多様化していく。しかし時間を問題にすれば、形態の選択肢は狭まり、建築の輪郭ははっきりしてくる。

建築が生まれてくるプロセスと、やがては帰っていく廃墟に、「素形」は見やすい姿で存在する。そして、これら建築の始めと終わりを結ぶ長い時間を、日常的な風景の背後で生き続ける。ふつう、建築はこの「素形」の持つ原初的な美しさを、様々な表層の意匠で覆い隠し、わかりにくくしてしまっている。

「素形」を眼前の建築において明らかにしたい。

なぜなら、そうすることによってのみ、我々の生命を超えたより長い時間、つまり過去でもなく未来でもない、自然と共にある「失われた時」のなかに建築を置くことができるのではないか……と思うからだ。

In Search of A Lost Moment

Hiroshi Naito

When I take people to this museum, each one seems to imagine various things. The inside of a whale's stomach, or the keel of a ship. The exterior of the repository resembles that of a "Kura", a traditional Japanese warehouse, and the exhibition hall is a large "Naya", a Japanese style barn. All these impressions are not inaccurate. Each of these images passed through my mind during the model study stage and the actual construction of the museum. It is interesting to see the similarity between the actual result and these images. However, it was not that these images first occurred in my mind and the buildings designed to resemble them.

The repository, in fact, has a structure similar to a "Kura". The framework uses precast concrete and post-tensioning, and as metal roofing materials could not be used due to salt damage, Japanese roofing tiles were placed onto the separate wooden roof in the same way as for "Kura". The exterior of the exhibition hall has wooden panels coated with tar paint. These buildings remind us of the houses and fish net storages of this area in the past painted with pitch black whale's oil.

The keel-like structure of the repository is the result of the consideration given to the overall stress to be conveyed naturally to the ground without generating bending stress. The result of an attempt at a new structural form can be seen in the exhibition hall. All stress converges into one spot of the spine like the bones of a snake, and from this spot, thin ribs convey the stress to the ground.

It is only natural that these factors rouse an organic image. However, these standards were chosen strictly for their rationality and economy.

What was unusual about this architecture was that although it was built with consideration given for the most part to its cost and functionality, there are people who look at it with nostalgia or swear they have seen it somewhere before. The reasons appear ambiguous. It is not the tangible elements such as the roofing tiles or the walls, the framework, or the exhibits, which makes the people feel this way. It seems that the air effused throughout the museum provokes a false view of paramnesia hidden behind the people's eyes accustomed to seeing daily an ordinary scenery.

Being involved for a long period of time with a building of a size not too big to fit into the palm of my hand, what lies deep in one's consciousness gradually begins to show itself. It is not something that easily changes but remains deep inside the brain beyond consciousness, even with the change of times, a kind of protoplasm which continues to surface unchanged. When I sorted out all the sketches and notes dating back to the beginning of this project, I realized that decisions which were made just to suit the conditions at the time were surprisingly all geared toward one direction. Beginning about two years ago when the museum was near completion, I felt like using the word "protoform" to describe the final destination to be reached by these factors.

Looking at the stored items in the museum, the "protoform" can clearly be located, particularly in the shape of a boat. The collection of vessels here is entirely of wooden fishing craft ranging from a canoe which was made by hollowing out a large log to a large size skipjack. Each one, from large to small, is the best suitable solution within the possible range of technology of the times. The least deficiency in performance would result in losing to the competition. Insufficient consideration toward withstanding waves would lead to the hell lying just beneath the garboard, and the potential loss of life in a stormy sea. For these reasons, all the parts are made with ingenuity, carefully weighing every possibility.

The form stemming from all these considerations, despite its being a man-made product, evokes beyond the physical object an image of the harsh nature it once confronted. The nostalgia we feel does not come from what we see before our eyes. It is nothing but a recollection of what is behind the object, "a lost moment" fostered along with nature. The simple beauty and strength that appears in the primitive forms of architecture such as the villages along the Mediterranean Sea and the station houses and factories of the past are cherished also in the lost moment of this time.

One cannot deny a similarity between the making of a ship and our design work which seeks the best suitable solution from the given conditions. There was no room at all for any intentional manipulation in designing the forms. Fortunately or not, I had been placed in a position whereby the only way to project my architectural expression was to build up a working hypothesis towards the "protoform".

In the planning of an architectural form, setting a time frame clarifies various things. The shorter the time span is set for the existance of the building, the more and endlessly the options expand. On the other hand, the wider the time frame is stretched for its existence, the narrower the options become. Perhaps, the "protoform" would be the one left last at the end of the narrowing options. Excessive consciousness of space diversifies architectural forms. However, if importance is placed on time, the options for formation would be narrowed and the building outlines become clear.

The existence of the "protoform" can be easily recognized in the planning process up to the birth of a building as well as in the ruins to which it is destined to fall. The "protoform" continues to live within a long time span between the beginning and the end of a building set against a backdrop of ordinary scenes. The fundamental beauty of this "protoform" is difficult to perceive since the buildings in general conceal their beauty covering it with various surface designs.

I wish to reveal the "protoform" in a building that stands before my eyes. For only by doing so can we place an architecture in "a lost moment", regardless of the past or future, which continues to live on with nature for a longer period of time than the life of man.

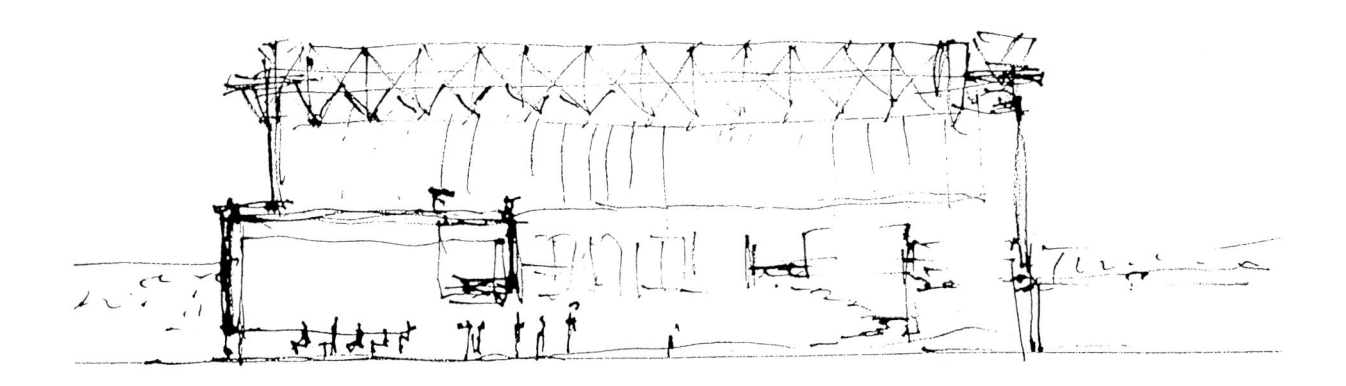

■データ

海の博物館
　　　　　　　施主：財団法人東海水産科学協会
　　　　　　所在地：三重県鳥羽市浦村町大吉1731-68　〒517-0025
　　　　　主要用途：博物館
　　　　　　　設計：内藤廣建築設計事務所　担当／内藤廣　渡辺仁　川村宣元
　　　　　　　構造：構造設計集団〈SDG〉　担当／渡辺邦夫　岡村仁
　　　　　　扉装飾：松田研一
　　　モニュメント制作：小清水漸
　　　　　展示計画：里見和彦
　　　　　家具制作：須賀忍

	展示棟	重要有形民俗文化財収蔵庫
設計期間	1988年10月－1991年2月	1985年11月－1988年2月
施工期間	1991年3月－1992年6月	1988年3月－1989年6月
施工	建築：大西種蔵建設　担当／大西勝洋 外構：石吉組	建築：鹿島建設　名古屋支店　担当／小林能史，田口寛人 　　　大西種蔵建設（木工事）　担当／大西勝洋 外構：石吉組
面積	敷地面積　　　　　　　　　　　18,058.00m² 建築面積　　　　　　　　　　　 1,487.00m² 延床面積　　　　　　　　　　　 1,898.00m²	敷地面積　　　　　　　　　　　18,058.00m² 建築面積　　　　　　　　　　　 2,173.00m² 延床面積　　　　　　　　　　　 2,026.00m²
寸法	最高高さ　　　　　　　　　　　　13,250mm 軒高　　　　　　　　　　4,000mm，7,000mm 主なスパン　　　　　　18,600mm×37,800mm	最高高さ　　　　　　　　　　　　 9,400mm 軒高　　　　　　　　　　　　　　4,000mm 主なスパン　　　　　　18,700mm×42,750mm
構造	木構造（集成材：ベイマツ） 一部鉄筋コンクリート造 基礎：深礎，ラップルコンクリート	プレキャストコンクリート・ポストテンション組み立て構法 風除室部分：鉄筋コンクリート造
外部仕上げ	屋根　：銀黒色系粘土掛土桟瓦（JIS 53A） 　　　　引掛桟工法ステンレススクリュー釘止め 外壁　：スギ板 t=32mm　縦横二重張りの上，タール塗装 開口部：木製扉：鉛シート貼りの上，樹脂系特殊塗装 　　　　ジャロジー：焼付塗装 　　　　アルミサッシュ：フッ素樹脂塗装 　　　　スティールサッシュ：フッ素樹脂塗装 外構　：黒色砂利 25φ　t=100mm 　　　　黒色割栗石 150φ積み 　　　　RC金ゴテ仕上げ，芝，自然石積み	屋根　：銀黒色系粘土掛土桟瓦（JIS 53A） 　　　　引掛桟工法ステンレススクリュー釘止め 外壁　：PC板素地の上，合成樹脂エマルジョン砂壁状吹付け 開口部：木製扉：鉛シート貼りの上，タールエポキシ特殊塗装 　　　　アルミガラリ：焼付塗装 外構　：黒色砂利 25φ　t=100mm 　　　　黒色割栗石 150φ 　　　　那智石洗い出し，RC小叩き仕上げ
内部仕上げ	エントランス 　　床：RC金ゴテ仕上げ t=100mm 　　　　グレーチング敷 　　　　黒色砂利 25φ　t=100mm 　　庇：鉄板亜鉛塗装 展示室 　　床：タイルカーペット敷 　　壁：スギ板 t=32mm張り　防火塗装（難燃仕様） 　　　　コンクリート打放し 　天井：スギ板 t=15mm張り　防火塗装（難燃仕様） 特別展示室 　　床：タイルカーペット敷 　　壁：コンクリート打放し 　天井：ワイヤーメッシュ　フッ素樹脂塗装 映像室 　　床：タイルカーペット敷 　　壁：コンクリート打放し 　天井：コンクリート打放し	風除室 　　床：真砂土叩き仕上げ t=150mm 　　　　那智石洗い出し　砂利敷 　壁・天井：モルタル金ゴテ仕上げVP A室（網の収蔵庫）・B室（布・紙の収蔵庫） 　　床：ナラ乱尺フローリング t=15mm（無塗装） 　　壁：スギ板 t=24mm 樋部倉匇加工落とし込み 　天井：スギ板 t=24mm張り C室（桶・樽・籠の収蔵庫） 　　床：真砂土叩き仕上げ t=150mm 　　壁：スギ板 t=24mm 樋部倉匇加工落とし込み 　天井：スギ板 t=24mm張り D室（桶・樽・籠の収蔵庫） 　　床：ナラ乱尺フローリング t=15mm（無塗装） 　壁・天井：PC板素地 　　　　木片セメント板打ち込み E室（船の収蔵庫） 　　床：真砂土叩き仕上げ t=150mm 　壁・天井：PC板素地 　　　　木片セメント板打ち込み

■DATA

Sea-Folk Museum

- Client : The Foundation of Tokai Suisan Kagaku Kyokai
- Address : 1731-68, Ogitsu Uramura-cho Toba-shi, Mie 517-0025
- Use : Museum
- Architectural Design : Naito Architect & Associates / Hiroshi Naito, Hitoshi Watanabe, Nobuharu Kawamura
- Structural Engineering : Structural Design Group Co.,Ltd. (S. D. G.) / Kunio Watanabe, Satoshi Okamura
- Door Artwork : Ken-ichi Matsuda
- Monument : Susumu Koshimizu
- Display Design : Kazuhiko Satomi
- Furniture : Shinobu Suga

	Exhibition Hall	Repository
Design Period	Oct.1988—Feb.1991	Nov.1985—Feb.1988
Construction Period	Mar.1991—Jun.1992	Mar.1988—Jun.1989
Contractor	General Contractor : Onishi Tanezo Construction Co., Ltd. Katsuhiro Onishi External Work & Landscaping : Ishikichi-gumi Group	General Contractor : Kajima Construction, Nagoya branch Yoshifumi Kobayashi, Hiroto Taguchi Onishi Tanezo Construction Co., Ltd. (Carpentry) Katsuhiro Onishi External Work & Landscaping : Ishikichi-gumi Group
Area	Site Area　　　　　　18,058.00m² Building Area　　　　1,487.00m² Total Floor Area　　　1,898.00m²	Site Area　　　　　　18,058.00m² Building Area　　　　2,173.00m² Total Floor Area　　　2,026.00m²
Dimension	Maximum-Height　　　　13,250mm Eaves Height　　4,000mm, 7,000mm Span　　　　18,600mm×37,800mm	Maximum-Height　　　　9,400mm Eaves Height　　　　　4,000mm Span　　　　18,700mm×42,750mm
Structure	Laminated timber(Douglas fir) Reinforced concrete	Precast concrete and Post-tensioning build up system
Basement Structure Foundation	Reinforced concrete Rubble concrete	Reinforced concrete
Exterior Finishing	Roof : Japanese roofing tile fasten with stainless nails Wall : Japanese cedar board t=32mm tar coating	Roof : Japanese roofing tile fasten with stainless nails Wall : Acrylic resin emulsion coating
Interior Finishing	Main Entrance 　Floor : Reinforced concrete trowel finish t=100mm 　　　　Granting 　Canopy : Steel plate, zinc dust anticorrosive paint Exhibition Room 　Floor : Carpet tile 　Wall : Japanese cedar board t=32mm, fire retardant paint 　　　　Exposed reinforced concrete 　Celling : Japanese cedar board t=15mm, fire retardant paint Special Exhibition Room 　Floor : Carpet tile 　Wall : Exposed reinforced concrete 　Celling : Welded wire mesh, fluorine resin paint Projection Room 　Floor : Carpet tile 　Wall : Exposed reinforced concrete 　Celling : Exposed reinforced concrete	Entrance Room 　Floor : Hammered soil t=150mm 　Wall, Ceiling : Mortar trowel finish, vinyl paint Room-A (fishing nets storage), Room-B (storage of clothes, papers) 　Floor : Japanese oak strip flooring block t=15mm, shiplap joint 　　　　(natural grain finish) 　Wall : Japanese cedar board t=24mm, herringbone joint 　Celling : Japanese cedar board t=24mm, tongue and groove V-joint Room-C (storage of tubs, casks, baskets) 　Floor : Hammered soil t=150mm 　Wall : Japanese cedar board t=24mm, herringbone joint 　Celling : Japanese cedar board t=24mm, tongue and groove V-joint Room-D (fishing tools storage) 　Floor : Japanese oak strip flooring block t=15mm, shiplap joint 　　　　(natural grain finish) 　Wall, Ceiling : Precast concrete undisguised finish, 　　　　wood chip cement board t=30mm attached Room-E (ships storage) 　Floor : Hammered soil t=150mm 　Wall, Ceiling : Precast concrete undisguised finish, 　　　　wood chip cement board t=30mm attached

CHIHIRO ART MUSEUM AZUMINO

Chihiro Art Museum Azumino

安曇野ちひろ美術館

PROCESS
1993-1996

模型 | MODEL

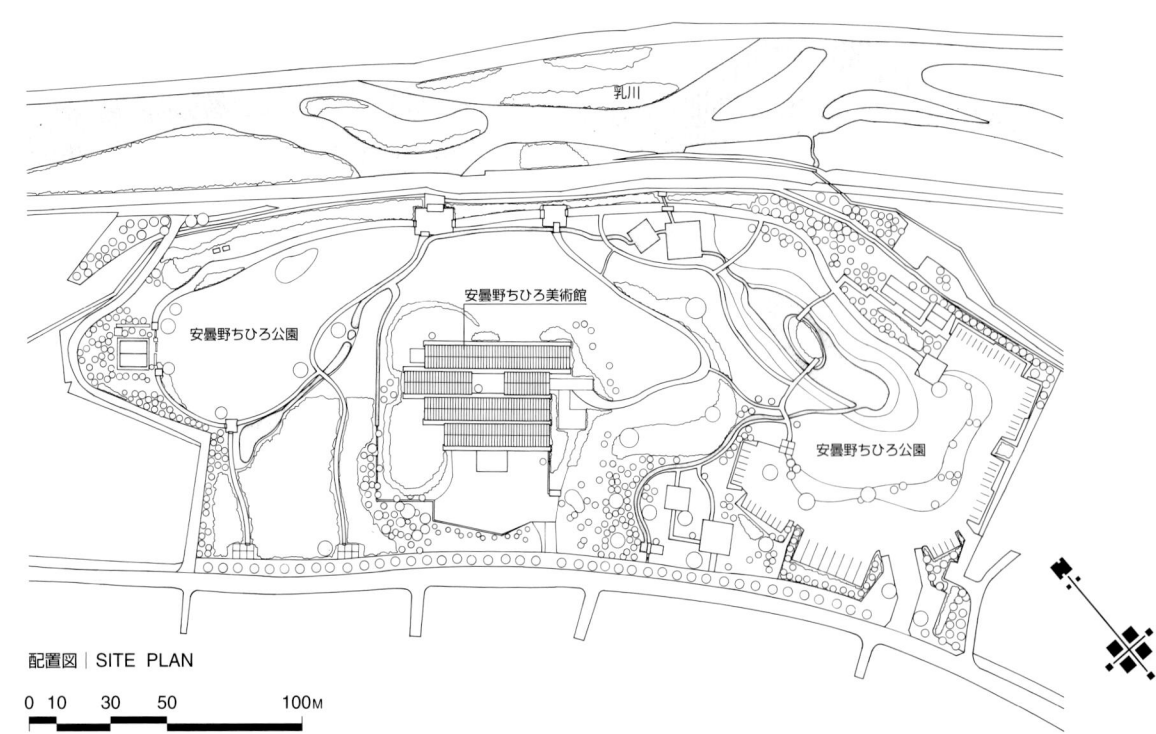

Photo : NAITO ARCHITECT & ASSOCIATES

配置図 | SITE PLAN

0 10 30 50 100M

北立面図 | NORTH ELEVATION

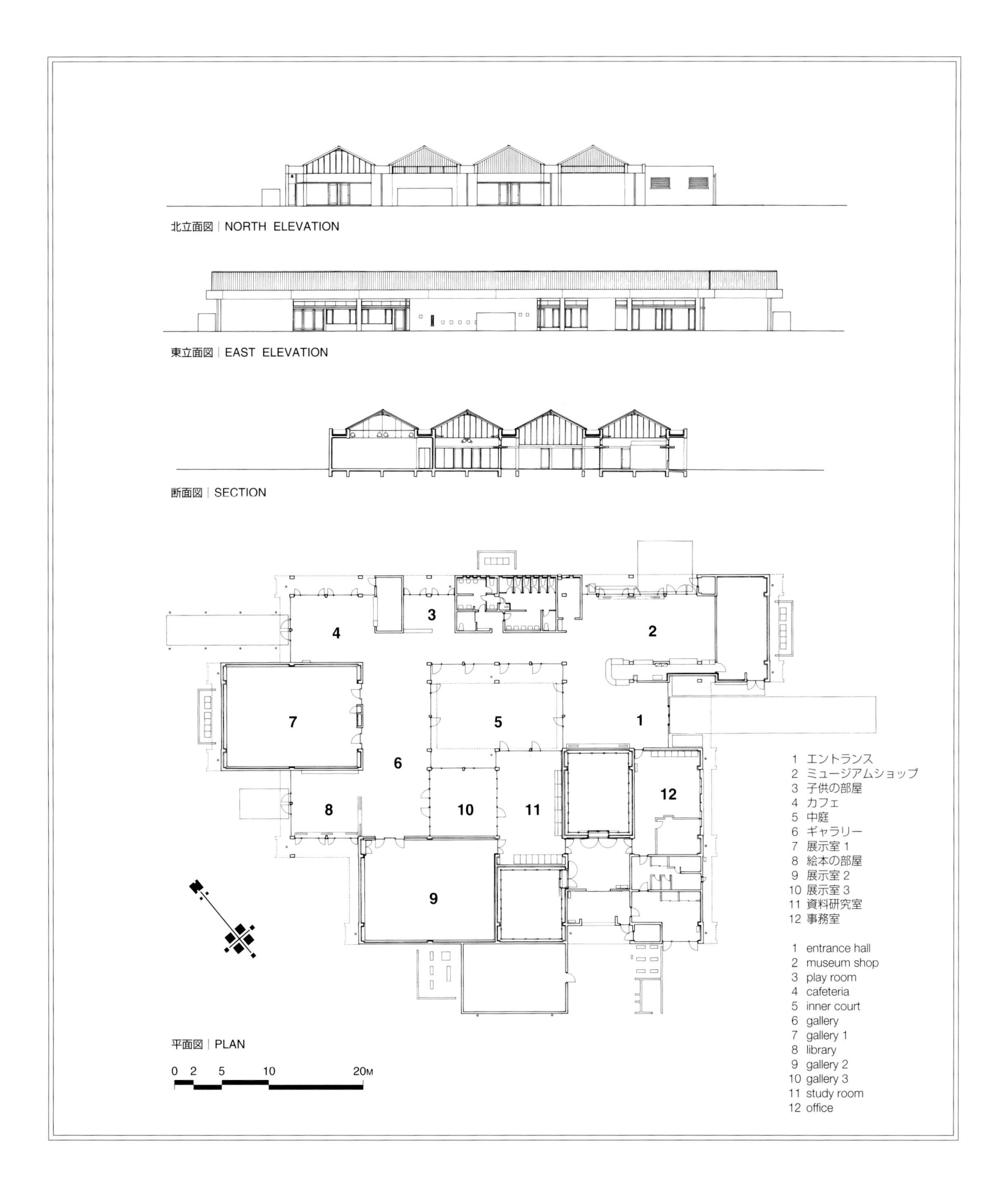

東立面図 | EAST ELEVATION

断面図 | SECTION

平面図 | PLAN

0 2 5 10 20M

1 エントランス
2 ミュージアムショップ
3 子供の部屋
4 カフェ
5 中庭
6 ギャラリー
7 展示室1
8 絵本の部屋
9 展示室2
10 展示室3
11 資料研究室
12 事務室

1 entrance hall
2 museum shop
3 play room
4 cafeteria
5 inner court
6 gallery
7 gallery 1
8 library
9 gallery 2
10 gallery 3
11 study room
12 office

東京・練馬にある「ちひろ美術館」は，多くの支持者を得ながら，長年にわたって活動を続けてきた美術館です。開館20年を期に，いわさきちひろのゆかりの地である安曇野に姉妹館を作ることになりました。地元の松川村が計画していた4ヘクタールあまりの公園の中に敷地を取得し，1993年夏，美術館を運営する財団法人いわさきちひろ記念事業団が自主コンペを企画した結果，当事務所が設計に当たることになりました。公園の設計も同時に進め，環境と建物の一体化を図ることが出来ました。
　図書館と美術館の中間のような建物にしてはどうか，周囲の環境とどうしたら馴染みの良い建物になれるか，ということをテーマとして，いくつもの提案を重ねました。無数の試行錯誤を経て，建物外観の大きさがもっとも抑えられることから，最終的に切妻の連続屋根を選択しました。建物の存在感を最小に留めることで，伸びやかな環境が出来たのではないかと思っています。

■

　The Chihiro Art Museum in Tokyo's Nerima district has enjoyed a continually expanding circle of supporters through its years of activity. On the occasion of its twentieth year, a plan was set in motion to establish a sister museum in Azumino, a region known for its connection with Chihiro Iwasaki. A site would be acquired, and a building constructed, it was decided, in a four hectare park scheduled for development by the community of Matsukawa Village. In the summer of 1993, the Museum launched a design competition, with the outcome that our office received charge of the design. Because of the necessity to advance the building design as an integral element of the park, we were also awarded the task of designing the park.
　We drew up a number of proposals focusing on a building classifiable, in function, somewhere between a museum and library, and exploring how this building might obtain a sense of unity with its environment. After building several models to investigate a composite of several roofs, we finally settled on a continuous series of gable roofs. The exterior appearance of the building would be restrained to the utmost, in order to minimize the visual presence of the building in the park.

詳細図 | DETAIL scale 1:30

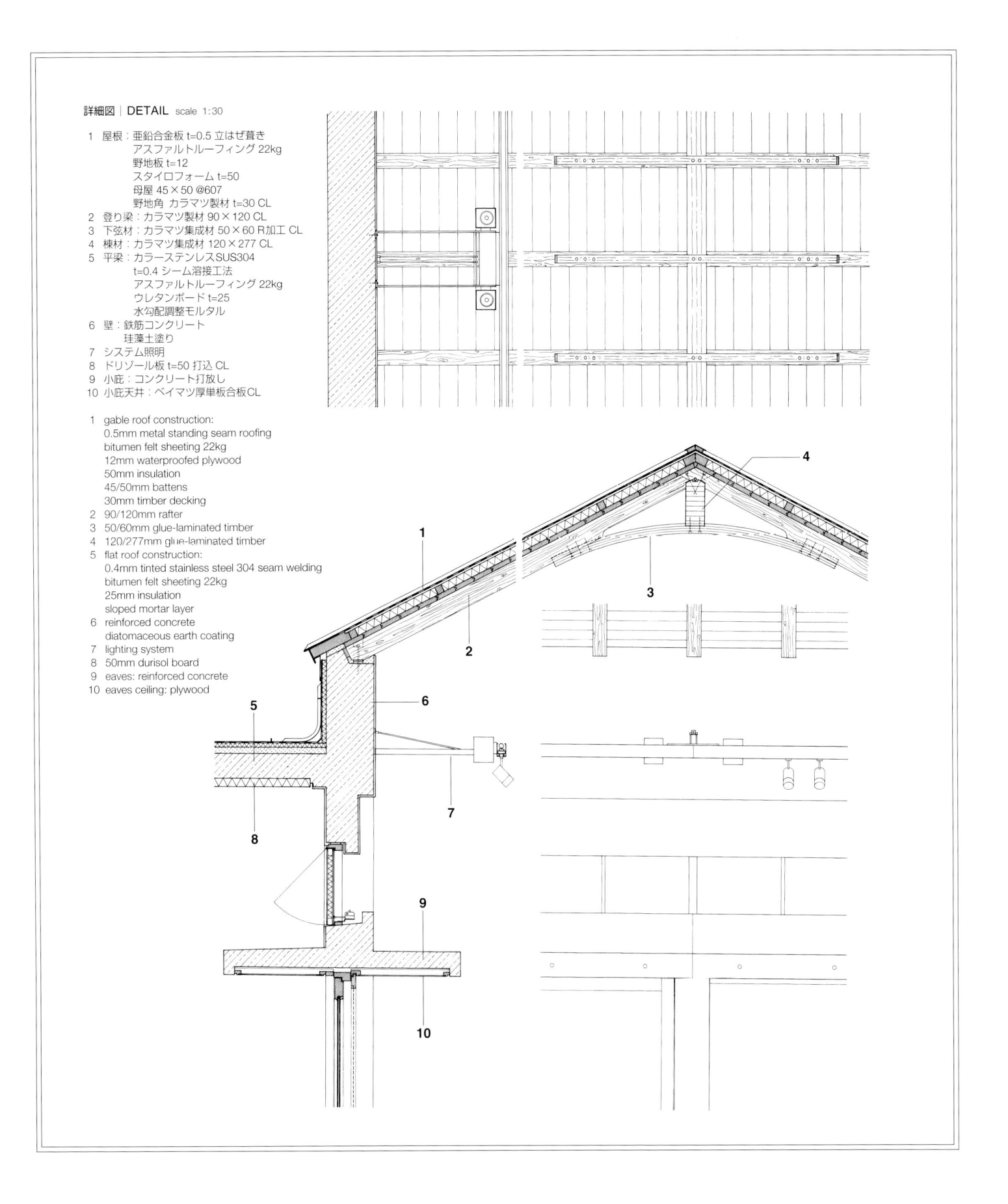

1 屋根：亜鉛合金板 t=0.5 立はぜ葺き
　　アスファルトルーフィング 22kg
　　野地板 t=12
　　スタイロフォーム t=50
　　母屋 45×50 @607
　　野地角 カラマツ製材 t=30 CL
2 登り梁：カラマツ製材 90×120 CL
3 下弦材：カラマツ集成材 50×60 R加工 CL
4 棟材：カラマツ集成材 120×277 CL
5 平梁：カラーステンレスSUS304
　　t=0.4 シーム溶接工法
　　アスファルトルーフィング 22kg
　　ウレタンボード t=25
　　水勾配調整モルタル
6 壁：鉄筋コンクリート
　　珪藻土塗り
7 システム照明
8 ドリゾール板 t=50 打込 CL
9 小庇：コンクリート打放し
10 小庇天井：ベイマツ厚単板合板CL

1 gable roof construction:
   0.5mm metal standing seam roofing
   bitumen felt sheeting 22kg
   12mm waterproofed plywood
   50mm insulation
   45/50mm battens
   30mm timber decking
2 90/120mm rafter
3 50/60mm glue-laminated timber
4 120/277mm glue-laminated timber
5 flat roof construction:
   0.4mm tinted stainless steel 304 seam welding
   bitumen felt sheeting 22kg
   25mm insulation
   sloped mortar layer
6 reinforced concrete
   diatomaceous earth coating
7 lighting system
8 50mm durisol board
9 eaves: reinforced concrete
10 eaves ceiling: plywood

外には大きなスケールの景観が広がっています。それに対して，求心的な中庭を建物の中心に据え，建物にまとまりを持たせることを考えました。この中庭を中心に来館者の主導線を巡らせ，その外側に展示室や各種のコーナーなどの諸室を配置しています。中庭を介して視線が交差し，建物の中のさまざまな人の動きが，どの空間からも視覚的にわかるようになっています。

　建築的には，どうしたら平易で親しみやすい空間を作り出すことが出来るか，が最大のテーマでした。壁と梁を鉄筋コンクリートで立ち上げ，少し赤みを帯びた安曇野の土を珪藻土に混ぜて，左官で仕上げました。それを土台として，これも赤みのある地場産のカラマツ材で架構をかけ渡しました。屋根頂部の小さなアーチは，この架構を結び合わせる重要な役割を果たしています。施工の精度が素晴らしく，単純で無駄がなく，全体としてスリムな架構を組むことが出来ました。地域の素材を積極的に使うことにより，周囲の風景と馴染みの良い建物になったのではないかと思っています。

∎

　The scenery encompassing the site was expansive and large in scale. We responded by giving the building a central court, centripetal in its effect on the design, and organizing the building around it. The path of movement for visitors was led around this inner court, and the functional spaces — the exhibit rooms and displays — placed outward of that. Through this inner court, the lines of sight intersect, and the movement of people through the building can be appreciated from each space.

　Architecturally, our greatest theme was how to create a simple, accessible space. Establishing walls and beams of reinforced concrete, we had plasterers finish them with a diatomaceous earth coating, tinted by mixing in red-hued Azumino soil. This basic structure we spanned with roof trusses built of locally grown larch timber, also reddish in hue. Small arches placed at the peak of the roof serve the important function of integrating the trusses. The precision of the construction work was superb. A roof frame, simple and spare, and quite lean in overall appearance, was achieved. By aggressively employing local materials, we obtained a building that responds harmoniously to its surroundings.

架構組立図 | STRUCTURAL SYSTEM

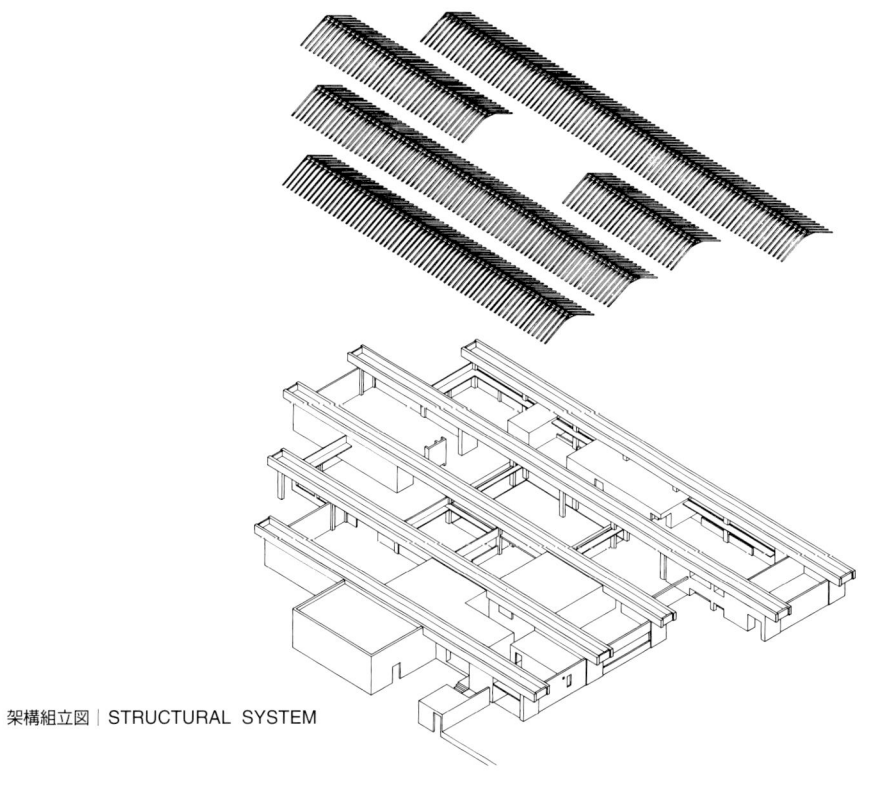

倉庫のようなもの・・・
■ 内藤　廣

　何気なく野原に建つ倉庫のようなものを作りたい，とどこかで思ったかもしれません。必要だから建てられたという，事実だけを背負ったようなもの，に憧れる気持ちがあります。建築をめぐる状況が，あまりに複雑になってしまったからかもしれません。

■ そっけない模型
　「安曇野ちひろ美術館」は，切妻の連続屋根のシルエットを持っています。敷地との関係から，この形態がいちばん建物が低く見え，敷地に対する座りが良いことから決定しました。模型の段階から，倉庫のようだね，と関係者の方々には言われていました。設計する側の意識としては，倉庫を形態的なアナロジーとして考えたことなど微塵もなかったので，その時は別に気にも留めませんでした。

　それから一年後，私の事務所で進んでいるプロジェクトの模型ばかりを並べた展覧会を催す機会がありました。この美術館の模型も当然その中にありました。そのとき，大方の模型を見て，倉庫のようだね，という方が何人かいました。言われた方の人柄からすれば，皮肉でもなんでもない，素直な印象だったのだと思います。嫌な気持ちになったという記憶はありません。事実，そこに並べられた模型たちは，切妻屋根を組み合わせたようなものばかりで，架構方法や素材に小さな差異は在るものの，そっけないことこの上ありませんでした。

■ 倉庫と納屋
　自分自身は，構法上の整合性や，内部の空間の質のみを気にしながら，建物をまとめたつもりでした。形態や素材を決定する要因を，自らの意識の外部に設定することは，「海の博物館」以来自らに課してきたことでした。その結果として現れるものが，退屈であろうとなかろうと，それには頓着しない，という姿勢を通して来たつもりです。拡散する意識を物によって収斂していく，というスタンスは，いわば自分自身の精神に対する自分自身によるカウンセリングに近いものだった，と思っています。

　しかし，それはこちらの側のいわばインサイドワークの事情であって，外から見ればどうなのか，ということは，設計という作業が終わり，建物が完成した以上，冷静に見直してみなければならないでしょう。「ちひろ美術館」の関係者だけではなく，もっと多くのいろいろな種類の人達から同じ印象を聞かされたわけですから，一度そのことについて考えてみなければ，と思い始めていました。倉庫のようだ，という言葉の意

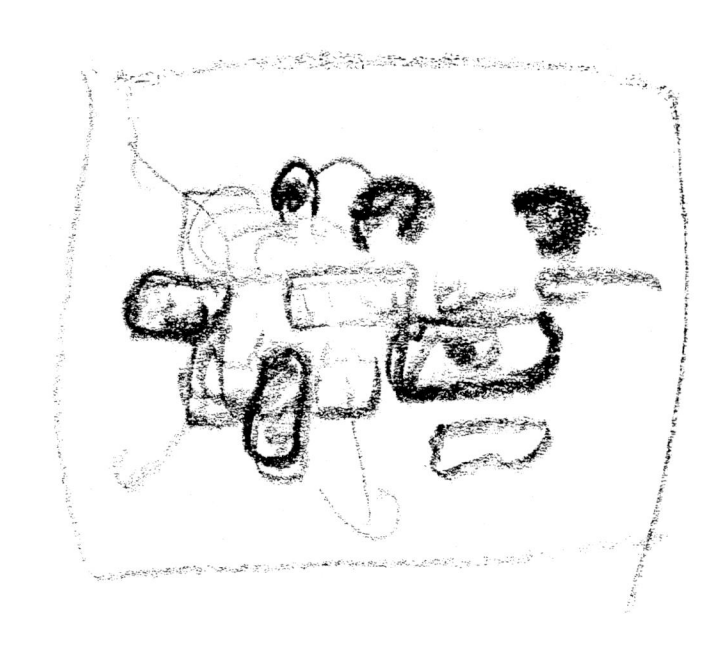

味するところをどう考えたらよいのか。積極的に捉えれば，それらに象徴される何かを，その模型たちは持っていた，ということになります。それは，私自身の意識の奥底の願望のようなものをいい当てているような気もしました。素形のことです。

　倉庫のことを考え始めてみて，求めているのは倉庫のような形態ではなくて，倉庫のようなもののなかに立ち上がる，納屋のような空気だったのではないか，と気がつきました。倉庫と納屋は，建物だけを見れば似たようなものです。両方とも機能的で無駄がなく，質素でつましいものです。倉庫も納屋も，外見の形や素材の在り方に関して，つまり物質的な側面からはさしたる違いはありません。しかし，その内容は本質的にはまったく異なるものです。

　倉庫は，物が蓄積されるためにあります。そこでは，時間は日常よりゆっくりと経過する方向に向かいます。一方，納屋は生産の場であって，鳥や牛や馬などの動物がいたりします。そこでは時間は減速せず，再生産されるのです。倉庫では，かびの匂いで満たされた冷たい空気が支配しています。その暗闇の中には，過去のさまざまな因果や記憶が塗り込められています。一方，納屋では，動物の息遣いと糞の臭いが立ち籠めた，暖かい空気が支配しています。「倉庫は過去に対して開いていて，納屋は未来に対して開いている」と言ってもよいかもしれません。

■納屋への兆し
　建築的な言葉，すなわちわれわれ設計に携わるものの修辞は，そこに訪れる普通の人達にとってはわかりにくいものです。多くの場合，設計に込めた建築上の言葉は，そこに訪れる方達に対して，視覚的にわかるように翻訳されなければ，何の意味も持ち得ません。建物だけは出来ましたが，それをどのようにして翻訳してよいか，考えあぐねていました。倉庫のようなもの，をつくり得たとしても，それがここで繰り広げられる活動と，どういうかかわりをもち得るのか。言葉で説明しなくても納得できるような，具体的につながる回路が必要です。

　中村好文は住宅を中心に活動してきた優れた建築家です。彼とは面識はありましたが，これといった付き合いはありませんでした。建物がほぼ完成した頃，彼から突然手紙をもらいました。現場の前をよく通る，この建物の家具にかかわりたい，という丁重な申し入れでした。まったく違った視点から，家具が建物の翻訳をしてくれるのではないか，とい

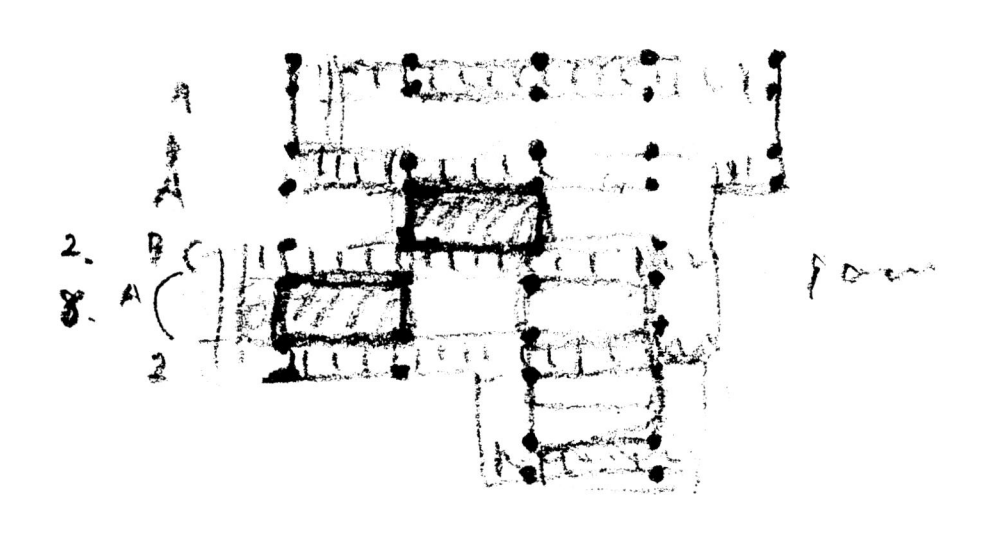

う期待が生まれました。さっそく建物を見てもらい，すべてを託すことにしました。

　ほとんどの家具はぎりぎりまで制作が続けられ，直前になって建物に運び込まれました。全貌を目にしたのはオープン当日です。生硬な建築空間の中で，優しく繊細な表情の家具たちが来館者を迎え入れていました。それらは，ちひろの周囲に漂っていたであろう空気を表現していました。この建物を訪れる人たちが，これがちひろの建物だと胸に落ちるものがあるとしたら，それはここに置かれた家具たちが，建物との仲立ちをしてくれたことに負うところが多いと思います。

　倉庫のようだ，と言った人は正しかったのだと思います。私の建物のつくり方はいかにもそっけないものです。使い手がその空間に対して何も行動を起こさなければ，たちまちただの倉庫になってしまいます。使い手の側に委ねる部分が多い，といえば聞こえは良いのですが，それだけ使い手に問題を預けている部分があります。使い手に対して親切ではないかもしれません。家具が置かれた風景を見て，空間にざわめきとかすかな揺らぎが生じ，この建物は倉庫のままであることを免れ，納屋のようなもの，になる兆しを得たのではないかと感じました。

■倉庫・シェルター・素形

　素形，シェルター，倉庫のようなもの。「海の博物館」を完成させてから，建築を語るとき繰り出したこれらの言葉は，一見脈絡なく飛躍しながらも一直線上に並んでいます。この流れは変っていません。素形は遥か彼方にあり，それ以後の言葉は，それを手前に引き寄せて考えるための方便です。俯瞰してみると，抽象的でとらえどころのない意識に，だんだんと質感のようなものが加わってきているかもしれません。素形は無意識の中にある，といったところで，当たり前すぎてどうなるわけでもありません。それに対して，倉庫のようなもの，を俎上に載せることは，少し違ったトーンを帯びているはずです。

　素形，シェルター，倉庫のようなもの，という脈絡は，イデー，手段，現象というように置き換えられます。自分では意識していなかったのですが，これは私自身の内的なものが，外在化するプロセスといえるかもしれません。もしそうなら，素形という一人称のイデーから始まった筋立てに，シェルターという二人称の手段が加わり，その道筋から生まれたものが三人称の他者にとってどういう現象に映るのか，ということでしょう。建物をつくっている最中は，建物を構成する無数の物質の理路を立てるのに必死で，他人の目など気にしていられません。出来上がっ

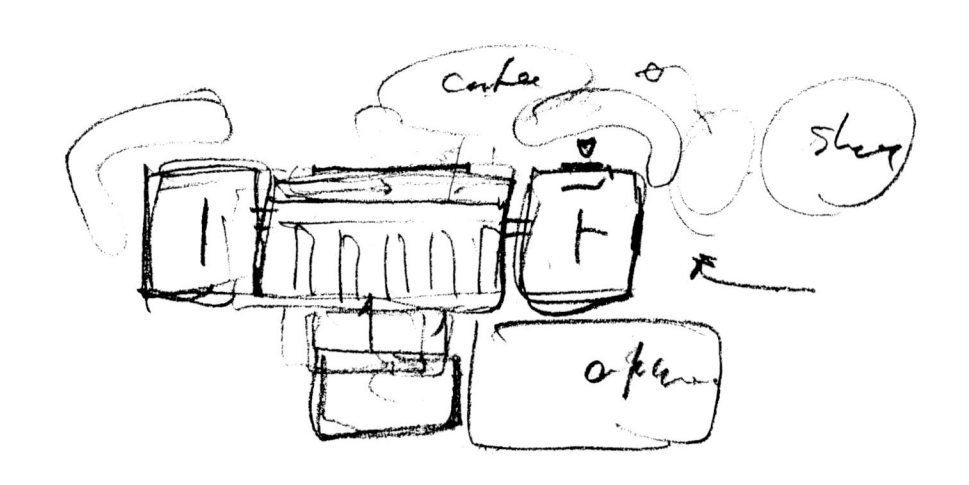

てみれば，現実になったものを第三者の目を介して客観化してみよう，というのも自然なことかもしれません。こちらから一歩踏み込んで，その目に対して問い返してみたい気持ちもあります。つくり手にとっては倉庫のような建物でも，外から見ればそこに希望はあるのだろうか，と。

■柔らかな倉庫

　出来上がって改めてこの建物を眺めてみると，この美術館のある風景には優しい雰囲気が漂っています。公園の修景にしても建築内部の空間にしても，どこか柔らかな空気があります。「海の博物館」が持っている男性的な強さとは違った雰囲気があります。これは自分でも予測していなかったことです。ちひろの美術館だから，と具体的に意識したわけではありません。たぶん，ちひろの作品を生み出した心の所在は安曇野の風景の中にあったのでしょう。まったく違うところから倉庫のようなものをつくろうとした私も，安曇野の風景や風土に対して答えを出す中で，結果として同質の何かに引き寄せられたのかもしれない，と今では想像しています。

　竣工してから，この建物を倉庫のようだ，と言った人はいません。それも不思議なことです。現実の倉庫とフィクションである模型とをつなぐ回路はあるのに，倉庫とこの現実の建物をつなぐ回路は，人の意識にはないのかもしれません。妙なもので，今になって私には，倉庫のように見えてほしい，という気持ちが芽生え始めています。実際の建物が倉庫のようにはならなかったからかもしれません。もっと突き放して，厳密に倉庫のようなものを目指したなら，建築に出来ることと出来ないことの境界が，もっとはっきり見えたでしょう。状況を考慮して，一歩手前で手を緩めたところもあります。辻褄合わせに手を出して意識的に形を操作してしまった部分もあります。この建物は，そうした部分に曖昧さを残しています。しかしその曖昧さが，納屋のようなものになり得る初速を，生まれたばかりの建物に与えているような気もします。

　ただの建物が，過去からの思いを受け止める倉庫のようなものから，それを未来へと再生する納屋になり得るかどうか。最終的な結果は無数の来館者と時の経過に委ねるしかありません。

A Building Like a Storehouse...
Hiroshi Naito

Deep down inside, I may have wanted to create something like a storehouse, sitting casually in a field. I feel drawn to structures built to meet a necessity and entrusted only with hard facts. Perhaps because the situation encompassing architecture has grown so complex.

■Impassive Models

The Chihiro Art Museum Azumino has a silhouette of continuous gabled roofs, a form chosen to best give the building a low, unobtrusive appearance, so that it sits well in its place.

Even when the design had only taken form as a model, people around the project were commenting on how the building reminded them of a storehouse. As the designer, the idea of making a formal analogy to a storehouse never occurred to me, so I paid these comments little notice, at the time.

A year passed. We had occasion to hold an exhibition and display all the models for projects underway at our office, and of course, the model for this museum was included. At this time, several people who came to the exhibition looked around at the models and said, "They look like storehouses." These comments, considering the character of the people giving them, were not meant to be ironical but simply the expression of a frank opinion. I do not remember feeling bothered at all. In reality, all the models featured combinations of gabled roofs, and despite small differences in the style of their roof frames or in their materials, they could not have looked more impassive.

■Storehouse and Barn

I tried to compose the building by focusing purely on consistency among the construction methods, the quality of the interior space, and so on. Since the Sea-Folk Museum, I had been able to establish outside the periphery of my consciousness the elements that would decide building forms or materials. Throughout this time, I maintained a stance of not paying heed to whether the result would appear boring or not. This habit of employing physical things as a vehicle for focusing my consciousness I considered a way of providing consultation to myself.

These are nonetheless the circumstances of my "inner work." As to how the building has actually turned out in appearance, I perhaps need to take an objective look, after the design is finished. Since I was hearing the same comment not just from people at the Chihiro Museum but from many people of different backgrounds, I began to think I should stop and consider what it meant. But how does one think about an expression such as "It looks like a storehouse"? If I really thought about it, it seemed to indicate the presence of something symbolic in those models. And this, I began to think, could only be a particular wish or desire that I embraced in the depths of my consciousness — a protoform.

As I thought about storehouses, I realized that what I was after was not a storehouse-like form but rather the kind of space found inside a storehouse. A barn-like space. Storehouses and barns look quite similar, as buildings. Both are functional, spare, and simple. Their outer forms and the manner of their materials — their physical aspects — reveal few differences. But when it comes to content, the difference is essential and complete.

A storehouse is for storing things. Times passes more slowly than is usual in a storehouse. A barn is for producing things. There are animals, such as chickens, cows, and horses. Time is reproduced in a barn, without ever slowing down. In a storehouse, a cold, moldy air holds dominion, and the darkness is imbued with the memories and residue of past events. A barn, on the other hand, traps in odors of animal breath and dung, and an atmosphere of warmth prevails. A storehouse, let us say, opens on the past, and a barn, on the future.

■An Omen of a Barn

The language of architecture or, in other words, the rhetoric we use in the design world, is hard to understand for ordinary visitors to this world. In many cases, the words we entrust to a design mean nothing to the layman, unless we can translate them so that they can be visually understood. The building is done; Now, how do I translate it? This is a question I have played with to exhaustion. I have created a storehouse-like building — what kind of relationship is possible with the activities that will unfold in it? A connection with something concrete is demanded, something that can be persuasive without resorting to a verbal explanation.

Yoshifumi Nakamura is an outstanding architect whose career has revolved around residential architecture. I had only a passing acquaintance with him. When the building was approaching completion, however, I suddenly received a letter from him, a politely worded request — he often passes by the site and would like to be involved in producing the building's furniture. This awoke a sense of expectation in me — Nakamura's furniture might provide the translation I needed, from an entirely different perspective. I had him look over the building right away, and left everything to him.

Most of the furniture remained under production until the last minute, and was not delivered until right before the opening. My first chance to see the full effect of the completed building was on opening day. There, in the harsh architectural space of the new building, visitors were received by a furniture of gentle and sensitive expression. The furniture seemed to lend a voice to the aura that one imagined had surrounded Chihiro Iwasaki. Ultimately, if the notion ever comes into someone's mind that here is a proper Chihiro building, then, in many ways, it will have been because the furniture intermediates so well.

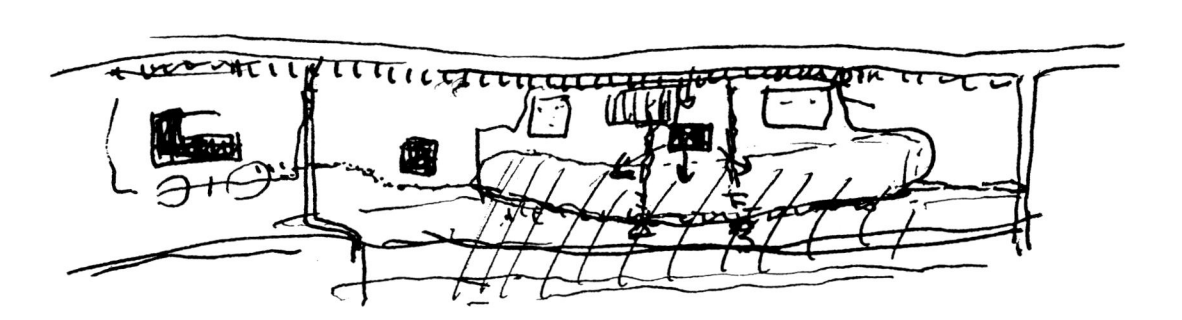

When they said of this building, "It is like a storehouse," they were right. My method of building design is, by nature, impassive. If the user is not aggressive in his approach to the building, it suddenly becomes a mere storehouse. To say that much is left to the user has a nice ring, but in many ways, what is left to the user is problematic. I am, perhaps, unkind to the user. Seeing the effect the furniture produced on the building — sensing a stir, a slight quiver in the air — I felt as if receiving an omen that the building would not remain a storehouse but would obtain life as something more like a barn.

■Storehouse, Shelter, Protoform

Protoform, shelter, something like a storehouse . . . These terms I have used repeatedly in order to talk about architecture, ever since finishing the Sea-Folk Museum, might appear a string of words without logical connection. But their order has never changed. The protoform is in the obscure reaches of the consciousness, and the terms that follow are expedients for bringing it closer to think about it. This way of visualizing abstractly something not consciously identifiable seems to help flesh it out. Of course, one could just say it is out of reach in the subconscious and let it go at that. But this way of putting something like a storehouse on the chopping block helps cast it in a different light.

We can replace these terms protoform, shelter, and something like a storehouse, in their logical sequence, with the words idea, means, and phenomenon. While not conscious of it, myself, this may be a process I use to externalize things latent within me. If so, it would mean a line of reasoning that begins with the protoform (in the first-person singular), then adopts shelter (second-person singular) as a means of producing a phenomenon that appears in a way unknown to me in the eyes of someone else (third-person singular). In the middle of creating a building, one is utterly taken up in assembling the countless material logics that compose a building, and can spare little of one's attention for what others see. It is perhaps natural, then, to want to see the final result, objectively, through the eyes of the third-person singular. I almost feel an urge to approach someone in that position and ask — what do you really think? Does this building, which for the designer is something like a storehouse, evince inspirational power, when viewed from out there?

■A Soft Storehouse

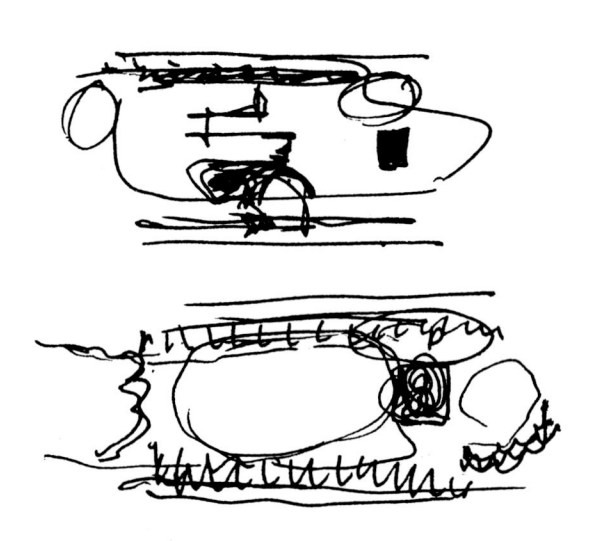

Looking at the building, now that it is completed, one notices an aura of softness about the art museum. A supple quality pervades the park scenery and the building's interior spaces – an atmosphere unlike the masculine strength of the Sea-Folk Museum. I did not expect this — it does not result from a conscious attempt to create a Chihiro-like museum. Likely, the spirit that motivated Chihiro's artworks inhabits the landscape of Azumino. Although setting out to create something like a storehouse for a different set of reasons, I eventually arrived at something kindred in nature to the scenery and atmospheric conditions of Azumino, perhaps from having to respond to them. Or, at least, I so imagine.

Now that the building is completed, no one tells me it is like a storehouse, anymore. This also seems odd. A resemblance exists between the fictional model and an actual storehouse, but it seems people are unaware of any resemblance of the actual building to a storehouse. In a funny way, I find myself wishing it looked more like a storehouse, perhaps because the completed building is not enough like a storehouse. If I had set out with more abandon to create something like a storehouse, I might have made a clearer statement about what architecture can do and cannot do. But, extending consideration to the needs of the situation, I faltered before the threshold of my ideal. I also resorted, at times, to a conscious manipulation of form in order to ensure consistency. Thus, the building exhibits some ambiguity, but an ambiguity, I sense, that will nudge the newly born building on its way to finding a barn-like existence.

Ultimately it will rest on the stream of visitors and on the process of time to determine whether a building — just a building — can change from a storehouse for the thoughts of the past into a barn that offers new life to the future.

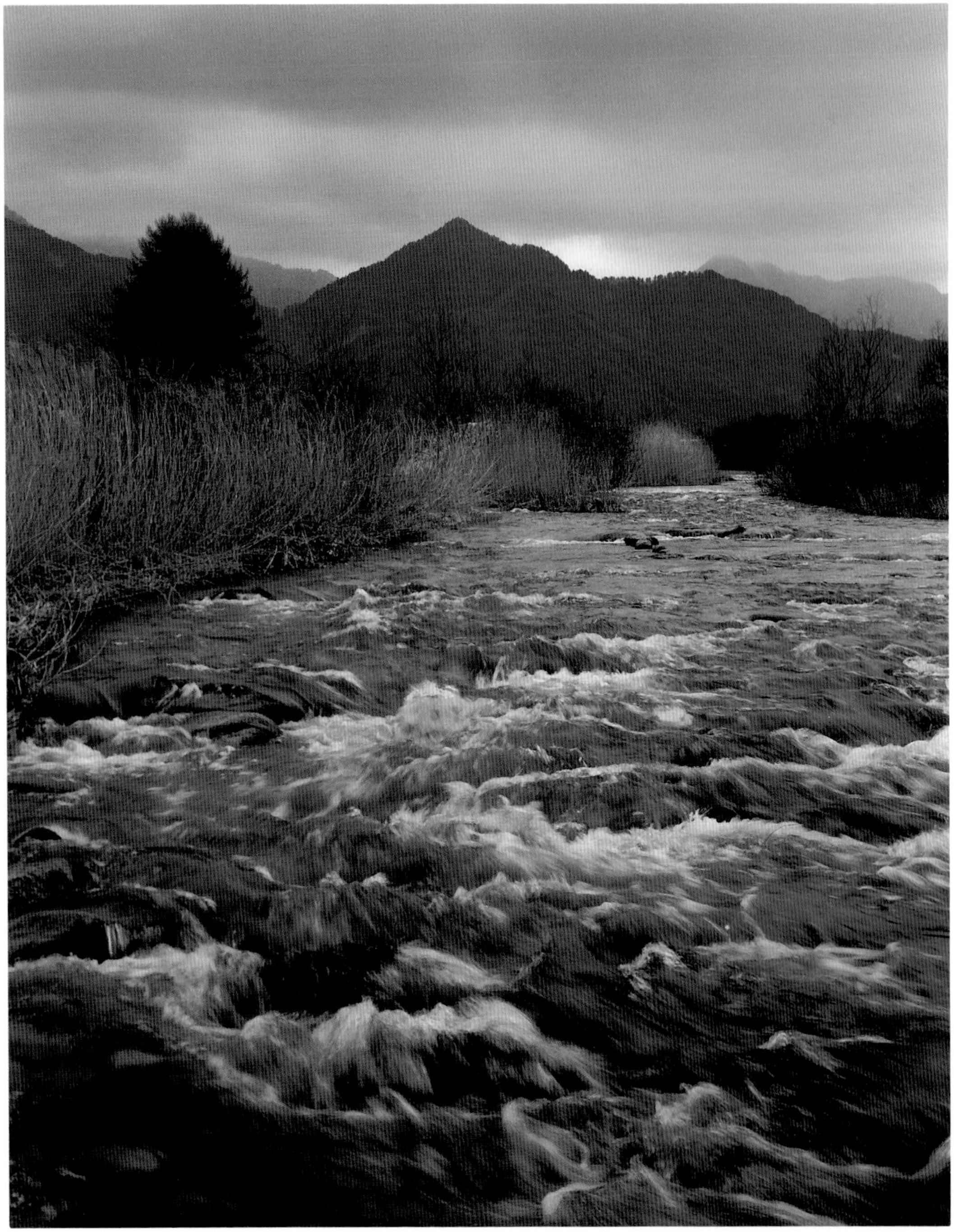

■データ

安曇野ちひろ美術館
- 施主：財団法人いわさきちひろ記念事業団
- 所在地：長野県北安曇郡松川村西原 〒399-8501
- 主要用途：美術館
- 設計：内藤廣建築設計事務所　担当／内藤 廣　古野洋美　横井 拓
- 構造：構造設計集団〈SDG〉　担当／渡辺邦夫　中田琢史
- 設備：明野設備研究所　担当／小川津久雄　下原秀彦
- 照明計画：ライティング プランナーズ アソシエーツ〈LPA〉　担当／面出 薫　泉 ルミ
- 家具デザイン：中村好文　開發智子
- サイン：佐藤卓デザイン事務所　担当／佐藤 卓

設計期間	1993年9月－1995年4月
施工期間	1995年5月－1996年6月
施工	前田建設工業 長野支店　担当／太刀川久夫　筒井 忍　朝日 勝 小屋組：信州林産
面積	敷地面積　8,000.09m² 建築面積　1,768.42m² 延床面積　1,581.01m²
寸法	最高高さ　6,170mm 軒高　4,250mm 主なスパン　7,200mm×7,200mm
構造	下部：鉄筋コンクリート造 小屋組：木造（カラマツ）
外部仕上げ	屋根：亜鉛合金板立てはぜ葺き@213mm 外壁：鉄筋コンクリート壁の上珪藻土塗り 開口部：木製サッシュ，スチールサッシュ，アルミサッシュ 外構：アプローチ・テラス／せっ器質タイル 210×340mm 貼り
内部仕上げ	エントランス，ギャラリー 　床：カラマツ縁甲板 t=25mm張り 　壁：鉄筋コンクリートの上珪藻土塗り 　妻面：ベイマツ厚単板合板（おびのこめ） 　天井：カラマツ野地角 t=30mm 張り小屋組カラマツ現し 展示室1 　床：ブナモザイクパーケット張り，カットパイルカーペット敷 　壁：ドンゴロス貼り 　天井：ベイマツルーバー50×75mm，一部木片セメント板 t=50mm 展示室2 　床：タイルカーペット敷 　壁：フレックスコート塗り 　天井：ベイマツルーバー50×75mm，一部木片セメント板 t=50mm

安曇野ちひろ公園
- 施主：松川村
- 所在地：長野県北安曇郡松川村西原 〒399-8501
- 主要用途：公園
- 設計：内藤廣建築設計事務所　担当／内藤 廣　古野洋美
- 屋外彫刻：クヴィエタ・パツォウスカー

設計期間	1993年10月－1994年8月
施工期間	1994年12月－1997年3月
施工	相模組，白澤組
面積	敷地面積　35,316.00m²
仕上げ	歩道：インターロッキング 散策路：自然砂舗装 せせらぎ：花コウ岩 φ150～φ300
植栽	芝生：野芝 低灌木：サツキ　ツツジ　レンギョウ 高木：ケヤキ　シラカシ　ソメイヨシノ　アカマツ

■DATA

Chihiro Art Museum Azumino
- Client：Chihiro Iwasaki Memorial Foundation
- Address：Nishihara Matsukawa-mura Kita-azumi-gun Nagano 399-8501
- Use：Art Museum
- Design：Naito Architect & Associates / Hiroshi Naito, Hiromi Furuno, Hiraku Yokoi
- Structural Engineering：Structural Design Group Co.,Ltd. / Kunio Watanabe, Takushi Nakata
- Engineering：Akeno Engineering Consultants Inc. / Tsukuo Ogawa, Hidehiko Shimohara
- Lighting：Lighting Planners Associates Inc. / Kaoru Mende, Rumi Izumi
- Furniture Design：Yoshifumi Nakamura, Tomoko Kaihotsu
- Sign：Taku Satoh Design Office Inc. / Taku Satoh

Design Period	Sep.1993－Apr.1995
Construction Period	May 1995－Jun.1996
General Contractor	Maeda Corporation Nagano branch Hisao Tachikawa, Shinobu Tsutsui, Masaru Asahi Roof frame : Shinshu Rinsan Co., Ltd.
Area	Site Area　8,000.09m² Building Area　1,768.42m² Total Floor Area　1,581.01m²
Dimension	Maximum-Height　6,170mm Eaves Height　4,250mm Span　7,200mm×7,200mm
Structure	Reinforced concrete Roof frame : Wood truss (Japanese larch)
Exterior	Roof : Metal standing seam roofing Wall : Reinforced concrete and diatomaceous earth coating
Interior	Entrance, Gallery 　Floor : Japanese larch strip flooring t=25mm 　Wall : Reinforced concrete and diatomaceous earth coating 　Ceiling : Japanese larch decking t=30mm Gallery 1 　Floor : Parquet flooring, Cut pile carpet 　Wall : Linen covering 　Ceiling : Douglas fir louver 50×75mm, wood chip cement board t=50mm Gallery 2 　Floor : Carpet tile 　Wall : Acrylic emulsion coating 　Ceiling : Douglas fir louver 50×75mm, wood chip cement board t=50mm

Azumino Chihiro Park
- Client：Matsukawa-mura
- Address：Nishihara Matsukawa-mura Kita-azumi-gun Nagano 399-8501
- Use：Park
- Design：Naito Architect & Associates / Hiroshi Naito, Hiromi Furuno
- Sculpture：Květa Pacovská

Design Period	Oct.1993－Aug.1994
Construction Period	Dec.1994－Mar.1997
General Contractor	Sagamigumi Co., Ltd., Shirosawa-gumi
Area	Site Area　35,316.00m²
Finish	Lane : Interlocking blocks Path : Natural sand pavement Little stream : Granite stone φ150～φ300
Plants	Grass Azalea, Asiatic azalea, Forsythia Zelkova tree, Oak, Cherry tree, Pine tree

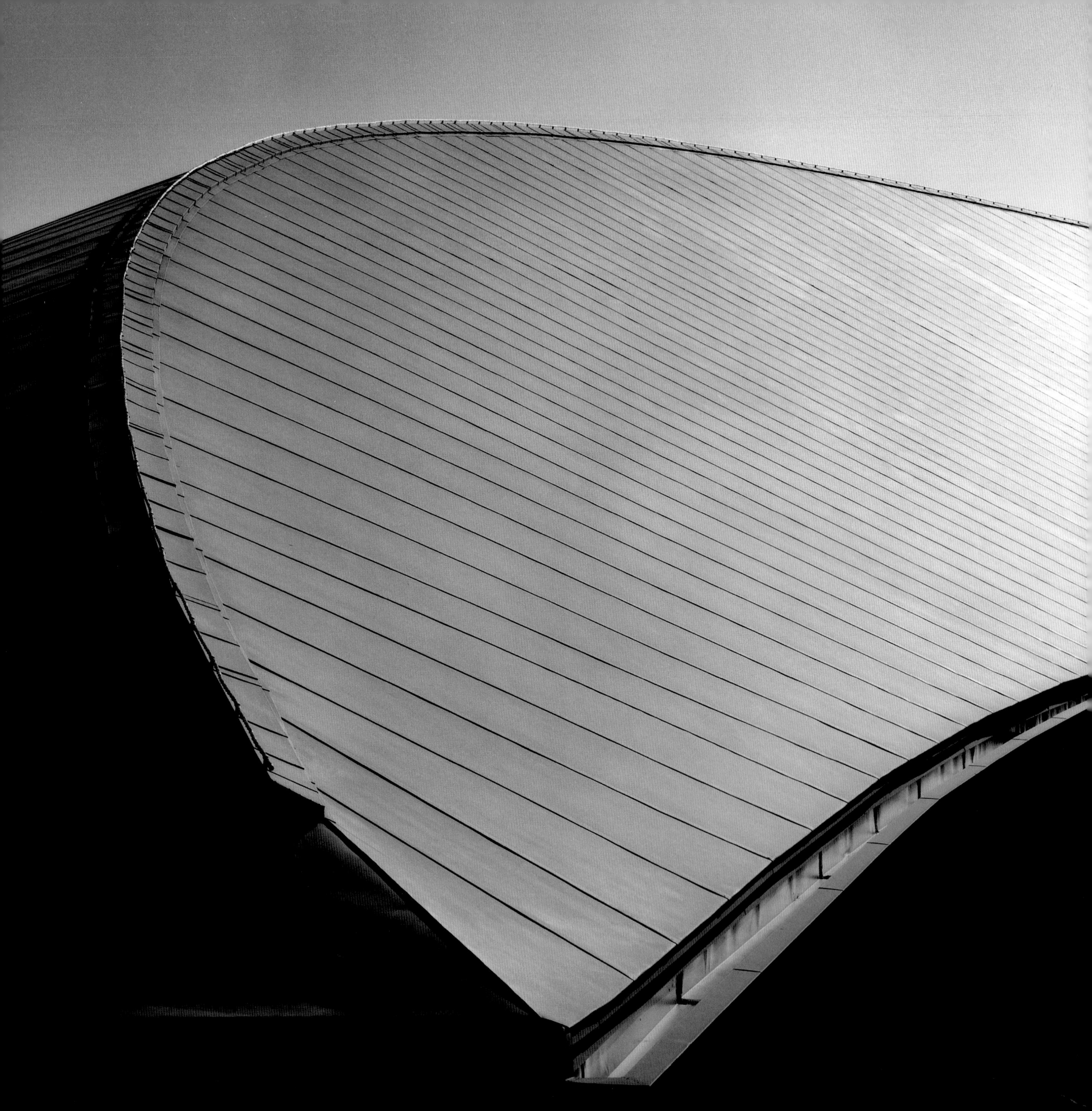

Makino Museum of Plants and People
牧野富太郎記念館

PROCESS
1994-1999

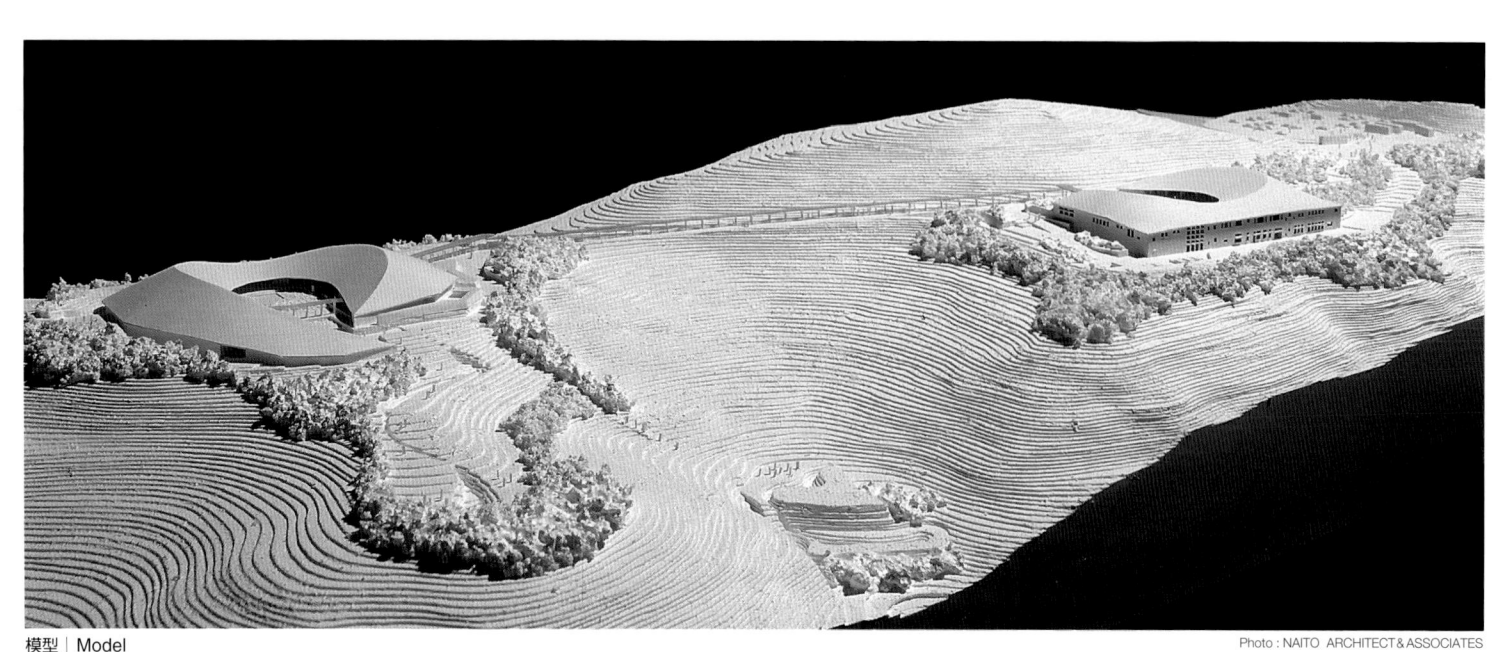

模型 | Model

Photo : NAITO ARCHITECT & ASSOCIATES

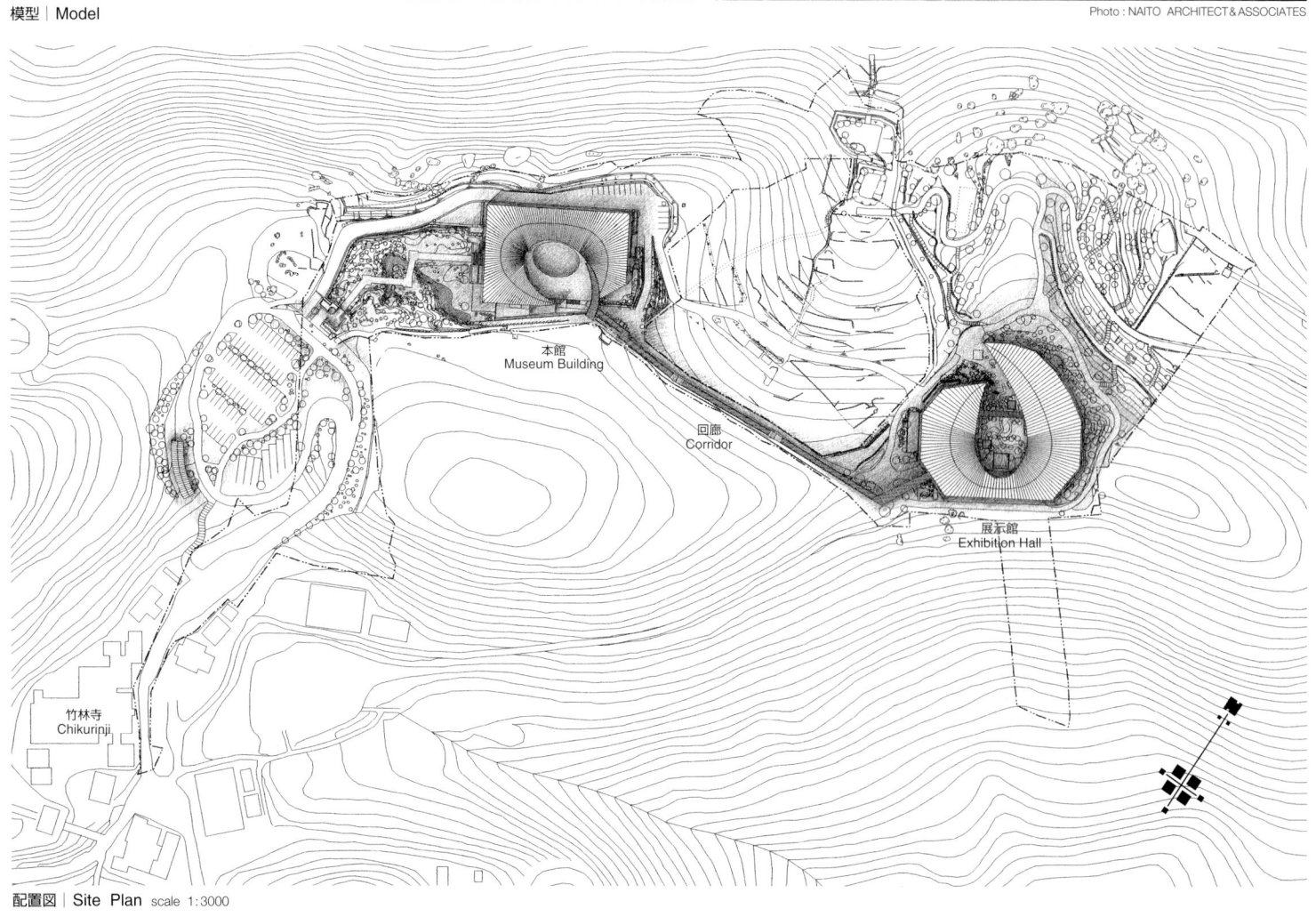

本館 | Museum Building
回廊 | Corridor
展示館 | Exhibition Hall
竹林寺 | Chikurinji

配置図 | Site Plan scale 1:3000

■本館 | Museum Building scale 1:1000

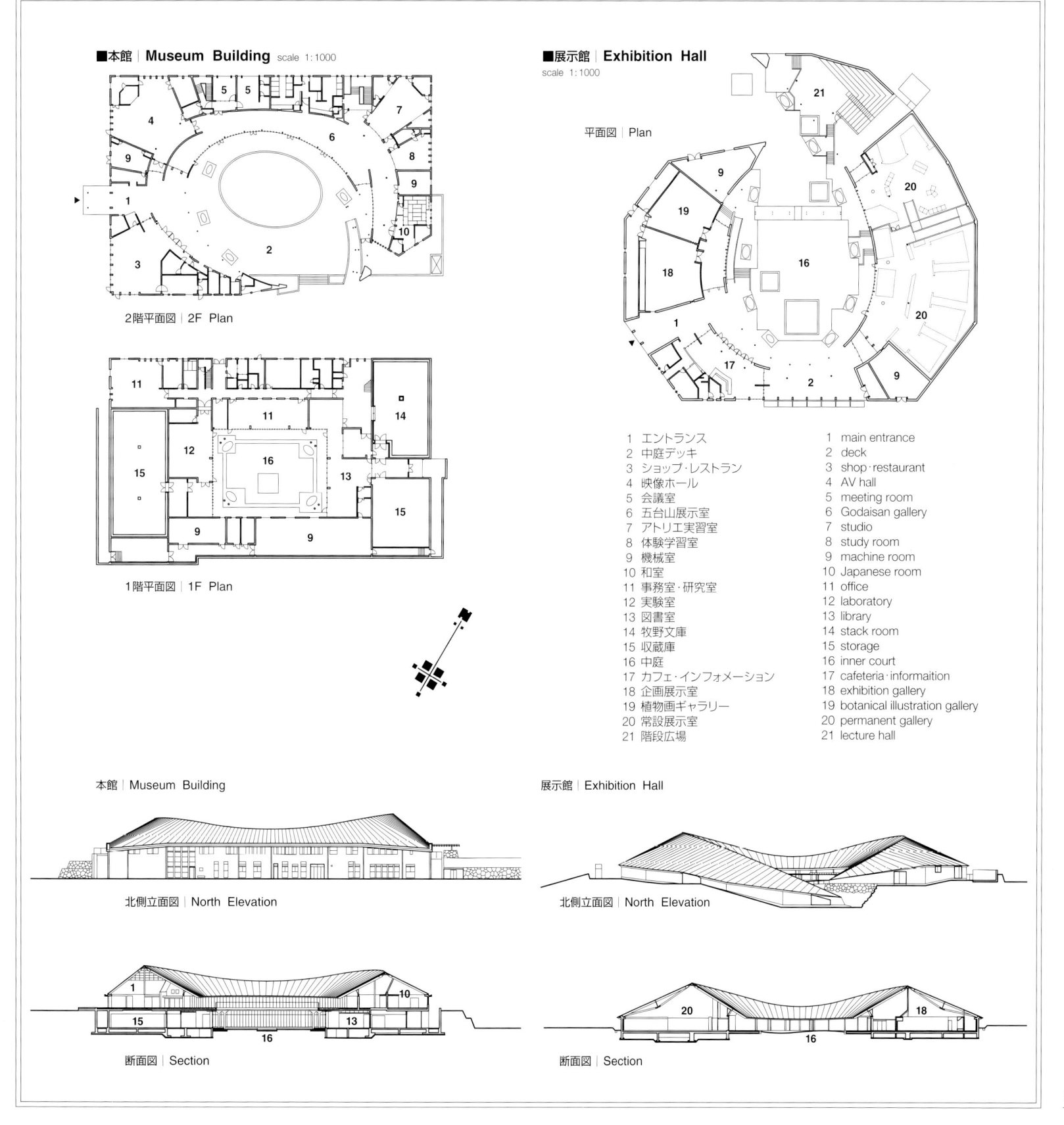

2階平面図 | 2F Plan

1階平面図 | 1F Plan

■展示館 | Exhibition Hall scale 1:1000

平面図 | Plan

1	エントランス	1	main entrance
2	中庭デッキ	2	deck
3	ショップ・レストラン	3	shop・restaurant
4	映像ホール	4	AV hall
5	会議室	5	meeting room
6	五台山展示室	6	Godaisan gallery
7	アトリエ実習室	7	studio
8	体験学習室	8	study room
9	機械室	9	machine room
10	和室	10	Japanese room
11	事務室・研究室	11	office
12	実験室	12	laboratory
13	図書室	13	library
14	牧野文庫	14	stack room
15	収蔵庫	15	storage
16	中庭	16	inner court
17	カフェ・インフォメーション	17	cafeteria・informaition
18	企画展示室	18	exhibition gallery
19	植物画ギャラリー	19	botanical illustration gallery
20	常設展示室	20	permanent gallery
21	階段広場	21	lecture hall

本館 | Museum Building

北側立面図 | North Elevation

断面図 | Section

展示館 | Exhibition Hall

北側立面図 | North Elevation

断面図 | Section

高知県は全国有数の林産県であることから，木造の建物とすることが求められた。植物園の建物であること，我が国の植物学の基を築いた碩学牧野富太郎を顕彰する意味でも，木造の建物が良いのではないか，ということから設計が始まった。複雑な土地所有のために，管理研究部門と展示部門に建物を二つに分け，これらを約170mの回廊で結ぶ分棟配置をとった。歴史的に重要な山である五台山の地形を可能な限り残しながら，7300m²の建物を樹木の高さを超えないように配した。外周をRCで固め，直径約35cmと26cmの鋼管を棟と軒に流し，それに集成材の梁を掛け渡している。422本の集成材の梁は，常に変化する屋根面に合わせているので，すべて長さも角度もジョイントの接続の仕方も違う。棟の頂部を走る鋼管と集成材の梁とをつなぐジョイントには鋳物を使って，木材と鋼材のより合理的な接合を画ると共に，ある程度の角度の変異にはジョイント自身で対応し得るようなディテールを作った。また，風洞実験を行い，200年周期の台風に対するシミュレーションを行った。この結果，屋根の一部に1t/m²を超える風の負圧が算出された。この数値をもとに架構を修正し，屋根の材料や下地のディテールを決めた。

■

　A building of wood construction was desired, as would befit the character of Kochi Prefecture, a major Japanese timber producing region. This provided the point of departure for design, along with the fact that a wooden building felt appropriate for a botanical garden, especially one that commemorates Dr. Tomitaro Makino, the eminent scholar and father of Japanese botany. Because of complex land ownership, the building would be split in two volumes connected by a 170m corridor — one for laboratory research and the other for a museum and gallery. While respecting as much as possible the land form of Mt. Godai, an historically important mountain, we situated the 7,300 square-meter building so that it would not stand taller than the surrounding trees. Enclosing its circumference with an RC wall, we ran steel pipe of roughly 35cm- and 26cm-diameter along the ridge and eaves, spanning them with laminated timber roof beams. Since the 422 laminated beams are positioned in response to the continuous change of the roof surface, each differs in length, angle, and method of joint connection. Seeking a more rational means of wood-to-metal attachment, we employed cast metal joints to connect the laminated beams to the steel pipe at the ridge, providing details that allowed some response to angle variation with the joint itself. In wind tunnel tests, we simulated the potential effect of a two-century-class typhoon, determining a wind load of over a ton per square meter for some parts of the roof. Adjusting the building frame based on these calculations, we made decisions concerning roof system materials and groundwork details.

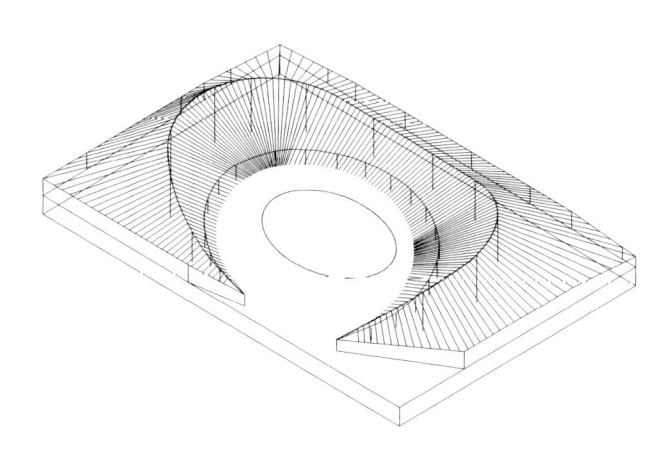

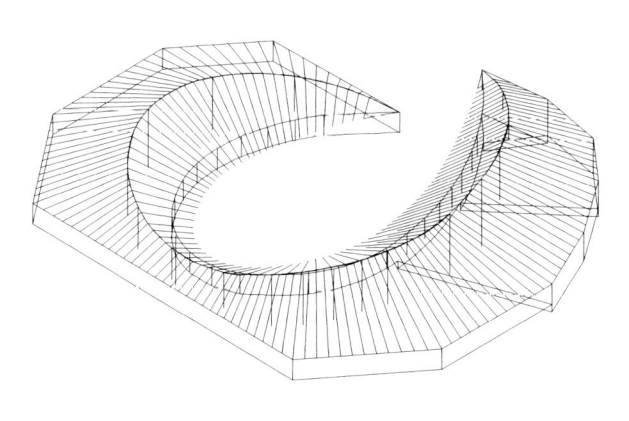

架構モデル | CAD Model

海からの潮風が予測されるため，屋根材には亜鉛とステンレスの複合板を使った。1t/m²の負圧に耐えるため，全面接着貼りとし，端部をビスで細かく止め付ける方法を採った。三次曲面で一枚ずつ寸法の違う屋根材の裁断は，CAD／CAMを使って工場で行われた。高知の雨と風は尋常ではなく，これに対する対応は慎重を極めた。板と板の間は，二重の内樋機能を持つ複雑な断面形状を持ったアルミの引き抜き材を使用し，さらにそれをバックアップする内樋を設け，全部で三重の内樋を作って対応した。天井の仕上げにもなる野地板や間仕切り壁は県産材の杉を使った。通常とは違う赤みの強い木裏を仕上げ面に使用したので，材の色が整い，赤みのある米松の集成材とも相性がよかった。また，外部のデッキにも県産材の檜を使った。こうした複雑で有機的な仕組みを持った建物は，細部の調整が難しい。排煙窓，サッシ，左官，RCの施工精度など，仕上げのディテールが一定の密度を保っているのは，製作・施工を通した最新技術による精度管理と職人の経験値による手作業が絶妙に補完し合った結果にほかならない。

■

　Assuming salt breezes from the ocean, panels of zinc and stainless steel laminated sheet were chosen for the roofing material. In order to withstand a wind load of a ton per square meter, the entire surface of each panel was secured with adhesive and its extremes fastened with screws at small intervals. Fabrication of the panels, each of which formed a cubic curve and had unique measurements, was undertaken using CAD/CAM at the factory. Extra precaution was taken in response to Kochi's uncommon winds and rains by devising a three-channel gutter system between each panel, comprised of a two-channel inner gutter of solid-drawn aluminum and an additional back-up inner gutter. Kochi-grown Japanese cedar (sugi) was used for the roof sheathing, which also provided the final ceiling surface, and for interior partitions. The inner surface of the planks, which have a stronger reddish tone than unusual, was employed on final interior surfaces to obtain uniformity of interior color and agreement with the red-toned laminated timber of Douglas fir. Local Japanese cypress (hinoki) was used for the exterior deck. Obtaining consistency of detail in a building of such a complex, organic organization is difficult. An even consistency was nevertheless achieved in finish details such as vents, sashes, and plastering, something that can only be laid to a superb alliance of the precision of advanced technology with the handiwork of the seasoned craftsman in all stages of production and construction.

詳細図 | Detail scale 1:50

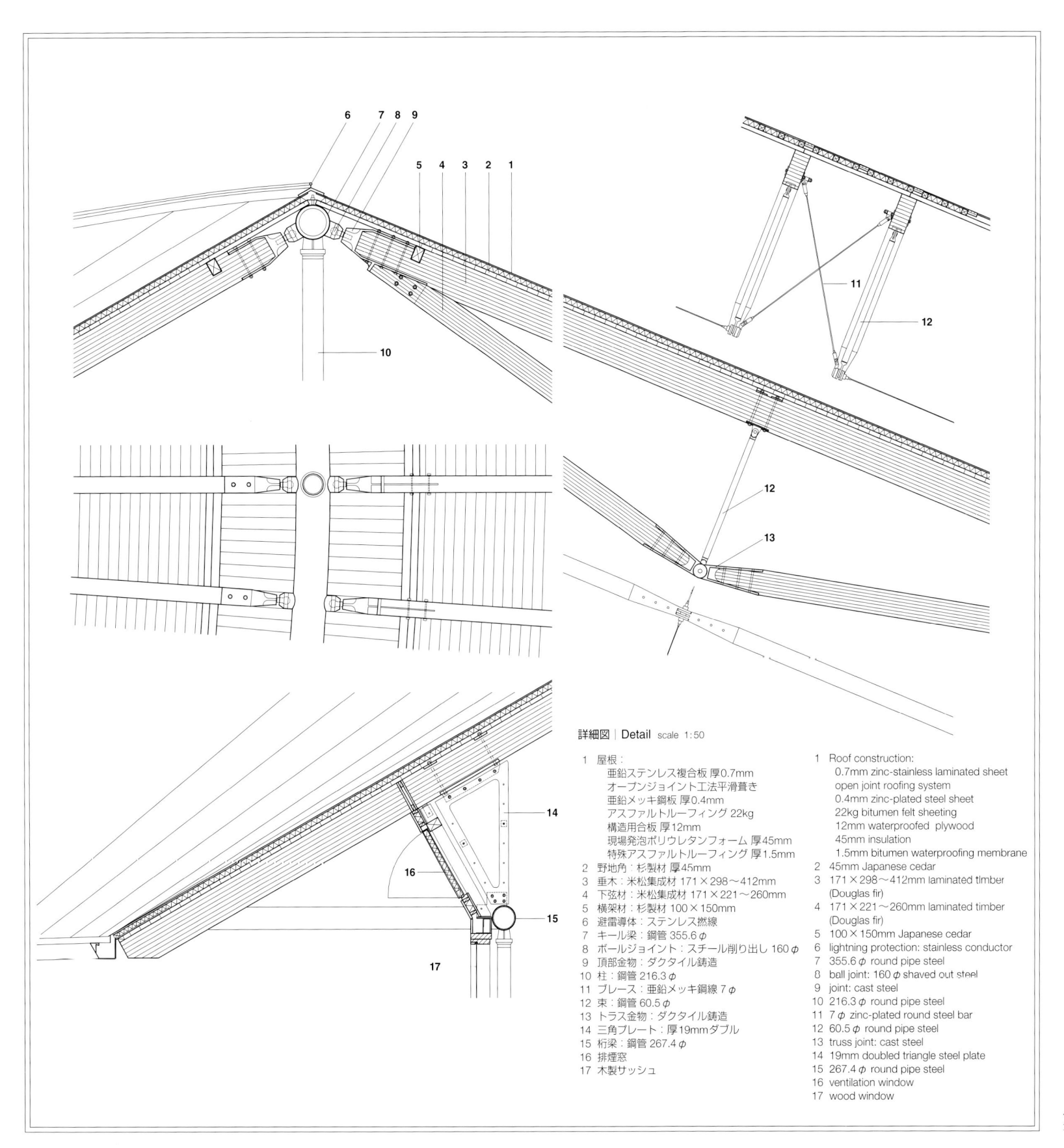

1 屋根：
　　亜鉛ステンレス複合板 厚0.7mm
　　オープンジョイント工法平滑葺き
　　亜鉛メッキ鋼板 厚0.4mm
　　アスファルトルーフィング 22kg
　　構造用合板 厚12mm
　　現場発泡ポリウレタンフォーム 厚45mm
　　特殊アスファルトルーフィング 厚1.5mm
2 野地角：杉製材 厚45mm
3 垂木：米松集成材 171×298〜412mm
4 下弦材：米松集成材 171×221〜260mm
5 横架材：杉製材 100×150mm
6 避雷導体：ステンレス撚線
7 キール梁：鋼管 355.6φ
8 ボールジョイント：スチール削り出し 160φ
9 頂部金物：ダクタイル鋳造
10 柱：鋼管 216.3φ
11 ブレース：亜鉛メッキ鋼線 7φ
12 束：鋼管 60.5φ
13 トラス金物：ダクタイル鋳造
14 三角プレート：厚19mmダブル
15 桁梁：鋼管 267.4φ
16 排煙窓
17 木製サッシ

1 Roof construction:
　　0.7mm zinc-stainless laminated sheet
　　open joint roofing system
　　0.4mm zinc-plated steel sheet
　　22kg bitumen felt sheeting
　　12mm waterproofed plywood
　　45mm insulation
　　1.5mm bitumen waterproofing membrane
2 45mm Japanese cedar
3 171×298〜412mm laminated timber (Douglas fir)
4 171×221〜260mm laminated timber (Douglas fir)
5 100×150mm Japanese cedar
6 lightning protection: stainless conductor
7 355.6φ round pipe steel
8 ball joint: 160φ shaved out steel
9 joint: cast steel
10 216.3φ round pipe steel
11 7φ zinc-plated round steel bar
12 60.5φ round pipe steel
13 truss joint: cast steel
14 19mm doubled triangle steel plate
15 267.4φ round pipe steel
16 ventilation window
17 wood window

伏せる様態

内藤 廣

　海の博物館を発表した頃，「素形」という言葉を使って自分の建築に対する思いと立場を語りました。内省し，検証し，自制するといった建築のつくり方です。この建物は，一見，それに反しているように見えます。ここで試みたのは，元来周囲から孤立しがちな建築の存在を，環境や景観といったより大きな枠組みに積極的に還元していこうとしたことです。自然や地形のダイナミズムを抱え込もうとした結果，形態や空間に動きを胚胎することになったのだと思います。

　われわれは言葉によって思考し，物事を理解します。一方，自然や風土は饒舌ですが，言葉を持ちません。建築の設計という作業は，この狭間にあって，直観によってその目に見えない価値を捉え，誰にでもわかる形で提示することではないか，と考えています。気候，土地の形状，景観の潜在力，時代の様相。建物が建ち上がる前にはおよそ見えにくかった様々な力や動きを顕在化させ，知覚に訴える現実のものとします。その意味で設計は，異なる言葉を行き来する翻訳という作業に似ています。この建物での翻訳の対象は，大きく言えば高知という風土から発する何か，です。この豊かな大地と共にあるような建物，それが五台山の尾根筋にある敷地を最初に訪れたときに抱いたイメージでした。

　普通なら何気なく見過ごしてしまうようなものが，設計に啓示を与えてくれることがあります。数十に及ぶ模型を作り，この敷地にふさわしい建物の在り方を試行錯誤していました。そんなある日，小雨のなか，あれこれ考えながら敷地を歩いている時，森の中に突出した大きな岩の表面に濡れ落ち葉がぴったりと貼り付いているのが目に留まりました。岩肌に浮かび上がったその葉脈の美しさに，何故か見入ってしまいました。同じ時期，ある博物館で，ヒラメの骨の展示に魅入られました。背骨から平たく伸びた骨は，三分の二ほどのところでさらに細かい骨と接続され，いかにも柔らかく優美な美しさを持っていました。

　濡れ落ち葉は有機物である生命が，分解され自然に帰っていく直前の様態です。ヒラメは海底の砂地に伏せて身を隠すため様態です。伏せること，というのがこの二つの対象物の存在の仕方に共通しています。これらを直感的に美しいと思ったことを出発点に建物の在り方を模索して

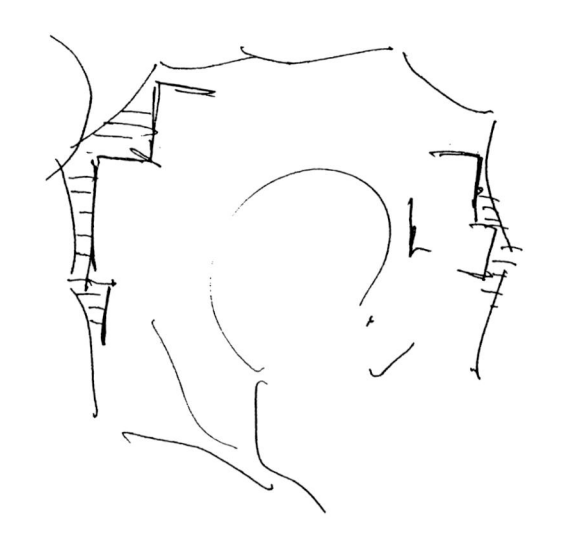

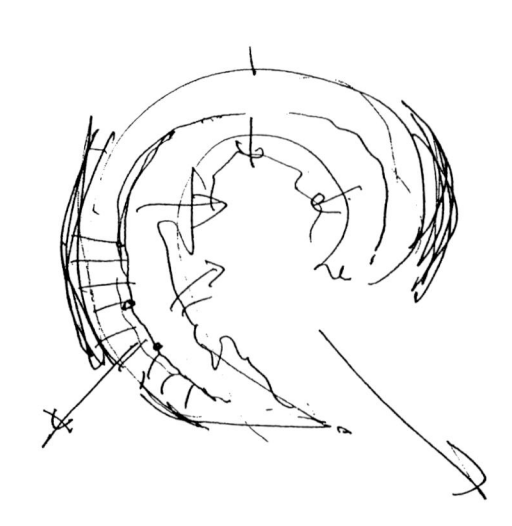

いきました。具体的にそれらの形をトレースしたわけではありません。建築の形式は全く違った次元にあります。しかし，伏せる様態の中に現れる合理性や美しさもあるのだ，と確信できたことが何よりも大きかったように思います。しっかりとした背骨を通して，そこから軸組が拡散していく，それも地形に添った形で柔らかく，フレキシブルなシステムが設定できれば，五台山の地形に対しても，高知の荒々しい自然条件にも適合した建物になるはずです。

　RCの壁で外周を閉じ，地表面の延長のような木造屋根で空間を覆い，深い庇で囲まれた中庭側はすべて開け放す，という構成としました。鋼管のキールを棟とサッシが来るあたりに配し，これらをガイドラインとして架構をまとめ上げました。不連続面や特異な部分が出てこないように棟の位置を平面と調整しながら，連続的で柔らかな屋根面ができるよう，模型を作りながらスタディを重ねました。最終的に出来上がった建物の架構や屋根の形状は，幾何学的な整合性や建築的な整合性を持つには至っていません。その結果，中庭に向かって張り出した屋根の下には，様々な質の半外部の空間が出来ることになりました。平面と屋根とのズレや歪みが面白い空間を創り出しています。建物に風の通り抜ける隙間やゆとりを生んでいるのは，この中庭沿いの半外部の空間です。この空間が，建物の内部と外部の繋ぎ役を果たしています。また，建物全体の動きや空間の流れも，ここを通して表出されています。

　五台山はそれほど大きな山ではありませんが，その山中に入ると独特の雰囲気があります。植物の生命力が違います。特に春先はそれらが発する息吹がそこら中に充満しています。この大気と一体になり，共に環境を育むような建築を目指しました。数年すれば，高知の旺盛な自然に育まれた植物たちは，この建物を覆い隠していくでしょう。建設の傷跡が癒えるにつれ，建物を建ち上げるという宴は終わり，山は元の佇まいに戻っていきます。建物は森の中に埋もれ，中庭とそれを取り囲む屋根に覆われた内部の空間だけが残るはずです。その時，建物という異物は，より大きな枠組みである環境や景観に還元され，切断された時間と和解します。本当の意味で我々が目指した翻訳が完了するのはその時です。

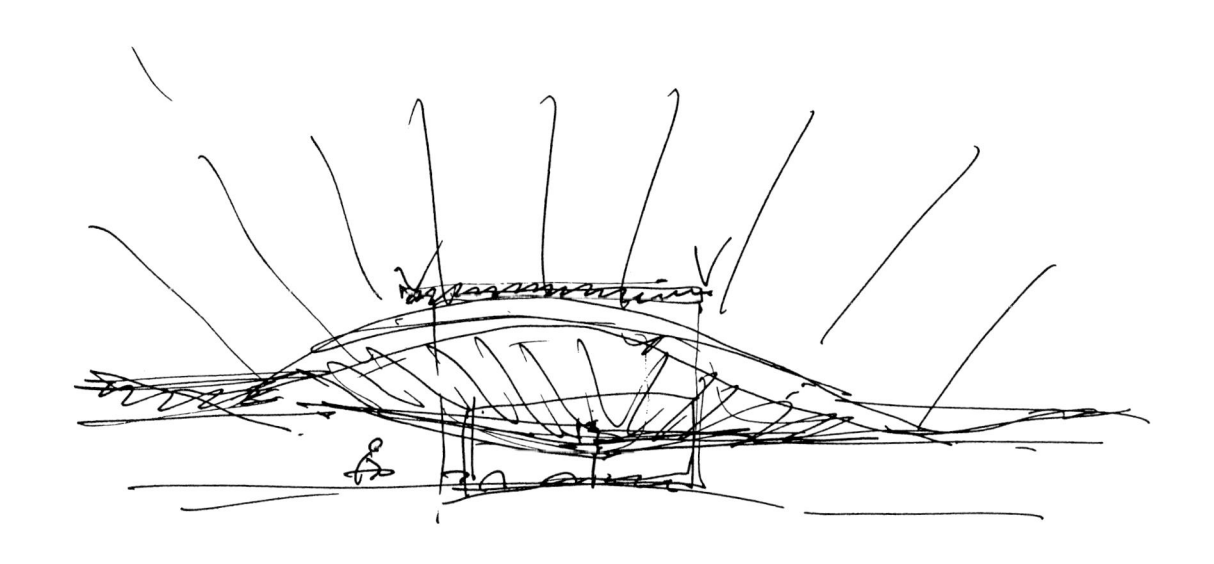

Embracing the Ground

Hiroshi Naito

Around the time I produced my design for the Sea-Folk Museum, I was using the word "protoform" to communicate my perspective on architecture. Architectural creation, I intended, is a process of introspection, verification, and control. The present building will initially appear to contradict that approach. My endeavor this time was an aggressive attempt to restore the presence of architecture, which tends to stand isolate in its surroundings, to the larger frame of its environment and scenery. I sought to embrace the dynamism of nature and topography and, as a consequence, awoke movement in architectural form and space.

Through words we ponder and understand phenomena. Nature, or the land, however, although a garrulous talker, does not possess words. The labor of architectural design, I find, takes place in the interval between. One relies on intuition to capture that invisible quality, then delivers it into a form readily apparent to everyone. Climate, land form, the latent power of scenery, the character of the times. Before a building can stand, hard-to-perceive forces and movements must be raised to prominence and made visible, tactile aspects of reality. In this sense, design is like translation, a labor of shuttling back and forth between different languages. The object of translation in the design labor of this building, broadly speaking, was something emanating from the land in this region known as Kochi. A building that would become one with this abundant landscape — that was the image I received when I first visited the site on a spur of Mt. Godai.

At times, something that one might overlook in ordinary circumstances will present itself as a revelation to the designer. I had created dozens of models as I sought, through trial and error, the appropriate building for the site. Then, one day, as I walked the site in the drizzling rain, my mind rambling from this thought to that, my glance fell on some damp fallen leaves, clinging flat to a large rock that stood in the forest. As I looked, I became absorbed in the beauty of their veins, which stood out clearly against the stone surface. Around the same time, I had been mesmerized by the skeleton of a flatfish on display in a museum. Its bones extended in a flat manner from the spine, interconnecting with a row of more delicate bones two thirds of the way out, in a skeletal structure of grace and supple beauty.

Damp fallen leaves represent a state of organic life on the verge of decomposing and returning to nature. A flatfish skeleton represents a state of self-concealment by lying prone on the sandy ocean floor. Common to both is a state of hugging the ground. Taking my intuited glimpse of their beauty as my point of departure, I began to grope toward the figure of the building. In actual terms, this did not entail the tracing of their forms. Architectural form belongs to an entirely different dimension. Still, my realization of the rationality and beauty existent in a structure that embraces the ground was perhaps more significant than anything. If, by providing a sturdy spine, I could transmit the framework from there and construct a flexible system that responded closely to the land form, a building might result that conformed to the topography of Mt. Godai and the harsh temperament of nature in Kochi.

Toward this end, I enclosed the outer circumference with an RC wall and covered this interior with a wooden roof that appears as an extension of the ground, leaving open under deep eaves the entire side that wraps around a central court. Locating a "keel" of steel pipe at the ridge and at the position of the sash, I used these as my guidelines in organizing the building frame. To create a continuous, flexible roof surface, I made repeated studies and built models constantly, meanwhile adjusting the position of the ridge relative to the plan so as to avoid producing discontinuous surfaces or parts. As a result of these repeated adjustments, neither the building frame nor roof arrived at geometric rationality or architectural rationality in their final form. This enabled me to create semi-exterior spaces of varying character under the projection of roof over the court. The disparity or distortion in the relationship of the plan to the roof has ultimately produced interesting spaces. These semi-exterior spaces along the court provide crevices for the wind to blow through and allow the building to breath. They give interconnection to its interior and exterior, and expression to the movement of the overall building and the flow of its spaces.

Mt. Godai is not a large mountain, but the visitor discovers a unique atmosphere within its environs. The plants have more vitality. In the early spring, the breath they exude fills the air. I sought a building that would respond naturally to this air and conjoin with it to foster the environment. So many years from now, Kochi's lush greenery will likely cover and conceal this building. As the wounds left by construction heal and this extravagant event of building erection ends, the mountain will return to its original state of repose. The building will be buried in the forest, leaving only its central court and interior spaces, encompassed by roof. At that time, this foreign element, a building, will be restored to its larger framework of environment and scenery, finding reconciliation with the flow of time it disrupted. Only then will the translation we set out to achieve truly be complete.

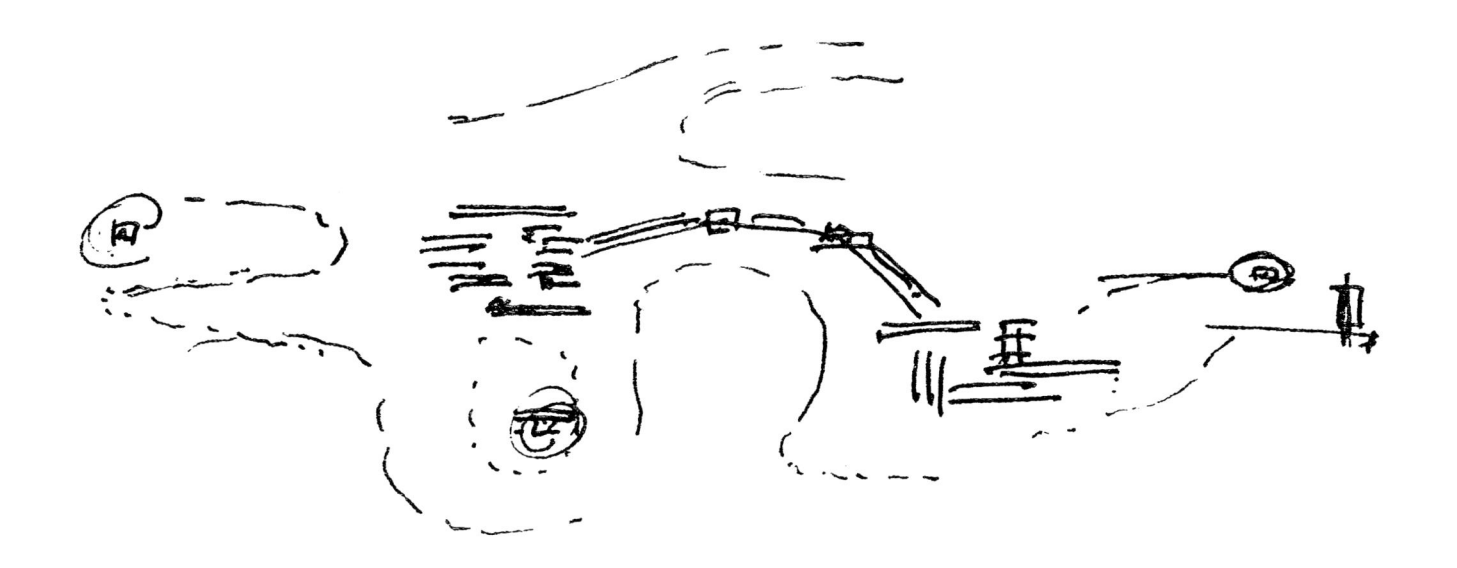

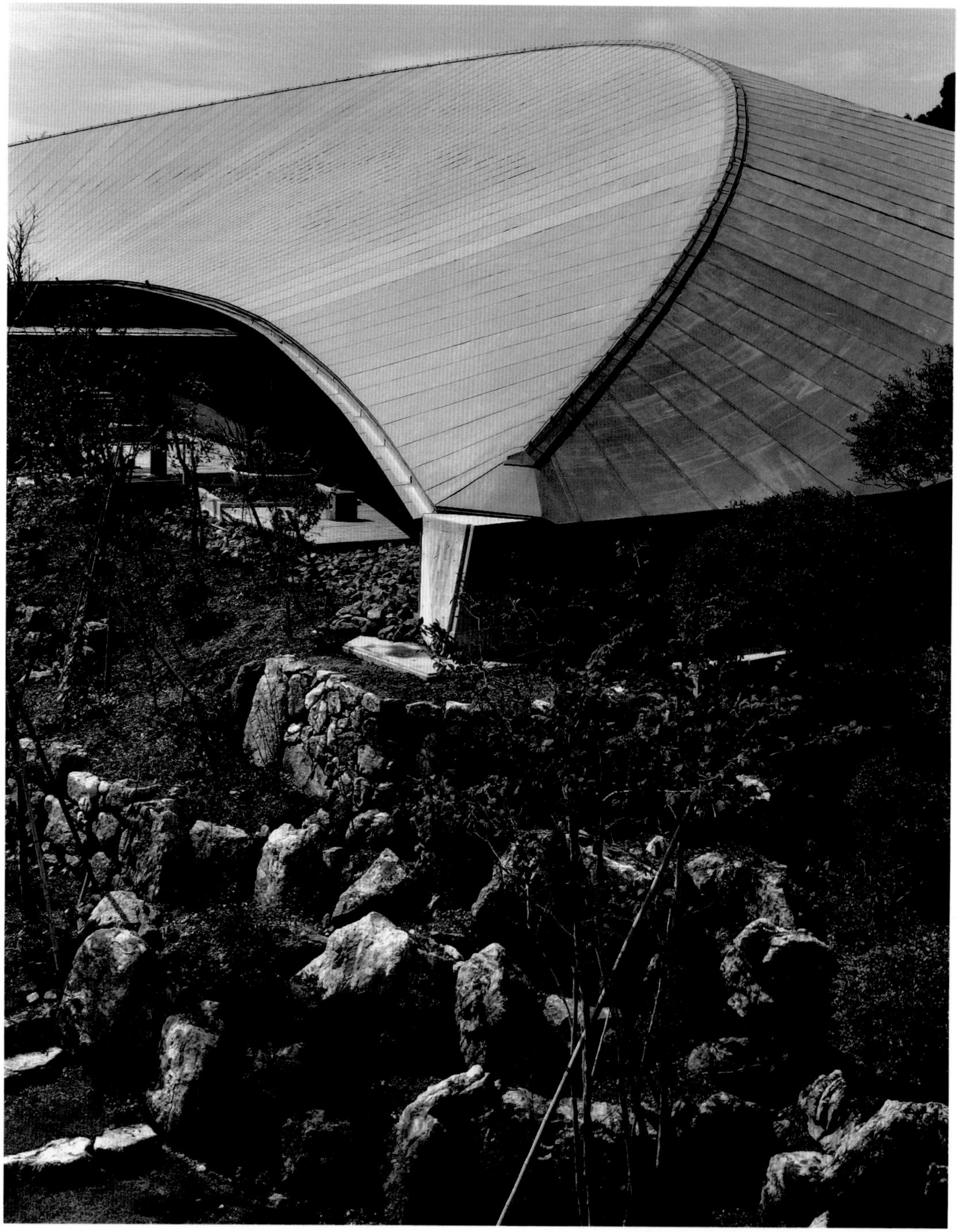

■データ

牧野富太郎記念館

施主	高知県
所在地	高知県高知市五台山4200-6 〒780-8125
主要用途	博物館
設計	内藤廣建築設計事務所
	担当／内藤 廣　川村宣元　神林哲也　高草大次郎
	加藤成明　好川 拓　吉田多津雄　玉田 源
構造	構造設計集団〈SDG〉　担当／渡辺邦夫　アラン・バーデン
	中村由美子　腰原幹雄
設備	明野設備研究所　担当／吉本健二　小川津久雄
風洞実験	風工学研究所　担当／藤井邦雄
ランドスケープ・アドバイザー	ウイン　担当／稲田純一
展示	サザンクロス・スタジオ　担当／里見和彦　明石真子
サイン	南雲デザイン事務所　担当／南雲美恵
中庭・作品	田窪恭治

設計期間	1994年9月ー1996年9月
施工期間	1997年8月ー1999年3月
施工	建築：竹中工務店・香長建設・中勝建設 建設共同企業体 担当／片岡勝
	空調：エルゴテック・アセイ設備 建設共同企業体 担当／森田邦夫
	衛生：四国水道工業 担当／有友伸之
	電気：斉藤電工・相互電設・門田電機商会 建設共同企業体 担当／釣井保広
	浄化槽：日本化工 担当／石神一雄
	エレベータ：フジテック 担当／東光男
	展示：丹青社 担当／安田篤史
	屋根：藤田兼三工業、三井金属鉱業、三洋金属
	集成材：ハマシュウセイ、ダイリツ
	架構金物：旭テック　木工事：ネクストオカモト
	鉄骨工事：川田工業　鉄骨曲げ加工：第一高周波工業
	家具：モリサキ工芸、野本木工所、ヤマサキ工芸
	AV：四国日立ビジネス機器
	木製サッシ：ノルド　外構：藤田建材工業
	造園：石勝エクステリア、日比谷アメニス
	造園協力：第一コンサルタンツ
面積	敷地面積　44,596.30m²
	建築面積　5,683.73m²
	延床面積　7,362.26m²
寸法	最高高さ　13,000mm
	軒高　7,000mm
構造	鉄筋コンクリート造　小屋組：鉄骨造＋集成材
外部仕上げ	屋根　：亜鉛ステンレス複合板 t=0.7mm オープンジョイント工法
	外壁　：アクリル合成樹脂砂壁状吹き付け，コンクリート普通型枠打放し
	開口部：木製サッシ，スチールサッシ，アルミサッシ
	外構　：ウッドデッキ／ヒノキ t=36mm（高知県産），砕石モルタル洗い出し
	植栽　：牧野博士命名樹木
内部仕上げ	**五台山ホール**
	床：タイルカーペット敷
	壁：コンクリート普通型枠打放し
	天井：ベイマツ集成材現し，スギ野地板 t=45mm 張り（高知県産）
	牧野文庫・収蔵庫
	床：ブナ縁甲板 t=15mm 張り（無塗装）
	壁：スギ板 t=15mm 目透かし張り（高知県産），無機質調湿板
	天井：スギ板 t=9mm 張り（高知県産）
	常設展示室
	床：タイルカーペット敷，ブナ縁甲板 t=20mm 張り
	壁：スギ板 t=18mm 張り（高知県産），コンクリート普通型枠打放し
	展示壁／土佐漆喰塗り
	天井：ベイマツ集成材現し，スギ野地板 t=45mm 張り（高知県産）
	植物画ギャラリー
	床：ブナ縁甲板 t=20mm 張り
	壁：スギ板 t=18mm 張り（高知県産），草木染紙布貼り
	天井：ベイマツ集成材現し，スギ野地板 t=45mm 張り（高知県産）

■DATA

Makino Museum of Plants and People

Client	Kochi Prefecture
Address	4200-6, Godaisan Kochi-shi Kochi 780-8125
Use	Museum
Architectural Design	Naito Architect & Associates / Hiroshi Naito, Nobuharu Kawamura, Tetsuya Kambayashi, Daijirou Takakusa, Nariaki Kato, Taku Yoshikawa, Tatsuo Yoshida, Gen Tamada
Structural Engineering	Structural Design Group Co.,Ltd. / Kunio Watanabe, Alan Burden, Yumiko Nakamura, Mikio Koshihara
Engineering	Akeno Engineering Consultants Inc. / Kenji Yoshimoto, Tsukuo Ogawa
Wind tunnel test	Wind Engineering Institute Co.,LTD. / Kunio Fujii
Landscape Adviser	WIN Landscape Architects & Planners / Junichi Inada
Display Design	Southern Cross Studio / Kazuhiko Satomi, Mako Akashi
Sign	Nagumo Design Office / Mie Nagumo
Art work	Kyoji Takubo

Design Period	Sep.1994－Sep.1996
Construction Period	Aug.1997－Mar.1999
Contractor	General Contractor : Takenaka Corporation, Kacho Construction, Nakakatsu Construction, JV / Masaru Kataoka
	HVAC : Ergotech, Asei, JV / Kunio Morita
	Plumbing : Shikoku Suido / Nobuyuki Aritomo
	Electric Services : Saitec, Sougo, Kadota, JV / Yasuhiro Tsurii
	Purification Plant : Nihon Kakoh / Kazuo Ishigami
	Elevator : Fujitec / Mitsuo Higashi
	Display : Tanseisha / Atsushi Yasuda
Area	Site Area　44,596.30m²
	Building Area　5,683.73m²
	Total Floor Area　7,362.26m²
Dimension	Maximum-Height　13,000mm
	Eaves Height　7,000mm
Structure	Reinforced concrete
	Roof frame : Steel+Laminated timber (Douglas fir)
Exterior	Roof　：Zinc-stainless laminated sheet (Open joint roofing system)
	Wall　：Acrylic emulsion coating, Exposed reinforced concrete
	Wood deck : Japanese cypress t=36mm (Locally grown)
	Plants: Plants named by Dr.Makino
Interior	**Godaisan gallery**
	Floor : Carpet tile
	Wall : Exposed reinforced concrete
	Ceiling : Laminated timber (Douglas fir)
	Japanese cedar t=45mm (Locally grown)
	Stack room, Storage
	Floor : Japanese beech strip flooring t=15mm
	Wall : Japanese cedar t=15mm (Locally grown)
	Ceiling : Japanese cedar t=9mm (Locally grown)
	Permanent gallery
	Floor : Carpet tile, Japanese beech strip flooring t=20mm
	Wall : Japanese cedar t=18mm (Locally grown)
	Exposed reinforced concrete
	Exhibition wall: Plaster (Tosa-sikkui)
	Ceiling : Laminated timber (Douglas fir)
	Japanese cedar t=45mm (Locally grown)
	Botanical illustration gallery
	Floor : Japanese beech strip flooring t=20mm
	Wall : Japanese cedar t=18mm (Locally grown)
	Plants dyed wallpaper
	Ceiling : Laminated timber (Douglas fir)
	Japanese cedar t=45mm (Locally grown)

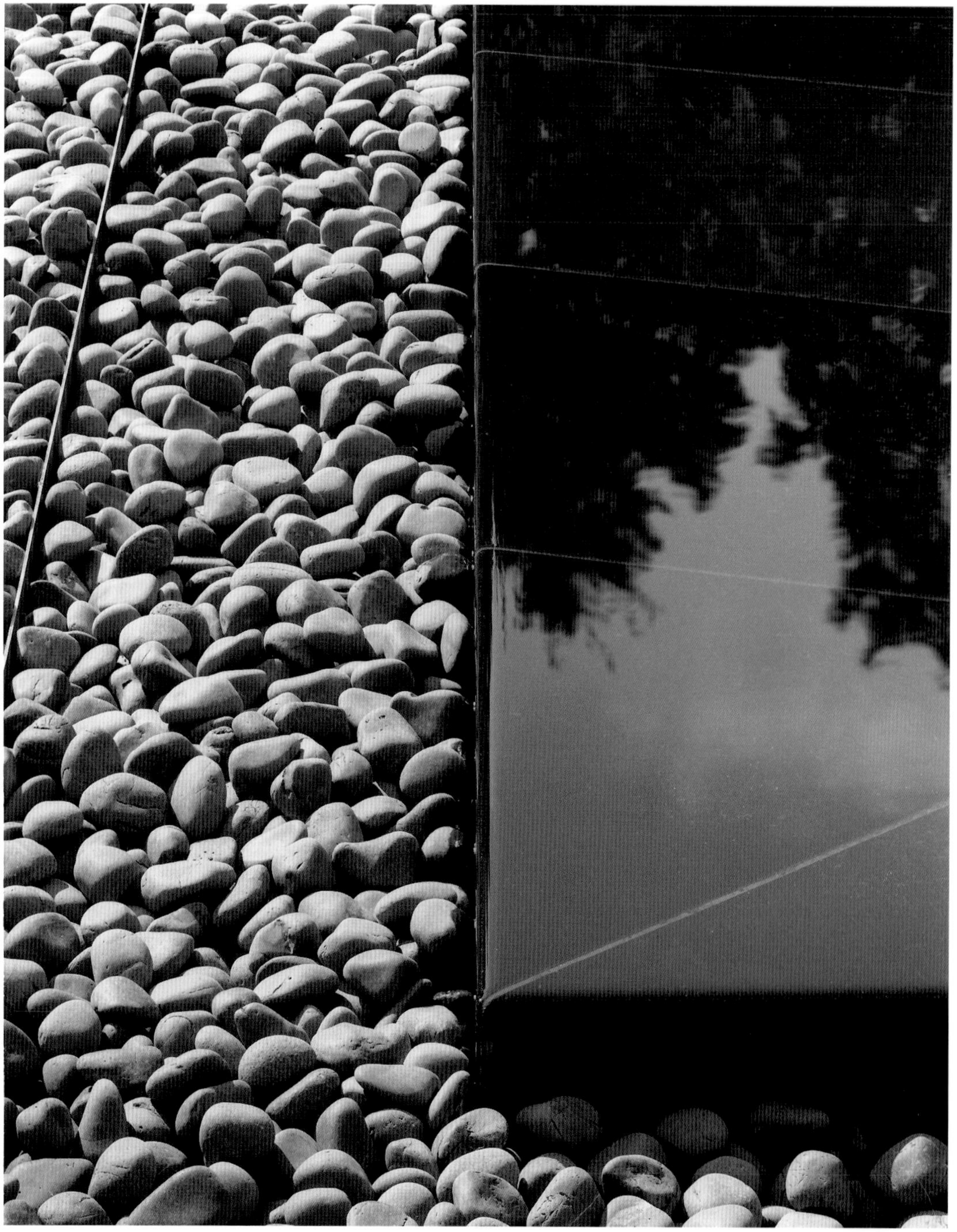

Fuji RINRI Seminar House
倫理研究所富士高原研修所

PROCESS
1998-2001

模型 | Model

Photo : NAITO ARCHITECT & ASSOCIATES

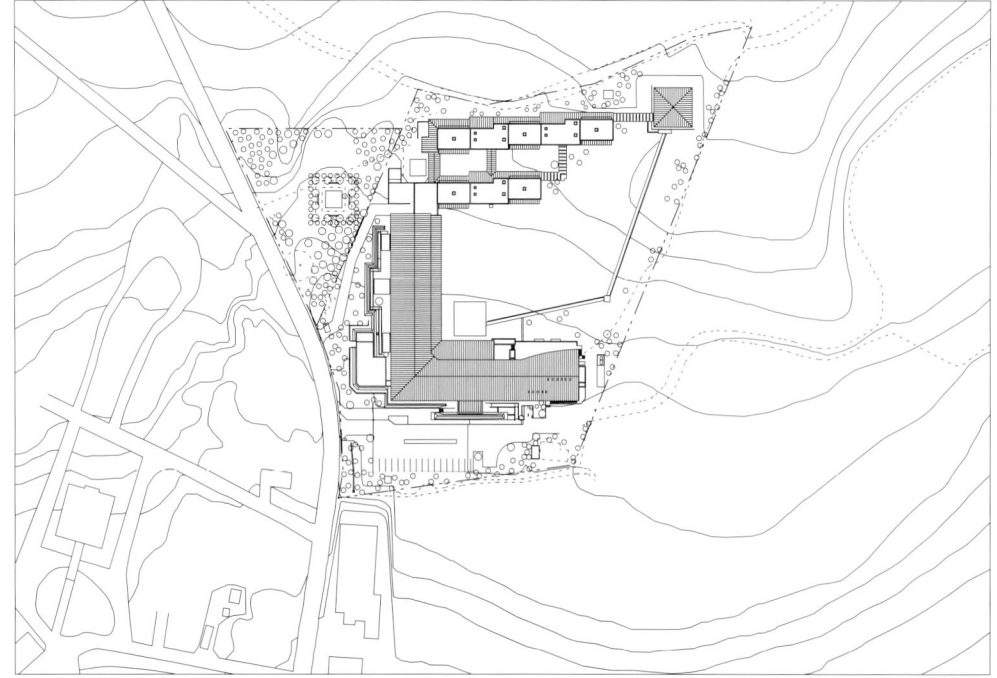

配置図 | Site Plan scale 1:3000

1階平面図 | 1F Plan scale 1:1600

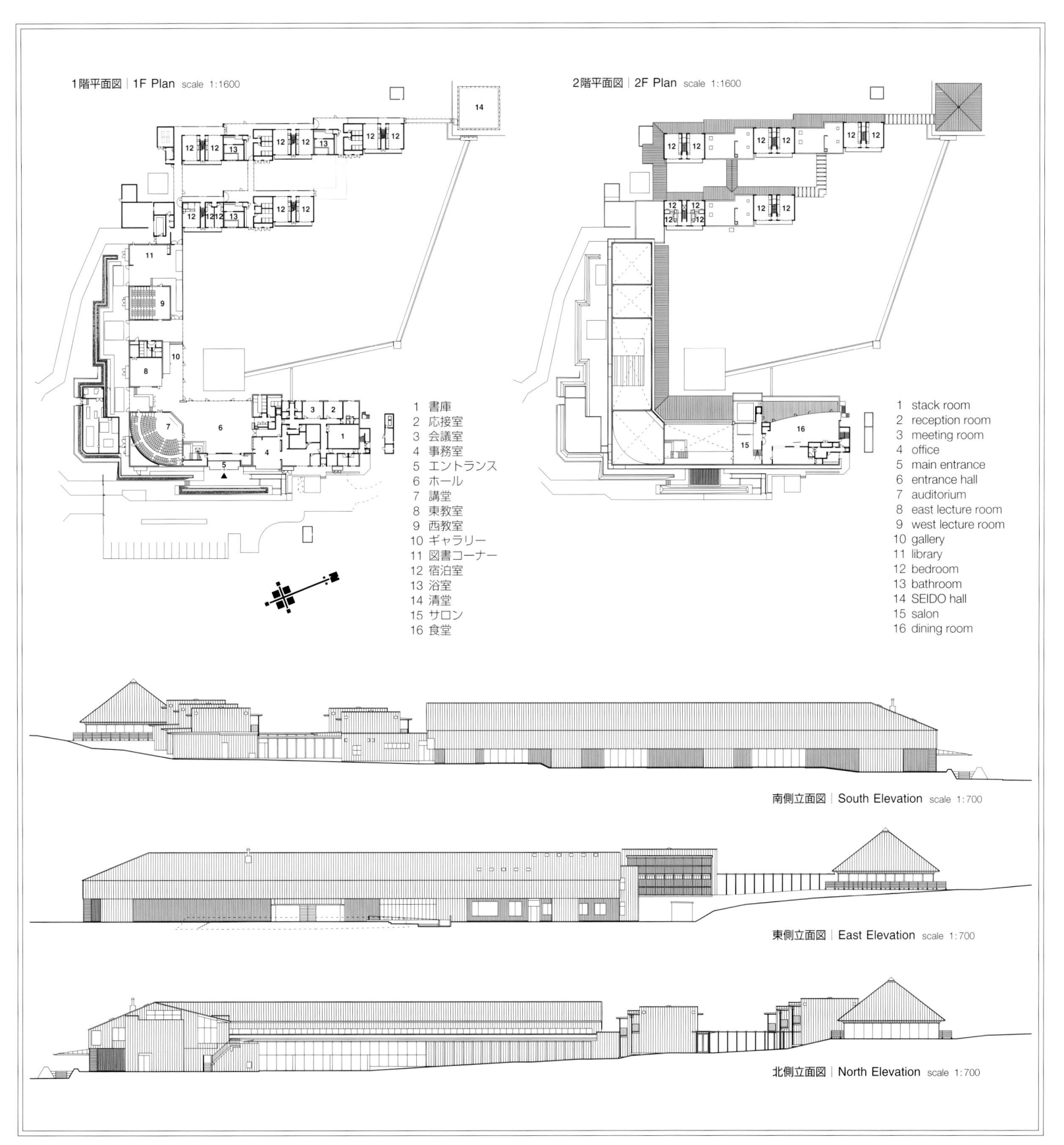

2階平面図 | 2F Plan scale 1:1600

1 書庫
2 応接室
3 会議室
4 事務室
5 エントランス
6 ホール
7 講堂
8 東教室
9 西教室
10 ギャラリー
11 図書コーナー
12 宿泊室
13 浴室
14 清堂
15 サロン
16 食堂

1 stack room
2 reception room
3 meeting room
4 office
5 main entrance
6 entrance hall
7 auditorium
8 east lecture room
9 west lecture room
10 gallery
11 library
12 bedroom
13 bathroom
14 SEIDO hall
15 salon
16 dining room

南側立面図 | South Elevation scale 1:700

東側立面図 | East Elevation scale 1:700

北側立面図 | North Elevation scale 1:700

■集成材の加工について
　これまで幾つもの木造の建物を作ってきた。その都度，ジョイント部に工夫を凝らしてきたが，なかなか満足がいくものが出来なかった。かねてより，木と木が直接力を伝えあうジョイントが出来ないかを模索してきた。この建物では構造家の岡村仁さんとこのことに挑戦することが出来た。在来木造の仕口の中にある木の性質に対するアイデアを，現代的な構造計算技術と加工技術を使って活かす事はできないか，というのが取り組みの内容だ。木の繊維と繊維が直接幾つかの力を伝え合うようにするためには，ジョイントの形状は立体パズルのような複雑なものになる。コンピュータのデータを工作機械に直結させて切り出すCAD／CAMのシステムをフルに活用して部材を製作することにした。大教室，清堂など，この施設の要となる空間では，この仕組みを最大限活用して，建物内の有機的な力の流れを視覚化することができた。仕口の形状を決定する際，木の乾燥縮みの具合や微妙な所は，経験のある人たちの知恵を活かしたことは言うまでもない。

■Laminated Timber Beam Fabrication
　I have designed a number of wood buildings. In each case, I have applied considerable thought and contrivance in the design of the joint, but never quite to my satisfaction. For some time, I had been seeking some way to devise a joint whose members would directly counteract each other with their force. In this building, I could attempt to design such a joint, together with structural engineer Satoshi Okamura. In substance, our endeavor was to introduce traditional Japanese joinery, with its reliance on the natural strengths of the wood, to contemporary structural calculation and fabrication technology. So that the wood members would directly exert force on each other, in a direction parallel to their grain, it was necessary to give the joint a very elaborate form, like a child's puzzle of interlocking wood pieces. In fabricating the members, we fully employed a CAD/CAM system that inputs computer data directly into the shop machine to cut the joints. In the main utility spaces of this facility, such as the large classroom and SEIDO hall, we used this construction to maximum application in giving visual expression to the variations of organic strength in the building's interior. Needless to say, when determining the shape of each connection, we applied the knowledge of seasoned experts with regard to the timber's potential for drying shrinkage and other difficult factors.

■熱押出形鋼について
　中庭に面するギャラリーの部分は，大きなスパン割りが要求される所で，PCを使ってポストテンションをかけて組み上げている。高さ5mの中庭側の開口部は，鉛直力だけ支えればよいので，PCのピースごとに細かい柱を並べることにした。敷地は零下20度まで気温が下がることもある酷寒冷地なので，ヒートブリッジを嫌って木製サッシでペアガラスを用いることにしていた。木製サッシなので，風に対して抵抗するにはどうしてもサッシマリオンが必要になってくる。検討を重ねるうちに，サッシマリオンとPCを支える柱のサイズが近いことに気付いた。ならば一緒にすることが出来ないか，それも最小限の部材構成で，ということから，数量さえ揃えば自由に断面を設計できる熱押出形鋼を使ってはどうか，ということになった。熱押出形鋼を柱として使うのは初めてのことだ。サッシがダイレクトに納まるよう，また，柱としてのバランスや製造プロセスなども検討して，十字形の断面を設計した。

■Hot Extruded Steel Columns
　The gallery, a space which looks out on the central court, required a long span. I therefore employed precast concrete planks with post-tensioning. The five-meter-high openings along the central court needed to be supported only by vertical force, so I established a row of slender columns, one below each precast concrete plank. The building site is in a region of severe cold, where temperatures fall to 20 degrees below zero centigrade, so to prevent heat transfer, I chose to employ pair glass with a wood sash. With a wood sash, structural mullions are inevitably necessary to provide resistance to wind loads. While studying the matter, I noticed that the sash mullions were similar in size to the columns supporting the precast concrete planks. This being so, I wondered if I could not combine them, and moreover, using a minimum of constituent parts. Here, it occurred to me that I might use hot extruded steel — a material offering freedom in the design of the column section — if I simply employed such columns in sufficient quantity. It would likely be the first use of hot extruded steel in a structural column. After investigating a balanced column design and column production, I designed a cross-shaped section that enables direct integration of the sash.

■発熱ガラスについて

　中庭に面した開口部にペリメータゾーンを形成するために，発熱ガラスを使った。これはガラスの表面に金属膜を0.3ミクロンの厚さで蒸着させ，微電流を通すことによって発熱させるものだ。これまで実験施設での使用に留まっていたものだが，この建物が置かれている気象条件やここの部分の開口部の在り方を考えると，この方法が最適だと考えた。このガラスを使うことによって，開口面のディテールを格段とスッキリさせることが出来た。

■ライフラインについて

　建物の中で，設備はもっとも消耗が速く，そして人間と密接な関係を持っている。この建物での試みの特徴は，電気・空調のライフラインを外壁ファサードの中に明確に設けたことだ。この部分に設備的な幹線が集中しているのでメンテナンスがしやすい。また，人が長時間滞留する教室で使われた空気を廊下や床下で使い，最後にライフラインの中を通して排気し，バッファゾーンとして有効利用している。いわば，熱と空気の使いまわしが，この建物の空気環境の特徴になっている。

■Thermal Glass

　In forming a perimeter zone along the openings facing on the central court, I used thermal glass. This glass features a metal membrane of 0.3-micron thickness bonded on its surface that generates heat by means of a slight electric current. Until now, its use has been restricted to experimental facilities, but considering the climatic conditions of the building site and the positioning of the openings, this method was well suited, I felt. The use of this glass allowed me to greatly simplify window detail.

■Lifeline

　Of a building's parts, its mechanical and electric systems have the shortest life and the most direct bearing on the comfort of users. In this building, I incorporated a distinct electricity and air-conditioning lifeline in the exterior facade. The main distribution lines for the mechanical and electric systems are concentrated in this lifeline, allowing easy maintenance. Air from the classrooms, where people spend long hours, is used in hallways and under floors, and ultimately passed through the lifeline for expulsion. Thus, the lifeline is also effectively utilized as a buffer zone. In a sense, the circulation of heat and air is the special feature of this building's air environment.

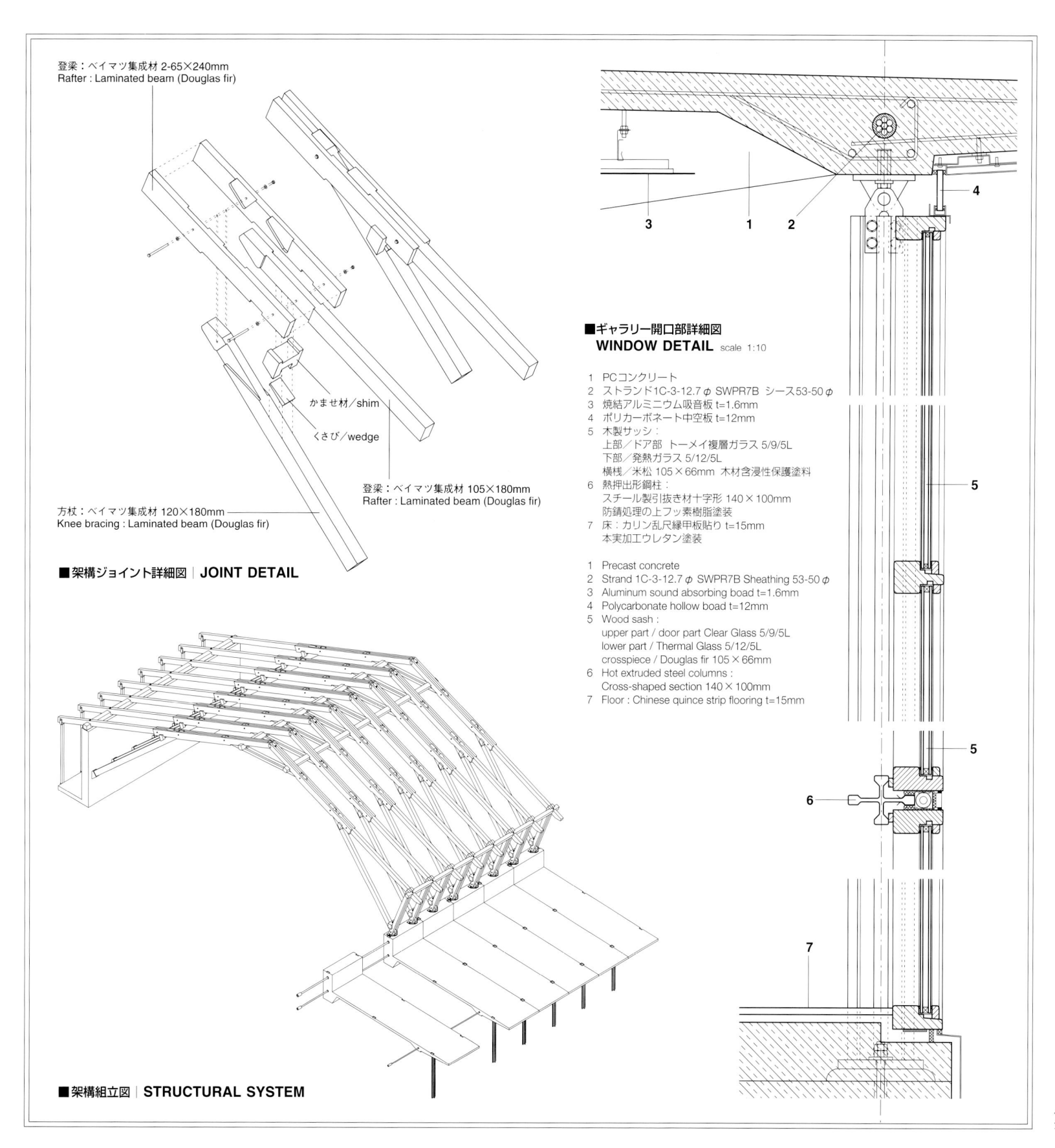

登梁：ベイマツ集成材 2-65×240mm
Rafter : Laminated beam (Douglas fir)

かませ材／shim
くさび／wedge

登梁：ベイマツ集成材 105×180mm
Rafter : Laminated beam (Douglas fir)

方杖：ベイマツ集成材 120×180mm
Knee bracing : Laminated beam (Douglas fir)

■架構ジョイント詳細図｜JOINT DETAIL

■架構組立図｜STRUCTURAL SYSTEM

■ギャラリー開口部詳細図
WINDOW DETAIL scale 1:10

1　PCコンクリート
2　ストランド1C-3-12.7φ　SWPR7B　シース53-50φ
3　焼結アルミニウム吸音板 t=1.6mm
4　ポリカーボネート中空板 t=12mm
5　木製サッシ：
　　上部／ドア部　トーメイ複層ガラス 5/9/5L
　　下部／発熱ガラス 5/12/5L
　　横桟／米松 105×66mm 木材含浸性保護塗料
6　熱押出形鋼柱：
　　スチール製引抜き材十字形 140×100mm
　　防錆処理の上フッ素樹脂塗装
7　床：カリン乱尺縁甲板貼り t=15mm
　　本実加工ウレタン塗装

1　Precast concrete
2　Strand 1C-3-12.7φ SWPR7B Sheathing 53-50φ
3　Aluminum sound absorbing boad t=1.6mm
4　Polycarbonate hollow boad t=12mm
5　Wood sash :
　　upper part / door part Clear Glass 5/9/5L
　　lower part / Thermal Glass 5/12/5L
　　crosspiece / Douglas fir 105×66mm
6　Hot extruded steel columns :
　　Cross-shaped section 140×100mm
7　Floor : Chinese quince strip flooring t=15mm

■ 断面図 | Section scale 1:700

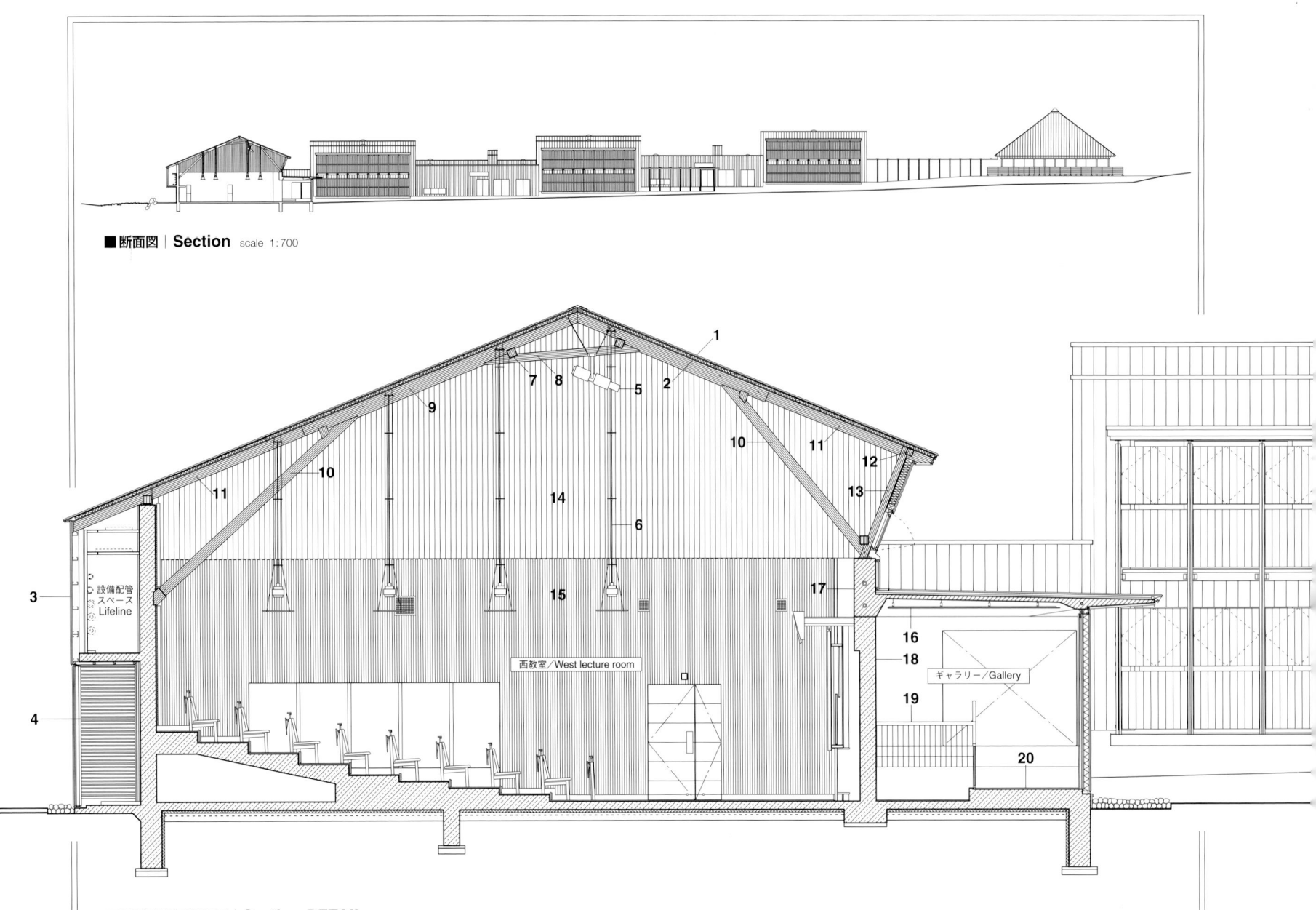

■ 西教室断面詳細図 | Section DETAIL scale 1:100

1 屋根：
　ガルバリウムフッ素樹脂塗装鋼板 t=0.5mm
　一般工法竪はぜ葺き＠225mm
2 天井：杉縁甲板難燃（一部準不燃）処理材
　　t=15mm w=90mm 本実加工
3 外壁：
　ガルバリウムフッ素樹脂塗装鋼板 t=0.4mm
　一般工法竪はぜ葺き ＠225mm
4 外壁：
　米松無垢材竪羽目張り t=33mm w=75mm
　スクリューボルト止め チークオイル塗布
5 デリベントファン
6 吊り下げ照明
7 棟木：米松集成材 150×150mm
8 つなぎ材：米松集成材 105×150mm
9 登梁：米松集成材 2-65×240mm
10 方杖：米松集成材 120×180mm
11 登梁：米松集成材 105×180mm
12 軒桁：米松集成材 150×150mm
13 束：米松集成材 2-75×120mm
14 妻壁仕上：
　杉縁甲板竪羽目張り t=15mm w=90mm
　本実加工 難燃処理
15 壁仕上：
　ルーバー竪張り杉 60×45mm 難燃処理
　亜鉛メッキボルト止め（穴は同材で埋木）
　ガラスクロス貼グラスウール吸音板 t=50mm
16 天井仕上：
　焼結アルミニウム吸音板 突付け張り
　t=1.6mm 接着張り 一部PCコンクリート顕し
17 PCコンクリート顕し
18 コンクリート打放し（杉板本実型枠）
19 手摺：ナラ集成材 62×40mm上部曲面仕上げ
20 床仕上：ロールカーペット張り t=7.5mm

1 Roof construction:
　Galvalume metal standing seam roofing
　t=0.5mm @225mm
2 Ceiling:
　Japanese cedar 15×90mm
　(tongue and groove)
3 Exterior wall:
　Galvalume metal standing seam cladding
　t=0.4mm @225mm
4 Exterior wall:
　Douglas fir 38×75mm fastened with stainless
　screw bolt
5 Axial fan
6 Pendant lamp (special order)
7 Ridge:
　Laminated timber (Douglas fir) 150×150mm
8 Bottom chord:
　Laminated timber (Douglas fir) 105×150mm
9 Rafter:
　Laminated timber (Douglas fir) 2-65×240mm
10 Knee bracing:
　Laminated timber (Douglas fir) 120×180mm
11 Rafter:
　Laminated timber (Douglas fir) 105×180mm
12 Lateral beam:
　Laminated timber (Douglas fir) 150×150mm
13 Web:
　Laminated timber (Douglas fir) 2-75×120mm
14 Laminated timber (Douglas fir) 15×90mm (tongue and groove)
15 Japanese cedar louver 45×60mm
16 Aluminum sound absorbing boad t=1.6mm,
　Exposed precast concrete
17 Exposed precast concrete
18 Exposed reinforced concrete
　(formwork:Japanese cedar)
19 Handrail:
　Laminated timber (Japanese oak) 62×40mm
20 Cut pile carpet t=7.5mm

217

「形」から「仕組み」へ
内藤　廣

　この建物の設計の依頼を受けたのは，牧野富太郎記念館の設計を終えた頃でした。この記念館では，要求されている建物の機能，高知という風土，五台山という山の地形，牧野富太郎という人の自然観，といった様々な要素を，建物の中で一挙に昇華しなければなりませんでした。したがって，それらすべての要素を巻き込んでいくような有機的な全体，それが周囲の環境に融けていくような動きのある形態，を求めることになりました。建物の全体と部分との整合性をどのようにバランスさせるか，構成する部材の処理の仕方をどのように合理的に処理するかなどにほとんどのエネルギーを使いました。作り上げる過程では，設計は変化に富む形態の動きを現実の建物へとまとめていくのが精一杯でした。

　しかし，この建物ではそうした流れに身を任せるわけにはいきません。文化の中にある生活規範を基に日常生活を正していくことを目的に活動している研究所の活動内容からすれば，全体から部分に至るまで「折り目正しい均衡」を保っていることの方がはるかに重要なのではないかと考えました。作るプロセスに整合性があり，そのプロセスが形となって意匠にまで痕跡として残り，それが建築空間を支えている，という在り方です。言い換えれば，建物を作り上げる様々な部材の整理のされ方，構成のされ方の積み上げが建築の全体像になるという構図を思い描きました。ここでは建物の「形」が建築的な意志を成立させるのではなく，作られる「仕組み」がその精神的な支えとなることを求めました。

　新しいものを追い求める気持ちは人一倍強くあります。しかし，今，新しさについては慎重でありたいと思っています。建築は見た目の新しさを追いがちです。視覚的に人目を引くのは効率がいいからです。本質的なものを先送りして見た目の「新しさのようなもの」を捏造する習慣が，政治から生活まで，もちろん建築にまで，すっかり染み付いてしまっています。目は素早く形に反応します。形が目に媚びれば媚びるほど，自己主張すればするほど，建築は誤解を生み，幻想を生み，現実から遠のくことを忘れてはなりません。「新しさのようなもの」を装い，本質を隠蔽する役割を果たすような意匠は犯罪に近いのです。

　誰もが「新しさ」を性急に追い求め過ぎています。建築はその度ごとの個別の解答ですから，その根底にある何かが劇的に変わるなどということはめったにありません。そういうものは，自分の意志とは無関係に，時代や巡り合わせが恩寵のようにくれるものです。精一杯目前の仕事に

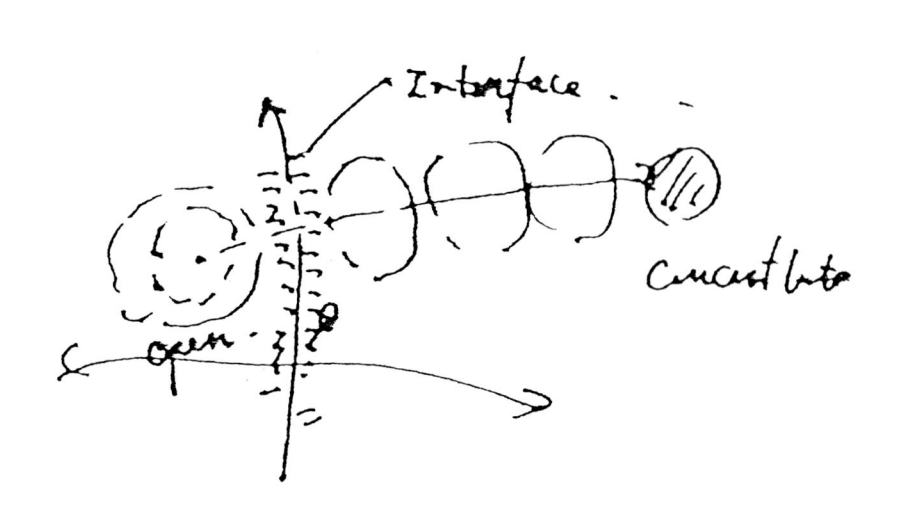

取り組んでいる中で，思いもかけず突然やって来る類いのものです。たぶん，本質的に新しい形や形式とは，個人の思いを超えたそういう訪れ方をするはずです。ですから，われわれは日々の積み上げを営々とやっていくしかないのです。

　現代はデジタル革命の最中にあります。コンピュータの能力は年々倍のスピードで進化し続けています。十年後には千倍近い能力の道具をわれわれは手にすることになるでしょう。それが何をもたらすのかは誰にも予測がつきません。近い将来，建築の形態的な可能性や面白いアイデアなら幾らでも描けるようになるはずです。しかし，冷静になって考えてみれば，そんなものに何程の価値があるというのでしょうか。デジタルだバーチャルだと言っても，目の前にあるのは相も変わらぬ疲れた現実の風景だけです。

　建築という価値に付け加えるべきは，後戻りしないわずかな前進なのです。後戻りしない確かなものは何か。それは技術だと思っています。目に見える形は時代の流行り廃りで流転しますが，技術の進化はけっして後戻りしません。今は，たとえ小さな一歩でも技術を積み上げるべきです。世の中がどうあろうと，それをベースに少しずつでも現実を改善していく意志を持ち続ける方が，ヒロイックな建築像を夢見るよりはるかに勇気のいることです。

　この建物には技術的に新しい試みがいくつかなされています。海の博物館以降，プロジェクトを重ねる度に，もう少し改善できないか，と懸案にしてきたものに取り組むことが出来ました。検証を重ねればもっと性能的に良くなるのに，と思うことでも，現実の仕事の中ではなかなかままなりません。エンジニアリングで新しいことに取り組むには，それなりの周到な準備と試行錯誤が必要だからです。この建物では，施主の理解も得られ，施工者との施工全体のオーガナイズもスムーズでした。それ故，こうしたことに取り組む精神的なゆとりがありました。めぐまれたプロジェクトだったと思います。

　新しい技術を伝統の中で培われた知恵で現実のものにする。それを整然としたプロセスで組み上げる。その「仕組み」の在り方がこの建物の目に見えないオリジナリティなのだと思っています。

From "Form" to "Construction Method"
■ Hiroshi Naito

I received the commission for the design of this building around the time I completed my design for Makino Museum of Plants and People. In Makino Museum, I had faced several distinct elements—the required building functions, the harsh climate of Kochi Prefecture, the topography of Mt. Godai, and Dr. Tomitaro Makino's vision of nature—which I had needed to fuse in a single essence in the building. This meant finding an organic totality able to draw all these elements into involvement, one whose dynamic form would visually meld with its surroundings. Most of my energy went to determining a balance that would ensure the consistency of the parts with the overall building, and to developing a rational means of assembling the constituent members of the framework. In the design process, the task of translating into an actual building the dynamic vitality of a form rich in variation commanded my entire attention.

I could hardly take the same approach with Fuji Rinri Seminar House. Judging from the activities of an institute aimed at correcting our way of living based on models for disciplined living fostered within traditional culture, it would be far more important, I felt, to maintain a "correct balance" throughout the design, a balance that would pervade the building from its whole to its parts. The consistency that informed the design process would engender form, making its presence felt even in the visual design, and support the integrity of the architectural spaces. In other words, the accumulative result of how I distributed and assembled each of the various framework members that comprise the building would produce the overall figure of the building. This is how I pictured it in my mind. Here, architectural form would not motivate the designer's intent. Rather, a "Construction Method"—"how it is put together"—would provide this psychological impetus.

I am strongly attracted to new things. These days, however, I am cautious in my approach to newness. There is a tendency in architecture to chase an appearance of newness. Visual appeal, after all, is our most effective means to capture an audience. A habit of postponing substance and fabricating an appearance of newness has taken root in architecture, as in all areas of society, from politics to daily life. The eye responds instantly to form. For this very reason, we must give care in our handling of form. We must remember that the more form teases the eye and asserts itself, the more architecture will invite misunderstanding, engender illusion, and deviate from reality. Design that pretends to newness while serving to conceal substance is nearly criminal.

We have become irrational in our pursuit of newness. Architecture is a solution to the needs of each building program, so rarely does the design process awaken a fundamental change, dramatic in its implications. Such a change comes as a gift of providence or the times, quite apart from what we consciously intend. Newness is the kind of thing that visits unexpectedly, while we are entirely absorbed in the work at hand. Likely, substantially new form, when it comes, visits as something that transcends our mental energies. As such, all we can do is build on our progress with slow, patient effort.

Our society is experiencing a digital revolution. Computer capability is evolving at double the speed, every year. In ten years, we will command computer capability a thousand times more advanced than what we know today. No one can predict what this will bring about. In the near future, we may enjoy complete freedom in visualizing the formal possibilities of architecture and interesting new ideas. When viewed with cool objectivity, however, how much value does this kind of thing have? Despite the excitement generated by digital and virtual technologies, the end result of their application is the same tired reality as ever before.

What we need to contribute to architecture in its present condition are small advances of lasting value. What could be so indubitable and lasting? I think the answer is technical innovation. The visible form of architecture is subject to the whims of fashion, but technical innovation endures. Our endeavor now should be to foster our technology, if only in small steps. An unflagging resolve to face reality and make incremental improvements, undisturbed by the commotion of the times, takes far more courage than to dream of a heroic architecture.

This building incorporates a number of technical innovations. Each new project since Sea-Folk Museum has enabled me to explore more thoroughly my thematic design concerns, seeking improvements. Through repeated testing and verification, one endeavors to obtain better performance, but in the context of an actual project, things never go quite as one expects. After all, to employ engineering in the development of new technology requires just that much careful preparation and trial and error. In this building, I enjoyed both the client's understanding and a smoothly functioning system of execution with the builder; this allowed me the mental freedom to undertake such challenges. I was blessed in this project.

In Fuji Rinri Seminar House, I have been able to realize new technology from a meditation on traditional knowledge, and to apply these innovations to the formation of structure within a tightly regulated design process. In the "Construction Method" of this building, as such, lies the nonvisual originality of its design.

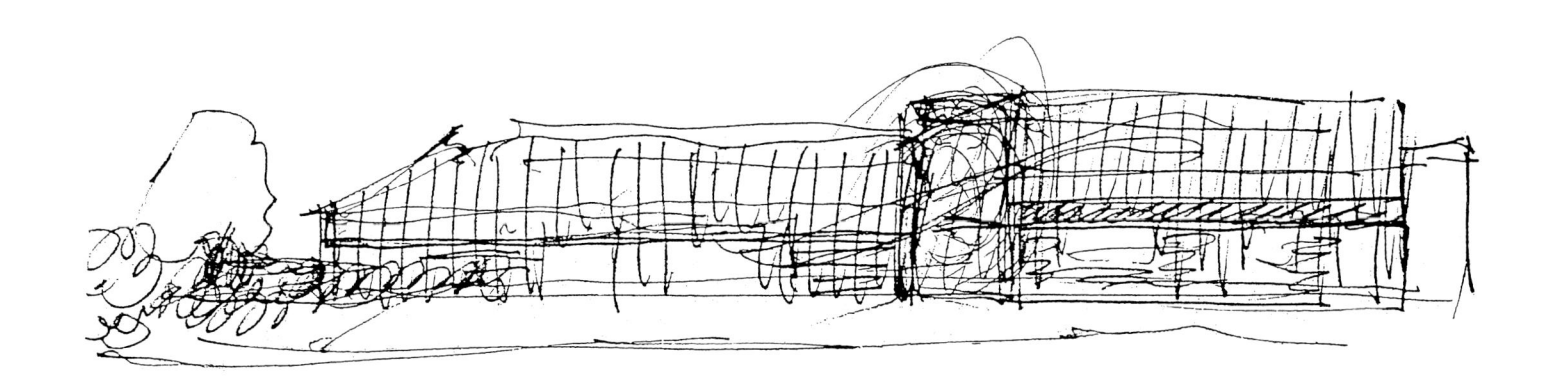

■データ

倫理研究所 富士高原研修所

施主	：社団法人倫理研究所
所在地	：静岡県御殿場市印野1383-9 〒412-0008
主要用途	：研修所
設計	：内藤廣建築設計事務所
	担当／内藤 廣 川村宣元 浅野恭子 古野洋美 好川 拓
	玉田 源 太田理加 宮崎俊行
	沼田恭子 田井幹夫 高草大次郎 大西直子
構造	：空間工学研究所 担当／岡村 仁 泉 圭市
設備	：明野設備研究所 担当／吉木健二 小川津久雄
サイン	：イスケ・インク 担当／大久保 學

設計期間	1998年8月－1999年6月
施工期間	1999年10月－2001年6月
施工	建築：鹿島建設 担当／青島淳典 箕浦達也 佐藤憲一
	設備：ダイダン 担当／家城洋次
	電気：関電工 担当／岩村圭一
	外構：鹿島道路
	集成材小屋組：斉藤木材工業
	熱押鋼製作：ニッコー，新日本製鐵光製作所，シラヤマ
	教室椅子：カッシーナ・インターデコール ジャパン
	木製サッシ：アイランドプロファイル
	特殊照明：ヤマギワ
	発熱ガラス：フィグラ
	AV：サウンドクラフト 担当／佐藤清美 栗木善治
	造園：岩城造園 担当／桜井芳夫
	家具：ユーロデザイン
	サイン工事：寿インテリア
面積	敷地面積　　　　　　　　　　　　　　19,510.37m²
	建築面積　　　　　　　　　　　　　　 5,192.78m²
	延床面積　　　　　　　　　　　　　　 5,777.19m²
寸法	最高高さ　　　　　　　　　　　　　　 9,112mm
	軒高　　　　　　　　　　　　　　　　 8,567mm
構造	下部：鉄筋コンクリート造，一部PC造
	小屋組：木造
外部仕上げ	屋根　：ガルバリウムフッ素樹脂鋼鈑 t=0.5mm 立てはぜ葺き@225mm
	外壁　：ガルバリウムフッ素樹脂鋼鈑 t=0.4mm 立てはぜ葺き@225mm
	ベイマツ無垢材38×75mm 縦張り スクリュウボルト締め チークオイル塗装
	開口部：木製サッシ（一部発熱ガラス仕様），スチールサッシ，アルミサッシ
	外構
	広場：磁器質タイル 69×69mm
	テラス：せっ器質タイル 227×60mm，200×44mm
	擁壁：溶岩積み（現場出土）
	建物廻り：溶岩敷（現場出土）
	水盤：コンクリート打放し（スギ板本実型枠）ブラックスレート敷
内部仕上げ	ホール
	床：カリン縁甲板 15×90mm 張り 本実加工
	壁：コンクリート打放し（スギ板本実型枠），
	一部スギ縁甲板 15×90mm 縦張り（準不燃処理木材）
	天井：ベイマツ集成材梁現し，野地板スギ縁甲板 15×90mm 縦張り（準不燃処理木材），
	PC梁現し，焼結アルミニウム吸音板張り
	講堂・教室
	床：長尺ループカーペット張り
	壁：グラスウール吸音材ガラスクロスの上 スギ板ルーバー 45×60mm（難燃処理木材）
	一部スギ縁甲板 15×90mm 縦張り（難燃処理木材）
	天井：ベイマツ集成材梁現し，野地板スギ縁甲板 15×90mm 縦張り（難燃処理木材）
	清堂
	床：ヒノキ板目縁甲板 15×90mm 張り 本実加工
	壁：木製サッシュ（発熱ガラス仕様）
	天井：ベイマツ集成材梁現し，野地板スギ縁甲板 15×90mm 張り

■DATA

Fuji RINRI Seminar House

Client	: RINRI Institute of Ethics
Address	: 1383-9, Inno Gotemba-shi, Shizuoka 412-0008
Use	: Seminar House
Architectural Design	: Naito Architect & Associates / Hiroshi Naito,
	Nobuharu Kawamura, Kyoko Asano, Hiromi Furuno, Taku Yoshikawa,
	Gen Tamada, Rika Ota, Yoshiyuki Miyazaki,
	Kyoko Numata, Mikio Tai, Daijirou Takakusa, Naoko Ohnishi
Structural Engineering	: Space and Structure Engineering Workshop Inc.
	Satoshi Okamura, Keiichi Izumi
Engineering	: Akeno Engineering Consultants Inc.
	Kenji Yoshimoto, Tsukuo Ogawa
Sign	: Isuke Inc. / Gaku Okubo

Design Period	Aug.1998－Jun.1999
Construction Period	Oct.1999－Jun.2001
Contractor	**General Contractor** : Kajima Corporation / Junsuke Aoshima,
	Tatsuya Minoura, Ken-ichi Sato
	Equipments : Daidan / Yoji Ieki
	Electric Services : Kandenko / Keiichi Iwamura
	Outward structure : Kajima Road
	Wood frame : Saito Wood Industry Co., Ltd.
	Hot extruded steel columns :
	Nikko, Nippon Steel Corporation Hikari Works, Shirayama
	Special order Chair : Cassina Inter-Decor
	Wood sash : Island Profile Inc.
	Special order Light : Yamagiwa
	Thermal Glass : Figla
	AV : Sound Craft Inc. / Kiyomi Sato, Yoshiharu Kuriki
	Landscape gardening : Iwaki Zoen / Yoshio Sakurai
	Furniture : Euro Design
	Sign : Kotobuki Interior
External Work & Landscaping	
Area	Site Area　　　　　　　　　　　　　　19,510.37m²
	Building Area　　　　　　　　　　　　 5,192.78m²
	Total Floor Area　　　　　　　　　　　 5,777.19m²
Dimension	Maximum-Height　　　　　　　　　　　 9,112mm
	Eaves Height　　　　　　　　　　　　　 8,567mm
Structure	Reinforced concrete, Precast concrete and Post-tensioning build up system
	Roof frame : Laminated timber (Douglas fir)
Exterior	Roof　 : Galvalume metal standing seam cladding t=0.5mm @225mm
	Wall　 : Galvalume metal standing seam cladding t=0.4mm @225mm
	Douglas fir 38×75mm fastened with stainless screw bolt
	Window : Wood sash (Partry used thermal Glass), steel sash, aluminum sash
	Stone wall: Lava (dugout of the site)
Interior	Hall
	Floor : Chinese quince strip flooring 15×90mm
	Wall : Exposed reinforced concrete (formwork:Japanese cedar)
	Ceiling : Laminated timber (Douglas fir), Japanese cedar 15×90mm
	Exposed precast concrete, Aluminum sound absorbing boad
	Auditorium・Classroom
	Floor : Cut pile carpet
	Wall : Japanese cedar louver 45×60mm
	Japanese cedar 15×90mm
	Ceiling : Laminated timber (Douglas fir), Japanese cedar 15×90mm
	SEIDO Hall
	Floor : Japanese cypress strip flooring 15×90mm
	Wall : Wood sash (used thermal Glass)
	Ceiling : Laminated timber (Douglas fir), Japanese cedar 15×90mm

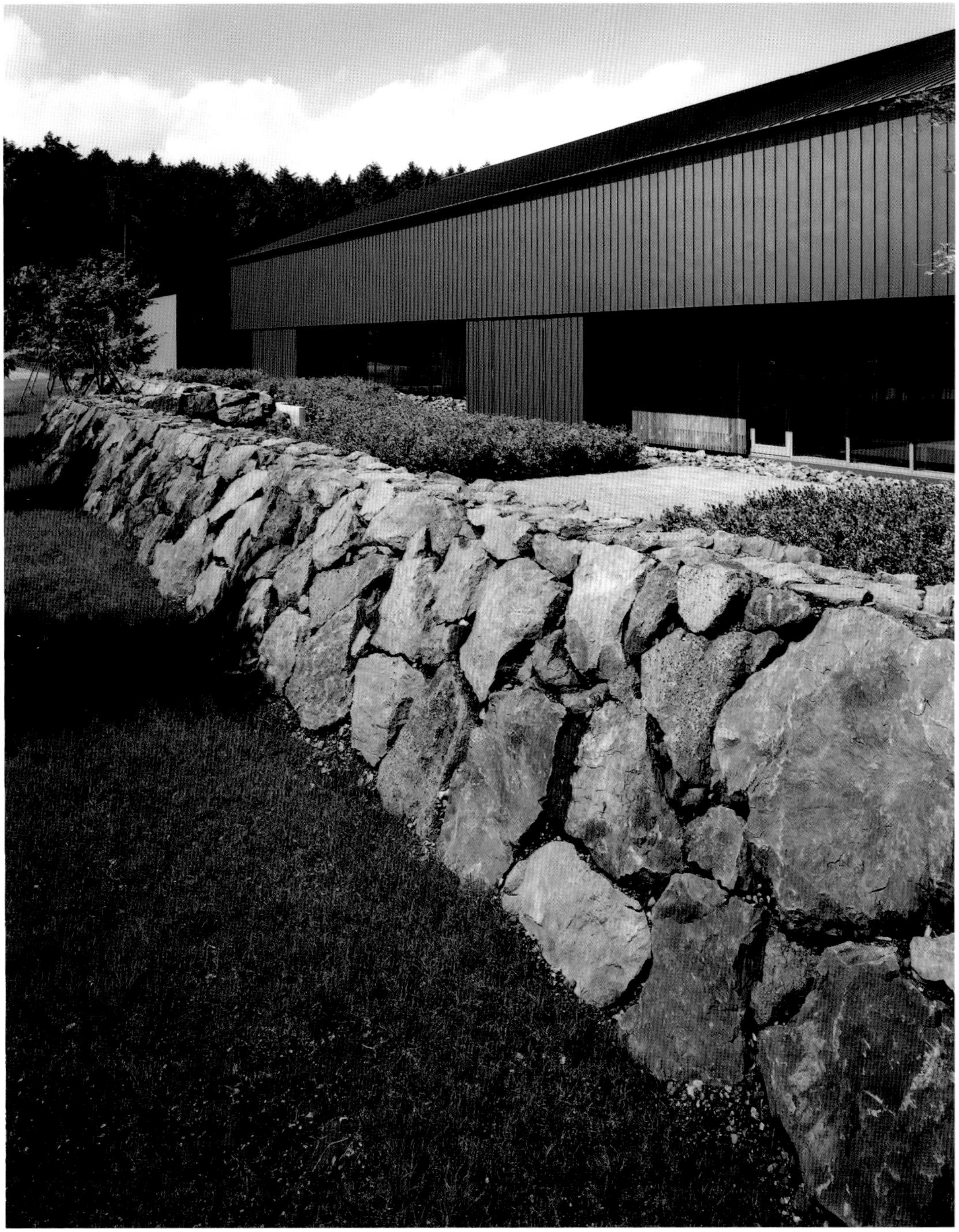

石元泰博｜Yasuhiro ISHIMOTO

■略歴
1921　6月14日農業移民の長男としてサンフランシスコに生まれる
1924　両親が家族を伴い郷里の高知県に帰国
1939　高知県立農業高校を卒業し、単身渡米
1942　コロラド州アマチ・キャンプ（日系人収容所）に収容される
1948　シカゴのインスティテュート・オブ・デザインの写真科に入学
1952　イリノイ工科大学卒業。翌年の3月に日本に戻り、桂離宮の撮影開始
1956　勅使河原蒼風に師事していた川又滋（本名：滋子）と結婚
1959-61　シカゴに滞在し精力的に写真撮影
1962-66　桑沢デザイン研究所、東京綜合写真専門学校で写真を教授
1966-71　東京造形大学写真科教授
1969　日本国籍取得
2012　2月6日東京にて死去

［主な作品（展覧会・出版）］
1955　NY開催の「The Family of Man」展に2点招待出品（日本展は翌年）
1958　『ある日ある所』（芸美出版社）
1960　シカゴ美術館で個展開催
　　　『桂　日本建築における伝統と創造』（イエール大学、造型社）
1961　ニューヨーク近代美術館で3人展
1962　「石元泰博写真展　シカゴ、シカゴ」（日本橋白木屋）
1969　『シカゴ、シカゴ』（美術出版社）
1971　『都市　映像の現代8』（中央公論社）
1973　「approach」（竹中工務店）表紙にカラー多重露光作品掲載開始
1975　『剣持勇の世界』（河出書房新社）に撮り下し写真掲載
1977　「石元泰博写真　曼荼羅展」（西武美術館ほか国内外を巡回）
　　　『伝真言院両界曼荼羅』（平凡社）
1980　『イスラム──空間と文様』（駸々堂出版）
1982　『湖国の十一面観音』（岩波書店）
1983　『桂離宮──空間と形』（岩波書店ほか米独伊同時出版）、『シカゴ、シカゴ
　　　その2』（キヤノンクラブ／リブロポート）
1988　『HANA』（求龍堂、翌年米国でも刊行）
1995　『伊勢神宮』（岩波書店）
1998　「石元泰博展──シカゴ、東京」（東京都写真美術館）
1999　「Yasuhiro Ishimoto : A Tale of Two Cities」（シカゴ美術館）
2000-01　「Yasuhiro Ishimoto : Photographs 1950-1995」（フランス）、
　　　「Yasuhiro Ishimoto Photographs : Traces of Memory」（クリーブランド
　　　美術館）
2001　「石元泰博写真展　1946-2001」（高知県立美術館）
2003　『色とかたち』（平凡社）
2004　『刻（moment）』（平凡社）
2007　『シブヤ、シブヤ』（平凡社）
2008　『COMPOSITION めぐりあう色とかたち』（平凡社）
2009　「Way of Seeing : The Photography of Yasuhiro Ishimoto」（ヒューストン
　　　美術館）、「石元泰博［多重露光］」（武蔵野美術大学美術館）
2010　「Katsura: Picturing Modernism in Japanese Architecture, Photographs
　　　by Ishimoto Yasuhiro」（ヒューストン美術館、図録が全米美術協会より
　　　Alfred H. Barr, Jr. Award受賞）、「石元泰博写真展」（水戸芸術館）、『桂離
　　　宮』（六耀社）
2011　「写真家・石元泰博の眼──桂、伊勢」（高知県立美術館）
2013　「追悼展　写真家・石元泰博の軌跡」（高知県立美術館）

［主な受賞］
1950　LIFE誌主催のヤング・フォトグラファーズ・コンテストに入賞
1951-52　モホイ・ナジ賞を連続受賞
1957　展覧会「日本のかたち」「桂離宮」で第1回日本写真批評家協会作家賞
1958　『ある日ある所』で日本写真批評家協会新人賞
1970　『シカゴ、シカゴ』で昭和44年度毎日芸術賞
1978　『伝真言院両界曼荼羅』で芸術選奨文部大臣賞、日本写真家協会年度賞、
　　　世界で最も美しい本展（ライプツィヒ）金賞
1983　紫綬褒章
1993　勲四等旭日小授章
1994　アルル国際写真フェスティバルで個展開催、マスター・オブ・フォトグラ
　　　フィー
1996　平成8年度文化功労者に選ばれる
2005　紺綬褒章、高知県文化賞
2012　正四位、旭日重光章を追贈される

■BIOGRAPHY
1921　Born in San Francisco on the 14th of June to Japanese immigrants
1924　Moved to Kochi Prefecture, Japan, with his parents
1939　Graduated from Kochi Agricultural High School, returned to the United States
1942　Sent to the Amache Camp, an internment camp for Japanese-American in Colorado
1948　Entered the Photography Department of the Institute of Design in Chicago.
1952　Graduated from The Institute of Design (Illinois Institute of Technology), and in the following year returned to Japan. Photographed for the first time Katsura Imperial Villa
1956　Married Shigeru(Shigeruko) Kawamata
1958-61　Traveled to the United States, staying in Chicago
1962-66　Lecturer, The Kuwasawa Design School and The Tokyo College of Photography
1966-71　Professor, The Tokyo Zokei University
1969　Obtained Japanese Citizenship
2012　Died in Tokyo on the 6th of February

[MAIN WORKS / Exhibitions and Publications]
1955　"Family of Man", Museum of Modern Art, New York
1958　*Someday, Somewhere* (Geibishuppan Sha)
1960　"Photographs by Yasuhiro Ishimoto", The Art Institute of Chicago, Chicago. *Katsura: Tradition and Creation in Japanese Architecture* (Yale University Press and Zokei Sha)
1961　Three-person exhibition "Diogenes with Camera", Museum of Modern Art, New York
1962　"Chicago, Chicago", Nihonbashi Shirokiya Department Store, Tokyo
1969　*Chicago, Chicago* (Bijutsu Shuppan-Sha)
1971　*Toshi: Eizo no Gendai 8* (Chuokoron Sha)
1973　*approach* (Takenaka Corporation) Start the series of multi exposure photographs on front cover
1975　*The World of Isamu Kenmochi* (Kawade Shobo Shinsha)
1977　"Eros + Cosmos in MANDALA, Photographed by Yasuhiro Ishimoto", Seibu Museum of Art, Tokyo
　　　Mandala of Two Worlds: The Legend of Shingonin (Heibonsha)
1980　*ISLAM SPACE AND DESIGN* (Shinshindo)
1982　*The Eleven - Faced Goddess of Mercy of Kokoku* (Iwanami Shoten)
1983　*Katsura Villa* (Iwanami Shoten). *Chicago, Chicago II* (Libro, Tokyo)
1988　*HANA* (Kyuryudo and Chronicle Books, San Francisco)
1995　*Ise Shrine* (Iwanami Shoten)
1998　"Yasuhiro Ishimoto: Chicago and Tokyo", Tokyo Metropolitan Museum of Photography, Tokyo
1999　"Yasuhiro Ishimoto; A Tale of Two Cities", The Art Institute of Chicago
2000-01　"Yasuhiro Ishimoto: Photographs 1950-1995", France
　　　"Yasuhiro Ishimoto Photographs: Traces of Memory", Cleveland Museum of Art, Cleveland
2001　"Yasuhiro Ishimoto Photographs 1946-2001", The Museum of Art, Kochi
2003　*Iro to Katachi* (Heibonsha)
2004　*Toki: moment* (Heibonsha)
2007　*Shibuya, Shibuya* (Heibonsha)
2008　*Composition: reuniting Form and Colour* (Heibonsha)
2009　"Way of Seeing: The Photography of Yasuhiro Ishimoto", Museum of Fine Arts, Houston. "Ishimoto Yasuhiro: Multi Exposure", Musashino Art University Museum
2010　"Katsura: Picturing Modernism in Japanese Architecture, Photographs by Ishimoto Yasuhiro", Museum of Fine Arts, Houston (Its catalogue was received the Alfred H. Barr, Jr. Award)
　　　"Yasuhiro Ishimoto", Art Tower Mito, Mito, Ibaraki. *Katsura* (Rikuyosha)
2011　"Photographer Yasuhiro Ishimoto's View: Katsura and Ise", The Museum of Art, Kochi
2013　"Photographer Yasuhiro Ishimoto", The Museum of Art, Kochi

[MAIN AWARDS]
1950　Young Photographer's Contest, Life Magazine
1951-52　Moholy-Nagy Prize
1957　Japan Photo Critics Association Artist Award
1958　Japan Photo Critics Association Newcomer's Award
1970　Mainichi Art Award
1978　Minister of Education Art Encouragement Prize
　　　Photographic Society of Japan Annual Award, International Competition of Best Designed Books from All Over the World (Leipzig) The Golden Letters
1983　Medal with Purple Ribbon from the Japanese Government
1993　Order of the Rising Sun, Gold Rays with Rosette
1994　Master of Photography Prize at the Rencontres d'Arles (Arles Photography Festival)
1996　Person of Cultural Merit
2005　Medal with Dark Blue Ribbon from the Japanese Government Kochi Prefecture Cultural Award
2012　Order of the Rising Sun, Gold and Silver Star

内藤 廣 | Hiroshi NAITO

■略歴
1950　神奈川県横浜市に生まれる
1974　早稲田大学理工学部建築学科卒業
1974-76　早稲田大学大学院にて吉阪隆正に師事，修士課程修了
1976-78　フェルナンド・イゲーラス建築設計事務所に勤務（スペイン・マドリッド）
1979-81　菊竹清訓建築設計事務所に勤務
1981　内藤廣建築設計事務所を設立
2001　東京大学大学院工学系研究科社会基盤工学の助教授に着任
2002-11　東京大学大学院工学系研究科社会基盤工学教授
2010-11　東京大学副学長
2011-　東京大学 名誉教授，総長室顧問

[主な作品]
1984　ギャラリーTOM（東京都渋谷区）
　　　住居No.1 共生住居（神奈川県鎌倉市）
1992　海の博物館（三重県鳥羽市）
1997　安曇野ちひろ美術館（長野県北安曇郡松川村）
　　　茨城県天心記念五浦美術館（茨城県北茨城市）
1999　十日町情報館（新潟県十日町市）
　　　牧野富太郎記念館（高知県高知市）
2001　倫理研究所富士高原研修所（静岡県御殿場市）
2005　島根県芸術文化センター（島根県益田市）
2007　日向市駅（宮崎県日向市））
2009　高知駅（高知県高知市）
　　　虎屋京都店（京都府京都市）
2011　旭川駅（北海道旭川市）

[主な著作]
1993　『海の博物館』（写真：石元泰博）
1995　『素形の建築』（INAX出版）
1999　『安曇野ちひろ美術館』（写真：石元泰博）
　　　『建築のはじまりに向かって』（王国社）
2000　『牧野富太郎記念館』（写真：石元泰博）
2002　『倫理研究所 富士高原研修所』（写真：石元泰博）
2004　『建築的思考のゆくえ』（王国社）
2006　『インナースケープのディテール』（彰国社）
　　　『建土築木1 構築物の風景』，『建土築木2 川のある風景』（鹿島出版会）
2007　『内藤廣対談集―複眼思考の建築論』（INAX出版）
2008　『構造デザイン講義』（王国社）
2009　『建築のちから』（王国社）
2010　『内藤廣対談集2―著書解題』（INAX出版）
2011　『環境デザイン講義』（王国社）
　　　『NA建築家シリーズ03 内藤廣』（日経BP社）
　　　『内藤廣と若者たち 人生をめぐる一八の対話』
　　　（東京大学景観研究室編，鹿島出版会）
2012　『内藤廣の頭と手』（彰国社）
2013　『内藤廣の建築 1992-2004 素形から素景へ1』（TOTO出版）

[主な受賞]
1993　芸術選奨文部大臣新人賞（海の博物館）
　　　日本建築学会賞（海の博物館）
　　　第18回吉田五十八賞（海の博物館）
1998　建設省選定公共建築100選（海の博物館）
2000　第13回村野藤吾賞（牧野富太郎記念館）
　　　IAA国際トリエンナーレ グランプリ（牧野富太郎記念館）
　　　第42回毎日芸術賞（牧野富太郎記念館）
2001　第42回BCS賞（牧野富太郎記念館）
2003　第4回織部賞
2004　第45回BCS賞（ちひろ美術館・東京）
2006　International Architecture Award（島根県芸術文化センター）
　　　土木デザイン賞2006 最優秀賞（牧野富太郎記念館）
2007　第48回BCS賞（島根県芸術文化センター）
　　　第52回鉄道建築協会賞 国土交通省鉄道局長賞（日向市駅）
2008　第10回ブルネル賞（日向市駅）
2010　第12回公共建築賞・特別賞（島根県芸術文化センター）

[主な展覧会]
1995　「素型の構図―還元する場のかたち」ギャラリー・間
1997　「Silent Architecture」Aedes West（ベルリン）
2005　「Hiroshi Naito - Innerscape」Museum of Finnish Architecture」（ヘルシンキ）

■BIOGRAPHY
1950　Born in Yokohama, Kanagawa Prefecture
1974　Graduated from Waseda University (B. Arch.) in Tokyo
1974-76　Completed studies under Prof. Takamasa Yoshizaka at the Graduate School of Waseda University (M. Arch.)
1976-78　Chief Architect at the office of architect Fernando Higueras (Madrid, Spain)
1979-81　Worked at the office of architect Kiyonori Kikutake (Tokyo, Japan)
1981　Established Naito Architect & Associates
2001　Associate Professor, Department of Civil Engineering, The University of Tokyo
2002-11　Professor, The University of Tokyo
2010-11　Executive Vice President, The University of Tokyo
2011-　Emeritus Professor and Senior Advisor to the Office of the President, The University of Tokyo

[MAIN WORKS]
1984　Gallery TOM (Shibuya, Tokyo)
　　　House No.1 (Kamakura, Kanagawa Prefecture)
1992　Sea-Folk Museum (Toba, Mie Prefecture)
1997　Chihiro Art Museum Azumino (Kitaazumi-gun, Nagano Prefecture)
　　　Tenshin Memorial Museum of Art, Ibaraki (Kitaibaraki, Ibaraki Prefecture)
1999　Tohkamachi Public Library (Tohkamachi, Niigata Prefecture)
　　　Makino Museum of Plants and People (Kochi, Kochi Prefecture)
2001　Fuji RINRI Seminar House (Gotemba, Shizuoka Prefecture)
2005　Shimane Arts Center (Masuda, Shimane Prefecture)
2007　Hyugashi Station (Hyuga, Miyazaki Prefecture)
2009　Kochi Station (Kochi, Kochi Prefecture)
　　　TORAYA Kyoto (Kyoto, Kyoto Prefecture)
2011　Asahikawa Station (Asahikawa, Hokkaido)

[MAIN PUBLICATION]
1993　*Sea-Folk Museum* (Photographer: Yasuhiro Ishimoto)
1995　*Protoform* (INAX Publishing)
1999　*Chihiro Art Museum Azumino* (Photographer: Yasuhiro Ishimoto)
　　　Toward the Beginning of Architecture (Okokusha / Japanese edition)
2000　*Makino Museum of Plants and People* (Photographer: Yasuhiro Ishimoto)
2002　*Fuji RINRI Seminar House* (Photographer: Yasuhiro Ishimoto)
2004　*The Directions of the Architectural Thinking* (Okokusha / Japanese edition)
2006　*Hiroshi Naito: Innerscape* (Shokokusha / Japanese edition), Birkhauser
　　　KENDOCHIKUBOKU 1, KENDOCHIKUBOKU 2 (Kajima Institute Publishing / Japanese edition)
2007　*Hiroshi Naito interview1, architect theory of compound eye thought* (INAX Publishing / Japanese edition)
2008　*Structure Design lecture* (Okokusha / Japanese edition)
2009　*Power of Architecture* (Okokusha / Japanese edition)
2010　*Hiroshi Naito interview 2, Annotated Bibliography* (INAX / Japanese edition)
2011　*Environmental Design lecture* (Okokusha / Japanese edition)
　　　The architect series 03 Hiroshi Naito (Nikkei Business Publication / Japanese edition)
　　　Hiroshi Naito, Dialogue with youths (Kajima Institute Publishing / Japanese edition)
2012　*Hiroshi Naito's perception and realization* (Shokokusha / Japanese edition)
2013　*Hiroshi Naito 1992-2004 From Protoform to Protoscape* (TOTO Publishing)

[MAIN AWARDS]
1993　Education Minister's Art Encouragement Prize for Freshman (Sea-Folk Museum)
　　　The Prize of Architectural Institute of Japan for Design (Sea-Folk Museum)
　　　Isoya Yoshida Memorial Prize (Sea-Folk Museum)
1998　100 Public Architecture Selected by Ministry of Construction (Sea-Folk Museum)
2000　Togo Murano Award (Makino Museum of Plants and People)
　　　World Triennial of Architecture, Grand Prix of the International Academy of Architecture (Makino Museum of Plants and People)
　　　Mainichi Art Awards (Makino Museum of Plants and People)
2001　Building Contractors Society Prize (Makino Museum of Plants and People)
2003　Oribe Award
2004　Building Contractors Society Prize (Chihiro Art Museum Tokyo)
2006　International Architecture Award (Shimane Arts Center)
　　　Civil Enginering Design Prize 2006 First prize (Makino Museum of Plants and People)
2007　Building Contractors Society Prize (Shimane Arts Center)
　　　Railway Construction Institute Architectural Award (Hyugashi Station)
2008　Brunel Award (Hyugashi Station)
2010　The 12th Public Building Award Special Prize (Shimane Arts Center)

[MAIN EXHIBITIONS]
1995　"Composition of the Protoform", GALLERY・MA, Tokyo
1997　"Silent Architecture", Aedes West, Berlin
2005　"Hiroshi Naito – Innerscape", Museum of Finnish Architecture, Helsinki

あとがき

　1992年，無謀にも「海の博物館」の写真集を石元先生の撮影で自費出版することにした。この手の話は皆目見当がつかないので，編集を森山明子さん，本のデザインを吉田カツヨさんにお願いした。序文を菊竹清訓先生，哲学者の市川浩さんに書いていただいた。女史お二人はボランタリーで参画，つまりこの企画の首謀者でもある。

　以後，めぼしい建物が出来上がると，石元先生の写真，森山さんと吉田さんのラインで自費出版を重ねた。写真の迫力に引き寄せられるように，完成度の高い写真集がその都度出来上がった。その後，苦心惨憺して完成させた島根県芸術文化センターを撮影していただいて，これまでの写真を合わせて合冊にしようと企てていたが，先生が体調を崩され，かなわなかった。

　今回，ADPの久保田啓子さんのご厚意で出版の運びとなったことは望外の歓びである。バブル経済にモミクチャにされ，翻弄され，崩壊後は，ひたすら設計に打ち込んで駆け抜けた時間が，陰影に富んだ写真を通して鮮やかに甦る。石元先生に出会えてよかった。厳しい眼差しに適うよう精進した十年だった。ここにあるのは，写真家石元泰博との言葉なき対話である。写真を見ていただければ，お分かりいただけるものと思っている。この本を石元先生と滋子夫人の墓前に献じたい。

内藤 廣

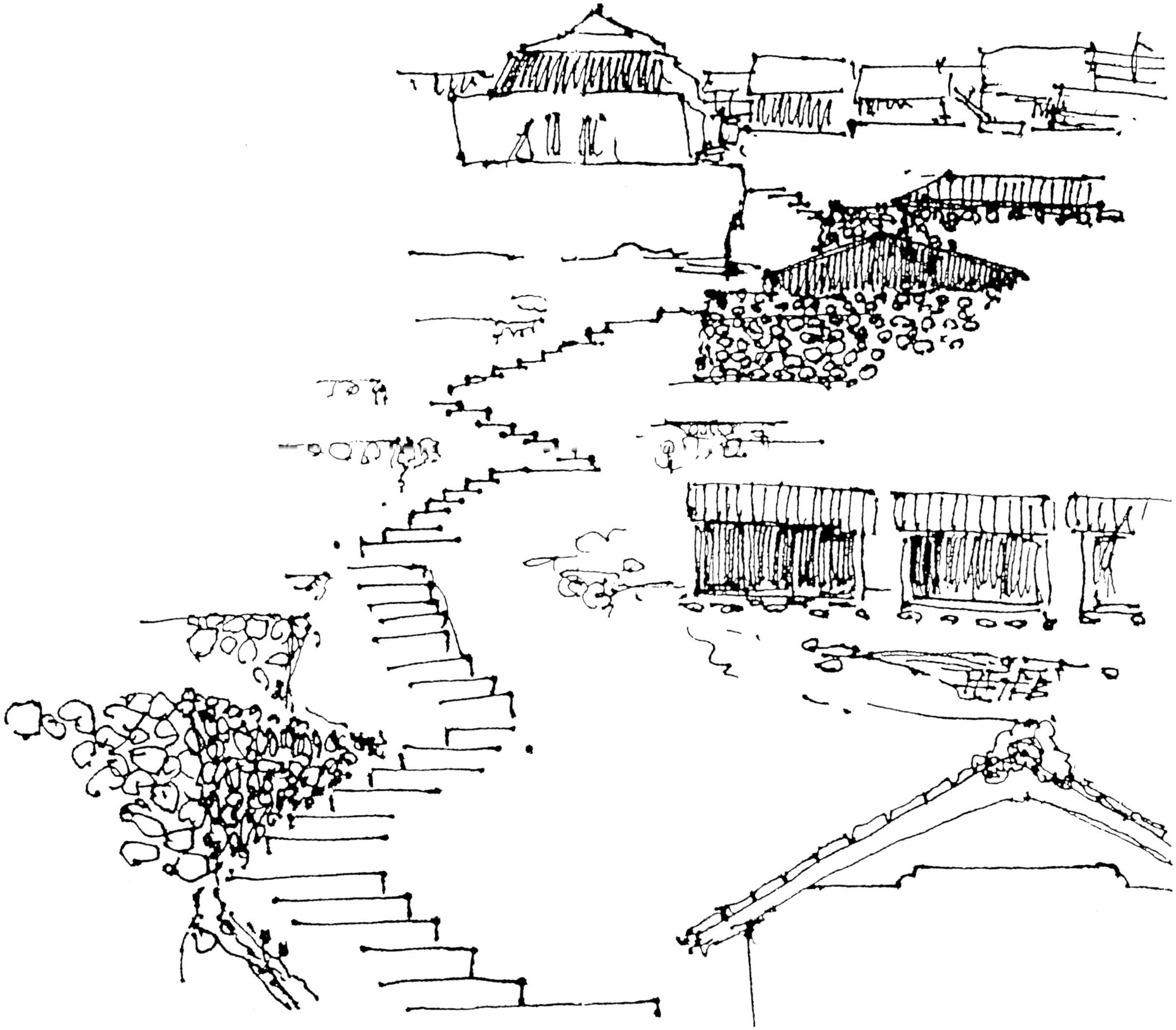

内藤 廣＋石元泰博　空間との対話

発行日	2013年4月30日

著者	内藤 廣
写真	石元泰博

編集	森山明子
編集協力	内藤廣建築設計事務所
翻訳	ブライアン・アムスタッツ
デザイン	吉田カツヨ　仲田延子
プリンティングディレクション	田中一也（凸版印刷）

発行人	久保田啓子
発行所	株式会社ADP	Art Design Publishing 東京都中野区松が丘2-14-12 〒165-0024 tel. 03-5942-6011　fax. 03-5942-6015 http://www.ad-publish.com

印刷・製本	凸版印刷株式会社

©Hiroshi Naito 2013
©Kochi Prefecture Photo by Yasuhiro Ishimoto
Printed in Japan
ISBN978-4-903348-33-9 C3052

写真家石元泰博氏が遺された写真作品及び著作権は、すべて高知県に寄贈され、高知県立美術館において写真作品を収蔵しています。

本書の収録内容の無断転載・複写（コピー）・引用などは、著作権法上での例外を除き、禁じられています。

■

NAITO Hiroshi + ISHIMOTO Yasuhiro　SPACE SPIRITS

Date of Publication	April 30, 2013

Author	Hiroshi Naito
Photographer	Yasuhiro Ishimoto

Editor	Akiko Moriyama
Editorial Cooperator	Naito Architect & Associates
Translator	Brian Amstutz
Book Designer	Katsuyo Yoshida, Nobuko Nakada
Printing Director	Kazuya Tanaka (Toppan Printing)

Publisher	Keiko Kubota
Publishing House	ADP Company	Art Design Publishing 2-14-12 Matsugaoka, Nakano-ku, Tokyo 165-0024 Japan tel. +81-3-5942-6011　fax. +81-3-5942-6015 http://www.ad-publish.com

Printing & Binding	Toppan Printing Co., Ltd.

©Hiroshi Naito 2013
©Kochi Prefecture Photo by Yasuhiro Ishimoto
Printed in Japan
ISBN978-4-903348-33-9 C3052

Photographer Yasuhiro Ishimoto left his photographic works and their copyrights as bequests to the Kochi prefectural government, and the photographic works are now stored by the Museum of Art, Kochi.

All right reserved. No part of this book may be reproduced without permission.